Black on the Block

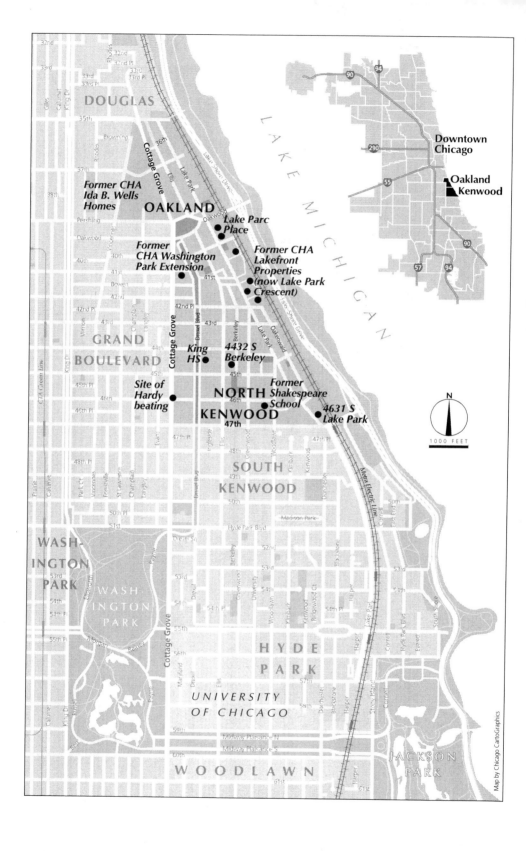

Map by Chicago CartoGraphics

The University of Chicago Press, Chicago 60637
The University of Chicago Press, Ltd., London
© 2007 by The University of Chicago
All rights reserved. Published 2007
Paperback edition 2008
Printed in the United States of America

17 16 15 14 13 12 11 10 09 08   2 3 4 5 6

ISBN-13: 978-0-226-64931-3 (cloth)
ISBN-13: 978-0-226-64932-0 (paper)
ISBN-10: 0-226-64931-8 (cloth)
ISBN-10: 0-226-64932-6 (paper)

Library of Congress Cataloging-in-Publication Data

Pattillo, Mary E.
    Black on the block : the politics of race and class in the city / Mary Pattillo.
        p. cm.
    Includes bibliographical references and index.
    ISBN-13: 978-0-226-64931-3 (cloth : alk. paper)
    ISBN-10: 0-226-64931-8 (cloth : alk. paper)
    1. North Kenwood (Chicago, Ill.)—Race relations. 2. Oakland (Chicago,
Ill.)—Race relations. 3. North Kenwood (Chicago, Ill.)—Social conditions.
4. Oakland (Chicago, Ill.)—Social conditions. 5. African Americans—
Illinois—Chicago—Social conditions. 6. Gentrification—Illinois—Chicago.
7. Community Life—Illinois—Chicago. 8. Social classes—Illinois—
Chicago. 9. Chicago (Ill.)—Race relations. 10. Chicago (Ill.)—Social
conditions. I Title.
F548.68.N65P37   2007
305.8960730773'11—dc22

                                                              2006017518

⊗ The paper used in this publication meets the minimum requirements of the
American National Standard for Information Sciences—Permanence of Paper for
Printed Library Materials, ANSI Z39.48-1992.

BLACK ON THE BLOCK

The Politics of Race and Class in the City

MARY PATTILLO

The University of Chicago Press | Chicago and London

CONTENTS

ILLUSTRATIONS

Figures

Table

ACKNOWLEDGMENTS

While acknowledgments are placed at a book's beginning, they are almost always written at the end of the process so that no one gets left out. The problem with this practice, for me at least, is that I have spent all my efforts at composing clever and creative prose on the book itself. All I have left are sincere and emphatic thank yous to lists of people and institutions who helped me undertake this investigation of race, class, and urban politics in Chicago, and to my wonderful friends and family, who provided me with much needed breaks from that obsession.

I was happy to work again with the University of Chicago Press, benefiting from the keen insight of Doug Mitchell, the expert organizational skills of Tim McGovern, and the smooth editing of Joel Score.

I was helped immensely by graduate research assistants Tennille Allen, Ellen Berrey, Cheryl Brown, Suzanne Hansford, Steve Hoffman, Carla Shedd, and Cheryl Ward, and by undergraduates Tiffany Berry, Jennifer Jones, Stephanie Kantor, Elizabeth Raap, and Terrenda White. Two people on this front get their own sentences: I would never have finished the book without the research and production assistance of Ife Finch, who thankfully convinced me that I did need help getting it all done. And my mother, Marva Pattillo, took hours from her retirement to transcribe boxes of interview tapes (I did pay her the going rate) and comment on several chapters of the manuscript, sharing her invaluable experience in urban development.

Many colleagues have read chapters or given especially helpful comments at presentations. My thanks to Martha Biondi, Xav Briggs, Cathy Cohen, John L. Jackson, Mark Joseph, Dan Lewis, Alex Polikoff, and Len Rubinowitz, and to anonymous reviewers from two different presses. I am indebted to Richard Iton for the title of the book, and to both Richard and Eric Klinenberg for reading the entire manuscript and giving detailed feedback that improved the book beyond measure. My colleagues, chairs, and friends (and luckily those aren't mutually exclusive categories) in the Sociology and African American Studies Departments at Northwestern University provided the kinds of departmental homes that make it a joy to come to work. I was also supported intellectually and financially (through time off from teaching) by the Institute for Policy Research and the WCAS Dean's Office at Northwestern, and by the Center for the Study of Race, Politics and Culture at the University of Chicago. But the bulk of the research funding came from the MacArthur Foundation, where Susan Lloyd has been a constant supporter while always acknowledging my scholarly independence.

In my archival and documentary research, I was assisted by the staffs at the Chicago Public Library (especially Lyle Benedict), the University of Chicago Library, the Northwestern University Library, the Newberry Library, University of Illinois at Chicago Special Collections, the Chicago Tribune (especially Yedida Soloff), the Cook County Recorder of Deeds (especially Ralph Albanito), the Chicago History Museum (especially Robert Medina), and the Chicago Department of Planning and Development (especially James Wilson).

Finally, the biggest thanks of all go to the people who live, work, and have a stake in North Kenwood–Oakland. I am especially grateful to Ms. Mary Thomas, the best landlord a displaced ethnographer could ask for; the past and present members of the Conservation Community Council and the residents of Berkeley Avenue, who gave freely of their time and knowledge in formal interviews and casual conversations; the late Izora Davis, a woman of real courage; and Shirley Newsome, by whose extraordinary commitment and wisdom I am eternally humbled.

As a professor, I am trained to be analytical, critical, and authoritative. But the truth is that the people of North Kenwood–Oakland allowed me to be their student, and so I have strived to carry out my academic duties with enduring respect for their generosity.

On the morning of November 25, 1987, Harold Washington, Chicago's first African American mayor, broke ground for a new housing development in the North Kenwood–Oakland neighborhood. That afternoon, he died. *Black on the Block,* set in the black South Side neighborhood where Washington made his last public appearance, builds its metaphors from these facts of death and new beginnings. At the city level, a short-lived era of black political power was buried with Washington, and a regime of white leadership with black and Latino consent was (re)born.[1] At the neighborhood level, what passed away were the vacant, trash-strewn lots that had marred North Kenwood–Oakland's landscape. Before long, the neighborhood's public housing high-rises would fall, and a cadre of community activists would rise up to tackle the social problems that had plagued the community since the 1960s—gangs, drugs, violence, and the font of poverty from which they sprang. North Kenwood–Oakland would be rejuvenated by people who rehabilitated its old houses and moved into new buildings like the ones for which Harold Washington turned the soil on that autumn day (see fig. 1). The residents who acted as the new neighborhood's symbolic midwives envisioned a revitalized, self-consciously *black* community. As a student of Chicago, of cities, and of black politics and social life, I was drawn to the transformation of North Kenwood–Oakland. In 1998, I became one of those new residents and began my research.

Figure 1. Mayor Harold Washington (fourth from left) breaks ground for new housing development in North Kenwood–Oakland, along with Kenwood Oakland Community Organization executive director Robert Lucas (far left) and former Alderman Timothy Evans (second from right), November 25, 1987. Special Collections and Preservation Division, Chicago Public Library. Photo by Peter J. Schultz.

There is another end and beginning described in *Black on the Block.* Building on the work of scholars like Cathy Cohen, Adolph Reed, and Kevin Gaines, I lay to rest the notion of a unitary black political agenda.[2] The story of the gentrification of North Kenwood–Oakland by middle- and upper-income African Americans—assisted by municipal, institutional, philanthropic, and corporate actors—makes clear the existence of divergent class interests within the black community. While blacks may, by and large, vote Democratic, support affirmative action, and agree on the need for some kind of reparations for slavery, their more immediate, daily concerns involve finding an affordable place to live in a safe neighborhood with good schools. People live locally. The most earnest political battles are played out when they face threats to their neighborhoods or try to fashion a new kind of neighborhood. Controversies then arise over control of and access to public spaces, streets, commercial ventures, jobs, schools, and housing. On these issues, *the* black position becomes *many* positions, split along lines of seniority in the neighborhood, profession, home ownership, age, and taste. Along any one of these axes, one side may launch efforts to shame, stigmatize, silence, or "disappear" the other. These struggles within the neighborhood are often waged between African Americans of different means and different perspectives, but this is by no means just a black-on-black affair. Alliances with and allegiances to whites outside the neighborhood add another layer of complexity to the ever more futile attempt to determine what course of action is in the best interest of the black community. In this way, middle-class blacks act as brokers—as "middlemen" and "middlewomen"—spanning the space between established centers of white economic and political power and the needs of a down but not out black neighborhood.

Internal fissures notwithstanding, the concept of "the black community" is *not* retired in *Black on the Block*, for while attempts to capture a single black politics, black perspective, or black agenda are dead (if they were ever really alive within the black community), I argue that the black community is forged in this engagement. The "Black Metropolis" of the 1930s and 1940s, which St. Clair Drake and Horace Cayton described in unparalleled detail, lives on. North Kenwood–Oakland attracts African Americans looking for a black residential space defined by institutions like Little Black Pearl Workshop and streets such as Muddy Waters Drive.[3] White-owned real estate companies pick up on this desire and give developments names like "Ellington Court" and "Jazz on the Boulevard"—where you can choose a model home to suit your musical tastes: the (Louis) Armstrong, the (Jelly Roll) Morton (see fig. 2). Even gang names—the Black Disciples, the El Rukns—connote black ownership of the neighborhood.

But it is more than just names and symbols (and relatively inexpensive real estate) that attract black middle- and upper-income newcomers to the neighborhood. They come, or come back, to North Kenwood–Oakland out of a sense of racial pride and duty, to be conduits of resources, to model "respectability." In this milieu, disputes between black residents with professional jobs and those with no jobs, between black families who have been in the neighborhood for generations and those who moved in last year, and between blacks who don fraternity colors and those who sport gang colors, are simultaneously debates over what it means to be black. Choosing participation over abdication and involvement over withdrawal, even and especially when the disagreements get heated and sometimes vicious, is what *constitutes* the black community.

Figure 2. New condominiums in North Kenwood named after Duke Ellington, 1998. Photo by author.

Black on the Block is also about North Kenwood–Oakland's history and position as a black neighborhood within a larger context of urban policies and projects.[4] A victim of discriminatory federal home appraisal practices in the 1930s and 1940s, recipient of thousands of units of public housing in the 1950s and 1960s, innocent bystander to urban renewal, and dead space on the radar screens of planners in the 1970s, North Kenwood–Oakland has been shaped by politicians and the businessmen and institutional leaders who influence them. The most recent interventions have been to undo the actions of previous generations of city leaders. Along with other U.S. cities, Chicago is in the midst of a major experiment in the provision and location of public housing, driven by federal initiatives such as the Homeownership and Opportunity for People Everywhere (HOPE) VI program, which aims to transform public housing for poor families into "mixed-income communities." It is in this policy context that the Chicago Housing Authority developed its "Plan for Transformation," which calls for the demolition of at least eighteen thousand units of public housing. Already, most of the concentrated public housing in North Kenwood–Oakland has been demolished to make way for row houses and apartment buildings. The hope is that these new developments—in which poor, less poor, and not poor families will live side by side—will be more palatable to the middle class than were the public housing high-rises of the 1950s and 1960s. The more pleasant design of public housing, the logic goes, will entice the middle and upper classes back to central city neighborhoods.[5] This process, more commonly known as gentrification, is happening in North Kenwood–Oakland, but with a decidedly black flavor. Since the neighborhood is not an island, this book situates the development activity in North Kenwood–Oakland within broader urban and national political and economic trends.

The Conservation of North Kenwood–Oakland

Along Chicago's south lakefront, a mile from the campus of the University of Chicago, and a ten-minute drive from downtown, North Kenwood–Oakland (NKO) has been rediscovered as ripe for new investment, as have many inner-city neighborhoods across the United States, and in many European cities as well. The City of Chicago is actively facilitating this process, having designated the neighborhood in 1990 as a "conservation area." That status, legally supported in both state and federal law, enabled community residents to work with city planners to develop a conservation plan. Ongoing advising and monitoring of the conservation area and its plan is done by the Conservation Community Council (CCC), a body of residents approved by the alderman—the community's elected representative to city government—and the mayor.[6] Meetings of the CCC are central sites of negotiation and contestation over visions of NKO's future.

The details of the making of a conservation area, plan, and council in North Kenwood–Oakland are complicated, multilayered, and, most importantly, intensely contested by the people who were involved, or—as some would have it—*claim* they were involved. There is hardly consensus about when discussions were initiated, who were the most vocal proponents, where the planning activity centered, or how the city bureaucracy was engaged and persuaded to support the designation. Perhaps the preface of a 1978 planning document by the Kenwood Oakland Community Organization (KOCO) best presented the challenges inherent in getting everyone to share one vision of community improvement. It stated, "There has been an adversary [*sic*], rather than a cooperative, relationship between local residents, governmental agencies and private developers. This has either frustrated planning processes or militated against the implementation of plans. . . . It is recognized that both governmental agencies and private developers have a stake in, a role to play, and resources to deploy in the redevelopment of the community area. Local residents can't go it alone."[7]

The constellation of people, organizations, and institutions that ultimately got involved in the planning process is the best proof that no one person alone made the conservation area happen. There were, rather, many key players, whose names will be familiar by the end of this book: Robert Lucas was executive director of KOCO, the organization that commissioned the document quoted above. KOCO was involved early on, calling for a conservation area, rehabilitating apartment buildings, and organizing block clubs and tenant organizations that gave human force to the revitalization efforts.[8] Shirley Newsome and her husband Howard Newsome also worked to organize block clubs, and made key contacts with representatives of the University of Chicago, members of the Hyde Park–Kenwood Conservation Community Council, and private developers. Both Lucas and Newsome formed relationships with real estate giant Ferdinand (Ferd) Kramer, whose designs for the neighborhood sparked as much controversy as the conservation plan itself. Izora Davis was one of the most consistent public housing activists and, along with many comrades, struggled to stay at the planning table throughout the process. Alderman Toni Preckwinkle was not elected until after the North Kenwood–Oakland Conservation Area was designated, but her participation in crafting the conservation plan and her obvious role as the neighborhood's elected representative makes her a key figure in these events.

There are so many others who organized subcommittees, did research on the neighborhood's history, demanded greater police services, and fought for decent recreational facilities. And of course there were those who were unflinchingly critical of the conservation process. "I guess I'm hopeful," said Mary Bordelon, perhaps the most ardent and long-suffering skeptic in the neighborhood, to a reporter from a Chicago weekly. "But I see monsters. I've been seeing them around here for a long time." Those monsters were the community outsiders, the big universities, the big developers, the big philanthropies, even the big researchers, whose enterprising overtures in the neighborhood were not always to be trusted.[9] These diverse perspectives come through in various parts of the story. Still, I am always mindful that, because I did not live through it, I can never fully grasp all of the effort and resistance that resulted in the "conservation" of North Kenwood–Oakland.

Two years into this research, after I felt I had done enough objective observation—taking notes without meddling, listening without asking—I submitted my name to sit on the CCC, and I was appointed. This position gave me access to information on nearly all facets of neighborhood development, but it also branded me in the eyes of some residents as beholden to the desires of the mayor and alderman who approved my appointment. As one critic argued, the CCC was nothing more than a "puppet board waiting to have its strings pulled."[10] I discuss the complexities of this role further in chapter 3, but in short it gave me a sense of the personal and political stakes of community development and it taught me that there are no easy answers.

Conservation areas stand in contrast to "slum and blighted areas." The goal in a conservation area is to salvage existing buildings and renew the neighborhood fabric, whereas slum and blighted areas are subjected to demolition, clearance of structures and people, and new construction. It was the latter classification that allowed for urban renewal and the expansion of downtowns across the country in the 1950s and 1960s. Urban renewal has a long and storied history in American cities, and Chicago's South Side has been an important main stage. Adjacent to North Kenwood–Oakland, the Hyde Park–South Kenwood area surrounding the University of Chicago was established as an avowedly middle-class and reluctantly, for some, interracial neighborhood using the tools of urban renewal. Attaining this balance required the disproportionate removal of African Americans who had then recently moved into Hyde Park–South Kenwood. These acts of aggression in the name of urban renewal left more than a bitter taste in the mouths of many black Chicagoans, especially with regard to the university, which reappears as a major player in contemporary gentrification.[11] It was in this era, the 1950s, that the Kenwood neighborhood was split in half. Forty-seventh Street became, in the words of residents, "the dividing line," "the invisible line," "the Mason-Dixon line." To the north of the line, North Kenwood and the neighborhood north of it, Oakland, languished. To the south, South Kenwood and its southern neighbors, Hyde Park and the University of Chicago, flourished (see frontispiece map).

Given its literal divisiveness and its association with dispossession and exclusion, present-day urbanists have disavowed "urban renewal" as a planning strategy. The move, however, seems more semantic than substantive. The contemporary lexicon favors words such as "renovation" and "rehab," when referring to specific buildings, or "revitalization," "conservation," and "gentrification," when speaking of entire neighborhoods. But the ghost of urban renewal is always present. "After all," anthropologist Arlene Dávila notes, "gentrification—whether called renewal, revitalization, upgrading, or uplifting—always involves the expansion and transformation of neighborhoods through rapid economic investment and population shifts, and yet it is equally implicated with social inequalities."[12] The line between revitalization and gentrification is a thin one. For some, gentrification is heralded as exactly what cities need, an infusion of tax dollars and disposable incomes. For others, gentrification suggests the kind of robbery of poor people's neighborhoods by elites that urban renewal came to symbolize. "Revitalization," on the other hand, often connotes a more bottom-up process, but in some respects it is just a more polite term since revitalization without the intervention or introduction of the gentry is rare. The common thread in all of these approaches is the desire to attract middle- and upper-income families to working-class or poor urban neighborhoods. In North Kenwood–Oakland this has entailed both the mass construction of new, high-end homes and condominiums by developers alongside the more piecemeal rehabilitation of existing old homes by individual investors. The result is a general upward trend in land, housing, and rental prices and the influx of people who can afford them. This sounds a lot like gentrification, so I use the term, along with words like revitalization, throughout this book.

Gentrification, however, is only half the story. Coincident with the planning and ongoing implementation of its conservation plan, NKO is making decisions about public and other subsidized housing in the neighborhood.[13] In the 1980s and early 1990s, nonprofit groups like the Kenwood Oakland Community Organization rehabbed hundreds of dilapidated and abandoned apartment buildings as affordable housing using an array of federal housing programs. This happened relatively quietly. The more contentious fight was over the future of six public housing high-rises referred to generically as the Lakefront Properties. The buildings, built in the 1950s and 1960s, were closed for renovation in 1986. The families that lived there were dispersed across the city with the promise that they would be able to return after the renovations. Two buildings were remodeled and reopened in 1991, but it soon became apparent that the other four high-rises would instead be demolished. Following protests from activist public housing residents, and after acrimonious negotiations and court proceedings, the Chicago Housing Authority was authorized to build 241 public housing apartments in North Kenwood–Oakland to partially replace the demolished high-rises. The process of getting the new public housing built in the neighborhood, placing families in it, and managing it has since been consistently on the agenda of the Conservation Community Council. Such agenda items almost always reopen the debate over the optimal socioeconomic mix for the neighborhood, and over the integration of poor families with their new neighbors, who have paid a pretty penny for their homes.

Extensive new construction is possible in NKO because of past depopulation and demolition. Between 1960 and 1990, Kenwood lost over half of its population, and Oakland lost two-thirds, following a pattern of decline and concentrated poverty experienced by many inner-city black neighborhoods across the country. In 1990, Oakland was the poorest of Chicago's seventy-seven official communities in terms of both median family income and the proportion of families who were poor: 70 percent of Oakland's families had incomes below the federal poverty line. North Kenwood was only slightly better off, with 51 percent of its families living in poverty. Between 1990, when the city recognized the neighborhood as a conservation area, and 2000, the overall demographic story shows considerable upward socioeconomic change. By 2000, 20 percent of the families in the neighborhood earned more than $50,000 per year, up from 6 percent a decade earlier. During the same period, the neighborhood's poverty rate declined precipitously, median family income more than doubled, the home ownership rate nearly doubled, and the cost of housing skyrocketed (see table).[14]

Despite these changes, Oakland was still the second poorest of Chicago's communities in terms of income and had the third highest neighborhood poverty rate in 2000. North Kenwood had the twelfth lowest median family income and the eighth highest poverty rate. Part of the reason for this is that in 2000 nearly 40 percent of North Kenwood–Oakland's housing stock—more than two thousand units—was publicly subsidized, either as public housing for families, the elderly, or the disabled or through other federal and state programs.[15] Eligibility for these units is based on household income, with cutoffs that include some moderate-income workers and people receiving various forms of public assistance, many of whom also work. The presence of subsidized

Demographic changes in North Kenwood–Oakland, 1990–2000

	1990	2000
Total population	10,938	9,987
Percent black	99	98
Median income (in 1999 dollars)	$9,391	$21,949
Percent with income over $50,000	6	20
Percent homeowners	10	17
Median home value (in 1999 dollars)	$44,160	$219,153
Percent of families that are poor	63	39

Source: 1990 and 2000 U.S. census, http://www.census.gov.

housing thus ensures the presence of poor and working-class families in NKO at least until the government contracts, which can range from fifteen to ninety-nine years, expire. When that time comes, landlords can either renew the contracts, thereby keeping their apartments affordable for the tenants who live there, or opt out of whatever subsidy program was used to finance the building. Those who opt out can then charge higher rents or convert the buildings to cooperatives or condominiums. During the course of this research, two subsidized buildings, with six apartments each, converted to for-sale condominiums.[16]

Amid significant income flux, North Kenwood–Oakland remains predominantly black. It has been so since the 1950s, and it is for the most part experiencing "black gentrification." Black professionals are moving in from other Chicago neighborhoods, from other cities, and back to the city from the suburbs.[17] For some African Americans, the move is motivated by what legal scholar Sheryll Cashin calls "integration exhaustion," the sociopsychological fatigue experienced especially by blacks who work in integrated environments or have been pioneers in white neighborhoods.[18] Respondents in North Kenwood–Oakland, though, talked more about factors that pulled them toward a black neighborhood than factors that pushed them away from whites.

This process is also fueled by the growing affluence of African Americans in Chicago. The proportion of black households in Chicago with incomes over $50,000 doubled between 1990 and 2000, from 14 percent to 28 percent. The share of black households earning $100,000 or more rose even more dramatically, albeit from a smaller base, from 1 percent to 6 percent over the same time period. The expansion of the black middle and upper classes outpaced the expansion of high-income earners in any other racial or ethnic group. These households (especially at the highest end) are the likely newcomers to North Kenwood–Oakland, where in 2006 a two-bedroom, two-bathroom condominium could cost as much as $300,000.[19]

Some whites have moved into the neighborhood, but the discourse among black residents concerning the imminence of whites' arrival is more extensive and more telling than their actual presence. North Kenwood–Oakland was less than 1 percent white in 1990, and 1.2 percent white in 2000. Still, residents are convinced of an impending white offensive; I choose the word "offensive" precisely because it suggests an organized purpose. "Quite frankly," one resident asserted, "we were never supposed to be here. Black people were never supposed to be here." Another concurred: "There's no way in the world they're gonna leave between McCormick Place [the Chicago convention center] and the Museum [of Science and Industry] to us. I mean, let's face it, you know, they're not going to leave it with us. If we don't make the money and build up our own community within ourselves, they gon' take it."

Low-income black residents are doubly threatened, first by the price of the new housing and second by the prospect of racial exclusion. Tying these two issues together, one public housing resident in Oakland said, "Well, the changes I see now, they tearing down all the buildings and they getting ready to build homes. You know how they say the white people moved all the way to the suburbs because they don't want to be around us? So now they building all these homes knowing damn well most of us cannot afford them. So they trying to get the white people back in. And that's the system. And they want this lakefront back." Another public housing resident had a simple but bleak forecast for the neighborhood: "No more blacks." "No more blacks?" I asked. "Couple. Coupla blacks. They got money." From this resident's perspective, the neighborhood's future owners were white, or black people with money. She was not included in either scenario.

There is no way to accurately predict the racial future of North Kenwood–Oakland, but there are signs that suggest more whites will move in. For example, the University of Chicago actively markets the neighborhood and offers incentives to employees who decide to buy a home there. Rising home prices throughout the city may encourage whites to look in areas that they would not otherwise explore. North Kenwood–Oakland's favorable location—near the lake, downtown, and the university—could recommend it to liberal whites looking for housing they can afford.[20] Furthermore, if real estate prices continue to escalate, there will be an ever smaller proportion of African Americans who can afford to buy homes in North Kenwood–Oakland. Even though black incomes rose over the 1990s, the pool of high-income white buyers is much larger than the equivalent pool of affluent African Americans. In 2000, 47 percent of white households in the city of Chicago had incomes over $50,000 compared to only 28 percent of black households. The disparity was even greater further up the income ladder, with 17 percent of white households, but only 6 percent of black households, earning $100,000 or more.[21] Given these factors, the anxieties of black residents seem warranted—simple math suggests that fewer blacks than whites will be able to buy in North Kenwood–Oakland. But history teaches us that figuring out where the races will live has little to do with math.[22] In the end, the question of the racial future of North Kenwood–Oakland hangs over the heads of residents, and ultimately of this book, without resolution. For the snapshot in time that this research represents, however, the issues are decidedly *intraracial*.

The Silent Salience of Class

The fact of racial homogeneity does not preclude the importance of difference, divisions, and distinctions. There are many ways to categorize people in North Kenwood–Oakland: men and women, Baptists and African Methodist Episcopalians, native Chicagoans and out-of-towners, people who went to different Chicago high schools. The categories that this book is most preoccupied with, however, are those that relate to *class*. Technical definitions of class, as framed by academics, government officials, and other definition makers, include some combination of how much money a person has, what kind of work he does, and how far she went in school. Common, everyday practices of determining if someone is in the lower, working, middle, or upper class are likely to be based on similar criteria. But people do not wear their diplomas on their sleeves or have their net worth written on their foreheads. Because we often cannot know the "hard facts" of class position, we usually settle for observing and making sense of "soft facts" instead. We express our own class standing and read others' class positions through signs of language, dress, demeanor, performance, and other objects and behaviors that have social meaning and that can be mapped onto the class hierarchy. This kind of stratification in the social order is what Max Weber called "status," where status groups are stratified according to the principles of their *consumption* of goods. The habits and manners with which people use the things they buy (or use their free time or deploy their bodies) constitute "styles of life," or lifestyles. Weber argues that the two spheres of *class* and *status* are closely connected. "The social order is of course conditioned by the economic order to a high degree," Weber writes, "and in its turn reacts upon it."[23]

The intertwined economic and social orders are both important in North Kenwood–Oakland. But as in American society more generally, discussions about lifestyles and status are more salient, whereas there is relative silence on the topics of class and the materiality of economic circumstances. Americans talk *around* class by using the vocabulary of status and lifestyles. Instead of referring to how much money someone makes, we describe their overseas vacations or their fancy cars. Instead of looking at a person's résumé to see if he or she attended college, we dismiss him because he has cornrows or her because she wears long press-on nails.

Many people also call this the realm of culture. Unfortunately, the word "culture" has been overly biologized. Ever since anthropologist Oscar Lewis proclaimed, dreadfully, that "by the time slum children are age six or seven they have usually absorbed the basic values and attitudes of their subculture and are not psychologically geared to take full advantage of changing conditions or increased opportunities which may occur in their life-time" there have been academic wars over just how much a pathological culture is to blame for poverty, and black poverty in particular. As a result of those debates, and despite many attempts to rescue the term, "culture" now conjures up notions of a way of life to which people are so attached that they cannot part with it or change it. Poor people's (and black people's) culture has been cast as a defective body part that causes debilitating stress on the entire collective organism. Because people are so stuck in a dysfunctional culture, one outside the "mainstream," they must be, goes the argument, *morally* deficient. From biology to morals, the word has taken on too much baggage. So while "culture" may be the more common rubric for the facets of life that I describe in this book, "lifestyle" is more *analytically* powerful because it avoids the preachy muck in which culture often gets stuck.[24] The lifestyle markers that take center stage in the debates about who should be included in and excluded from North Kenwood–Oakland can always be traced back to and mapped forward onto the hard facts of economic inequality, or the silent salience of class in American society.

There are three primary axes of differentiation in the realm of status and lifestyles that emerge as ways to talk about class without talking about class in North Kenwood–Oakland: (1) home owner/renter, (2) public housing resident/non–public housing resident, and (3) old-timer/newcomer. Each has obvious connections to the economic order: home ownership requires a level of financial security, public housing has become the housing for those with little money, and newcomers must be well-off to afford rising housing prices. These dichotomies operate both as ways that residents represent and organize themselves and their interests, and as analytical categories.

Still, while these categories are about class, they are not *all about class*. The categories neither correlate perfectly with class divisions nor consistently predict or predetermine the sentiments of their individual members. Indeed, the thesis of this book is that the primacy of race is often reasserted to overshadow these cleavages. When being black is the most important identity, there can be cross-category sympathy, empathy, and bonding. Furthermore, these groups are not mutually exclusive. Home owners, for example, represent a mix of old-timers and newcomers. Most old-timer home owners are senior citizens who moved to the neighborhood in the 1940s, 1950s, and 1960s, but some are young adults who inherited homes from the original residents. Newcomer home owners are mostly young and middle-aged individuals and families. In terms of actual class position, home owners represent a wide swath of working- to middle- to upper-class occupations—painters, lawyers, housewives, teachers, drugstore clerks, nurses, professors, mail carriers, bankers, and retirees—with the newer home owners clustering toward the upper end of the occupational and income spectrum. Hence, the category of home owners crosses those of economic class and neighborhood tenure. What home owners share is a financial investment in their homes and a desire to protect it.[25]

Renters can also be old-timers or newcomers. Most renters are poor or working class because the majority of rental housing in the neighborhood is supported by some kind of public subsidy program and is therefore reserved for low- and moderate-income families. The situation is continuously changing, but I first learned this when I searched for an apartment, trying to find one that did not put a ceiling on my income.

The public housing/non–public housing distinction is perhaps the most clear cut in terms of its connection to class, although a variety of residents (home owners and renters, newcomers and old-timers) speak about having lived in public housing at some point in their lives. More-over, work requirements and welfare reform rules have made it the case that many public housing residents work, but still for low wages. All of the caveats and confusion notwithstanding, these categories line up relatively neatly on the crucial dimension of class. On one side sit new-comer home owners—the newer they are, the more affluent—and on the other side, old and new renters and public housing residents. It is old-timer home owners who fall in between or outside of these catego-ries, and whose positions on neighborhood issues are the most variable.

Despite the fact that home owners are the minority in North Ken-wood–Oakland, they dominate the community organizations, and new-comers are also disproportionately represented at most community meetings. For example, when I lived on Berkeley Avenue in North Ken-wood all sixteen dues-paying members of the block club were home owners (and most were women, since among the old-timers the men died before the women). Old-timers I interviewed attributed their with-drawal from the block club to the disproportionate influence of new-comers who wanted to change so much. The participation of public housing residents in the community waned once the high-rise build-ings were demolished, but I have been able to capture their voices through archival research and interviews. The predominance of home owners in neighborhood organizations is related to a more generaliz-able point about urban processes made by sociologists John Logan and Harvey Molotch: "The 'better element' in an otherwise disadvantaged area can function as a vanguard for change. . . . Not surprisingly, those who ordinarily join and become leaders in a community organization tend to be the middle-class (or aspiring middle-class) homeowners."[26] The balance of power in neighborhood decision making favors home owners. Their values and norms about appropriate neighborhood deco-rum are most audibly expressed, and they frequently invoke their sta-tus as taxpayers to legitimate their demands for action. Home-owning newcomers and their old-timer allies translate their economic power into political voice.

Overview of the Book

Black on the Block uses ethnographic data to examine the interests and actions of four key stakeholders: (1) government officials, (2) private investors and developers, (3) institutions and community organizations, and (4) residents. I began research in North Kenwood–Oakland in 1998. I moved into the neighborhood and have observed it as both a home owner and a renter, gathering three notebooks of field notes plus a file cabinet and binders full of flyers, newsletters, community newspapers, plans, and political literature. I conducted 108 tape-recorded interviews with actors across the above four categories, each of which lasted one to two hours. As secretary of the Conservation Community Council, I took detailed minutes of its meetings. I obtained all council minutes and correspondences that predated my research through a Freedom of Information Act request to the city's Department of Planning and Development. I also attended the meetings of other neighborhood organizations like the Kenwood Oakland Community Organization and block clubs. In order to ground this research in urban politics and planning more broadly, I attended numerous meetings, conferences, and briefings outside of the neighborhood, including ones at the Chicago Housing Authority, the Metropolitan Planning Council, and the MacArthur Foundation, which is a major funder of neighborhood revitalization efforts in Chicago and the funder of my research. I also placed a graduate research assistant at Chicago's Department of Planning and Development for a summer to get a sense of the workings of the city agency charged with revitalizing the neighborhood.

Many of the quotes in this book are from transcriptions of the interviews I conducted, and many others come from the notes I took in public meetings, neighborhood gatherings, and casual conversations. When quoting from this original research, I have not included citations. Quotes drawn from secondary sources, such as community newspapers or the minutes of meetings I did not attend, are documented in the footnotes. Halfway into writing the book, I realized it would be impossible to conceal the identities of the key actors in this story, and I thought that many of them might want to be recognized. Thus, I sent portions of the draft manuscript to everyone who was quoted and asked whether they would prefer that I use their real name or a pseudonym. I honored their preferences, but for obvious reasons I cannot specify which names are real names and which are pseudonyms.[27]

Finally, much of the research in this book is historical. I consulted the collections and archives of the Chicago Historical Society (now the Chicago History Museum), the Newberry Library, the University of Chicago, the University of Illinois at Chicago, and the Chicago Public Library. I undertook significant legal research on the *Gautreaux* lawsuit, a racial discrimination case filed in 1966 that affects all new public housing in Chicago. All of the *Gautreaux* court files are located in the Office of the Clerk for the United States District Court, Northern District of Illinois. Since 1998, I have maintained a file of clippings from citywide and neighborhood newspapers, and I have searched the online archives of the major newspapers for the period preceding my research. I also utilize secondary data sources, such as the U.S. Census, and three neighborhood-specific surveys conducted at various times by other researchers in Chicago. From these voluminous data, I craft a story of urban power and politics suffused with racial and class tensions.

Black on the Block begins in the era before blacks were even allowed on the blocks of North Kenwood–Oakland. In 1998, I moved to 4432 South Berkeley Avenue. A short street only four blocks long, Berkeley Avenue was designated as the core of the North Kenwood Landmark District because so many of the homes built in the 1890s are still standing. This distinction makes the house a perfect narrator for the early history of the neighborhood, which is the subject of chapter 1. Over time, 4432 Berkeley and the other houses in the neighborhood passed from the rich industrialists for whom they were built to a mix of professional and laboring native-born and immigrant whites, then to working- and middle-class blacks, and then to the black poor. From the platting of Berkeley Avenue in 1890 to the conservation plan of 1990, I chronicle the weddings, the vacations, the improvement associations, the schools, the racial covenants, the music, and the murders in the neighborhood. This biography of one house previews how North Kenwood–Oakland fits into larger urban studies debates.

Chapter 2 uses the titles of two books by two noted black sociologists—E. Franklin Frazier's *Black Bourgeoisie* and William Julius Wilson's *The Truly Disadvantaged*—to signal *Black on the Block's* focus on the meeting of the black middle class and the black poor in North Kenwood–Oakland. These two texts allow for the exploration of a variety of relevant scholarly debates, from the importance of "respectability" in the representations of black identity, to the role of middle-class blacks as political and moral leaders, to the ideologies guiding contemporary urban policies promoting mixed-income communities. In this chapter, I introduce the concept of "black middlemen," and middlewomen, as a way to understand the workings of race and class in urban politics. The forebears of black middlemen were the subject of Frazier's reflections, but the group has grown in size and prominence since Frazier's time. These African American brokers have established themselves within networks of public and private power in Chicago and beyond. They exist within a system of coalition politics that fosters and requires both finesse and subterfuge in the back-and-forth translation of the demands of various interest groups. As the links between low-income African Americans and powerful white elites, black middlemen are the main characters of this book, and middleness is its dominating motif.

Chapters 3 and 4 give empirical form to the middleman concept. Black newcomers broker important resources for North Kenwood–Oakland, the most basic of those being mortgage capital. Their presence, and the demands they made to financial institutions, drew investments to this neighborhood, which had long been ignored. I also explore the participation of professional African Americans in "growth machine" politics, where the goal is to increase land values and subject land to its most profitable use. This is a brokerage function that does not always have a positive outcome for existing poor residents of the neighborhood. At the end of chapter 3, I interrogate my own role as a black middlewoman.

The politics of school reform is presented in chapter 4. Again newcomers have brokered school improvements that were desperately needed, but again not all residents have benefited equally. The resources these middlemen broker are of a particular kind, in line with a neoliberal, or entrepreneurial, approach to state governance, which puts significant responsibility on citizens to choose from a universe of public goods that are increasingly provided or managed by private entities.

Chapters 5 and 6 are companion chapters on the volatile controversy over the Lakefront Properties, the sixteen-story public housing buildings overlooking Lake Michigan in Oakland. The disputes surround the prospects of demolishing the buildings, the responsibility to residents who once lived there, and the logic of building new public housing as North Kenwood–Oakland revitalizes. In 1969, the federal courts found in *Gautreaux v. Chicago Housing Authority* that public housing in Chicago was intentionally and illegally concentrated in black neighborhoods, and that blacks were restricted to living in these segregated projects. In the mid-1990s, a group of North Kenwood–Oakland residents waged their case *against* public housing by focusing on this original finding in the *Gautreaux* case. Concentrations of public housing in black neighborhoods levy a negative economic toll on the neighborhoods and their black residents, they argued, and thus constitute racial discrimination. This gloomy reality would persist if new public housing was built in the neighborhood. It would stymie their struggle to reverse years of disinvestment, depopulation, and decay.

On the other hand, poor people have waged a decades-long fight to maintain a presence on Chicago's lakefront. Thwarting further injury to this most vulnerable of populations constitutes the case *for* public housing in North Kenwood–Oakland. Public housing residents have constantly feared permanent displacement and have repeatedly been promised that it would not happen. But their fears, which at times have seemed paranoid, have quite often proved justified. The failed promises made by public officials often beget revised promises, all cloaked in a rhetoric of kindhearted intentions. I present both sides of this debate without reconciliation to support the point made in chapter 2, namely that plans to transform public housing into mixed-income communities are but microremedies to problems rooted in larger structural forces of racial and class discrimination.

Chapter 7 is about crime. Geographer Neil Smith argues that contemporary gentrification has taken on the character of the French "revanchist city" of the late nineteenth century. *Revanche* means revenge, and Smith contends that revenge characterizes contemporary gentrification efforts. Marginalized groups—distinguished by race, class, sexuality, or other characteristics—are blamed for the decadence and decline of the American city, resulting in a stream of regressive, if not punitive, policies. In NKO, this vigilance is manifest first in the attribution of crime to public housing, which justifies condemning and ultimately demolishing it, and second through the progressive criminalization of quality-of-life issues. Activism is initially focused on lowering the incidence of serious violent or property crimes, and the political clout of new black middle-class brokers yields big payoffs in terms of improved safety. However, attention soon shifts to curtailing activities that straddle the line between licit and illicit or, lesser still, fall into the category of legal but *undesirable* behaviors. My focus on the actions taken by newcomers against poor residents who have different relationships to public and private space and are more subject to regulation through their reliance on publicly subsidized housing, highlights the bidirectionality of violence, both literal and symbolic, in gentrifying neighborhoods.

I conclude by reiterating the class fractures within black identity through a focus on lifestyles and tastes. Distinction making characterizes black communities, constantly challenging both the attempt at racial solidarity by organizational activists and the assumption of homogeneity by academic and other outsiders. Middlemen and women are especially crucial since they can either work toward tolerance and co-operation, or wield their influence to quash behaviors they find objectionable. In the conclusion, I elaborate a theory of the middle that goes beyond North Kenwood–Oakland to generalize the roles of middlemen in both fighting and perpetuating inequality.

Yet just as boundaries exist within this black community, they also work from without to contain its members within a community of solidarity. Alongside the work of difference, distinction, and sometimes even dislike exists the salience of race as a unifying social category, fostering allegiances across class and similar experiences of racial otherness. Residents of North Kenwood–Oakland are, for richer or for poorer, members of the black community. To resolve these contradictory pulls, I conceive of blackness as a collective *endeavor*, and the black community as an implicit agreement to persevere in that journey.

This Book Is . . . , This Book Is Not

Black on the Block is a work of sociology, anthropology, political science, legal criticism, and history, and is grounded in the interdisciplinary fields of African American studies and urban studies. But such a scope can be as confusing as it is elucidating. Therefore, I want to clearly identify the fields, debates, and questions to which I hope to make the strongest contribution—that is, to state what this book is and what this book is not—in order to guide readers' interests and expectations.

This book is not a study of the causes and consequences of gentrification. While I attend to many of the factors that have been raised in the literature as causing gentrification, such as the bottoming out of rents and home prices and the role of public sector inputs, I do not try to pinpoint what caused North Kenwood–Oakland to become attractive to middle- and upper-income African Americans at the particular time that it did. And whereas I am interested in some of the effects of gentrification, this is not a study of the most controversial purported consequence of gentrification—displacement. As a piece of ethnography, the book offers no quantitative measurements of displacement. Because I interviewed and observed people who still live in the neighborhood, I have little sense of the extent to which displacement might have occurred. When it is relevant, I report when people whom I interviewed have since moved away; if the reason was related to the socioeconomic upgrading of the neighborhood, then I state that too. But I have no findings that definitively weigh in on the heated debate about the displacement effects of gentrification.[28] Finally, this book is not an evaluation of the various policy approaches to improving public housing. There is a HOPE VI project in North Kenwood–Oakland, and the new mixed-income housing that will replace the Lakefront Properties high-rises mirrors the HOPE VI model. But I did not survey the public housing residents at the beginning of these experiments to track their moves or measure their outcomes. Nor have I analyzed the complex financing schemes that are required to bring one of these developments to fruition.[29] Public housing is an integral part of North Kenwood–Oakland, so much so that I tell and retell parts of its story from various vantage points. But I approach it with the eyes of a sociologist, not those of a policy analyst.

This book *is* about gentrification and public housing and mixed-income communities, but as contexts within which African American residents negotiate each other, the outside players, and the various layers of public (governmental and civic) decisions that frame what is preferable and what is possible. Recently, Monique Taylor, Sabiyha Prince, and John L. Jackson have done similar research on middle- and upper-income blacks moving back to Harlem, Michelle Boyd has written about these processes in Chicago, and Derek Hyra has studied both Harlem and black Chicago. Arlene Dávila and Gina Pérez offer engaging ethnographies about the gentrification of Spanish Harlem and Puerto Rican communities on Chicago's near northwest side.[30] In a rare and encouraging kind of qualitative verification, there are remarkable similarities in the scenarios portrayed and the sentiments expressed by gentrifiers and established residents across these settings. More than any of these books, however, I hope to develop the trope of the "middle" in my discussion of the brokering that newcomers do when they move back onto the blocks of North Kenwood–Oakland. I highlight the conflicted but pivotal frontline role that middle-class African Americans play in transforming the neighborhoods of poor African Americans who are sometimes dismissed and disparaged, while at the same time battling *on behalf of the race*, including the poor of the race, for the rights and resources that citizenship and municipal residency should, but do not always, automatically entail. This book is about the politics of blackness and the politics of cities in which African Americans are asserting their rights and wants.

1

4432 Berkeley

The Gilded Age (1889–1919)

The two-story, graystone row house at 4432 South Berkeley Avenue, in what is now North Kenwood, was built long before any of the drama narrated in this book unfolded, and it will likely stand well into the time when the events are forgotten (see fig. 3). Its persistence—through new owners and departing neighbors, two world's fairs and many block parties, feverish construction and wanton demolition—supplies a home base from which to recount the neighborhood's past and present.

> Architect Robert Rae: For G. S. Swift [*sic*], 8 two- and three-story dwellings to be erected on Berkeley between 44th and 45th streets. Furnaces, mantels, bathrooms, etc., to cost about $50,000.[1]

In 1891, on a newly created Chicago street that stretched for only four blocks, from 41st to 45th Streets through the hearts of both North Kenwood and Oakland, 4432 Berkeley Avenue came to life. It was designed by architect Robert Rae as one in a row of eight homes, all similar but each with attractive variations. He built the houses to the highest architectural standards of the time. "First-class in every respect," read a newspaper advertisement for the houses. "Best of plumbing throughout; walls all tinted and principal rooms artistically decorated; wired for electric

Figure 3. 4432 South Berkeley Avenue, 2005. Photo by author.

gas-lighting; electric bells and speaking tubes; pipes for fuel-gas to kitchen and mantel grate; elegant buffet in dining room. Hot and cold water and mantels on every floor; clothes chute from bath-room to laundry." Another notice described the exterior of "buff Bedford rock-faced stone" and the interior "finished in selected oak with plate-glass fronts . . ., genuine bronze hardware, [and] old copper finish."[2] Many of these distinctive details and stately antiques were still present over a hundred years later when I first visited 4432 Berkeley. The buffet still anchored the dining room waiting for a new set of china to be displayed. The door handles throughout the house had tarnished as only real bronze will. The floors, laid in an unusual ship's plank design accented with decorative treenails, had astonishingly few scratches or other signs of their age. The house's physical permanence testifies to the technological advances and quality craftsmanship that characterized the Industrial Age.

Between 1891, when 4432 Berkeley was built, and 1998, when I moved in, the six-foot wooden windows of the house provided a view of history as it was made. In 1889, just a year before construction started on Berkeley, the City of Chicago had annexed the Village of Hyde Park, which included the towns of Oakland and Kenwood and the entire area south of 39th Street and east of State Street. Soon after, Chicago hosted the World's Columbian Exposition of 1893. The annexation of Hyde Park and the world's fair set the stage for the transformation of North Kenwood and Oakland from bucolic, aristocratic commuter suburbs— "the embodiment of an elegant rural preserve"—into higher-density, middle-class urban neighborhoods. "By 1910," wrote the Commission on Chicago Landmarks, "the community was considered to be middle-class and slightly out-of-date."[3]

During the neighborhood's early development, architects of significant renown designed new homes for equally prominent industrialists. In 1886, on Drexel Boulevard, the grandest street in the neighborhood (two blocks west of Berkeley), Daniel P. Burnham, who would go on to design the grounds of the Columbian Exposition, made his mark on North Kenwood. His firm, Burnham & Root, crafted a mansion for William E. Hale, owner of the Hale Elevator Company, whose business was booming as Chicago pioneered the building of skyscrapers. In Oakland, architect Cicero Hine designed a row of houses that garnered the following quaint description from the 1887 *Chicago Inter Ocean* newspaper:

> Eleven Berkeley cottages on Berkeley avenue between 41st and 42nd streets. Some of them are built partially of stone and others entirely of stone. The houses embody in a marked degree the elements of the attractive and popular along with the economical and substantial. . . . Throughout, the Queen Anne architecture of all these houses is as attractive as it is diversified.[4]

Despite the modest size and charm of these cottages, the owners were principals in law firms, presidents of corporations, and high-ranking city officials. Such distinguished Chicagoans lived throughout North Kenwood and Oakland at the end of the nineteenth century. Acclaimed architect Louis Sullivan designed and lived in a house at 4575 Lake Park Avenue; lawyer Melville Fuller, who went on to become Chief Justice of the U.S. Supreme Court, had a home built at 3600 Lake Park; John G. Shedd, president of Marshall Field & Company, lived in two different North Kenwood homes, at 4628 Ellis Avenue and 4515 Drexel; Hannah Greenebaum Solomon, founder of the National Council of Jewish Women, lived at 4060 Lake Park; and paper magnate Lucius G. Fisher, who commissioned his own now-landmarked skyscraper in downtown Chicago, made his home at 4036 Ellis.

While grandeur and distinction surrounded 4432 Berkeley, its own early history is more the story of absentee investors who saw a chance to make money off the city's phenomenal growth. Chicago's population doubled between 1880 and 1890 (partially because of annexation), reaching the one million mark and surpassing that of Philadelphia, which until then had been the nation's second largest city (behind New York). Chicago's population doubled again by 1910. William H. Cairnduff, a financial investor in the development of Berkeley Avenue, remarked to a gathering of the Chicago Real Estate Board in 1893, "The growth of our city is marvelous. So marvelous that the resident of but a dozen years can claim the distinction of being an older resident than one-half the present population of the city." Even more, the coming world's fair would take place in Jackson Park, just a streetcar ride away from Berkeley Avenue. Whatever was built and couldn't be sold could surely be rented to the visitors who would descend upon the city for the fair. Cairnduff & Co. made such a pitch in its advertisement for a new house in Oakland: "P.S.—Don't forget the World's Fair. Our houses have six large and cheerful sleeping rooms, which you can turn to enormous profits in the next two years."[5]

The legal description of the land under 4432 is "Swift's Berkeley Avenue Addition to Chicago," Swift being Gustavus F. Swift, founder of the meatpacking empire Swift & Company.[6] Men like Swift, and the thousands of people who worked for them, inspired Carl Sandburg's 1916 poem "Chicago," which opens with the appellation "Hog Butcher for the World."[7] Swift bought and subdivided the plot on Berkeley when it became clear that the annexation of Hyde Park would bring growth to the area and handsome profits to its owners. Joining the rush, Leander Hamilton McCormick—nephew of the founder of McCormick Reaper Company (which became International Harvester, the forerunner of present-day Navistar Corporation)—took another part of Berkeley, just a bit north of 4432. Swift commissioned architect Robert Rae to build his development. Foreshadowing the more understated future of the block, Rae's designs "focused on small scale commercial buildings and residences in eclectic historical styles."[8] He was not an architect of particular distinction, although his solid and pleasing contribution to North Kenwood–Oakland's landscape now comprises the core of the historical landmark district. For Swift and the other landowners on Berkeley, Rae fashioned a sturdy row of single-family homes fronted with limestone and sandstone, ornamented with arched windows, gabled parapets, and detailed balustrades. The architectural survey of 4432 exalts that the block is "noteworthy due to excellence in design and craftsmanship."[9]

Yet despite its beauty and modern appointments, 4432 Berkeley changed hands from investor to investor in its early years and alternated between being rented out and sitting vacant.[10] Its owner by 1896, Willoughby Walling, by all accounts did not live in it. Willoughby Walling was a prominent Chicago physician, born of a prominent (slaveholding) Kentucky family and father to the prominent William English Walling. W. E. B. DuBois wrote a letter to William Walling in 1929 saying, "Personally, I know perfectly well that you are the real founder of the NAACP. I have kept still while others have scrambled unseemingly for the honor." In active repudiation of the ignominious racial practices of his forebears, William English Walling worked with DuBois to build the organization that championed the rights of African Americans.[11] Black history on Berkeley Avenue began with the Walling family long before any black people lived there. In announcements of weddings, travels, parties, and all the Gilded Age happenings of the 1890s and early 1900s, Willoughby Walling is listed as living at 4127 Drexel Boulevard, a few blocks north and west of the house on Berkeley. Most likely he owned 4432 as an investment property. By 1902, the *Tribune* ran the following ad: "To Rent—4432 Berkeley-Av., 8 room modern stone; $50."[12]

The rocky start of 4432 was likely the result of the Depression of 1893, which sobered the optimism that had motivated the development of Berkeley and the rest of the neighborhood. Banks across the country failed and double-digit unemployment riled workers everywhere. Chicago was a hotbed of labor unrest; train workers walked off the job in the Pullman Strike of 1894.[13] The early residents of North Kenwood and Oakland did not work on the railroad or in the stockyards, but they were a varied lot and weathered the economic storm in varying ways. Some of the better-off residents were Charles Pincus Monash at 4436 Berkeley, who was a partner in the Monash-Younker Steam Specialty Company, and Isaac Austin Freeman, a dentist, at 4438 Berkeley. Alongside them were grain dealers, lawyers, civil engineers, doctors, bookkeepers, and, on the corner at 4400 Berkeley, a "manufacturer of waists and dresses." Families like these were likely unaffected by the 1893 depression, at least if the ability to hire servants is any indication of financial comfort. In 1898, the occupants of 4432 searched for a "competent girl for general housework, German, Danish or Swedish."[14] Next door at 4434, the 1900 census listed Augusta Berg as the Swedish servant of the Reed family. All along Berkeley, there were servants from Ireland, Russia, and Bohemia, as well as some who came to Chicago from small U.S. towns. And at a time when African Americans comprised less than 2 percent of the neighborhood's population, there were three black servants on Berkeley—Gennie Thurman from Indiana, Ellis Oglesbee from Missouri, and Martha Shephard from Alabama—all marked as "literate" on the census forms.

Even earlier, there had been another black man working on Berkeley, who was a witness to one of the street's most newsworthy incidents. On June 12, 1895, a commotion arose when a servant, Mary Hall from Kentucky, ran frantically from 4430 Berkeley to tell the neighbors that her mistress, Mrs. Hooke, had tried to commit suicide. When the neighbors went to investigate, they found Hooke, her face cut and bruised, sitting dazed on the back porch, where the black man, identified by the newspapers only as "a negro named Steve," had been doing some chores. Contradicting her servant's story, Hooke claimed that Hall had beaten her and then run off. Hall was indicted, and the trial "attracted many of the fashionable neighbors in Hyde Park and Kenwood," maybe even the unknown tenants of 4432, given that they lived next door. The defense called several character witnesses for Mrs. Hall, whom the newspaper described as "an honest-looking servant of the better class." But Mrs. Hooke, who was deaf, pale-faced, and slender, also told a compelling story. The trial ended in a hung jury.[15]

Servants like Mary Hall and Steve lived with and worked for wealthy families, while working-class households supplemented their incomes, in order to make the rent or mortgage, by taking in boarders. It was no more than a year after buying 4430 Berkeley that the neighbors there, a "private family," tried to let a "nicely furnished room" to a single gentleman with references. The going one-room rent at the time was $12 a month.[16] In a three-story house across the street, at 4431, William Bray, a grocery clerk, lived with his wife and stepdaughter. Given Mr. Bray's small family, large house, and humble occupation, it makes sense that the Brays were renting rooms to two boarders at the time of the 1900 census. While the presence of both servants and boarders tells us something about the socioeconomic diversity of the families that lived on Berkeley, it also reflects the high tide of (im)migration, as people flooded into this newly acquired piece of Chicago at the end of the nineteenth century. The population of Ward 32, which stretched from 39th Street to 55th Street and State Street to Lake Michigan, more than doubled from 26,775 residents in 1890 to 69,202 in 1900.

As the centuries changed, so did Berkeley. During the 1900s and 1910s, the proportion of executives and professionals fell while that of midlevel workers rose. By 1920, there were hardly any servants, and boarders nearly outnumbered the official occupants. At 4431 Berkeley, where in 1900 William Bray and family lived with two boarders, Charles Barker now lived with his wife, his mother-in-law, and four boarders. The *Chicago Blue Book*, a compilation of "the most prominent householders of Chicago," listed fewer and fewer names on Berkeley Avenue. The neighborhood was not completely démodé, however, since some of the wealthiest residents stayed on. Millionaire John G. Shedd lived at 4515 Drexel for over twenty years while president of Marshall Field & Company, and almost until his death in 1926. And Willoughby Walling, who owned 4432 Berkeley, continued to receive guests on Wednesdays at 4127 Drexel until he died, shortly after Thanksgiving in 1916. Berkeley was still middle class, but now more lower than upper.

The census recorded that in 1910 fully 70 percent of the families on this stretch of Berkeley were renters, a not uncommon figure at a time when only 46 percent of Americans owned their homes. In 1912, 4432 Berkeley was rented by William Hirsch, a wholesale jeweler, and his wife, Mina, who fancied herself an entrepreneur of sorts. Responding to a newspaper feature on "profitable employment for women in occupations which they can carry on at home without interfering with their domestic duties," Mrs. Hirsch sent the following account: "I weave Indian work baskets made out of 5 cents' worth of reed and raffia, which I get at any seed store. Patterns I copy from oriental rugs. It takes me about a week to make one and I could sell them readily for from $5 to $6. —Mrs. William Hirsch, 4432 Berkeley avenue." Either she sold a lot of Indian baskets or Mr. Hirsch was a very successful jeweler, because on May 20, 1914, the family—mother, father, and son Joseph—sailed for Europe for the entire summer. Berkeley's cachet was fading but was not extinguished.[17]

After Walling died in 1916, 4432 Berkeley was finally sold to a family that would actually occupy it. In keeping with the neighborhood's moderating prestige, the new owner, Roy P. Donovan, was a painter and decorating contractor. Whereas the early residents of North Kenwood and Oakland had belonged to the exclusive Union League, Chicago, and Standard Clubs, Donovan was a Mason, an honor and mark of distinction indeed, but not one that conveyed the same high-society status. He had no children to fill the four-bedroom house on Berkeley, but he served his organization dutifully, as master of the Jackson Park Lodge #915 and secretary of the Woodlawn Chapter.

During the Donovans' tenure in 4432 Berkeley, Roy Donovan (who died in 1947), his first wife Una, and his second wife Genevra (who stayed in the house until 1952) were witnesses to, and ultimately parties to, the racial transformation of Kenwood, Oakland, and indeed the city of Chicago. They weathered a racial tempest in Chicago beginning with the Chicago Race Riots of 1919. The riots were touched off at a beach less than three miles up the lakeshore from their Berkeley home, and the violence spilled across the city's south and west sides. During this period, the residents of Kenwood and Oakland, along with their neighbors in Hyde Park to the south, were central architects of strategies to stem the tide of black migration to all-white neighborhoods, drafting racial restrictive covenants that were stubbornly defended, cleverly altered when challenged, and in the end reluctantly dismantled. The rhetoric in neighborhoods across the city was charged with anger, an anger made palpable in the form of house bombings, violent attacks, and mob actions. But ultimately none of it was enough to stop the inevitable. Throughout the tumultuous years that Roy Donovan and his wives lived at 4432 Berkeley, African Americans were knocking on North Kenwood and Oakland's door.

Knock, Knock (1919–1948)

Roy and Una Donovan moved into 4432 Berkeley in 1917. Two years later, just blocks from their home on the western border of North Kenwood, there was a murder. The newspaper noted the following.

Hardy, B.F., colored, 3136 Ellis avenue, skull fractured, Cottage Grove avenue and Forty-fifth street. Died at county hospital.[18]

The coroner's report said that Hardy was "beaten into a state of insensibility" (see fig. 4). This being an act of mob violence, during a period of general mayhem, the perpetrators were never apprehended.

The Chicago Race Riots were sparked by rumors about rocks being thrown across the informal color line at the 29th Street Beach, the drowning of a black boy, and the subsequent inaction of police at the scene; they ended with 38 people dead—15 whites and 23 blacks— and 537 injured (178 white, 342 black, 17 race unknown). Four black residents of Oakland and one white resident of North Kenwood were among those injured.[19]

B. F. HARDY (Col.)

STATE OF ILLINOIS, ⎫
COUNTY OF COOK ⎰ ss.

An Inquisition was taken for the People of the State of Illinois, at Cook County Morgue and 1124 Cook County Court House, in the City of Chicago, in said County of Cook, on July 30 and August 21, 22 and 30, A. D. 1919, before me, Peter M. Hoffman, Coroner, in and for said County, upon view of the body of B. F. Hardy (Col.), then and there lying dead upon the oaths of six good and lawful men of the said County, who, being duly sworn to inquire on the part of the People of the State of Illinois into all circumstances attending the death of said B. F. Hardy (Col.), and by whom the same was produced, and in what manner and when and where the said B. F. Hardy (Col.) came to his death, do say, upon their oaths, as aforesaid, that the said B. F. Hardy (Col.), now lying dead at Cook County Morgue, in said City of Chicago, County of Cook, State of Illinois, came to his death on the 29th day of July, A. D. 1919, at the Cook County Hospital, from hemorrhage, shock and internal injuries, all due to external violence. We find the deceased was a passenger on northbound street car 5789, on Cottage Grove Avenue, about 11 p. m., July 29, 1919, during race rioting, and when said car was at about 47th street a large mob of white men threw stones and other missiles at the street car, breaking the windows, and by pulling down the trolley pole brought the car to a stop at about 46th Place, where deceased attempted to escape from the car. He was grabbed by members of the mob, none of whom are known to this jury, and beaten into a state of insensibility.

We, the jury, recommend that the unknown white men composing said mob be apprehended and held to the Grand Jury upon a charge of murder, until discharged by due process of law.

IN TESTIMONY WHEREOF, the said Coroner and the jury of this inquest have hereunto set their hands the day and year aforesaid.

R. KEENE RYAN, *Foreman*   ROY C. WOODS
J. P. BRUSHINGHAM   O. W. McMICHAEL
WILLIAM J. DILLON   E. N. WARE
        PETER M. HOFFMAN, *Coroner*

Figure 4. Cook County Coroner's report on the beating death of B. F. Hardy on Cottage Grove Avenue during the 1919 Chicago Race Riots. Cook County Coroner.

The riot was not really about the unfortunate death of one young black man in Lake Michigan. The cause of racial conflagrations is never that simple. Instead, it was about the fact that Chicago's black population had more than doubled in the decade, from 44,103 in 1910 to 109,458 in 1920. And the migrants kept coming.[20] The new black families were looking for places to live, setting up churches and speakeasies, relishing the relative freedoms of the North—and they were eager to work. The Black Belt was taking shape. Of course, blacks were not moving into unoccupied territory, but rather into places already densely settled by whites. The white residents of the Douglas and Grand Boulevard neighborhoods—the heart of the congealing Black Belt—and Oakland, Kenwood, Hyde Park, Woodlawn, and Washington Park, along its periphery, were actively preparing to resist what was seen as a racial invasion. The violence of the 1919 riots was but an intensified version of the animosities that seethed daily in these changing neighborhoods.[21]

One particularly spectacular and deadly method used to intimidate blacks who dared to move into white areas, as well as the black and white real estate agents who ushered them in, was house bombings. In Oakland, the homes of four black residents and three black real estate agents were bombed in the period surrounding the riots, from 1917 to 1921. Two of the houses bombed were on Berkeley Avenue. The home of Mr. and Mrs. Jerry Anderson at 4141 Berkeley, three blocks north of the Donovans' new home, was bombed on October 12, 1918. The front door was torn away, windowpanes shattered, and items inside the house destroyed. No one was injured, but the blast was strong enough to damage the next-door home of Mr. and Mrs. Alfred Waller, who were also black and who had moved in just two weeks earlier. The city's black newspaper, the *Chicago Defender*, cited this as another example of the racially motivated "bomb culture" that was overtaking parts of the city, and it condemned the actions with righteous outrage: "This new brand of Hunnish activity is un-American, undemocratic and for atrocity it is unparalleled even by the Huns themselves." The bombings were reprehensible but produced the desired effect. Both the Andersons and the Wallers quickly moved from Berkeley Avenue and were replaced by whites.[22]

The 1919 Chicago Race Riots and the house bombings were a fiery prelude to decades of white organizing against black settlement on the South Side. Property owners' associations were the first line of defense. Perhaps the most notorious was the Kenwood and Hyde Park Property

Owners' Association, formed in 1918. It defended the area from 39th Street to 55th Street and Lake Michigan to State Street, and vowed to "make Hyde Park white." Its 1919 publication the *Property Owners' Journal* minced no words in stating the organization's position and outlining its plans to address the growing black presence in greater Hyde Park:

> Keep the Negro in his place, amongst his people, and he is healthy and loyal. Remove him, or allow "his newly discovered importance to remove him from his proper environment and the Negro becomes a nuisance." He develops into an overbearing, inflated, irascible individual, overburdening his brain to such an extent about social equality that he becomes dangerous to all with whom he comes in contact; he constitutes a nuisance of which the neighborhood is anxious to rid itself.... As stated before, every colored man who moves into Hyde Park knows that he is damaging his white neighbor's property. Therefore, he is making war on the white man. Consequently, he is not entitled to any consideration and forfeits his rights to be employed by the white man. If employers should adopt a rule of refusing to employ Negroes who reside in Hyde Park to the damage of the white man's property it would soon show good results.[23]

The tone of the property owners' association is eerily reminiscent of the language used by the U.S. Supreme Court in both the *Dred Scott* decision, which stated that blacks had "no rights which the white man was bound to respect," and in *Plessy v. Ferguson,* where Justice Billings Brown wrote for the majority: "If [Plessy] be a colored man and be so assigned, he has been deprived of no property, since he is not lawfully entitled to the reputation of being a white man." The Kenwood and Hyde Park Property Owners' Association saw blacks' in-migration as part of their growing sense of entitlement to rights, to work, and to property, a sense of entitlement that needed to be checked. The organization summoned whites—"Wake up, white voters! Come out of your dream"—to reestablish their dominance, stem the tide of black encroachment, and take back the areas into which blacks had already moved.[24]

Kenwood and Oakland were prized parts of the greater Hyde Park area because they fronted Lake Michigan and contained Drexel Boulevard, one of the city's grandest thoroughfares. It is not surprising, then, that they became a particular focus for organizing. Driven by an intense and crude antipathy to living near blacks and by widespread agreement that a black presence provoked falling property values, the area's white residents were particularly avid in adopting racial restrictive covenants—agreements written into property deeds that prohibited owners from selling or renting to blacks and sometimes other unwanted groups such as Jews and Asians. Restrictive covenants became especially common after the U.S. Supreme Court's review of *Corrigan v. Buckley* in 1926, which proponents of covenants read as tacitly supporting their constitutionality. The 1928 restrictive covenant covering the northernmost section of Oakland was one of the first such agreements recorded in Chicago. Not one but two restrictive covenants covered 4432 Berkeley—one in 1938 and another in 1944. By the time covenants were ruled unenforceable, in the 1948 case *Shelley v. Kraemer,* most of Chicago's South Side was covered by them. Adopting such restrictions required considerable time and money and would not have been possible without the financial investment and reputational influence of major Chicago institutions like the YMCA, the University of Chicago, and most notably the Chicago Real Estate Board, which developed standard text for restrictive covenants to be used by its member developers and real estate agents. As historian Wendy Plotkin uncovered, the Chicago Real Estate Board "voted unanimously to expel any member who rented or sold property on a white block to black people."[25]

Local elected officials were not at all neutral in the matter of keeping blacks out of white neighborhoods. In 1920, Ulysses S. Schwartz, alderman of Oakland and North Kenwood's Third Ward, buoyed the pride of members of the Kenwood and Hyde Park Property Owners' Association by telling them that their neighborhood was "the show place of Chicago." But, he warned ominously, it was clear that the area was under threat. He reported that $100 million had been lost in property values in the Oakland neighborhood alone. While the city council was doing what it could on the legislative side, its hands were tied by statutory constraints. So, he admonished them, "You yourselves must resurrect the South Side." Exhorting them to action in diplomatic, nonracial language that nonetheless echoed the antiblack sentiments of the day, he continued:

> You men and women . . . must stand together to save your homes, see
> that your homes are kept as fine places to live in, that your neighbors are

kept the most desirable neighbors in the city of Chicago, so that you may enjoy the benefit of that wonderful improvement that is to come.[26]

Stand together they did. White residents met throughout the area to devise strategies for keeping blacks out. Walter White attended one of these closed-door strategizing sessions, which was held at the Kenwood Club House on 47th Street. White, who was then the assistant secretary of the national NAACP, would obviously not have been welcome at such a meeting as a representative of the civil rights community. But Walter White was a black man who could pass for white, and thus could infiltrate racist gatherings. He reported on his undercover expedition among this "hysterical group of persons" in the NAACP publication *The Crisis:*

> Various plans were discussed for keeping the Negroes in "their part of the town," such as securing the discharge of colored persons from positions they held when they attempted to move into "white" neighborhoods, purchasing mortgages of Negroes buying homes and ejecting them when mortgage notes fell due and were unpaid, and many more of the same calibre.[27]

White Chicagoans were digging in their heels to protect the churches, businesses, and beaches of "their" neighborhoods using all available means. Street by street, the graystones, mansions, and apartment buildings on Oakenwald, Lake Park, Woodlawn, University, Greenwood, Ellis, Drexel, and Berkeley were blanketed with racial covenants, foreclosed by financing conspiracies, and martyred with incendiary reprisals (see frontispiece map).

Despite the best (or worst, in moral terms) efforts of the property owners' associations and their armies, the wall of intolerance was bound to be trampled by blacks desperate for space. Cottage Grove Avenue constituted the eastern edge of the Black Belt, separating the core of black settlement in Douglas and Grand Boulevard from Oakland, Kenwood, and Hyde Park. By the 1920s, African Americans began moving east of Cottage Grove Avenue, marching toward Lake Michigan. In the period following the Chicago Race Riots, Kenwood was more successful in keeping blacks out than Oakland. Because the Black Belt was pushing from the north as well, Oakland was first in its path. Oakland's black population doubled from 15 percent in 1920 to nearly 30 percent in

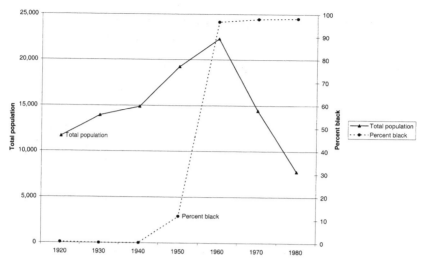

Figure 5. Total population and racial composition of North Kenwood, 1920–1980. Burgess and Newcomb 1931, 1933; Wirth and Bernet 1949; Hauser and Kitagawa 1953; Kitagawa and Taeuber 1963; Chicago Fact Book Consortium 1984.

1930, whereas the northern half of Kenwood's black population was still less than 1 percent in 1930 (see figs. 5 and 6). For the two decades flanking the Depression, Oakland maintained this integration, and Kenwood relished its all-whiteness.

In the face of insecurities about the changing racial makeup of the city and their neighborhoods, residents of North Kenwood and Oakland carried on with routine tasks and heartily celebrated the special occasions of neighborhood life. The year 1919 may have been marred by the race riots, but Chicago still celebrated the end of the Great War and honored its returning veterans. In his late 30s, Roy Donovan had been too old to fight in World War I, but he was well represented by his neighbors. Lieutenant George N. Holt returned to his wife and daughter (and the two boarders in their home, at 4436 Berkeley) after serving five months with the American Red Cross and establishing the first Red Cross station on the Rhine River. The Weiss brothers—Arthur, Theodore, Max, and Francis—all of whom served their country in the war, were the pride of their parents, Mr. and Mrs. Ignatius Weiss of 4159 Berkeley Avenue.

Through the 1920s and 1930s, people shopped and recreated in a neighborhood that was reaching its population maturity. Donovan and

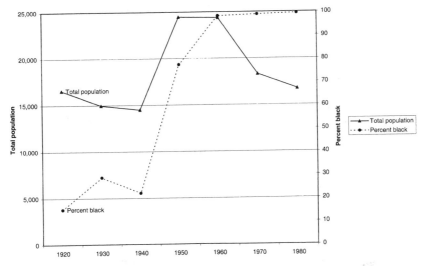

Figure 6. Total population and racial composition of Oakland, 1920–1980. Burgess and Newcomb 1931, 1933; Wirth and Bernet 1949; Hauser and Kitagawa 1953; Kitagawa and Taeuber 1963; Chicago Fact Book Consortium 1984.

his friends could shop at Harlan's Dry Goods and Men's Store on the corner of 43rd and Berkeley, where "boys blouses" and "men's athletic union suits" sold for 69 cents. For Mrs. Donovan, women's silk dresses were considerably more pricey at $15. Residents could catch a movie at any number of "picture houses" in the neighborhood: the Oakland at 3861 Cottage Grove; the Oakland Square, around the corner at the intersection of Drexel and Oakwood Boulevards; the Shakespeare at 43rd and Ellis; the Kenwood at 47th and Kimbark; or the Vista at 47th near Drexel.

During this time major institutions were transformed and expanded. Rebuilding after a devastating fire, Saint James Methodist Episcopal Church erected its imposing new eleven-hundred-seat edifice at the corner of 46th and Ellis in 1924, where it still stands today. Merging two different churches, it was expected to be the second largest Methodist congregation in Chicago. In 1925, an old hotel that had been used as a government hospital was bought and rechristened as the Sutherland. Its 200-plus residential suites were soon occupied by people who frequently made the society pages of Chicago's newspapers. Its ballroom hosted the meetings of area women's clubs and the Oakland Business Men's Association. In 1935, the neighborhood cheered Mayor Martin

Kennelly as he broke ground for the new Oakenwald School at 4070 South Lake Park Avenue. Classes for its 750 students had previously been held in fourteen portable units as Chicago struggled to keep up with the city's growing population, especially in areas in and near the Black Belt.[28]

In 1933, the neighborhood prepared for another world's fair, titled "A Century of Progress." The plans brought renewed civic energy to Oakland because the fairgrounds extended just into the neighborhood at 39th Street and the lakefront. "It is our intention," commented Mrs. George Robinson, head of a special subcommittee of the Central Shore Voters League that was preparing for the fair, "that every square foot of vacant ground in Oakland be converted into smooth green lawn, and that trees, bushes, and shrubs be planted in any unsightly places, so that visitors entering the Fair grounds through the 39th street entrance or by the new 35th street viaduct, will start the day with a picture in their minds of Oakland's tree-bordered streets, its trim, freshly painted houses, and spacious lawns." To marshal this energy, Mayor Anton Cermak addressed the Oakland Business Men's Association on the topic of "Oakland's Duty to Century of Progress Visitors" at the Sutherland Hotel in January of 1933. The neighborhood was slated to get new streetlights, repaved streets, and ornate shrubbery to assist in its efforts.[29]

Of course all was not rosy in North Kenwood and Oakland in these years, even aside from simmering racial issues. In the 1920s, Oakland had such a gambling and prostitution problem that the Committee of Fifteen, a private association that grew out of the mayoral-appointed Chicago Vice Commission, made Oakland a target of its anti-vice crusade. Earlier, in 1915, the Committee of Fifteen had boasted that it closed ninety-five houses of prostitution in the Oakland area alone. They apparently did not stay closed for long because in the early 1920s it was reported that the Oakland district contained ninety houses of prostitution, forty gambling houses, and forty to fifty bootlegging operations. In 1922, after teaming up with the Oakland Business Men's Association, the committee announced the formation of "an army 10,000 strong," with a $2,000 war chest, which would attack these immoral behaviors in Oakland. The war was fierce and held no one blameless. "Some of you men who are promoting these illegal places are sitting in the church before me now," said Samuel P. Thrasher, the chairman of the Committee of Fifteen, pointing his finger at some residents who attended a meeting at the South Congregational Church at 40th and Drexel Boulevard in Oakland. "I know who you are and I know some of you who think you are not known," he continued, and then promised the ultimate judgment. "If this practice is not stopped there will be a stir on the part of the wives, sons and daughters of these men."[30]

A particular target of the anti-vice coalition was the Ritz-Carlton, a speakeasy at 38th and Cottage Grove where the party didn't start until three in the morning. The Ritz-Carlton was guilty of two transgressions: selling liquor and race mixing. "Black and tans," as these nightclubs were called, referring to the skin colors of their interracial clientele, were the symbols of racial progress for some, but to others signaled a sure affront to white racial respectability. In a 1922 *Chicago Daily Tribune* article, reporter Genevieve Forbes paints a particularly racy picture of her night at the Ritz-Carlton (see fig. 7). The description is inflected with all of the racial and sexual fears and longings of the day. The writer gives special attention to the "blonde curls" and "'honest' pink and white complexions" of the white women patrons; the shaking, squatting, and shimmying of the black women; and the "perpetual motion of the dark skinned brethren" whose music drives the proceedings. The Committee of Fifteen charged that there were orgies going on at the Ritz. The club's owner, Eddie Rosenberg, was ultimately charged with violating the Prohibition Act, but most of the evidence against him concerned the "gross immorality of the black and white patrons." The club was closed soon thereafter, a certain victory for the anti-vice army and its partner against crime, the Oakland Business Men's Association.[31]

Berkeley also saw its fair share of action and tragedy. Mr. and Mrs. Shankle, the managers of the Walgreens drugstore at the corner of 43rd and Berkeley were held up in their store, threatened with a pistol, and robbed of $300. After what was surely a scary experience for the husband and wife, the robbers "courteously drove the Shankles to their home, left them at the door, and speeded away." In 1928, Eunice McElroy of 4146 Berkeley died after a botched abortion performed by a doctor on 43rd and Cottage Grove. In 1929, Helen Walsh, a young north-sider, died of a heart attack at a birthday party at 4402 Berkeley. And in 1939, Daniel C. Howe—a law student, WPA worker, and Berkeley resident—was fatally shot in the chest at the Submarine Tavern, a neighborhood bar on 43rd Street. The police charged that Adolphus Flemming, a black man, had wantonly shot into the establishment's windows after being

COLOR LINE LOST IN ABANDONED REVELS AT RITZ

"Black and Tan" Melting Pot Boils, Bubbles.

BY GENEVIEVE FORBES.

A "black and tan" that grew out of a song is the Ritz-Carleton, at 3842 Cottage Grove avenue, in the heart of the "Oakland district," the center of many drives against the ladies of facile ways and their gentlemen friends.

Formerly the Canary cottage of pre-prohibition days, the Ritz took its first step blackward when the manager grew angry with white musicians who beat a listless drum and struck a wearied piano along about 3 in the morning. Colored artists, he discovered, were just getting warmed up then.

Later, sold on the perpetual motion of the dark skinned brethren, he substituted brisk colored waiters for the less energetic white ones. But the audience was still white. Gradually, however, the guests grew dark. The fifty-fifty mark was passed and now the percentage wavers back and forth, but it is always a black and tan.

Knock Off at Breakfast.

The twilight of the black and tan does not come until at least breakfast time, so 3 o'clock in the morning is almost indecently early to arrive at the double doored entrance and pay the 50 cent admission tax.

Through a small passageway, into a room built in three wings about a small dance floor, past a wild, harmoniously discordant jangle of music, and to a table near the dance floor. No shower of bullets, no glimmer of razors, no scuffle of men. It seems just an ordinary cabaret, with a vaudeville sort of darkey who takes the order, mumbling something about "thirteen."

Sailor Friedman "Fund."

But the momentum is gathering. At a nearby table, a party of eight, all white but two colored girls, are discussing the "swell time" they had recently at the "grand defense benefit" given here for Sailor Friedman, the pugilist, and his companions involved in a "shooting." All the elite of this stratum of the world were there, and it was some party, the table companions allow.

The dancing starts. A little white girl deserts the party and rushes over to another table, grabs a large colored man by the waist as she cries, "Come on, dearie, I've gotta beat them other girls to it, for I want this dance."

She snuggles in under his arm and nestles her blonde curls against his coat. Arms interlocked, bodies pressed close together, she gets some of the "loving" she desired.

The dance is over: still embracing the dancers stumble to their seats.

Waiters turn out most of the lights as the entertainment begins. Three colored girls, at the sound of the drum, leave their white partners, with whom they have been lolling at the tables, and take their places on the dance floor.

Slowly, almost decorously, with a native rhythm that is not unpleasant, the dance begins. Faster and faster grows the music; more and more abandoned the dance; more colorful and definite the remarks of the audience about dancing, underwear and anatomy.

The short girl at the end crouches on the floor; the fat girl in the middle shakes and shimmies; the tall girl squats down as she half rolls, half crawls about the floor. Higher and higher do the girls pull their skirts, more and more definite do their actions grow. In a wild fanfare of syncopation syncopated and a revel of abandonment the dance ends.

As the girls roll about in the fifth encore, a white girl jumps hysterically out on the floor. She is drunk and ill. With a tragic imitation of the colored girls' motions, she attempts to join them. She wobbles, her hat falls to the side; her hair steals down about her bleary eyes; the cigaret falls out of her hand.

As they crouch, she crouches, but she is unable to get up. She is lifted up by one of the girls and she starts, vaguely, on her way to the ladies' parlor. She is assisted, here by a white hand, there by a black hand, and finally disappears.

Come Back Alone.

Two white girls, beautifully and expensively gowned, very young, with "honest" pink and white complexions, dance with their white escorts, but wink at the colored men. They leave with the white men about 4. In half an hour they are back, alone.

Dancing together, they go through a series of motions that rivals anything yet seen on the floor. As the dance closes their popularity is assured. Their table is crowded with colored men.

It is after 5 when the doorman, friendly and black, commiserates the neophyte at the black and tan on the lack of "thrills."

"We didn't see nothin' tonight," he admits, but, with a hopeful note: "Come back again Saturday night."

Everything is relative.

Figure 7. The thrill of race mixing in Oakland in the 1920s. Genevieve Forbes, "Color Line Lost in Abandoned Revels at Ritz," *Chicago Daily Tribune,* July 19, 1922.

denied service because he was black. Flemming claimed innocence but was found guilty and sentenced to fourteen years in prison.[32]

The Howe shooting no doubt shook the neighborhood and Berkeley Avenue, but it paled in comparison to a crime of the previous year and its aftermath. "Brick slayer," "sex killer," "colored moron," and "jungle beast" were among the terms used to describe eighteen-year-old Robert Nixon, who was accused of and ultimately executed for the May 27, 1938, murder of Mrs. Florence Johnson in her North Kenwood apartment. Johnson, who was white, died of multiple blows to the head with a brick after she awoke during what had started as a burglary. Her sister, who was sleeping in another room, caught a glimpse of the trespassers as they fled the apartment. Johnson was the mother of two small children and the wife of a Chicago fireman. Pictures of the children, with captions like "Orphaned by Crime" were run in the local newspapers, as were photographs of Johnson herself. The family had strong ties in the North Kenwood neighborhood. They were parishioners at Saint Ambrose Catholic Church at 47th and Ellis, and Johnson's brother lived nearby, at 44th and Drexel.

The police "solved" the crime swiftly and decisively. Just hours after Johnson was killed, they picked up Nixon—clothes bloodied and hands scratched—walking west on 47th Street. He immediately became the number one suspect, and eventually the police reported that all the evidence pointed to him. For two days in police custody Nixon maintained his innocence. Then, on the night of the second day, he "confessed." (Nearly every time the *Chicago Defender* reported on this case it put the word "confessed" in quotation marks.[33]) His lawyers would later argue, unsuccessfully, that the confession had been coerced with both pleasure—"numerous helpings of cocoanut [*sic*] pie and copious swigs of strawberry pop"—and pain. In the days following his initial purported admission of guilt, Nixon similarly "confessed" to the unsolved murders of four other white women in Chicago and Los Angeles. Some of the other crimes also featured a brick as the murder weapon, and in one of the cases the victim had been raped. The details of the multiple homicides pushed the media, the city, and the neighborhood into a frenzy.[34]

The white newspapers' descriptions of Nixon were particularly racist. By the second day, he was described by the *Tribune* as a "slow witted colored youth," and the label "moron" was quickly affixed to him. In gathering background information, Chicago police contacted the sheriff in Tallulah, Louisiana, where Nixon was born and spent his childhood. The sheriff informed them that Nixon had been a pickpocket and thief throughout his youth and that "nothing but death will cure him." Even more detestable than the depiction of Nixon as unintelligent and innately criminal were the references to his supposed bestiality. A full feature story was devoted to establishing Nixon's apelike qualities. "He is very black—almost pure Negro," the journalist wrote. "His physical characteristics suggest an earlier link in the species." The article described Nixon's "ferocious" tendencies when he worked on a Mississippi steamboat, the way he "swung himself over the [window] sill" in reenacting the crime, and the smacking of his lips when ate. Before the trial, Nixon's lawyers requested a change of venue because the "malicious publicity had made it impossible to hope for a fair trial within the area." The *Chicago Defender*'s characterization of the white coverage as "lurid and inflammatory" was an understatement.[35]

If these events sound familiar, it is because the Nixon case was a model for Richard Wright as he wrote the novel *Native Son*. Wright wrote in the essay "How Bigger Was Born": "So frequently do these acts [of charging black men with rape] recur that when I was halfway through the first draft of *Native Son* a case paralleling Bigger's flared forth in the newspapers of Chicago. (Many of the newspaper items and some of the incidents in *Native Son* are but fictionalized versions of the Robert Nixon case and rewrites of news stories from the *Chicago Tribune*)."[36]

The violence of the crime and its cross-racial and cross-gender character encouraged the belief among whites that the perpetrator, now "known" to be Nixon, was no better than an animal. On the afternoon of Sunday, May 29, two days after the killing, the police brought Nixon back to the crime scene, at 4631 Lake Park, to reenact the brutal events. Twenty policemen guarded the building, where a crowd of more than a hundred angry residents had gathered to hurl racist invective. The two shackled suspects, Nixon and his suspected accomplice Earl Hicks, were ordered to play out and narrate the crime just as it had happened. A woman in the crowd jeered, "Why don't they lynch them!" and the brother of Mrs. Johnson, who arrived with Johnson's husband and two small children, tried in vain to break through the police line to punish Nixon and Hicks himself. The two suspects challenged each other's stories as it came to the crucial fact of who had wielded the brick and done the killing, but the police were already on record as having "no doubt"

Figure 8. Robert Nixon "reenacts" the murder of Florence Johnson at 4631 South Lake Park in North Kenwood as police and residents watch. *Chicago Tribune* photo by Tribune Photos. All rights reserved. Used with permission. "2 Accuse Each Other in Brick Killing," *Chicago Daily Tribune,* May 30, 1938.

that it was Nixon. The reenactment was front-page news in the next day's paper. Above a picture of Nixon and Hicks was the caption "Two Re-enact Sex Slaying of Mrs. Johnson" (see fig. 8). As if the true story were not sensational enough the caption conjured a sex crime where none had occurred, erroneously, but no less effectively, reinforcing an all-too-common gendered and racist trope.[37]

Aside from its many tragic contours, the murder of Florence Johnson is significant because it represented and fueled the fears of white residents in neighborhoods that bordered the expanding Black Belt. The previously invisible but impermeable walls around these white neighborhoods now seemed dreadfully porous, allowing in blacks of all ilks. Indeed, white residents had frequently complained to the police about the growing number of "prowlers" in the area in the months preceding the murder.[38] The mere presence of blacks in Kenwood was regarded as a bad omen. This fear was exploited by shady real estate agents to scare whites into selling their homes cheaply so that they could resell them to blacks at a considerable markup, a practice known as blockbusting. The Johnson murder was the ultimate, albeit unplanned, blockbusting tragedy. It solidified the mental connections white residents made between crime, sexual perversity, and blackness, especially black men. Residents who felt that this heinous crime, and crimes like it, vindicated their racism thus doubled their efforts to protect the neighborhood from black incursion, paying their dues to the local property owners' associations and signing restrictive covenants. But at the same time, the murder shook whites' faith. Some worried that their battle was already lost and began their retreat, and the neighborhood began to change.

Between 1940, two years after the Johnson murder, and 1950, North Kenwood was "invaded." The war metaphor was pervasive in the rhetoric of community groups and scholars alike. Robert Park, a sociologist at the nearby University of Chicago, borrowed the concept of "invasion and succession" from plant biology to describe the transition from one type of urban land use or resident population to another. The university's early involvement in and support of property owners' associations was a likely route by which such rhetoric was disseminated. Following this theoretical tradition, sociologists Otis Dudley Duncan and Beverly Duncan analyzed 175 census tracts in Chicago and classified them in terms of stages of racial transition in 1950. They classified most of Oakland and the western part of North Kenwood as "invasion" areas from 1940 to 1950, when blacks were first making residential headway into the neighborhood. The eastern part of North Kenwood, where the Johnson murder occurred—tracts 594 and 595—was seen as being invaded by both blacks and Japanese.[39]

A more detailed study of the "Negro invasion" of Oakland makes the battlefield metaphors even more explicit.

> Conditions conducive to expansion of the Negro community may develop gradually, but the actual change from white to Negro occupancy has an abrupt beginning because it almost always involves the crossing of a "barrier." A physical object like a railway or park which marked the extent of some previous wave of expansion gradually assumes such symbolic significance as a boundary that any attempt at its crossing is viewed as a challenge by the dominant community. The successful crossing of such a barrier by a single Negro resident marks the first event of the physical invasion process.

The author, a master's student in sociology at the University of Chicago and thus well-trained in the invasion/succession terminology, goes on to identify the precise moment of invasion of the southern part of Oakland. "The public record shows that a parcel of land in sub-area 'A,' which is adjacent to the Cottage Grove Avenue barrier, was sold to a Negro in 1942." Even though the African American buyer did not move into the house he bought, this first purchase signaled a crack in the armor and, like dominoes, "Negro acquisition of one structure seemed to precipitate Negro occupancy of adjacent structures."[40]

But while some whites surrendered and sold, others countered the invasion with renewed zeal. In 1938, the same year that Florence Johnson was murdered in her apartment, the Oakland-Kenwood Property Owners' Association (OKPOA) was chartered.[41] Neighborhood improvement associations, like the sprawling Kenwood and Hyde Park Property Owners' Association that represented the area in the 1920s, were primarily instruments of racial exclusion. A survey of forty-five such organizations in Chicago and Detroit in the 1940s found that thirty-nine of them (or 87 percent) considered blacks to be "objectionable" and undesirable as neighbors.[42] These groups undoubtedly performed many other functions, which allowed them to present their activities as being as innocuous as their names suggested; they were simply associations of home owners concerned about and active in their neighborhoods. The *Chicago Daily Tribune* hailed OKPOA as a model for how to "prevent a high class residence district from becoming a slum." Worried about the exodus of middle-class families and property value depreciation, the home owners of the neighborhood did what any concerned citizens would do: they organized. Setting up an office at the corner of 43rd and Ellis Avenue, they repaved streets, cleaned up vacant lots, enforced no-peddling ordinances, lobbied for new park facilities, and instituted a youth recreation program.[43] Who could object to these civic activities?

As the years progressed, however, OKPOA became more aggressive in its "improvement" tactics. Newton C. Farr, president of OKPOA, and also president of the National Association of Real Estate Boards, said that neighborhood residents needed "new courage" to stem the rushing tide of blight. Farr was a strong supporter of racial segregation, calling the methods of the Ku Klux Klan in the South "extreme" but "justified" and "certainly effective." The *Chicago Defender* deemed Newton Farr "more than any single person, responsible for keeping the city's expanding Negro population packed 'in their place'" and characterized OKPOA as "the wealthiest and most active anti-Negro organization above the Mason-Dixon line." Hence, the "courage" Farr challenged his neighbors to exhibit likely entailed more than keeping the alleys clean and planting flowers. In one courage-building campaign, the organization set the goal of increasing its membership from 672 residents in 1940 to 1,000 in 1941. Just as desperate as blacks were to move into neighborhoods like Kenwood and Oakland, whites were to hold on to them, demonstrated by the rising organizational fervor of OKPOA and similar associations.[44]

By 1943, OKPOA was unabashedly antiblack. Its annual report listed the following accomplishments for the year:

1. The eviction of undesirables—Negroes—from dwellings at 4608 Drexel Boulevard, 44th and University, Northwest corner of 47th Street and Woodlawn Avenue;
2. Successful opposition, through appearances before the State Legislature, to a bill to nullify race restrictive agreements;
3. The initiation of suits to restrain sale to Negroes of four pieces of property between 39th and 40th streets on Ellis and Oak [sic] Park Avenues and on Oakwood Boulevard;
4. The initiation of suits to restrain sale to Negroes of seven pieces of property between 36th and 42nd Streets on Ellis and Lake Park Avenues;
5. The renewal of interest in restrictive agreements through organization of block-by-block anti-Negro contracts.[45]

In 1944, OKPOA spent over $3,000 in legal fees to enforce existing restrictive covenants barring black purchase of property in the neighborhood. These were defensive actions, but the group also went on the offensive that year, gathering signatures of more than 25 percent of the property owners to enact new restrictive covenants.[46]

When the OKPOA canvassers knocked on the door of 4432 Berkeley, they were favorably received by its owners. The document they carried spelled out "the restriction that no part of said premises [with the exception of servants' quarters] shall in any manner be used or occupied directly or indirectly by any negro or negroes." In book 40063, page 94, line 34, of the Cook County Recorder of Deeds' records are the signatures of Roy P. Donovan and his wife Genevra, amid the signatures of forty-seven of their neighbors, covering the houses on the east side of Ellis Avenue and the west side of Berkeley Avenue in the 4400 block (see figs. 9 and 10). The 1944 covenant was in fact the second such document covering 4432 Berkeley and the neighboring houses. In 1937, the Donovans had signed on to a restrictive covenant that then covered almost all of northern Kenwood. By 1939 all of Kenwood as well as Oakland and Hyde Park were covered by restrictive covenants that forbade sell-

IN CONSIDERATION of the premises and of the mutual covenants hereinafter made, and of the sum of Five Dollars ($5.00) in hand paid to each of the parties hereto by each of the other parties hereto, the receipt of which is hereby acknowledged, each party as owner of the parcel of land above described immediately under his name, does hereby covenant and agree with each and every other of the parties hereto, that his said parcel of land is now and until Jan. 1, 1960 and thereafter until this agreement shall be abrogated as hereinafter provided, shall be subject to the restrictions and provisions hereinafter set forth, and that he will make no sale, contract of sale, conveyance, lease or agreement and give no license or permission in violation of such restrictions or provisions, which are as follows:

1. The restriction that no part of said premises shall in any manner be used or occupied directly or indirectly by any negro or negroes, provided that this restriction shall not prevent the occupation, during the period of their employment, of janitors' or chauffeurs' quarters in the basement or in a barn or garage in the rear, or of servants' quarters by negro janitors, chauffeurs or house servants, respectively, actually employed as such for service in and about the premises by the rightful owner or occupant of said premises.

2. The restriction that no part of said premises shall be sold, given, conveyed or leased to any negro or negroes, and no permission or license to use or occupy any part thereof shall be given to any negro except house servants or janitors or chauffeurs employed thereon as aforesaid.

Figure 9. Restrictive covenant covering 4432 South Berkeley, 1938. Cook County Recorder of Deeds.

ing or renting to blacks.[47] This protection proved ineffective, however, as blacks moved into the northernmost sections of Oakland in the 1920s, and marched southward through the 1940s. They defied the strictures barring their entry and used an array of circuitous methods to acquire and inhabit homes. The new covenants of the 1940s—which added language prohibiting the conveyance of property to "any corporation which has one or more negro stockholders or to any trust which has a negro trustee or which has one or more negro beneficiaries"—were deemed necessary to forestall one of the more popular schemes. The new covenants were necessary, so white residents believed, but ultimately insufficient.[48] Roy Donovan died in 1947, a year before the restrictive covenant he signed was dealt the final blow by the Supreme Court.

With the demand for housing even more acute after World War II, even violence did not work to scare off African Americans in search of better quality housing. In May 1945, the Oakland home of the Reverend Theodore Dabney, at 4145 Drexel Boulevard, was bombed. A year later, Alton Baird, a white neighbor of Dabney's who was interviewed about the bombing, told the *Chicago Defender* that he "thought that was great!" Baird was the leader of the informal White Independent Citizens' Committee, formed to "do things the [Oakland-Kenwood] Property Association can't afford to do officially." His venomous diatribe against blacks and their alleged Jewish coconspirators illustrates the ferocity with which some residents were willing to protect their neighborhood.

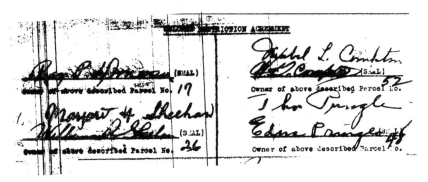

Figure 10. Signature of Roy P. Donovan on 1938 restrictive covenant (top line of left column). Cook County Recorder of Deeds.

I've been living here nigh on 12 years and now I got nigger neighbors on the north and on the south of me. And who do you think is to blame? The Jews. They're the greatest danger around here. They got no respect at all for restrictive covenants. You sell 'em some property, and they turn right around and sell it to the niggers. . . . [B]ombing don't do no good. We—er—they bombed and burned the niggers on Michigan Boulevard and they bombed 'em and burned 'em on Grand, and now the niggers are there anyway. You gotta fight it out in the courts. . . . We're fighting in the front lines here in Kenwood. Those Jews better get wise; if we lose, their Hyde Park is next.[49]

To signal their contempt, Baird and his compatriots hung signs in their windows that read, "This Property Is Not For Sale." They were the militant, fringe wing of OKPOA, dogged in their commitment to holding the line, but ultimately weakened by the reality of the many properties that were for sale.

Sensing the inevitability of black entry into Kenwood and Oakland, and having exhausted all other avenues, in 1948 OKPOA tried a new tactic: compromise. During the summer of 1947, OKPOA participated in a series of meetings convened by the Mayor's Commission on Human Relations that included representatives from the NAACP, the Urban League, and the Metropolitan Housing and Planning Council.[50] These were closed-door, invitation-only meetings, with no press allowed given the sensitivity of the topic. The meetings were to discuss the possibility of scrapping racial restrictive covenants in favor of *occupancy stan-*

dards, which would be in the service of "stabilizing population developments in the Oakland-Kenwood area." The new agreements would crack down on overcrowding, illegal conversions, absentee speculators, and unintended uses. "Occupancy standards," it was proposed, would promote "sound family living, irrespective of skin color, religious beliefs or nationality."[51]

The parties emerged from these meetings with a plan to replace restrictive covenants with "community conservation agreements." The *Chicago Daily Tribune* reported the story under the headline "Home Owners End Race Ban in Community." The article in the *Chicago Defender* included nearly identical content—both newspapers pulling heavily from the press releases issued by the organizations—but saw the agreements as having an impact beyond the small test area in the Oakland-Kenwood community: "Plan Spells End of Covenants," the *Defender* announced sweepingly (and only a bit prematurely: the Supreme Court decision striking down covenants would come just a few months later). Both articles emphasized that the new *conservation* approach was the result of interracial cooperation and a common commitment to property maintenance, and asserted that such black/white partnerships would be the model for other community groups across the city, "bringing about better living for all in our community."[52]

Despite the celebration and optimism, the community conservation approach was too little too late. Winds much stronger than those that swirled in tiny Kenwood–Oakland swept across the country. Southern blacks continued to make the journey north to Chicago, swelling the population of the already "hemmed-in" Black Belt. The construction industry continued feverishly building new housing, much of it in suburbs, to address the demand that had built up during World War II. OKPOA was having a hard time getting residents to sign on to the new community conservation agreements—why should they go on fighting when gleaming modern houses awaited them in the suburbs? The owners' association was in a near panic. "It appears likely that the Negro community will expand in an unhealthy fashion and it may be that the pressures will be such that all the work to date on the conservation agreement will be undone," stated OKPOA's president in May 1948. That same month, the Supreme Court ruled in *Shelley v. Kraemer* that racial restrictive covenants were unenforceable. OKPOA and residents of the neighborhood collectively raised the white flag. The invasion was too strong to combat. With waning participation, the organization was in heavy debt. Within five years, in 1953, the Oakland-Kenwood Property Owners' Association dissolved.[53]

The Black Golden Era (1948–1965)

In 1952, Genevra Donovan, the widow of Roy Donovan, moved from 4432 Berkeley to the northwest side of Chicago, far from the encroaching Black Belt. By the 1950s, it was rare for whites to move into Kenwood and Oakland. They were moving out, to the suburbs or, like Mrs. Donovan, to other Chicago neighborhoods less imperiled by integration. The black "invasion" of the 1940s was followed, in the 1950s, by "consolidation," to use the sociological terminology of the time, a period of "further increase in percent of population non-white."[54] After Genevra Donovan moved out, Leola Brown moved in. For a short time, Ms. Brown rented from Mrs. Donovan. Then in 1956, Leola Brown and her husband Earl bought the house, taking out a mortgage for $5,681.04. The surname of 4432 Berkeley's new owners could not have been more telling as the street "browned" with each new neighbor. By 1960, North Kenwood was 97 percent black.

"Ah, this is interesting. I hadn't been thinking about that for a long time," said Dorothy Smith when I asked her to take me back to Berkeley Avenue of the 1950s. Ms. Smith moved in at the age of ten, just as Genevra Donovan was moving out, so she couldn't tell me anything about the departing white woman. But she knew the general trend, summarizing the time period with the commonplace, "Well, it was undergoing a change." The white families who were left on the block seemed "lost" and "stuck," Smith observed, and all of the newcomers were black. She couldn't remember the name of her best friend next door, but oddly she could recall her friend's parents' names—Yuri and Joe. They were Japanese, and they didn't stay very long either. There were obvious tensions during this time of change, like when someone stuck a note to the young Ms. Smith's window threatening to murder her. She figured it was Patrick, a white kid who lived a few houses down. They were friends by day, but when Patrick's parents came home playtime was over since his "angry and abusive" father forbade the friendship. Patrick learned that anger from his father and took it out on the new black girl on the block. As the black kids came to outnumber the white kids, however, such intimidation tactics became less and less viable. Once most of the white kids were gone, the juvenile squabbles were no longer about race, but just about being kids, since everybody was black.

The 1950s and early 1960s were a golden era for North Kenwood–Oakland's new African American residents. Now with a black majority, NKO was no longer so separate from the areas west of Cottage Grove Avenue, or what had come to be known as Bronzeville. Chicago's Black Belt was not unlike black enclaves in other northern cities, the best known of which was Harlem. Like Harlem, Bronzeville was a wellspring of black businesses, vice, politics, religion, scholarship, and music, and it too experienced a romantic "renaissance" in the first half of the twentieth century. In the 1950s, the "piled up" Black Belt, to use yet another sociological descriptor, stretched out a bit, and places like North Kenwood–Oakland were embraced as part of the black community. Perhaps the most colorful example of North Kenwood–Oakland's new place at the center of black community life was the arrival of blues guitarist and vocalist Muddy Waters as owner of 4339 South Lake Park Avenue.[55] From 1954 to 1974, the house gave him, his wife, and their children easy access to the blues clubs along 43rd and 47th Streets, and gave the musicians a place to keep playing after the clubs were closed. In his biography of Waters, music journalist Robert Gordon vividly captures the energy at Waters's home:

> Muddy, accustomed to a sideline, quickly installed tenants upstairs and in the basement, adding three more kitchen areas. [Band pianist] Otis Spann claimed the basement's front room, [Muddy's best friend and bodyguard] Bo took the middle room, and Muddy put his uncle from Stovall [Mississippi], Joe Grant, in the back of the basement. The band rehearsed in the basement's common room. Band members and a valet rented the upstairs apartments.
>
> Several people could comfortably gather on the front stoop, and with a crowd spilling down the steps, maybe a chair or two at the bottom, there was room enough for two poker tables of people to gather, jive, and talk trash. A wino in the neighborhood went up and down the street with a cat on a leash and a recorder in his pocket, stepping around the tamale, watermelon, and Sno-Kone vendors. He'd have a trail of kids behind him, Muddy would see him, say, "hit it," and he'd blow a work song that sent the kids dancing. There was a patio in the backyard, and Muddy put two wrought-iron flamingoes on his front door, his name inverted beneath: Waters Muddy.[56]

Kids, men, and women, music, food, and drink filled the streets of the neighborhood during this time of post–World War II prosperity and optimism.[57] It's clear that Muddy Waters was not a private man; everyone could claim a piece of him and his house during his years in North Kenwood, and not just the musicians. Leroy Bowers delivered newspapers in the 1960s, and 4339 Lake Park was on his route. "I delivered papers to Muddy Waters and his wife," he declared proudly, going on to confirm the perpetual welcome mat at Waters's door. "And I would go down 43rd and I would hear him and his band playin'. 'Course they would shoo me away from the window 'cause I was still too young. And he'd say—ah, that's my paper boy. So those were fun days up and down Lake Park."

Muddy Waters's purchase in North Kenwood–Oakland (43rd Street is the boundary between the two neighborhoods, and Waters lived just south of it on the North Kenwood side) signaled his own personal ascent into the middle class. Waters moved his family from a cramped, bare apartment in Chicago's West Side black community to the spacious two-story brick home on the more well-regarded South Side. The houses were stately and well-kept, the businesses were plentiful and thriving, there was an abundance of nearby entertainment, and the neighbors were convivial. The old-timers who still live in the neighborhood remember those years with just such nostalgia.[58]

On Berkeley, the older residents especially remember when the block was free of fences. The black wrought iron fencing so popular today may look vintage and seem appropriate given the area's landmark status, but it is not authentic. Anne Boger moved to Berkeley in 1953, the same year that Leola Brown occupied 4432 Berkeley, and just three doors down. She pictures the block she played on as a child: "It was gorgeous. It didn't have no fences at all. And green grass. You could just look down, sit at the end of the block and look all the way down. And you see nothing, just green grass on both sides. No fence." Emma McDaniel's family moved two doors down from Boger in the 1950s, and she remembers the same thing. "You could just run from yard to yard. You basically had a football field here, because they had no fences. And I mean it was just amazing to me, you know?" The absence of fences—which now sharply delineate property lines—reflected a sense of shared ownership of the block. The commitment to high aesthetic standards is manifest in the reveries of adults who grew up there.

Seeing that there were so many young families with kids moving onto the block, there were bound to be problems with keeping up the grass and keeping down the trash. That's where the parents came in. Diane Hastings lived in an apartment in Oakland in the 1950s and bought a house on Berkeley in 1969 so that her children could have "a home to themselves." She exemplified the esprit de corps of the parents on the block: "I used to get all the teenage girls and boys and their little ones and we all would clean these lots and all. And we kept the lots clean and we kept the alleys clean." If Ms. Hastings kept the 4300 block of Berkeley clean, Bertha Brown, who lived across the street from Leola Brown, was the caretaker of the 4400 block. Indeed, her fastidiousness irked at least one of her neighbors: "Like I told Ms. Brown, 'I didn't know that Mayor Daley had hired you to clean up the streets. . . . You go all up and down the street. You can't stand filth, you can't stand this, you can't stand that. I didn't know the man hired you to do his work.'" Ms. Brown may have been rigid, but her kind of concern was what nourished and ensured the widespread pleasant memories of that golden era on Berkeley.

There was so much to do in the North Kenwood–Oakland of the 1950s and 1960s. Theaters still dotted the neighborhood, the same ones to which whites had flocked in previous decades—the Oakland Square, the "Ken," as the Kenwood Theater was called then, and the Shakespeare. There was a bowling alley on 47th Street just east of Cottage Grove Avenue. But the prize of the neighborhood, just as it had been for the white community, was the Sutherland Hotel. "Until 1952," chronicled a *Tribune* article, "the Sutherland catered exclusively to a white clientele. Its cuisine was famous, attracting people from other areas of the city. But there was a sharp decline in business, as the section's social landscape suddenly changed from white to Negro." Sharp and sudden. What did not change so rapidly, however, was the quality of the service, the fineness of the structure, and its all-around renown, albeit among a darker-hued clientele. Following a $300,000 renovation, the Sutherland—with a bar, barber shop, dining room, tailor, beauty parlor, travel agency, doctors' and dentists' offices, and "well-upholstered" lounges "where the community's celebrities gather"—remained a choice residential address and a place of fine music and food. Thelonious Monk, Max Roach, and Miles Davis (and his sidemen John Coltrane and Cannonball Adderley) all played the Sutherland Lounge. It is one of the few remaining venues of this heralded jazz age in black Chicago.[59]

Most of the residents' shopping needs were also met locally.[60] "I used to think 47th Street was like downtown. It's all those bright lights," remembered Leroy Bowers. Many residents thought of the 43rd and 47th Street commercial strips, which ran west from the lake through the core of the Black Belt to State Street, as their own Main Street. It was the downtown of Black Metropolis. "I didn't talk about 47th Street," said Dorothy Smith stopping herself excitedly as she realized she had skipped the most important part about the old days in the neighborhood. She reminisced about Christmas in the neighborhood and her family's visit to a department store on 47th Street. While some children went downtown to see Santa Claus, she went just a few blocks south where "they had a black Santa Claus. That was really important to my family. That's where I went."

The list of businesses that once thrived on 43rd Street echoed so frequently in old-timers' descriptions that I could almost see the street myself (see figs. 11a–e). "Down 43rd was our commercial street," Gladys McKinney instructed me, revealing a past that has long since been erased by vacant lots and abandonment. "We had, I never forget, we had a bakery called Theresa's. We had two beautiful bakeries. We had High-Low [Foods]. We had two beautiful butcher shops. We had a Harlan's Grocery Store. And we had a Walgreens right there on the corner of 43rd and Berkeley, right up there on the corner." Sometimes, as when Anne Boger described the street, the account was so convincing that I could smell, taste, and feel the street:

Down 43rd used to be a shopping area. . . . Bakery and shoe stores and a department store and a chicken place that had live chickens. And I tell you, you go in, it smelled like chickens. You come out with feathers all over you. But you chose your own chicken and they would kill it. Oh, girl, it was fantastic! And then a fish place. And then they had a Japanese store that had all kinds of stuff if you wanted to make an Oriental dish, you know. They had everything up there.

Forty-third Street had the feel of an international bazaar, with breads and meats and spices and clothes, Japanese, Jewish, and "American" chain stores, all with a teeming black clientele. Few of the establishments that residents remember so fondly were black-owned. Norman Bolden's father's businesses offered major exceptions. He ran (at various times) a record store, hardware store, beauty parlor, pool hall, and TV repair shop out of the storefronts he owned on 43rd Street between

Figure 11a. 43rd Street commercial district, Shakespeare Theater and other businesses, northwest corner of 43rd Street and Ellis Avenue, July 19, 1917. Chicago History Museum, film negative ICHi-39188. Photo by Chas E. Baker.

Figure 11b. 43rd Street commercial district, northwest corner of 43rd Street and Greenwood Avenue, April 4, 1964. Chicago History Museum, film negative ICHi-39189. Photo by Sigmund J. Osty.

Figure 11c. 47th Street commercial district, 1371 West 47th Street, April 18, 1956. Chicago History Museum, film negative ICHi-39182. Photo by Mildred Mead.

Figure 11d. 47th Street commercial district, Ken Theater, 1225 East 47th Street, April 19, 1956. Chicago History Museum, film negative ICHi-39187. Photo by Mildred Mead.

Figure 11e. 47th Street commercial district, 1357 East 47th Street, April 18, 1956. Chicago History Museum, film negative ICHi-39181. Photo by Mildred Mead.

Berkeley and Ellis Avenues. "I remember the days spending many spring breaks and summer breaks at Royal Flush, Dad's record shop, working," Bolden reminisced. Norman Bolden's dedication to the rebirth of North Kenwood–Oakland—"43rd Street is definitely my life"—is built upon the years his father spent serving its residents, right up to his death in 1994, in his shop. Bolden still owns the buildings where his father did business and plans to have them bustling again in the contemporary reprise of that golden era.

Joining Leola and Earl Brown in their move to North Kenwood–Oakland in 1953 were one hundred and fifty families bound for the newly constructed Victor Olander Homes at Oakwood Boulevard and Lake Park Avenue. The fifteen-story Olander Homes building was the tallest Chicago public housing project built to date, rising above Lake Michigan and a neighborhood of two- and three-story homes and apartment buildings. The building was exceptionally clean, almost sterile, and stood alone amid newly planted grass and freshly laid walkways (see fig. 12). Whereas the architectural promise of the suburbs was perfected in ramblers, ranches, and bungalows, arranged neatly with their private garages along miles of new winding streets, the physical form that would save the city was the modernist high-rise, distinguished by its heavy massing and the abundance of vertical and horizontal straight lines. Skyscrapers were common in Chicago in and near downtown, but only there. A new tall building like the Olander project on the south side was quite literally awesome. Its imposing design was a model for the wholesome aspirations, directed dreams, and high hopes of the new families who would move into it.

The project was a near paradise for the Carter family, who were the first to move into the second Olander building in 1956. Mrs. Carter gleamed and remarked, "The lovely view [of Lake Michigan] from my living room windows is the nicest Christmas present I could get." The Carters left behind a run-down, overpriced, stove-heated apartment where their children "seldom went outdoors because the only playground available to them was the street." At the Olander Homes there was a fully equipped and landscaped play area that the residents tended with such care that they won the Chicago Housing Authority's "Spruce Up" award in the summer of 1958, earning the coveted distinction of flying the royal blue and gold CHA banner in front of their development.[61]

Public housing came to North Kenwood–Oakland literally with a bang. At the dedication ceremony of the first Olander Homes building

Figure 12. First building of Victor A. Olander Homes, 1954. Chicago History Museum, film negative ICHi-39184. Photo by Mildred Mead.

in 1952, Mayor Martin Kennelly and other dignitaries were gathered at the base of the building, which was still under construction. As the program began a wooden plank came tumbling down from the partially built tenth floor. The debris landed five feet from the podium, sending the mayor and everyone else screaming and dodging.[62] The inauspicious inauguration was an unrecognized omen of the building's embattled future. The next year, construction began on a sister building just south of the first, with another 150 apartments. In the next decade four more high-rises were constructed, forming a nearly half-mile wall of public housing that came to be known as the Lakefront Properties. In all, nearly nine hundred families came to Oakland to live in the new projects. Some were refugees of "slum clearance" in the core of the Black Belt (see chapter 6); others were families like the Carters simply looking for clean and decent housing.

During this time, there was debate across the city, in the city council, among planners, and between black and white civic leaders about where to build the new public housing. The vacant land to be used for the Victor Olander Homes in Oakland was suggested by the neighborhood's alderman and had broad community support, with one very important exception. The Ken-Oak Improvement Association, which was formed when fifteen new black families moved to the neighborhood in 1945, opposed the construction of public housing at that location. They argued that the vacant land should be used to build middle-income housing rather than housing for the working class and poor, yet another eerie instance of foreshadowing.[63]

The most immediate impact of public housing in the neighborhood was acute population pressures. In the 1950s, the elementary schools were severely overcrowded. Students at Oakenwald School, located next door to the new Olander Homes, were in class for just four hours a day because the building could not accommodate all the children at the same time. Instead, administrators ran two four-hour shifts. In 1955, Shakespeare School in North Kenwood had the largest enrollment of any elementary school in Chicago. It got a twenty-one-classroom addition in 1953 to address its space issues, but was back on double shifts again by 1958. The Chicago Public Schools bought a former private school, Bousfield School at 46th and Drexel, and a former optometry institute, which it converted into Doniat School at 42nd and Cottage Grove, to try to ease overcrowding, but by 1959 additions and new schools were being constructed to take *their* overflow. "You just had people just mushrooming and blossoming around here," said Cyrus La-Salle, falling back on organic references to characterize the neighborhood's springtime: "I can't quote percentages but CHA housing was so full until they had so many kids in the neighborhood until they had to put a mobile unit at the corner of 39th and Lake Park. There were like four or five of them." The mobile units that LaSalle remembered were soon replaced by new school buildings. George T. Donoghue Elementary School was constructed in 1963, with thirty classrooms and two kindergartens, to "provide room for 1,050 pupils, who will move into three new high-rise buildings at 41st street and Lake Park avenue." Two other elementary schools were built in the neighborhood around the same time, followed by yet another elementary school and Martin Luther King Jr. High School in the 1970s.[64]

The bursting and bustling population also created a rich organizational life. The groups that filled the void after the collapse of the predominantly white Oakland-Kenwood Planning Association in 1953 were explicitly interracial or predominantly black. Forty-Seventh Street hardened as the divider between North and South Kenwood. The Ken-Oak Improvement Association, the organization of black home owners founded in 1945, set 47th Street as its southern boundary. And with urban renewal plans well under way in Hyde Park and South Kenwood, in 1950 the newly formed Hyde Park–Kenwood Community Conference established 47th Street as its northern border. The Kenwood-Ellis Community Center, at 46th and Greenwood, although inclusive of all of Kenwood in name, in practice concentrated on North Kenwood. Thus, while Oakland and Kenwood had for many years been sister neighborhoods in planning and action, after 1950 there was a stark distinction between North and South Kenwood. The names of some community groups, like the North Kenwood-Oakland Community Conference, and the North Kenwood-Oakland Community Conservation Committee, explicitly reflected this split. In addition to these neighborhood-wide organizations were the local groups specific to the public housing projects, like the Olander Y-Wives, and the Victor Olander Boys Club and its heralded marching band.[65]

Even during these golden years the panoply of neighborhood organizations in North Kenwood–Oakland was already mounting offensives against the specter of blight and the prospect of becoming a "slum." This was partly because of their exclusion from the Hyde Park–South Kenwood planning process, which, backed by the powerful and rich University of Chicago, was almost assured of success. But it was also because the population pressures were so powerful. The black population in Chicago was estimated to be growing by thirty thousand people every year from 1950 to 1955.[66] The neighborhood's black residents knew that what had drawn them to North Kenwood–Oakland despite restrictive covenants and racist sneers would similarly motivate more newcomers. This put serious strain on the neighborhood's infrastructure and housing stock. A 1957 study found that the number of housing units in the neighborhood had increased by 26 percent even though no new buildings had been erected, leading to the conclusion that "kitchenettes abound"[67] (see fig. 13). Population growth initially

Figure 13. Six-flat building at 3846 South Ellis advertising "kitchenette" apartments, 1954. Chicago History Museum, film negative ICHi-39180. Photo by Mildred Mead.

meant a thriving business district, packed churches (including some fourteen storefronts), and a lively street life, but by the mid-1960s the neighborhood's springtime was giving way to an oppressive summer heat (see fig. 14). There were too many bodies, too little space, and too little money (individual or institutional), and when the gangs came there were too many guns.

The Low End (1965–1988)

In the 1950s, Leola and Earl Brown probably walked a block down from their 4432 Berkeley home to do their grocery shopping, buy clothes,

Figure 14. Residents and neighbors of the Lakefront Properties as the buildings and neighborhood began to decline, 1968. Kenwood Oakland Community Organization. Used with permission.

or catch a movie on 43rd Street. By the mid-1960s, they might have thought twice.[68] In 1968, a reported "twenty gang members" were arrested at the corner of 43rd Street and Berkeley after a commotion. One of the teenagers, who lived in the neighborhood, had fired shots into a crowd. There were no injuries, but such a ruckus no doubt shattered the neighborliness that had before governed block life.[69] By the late 1960s, gangs were firmly entrenched in the neighborhood, the most notorious being the Blackstone Rangers (see fig. 15). As if to physically document

Figure 15. Graffiti in North Kenwood–Oakland marks the territory of the Blackstone Rangers gang, 1968. Kenwood Oakland Community Organization. Used with permission.

the replacement of commercial and social vitality with youthful lawlessness, the Oakland Square Theater, which had hosted performances and movies since 1916, became in 1978 the headquarters of the Blackstone Rangers, or the El Rukns, as the gang was called following the politico-religious conversion of its leader.

"The Low End" was the label affixed to North Kenwood–Oakland and the neighboring communities of Douglas and Grand Boulevard. With whites leaving for the suburbs, middle-class blacks moved south in the city, to 79th Street, 87th Street, 95th Street—the numbers just kept getting higher. For some people, then, the Low End simply referred to the lower street numbers. But the term equally reflected morale, behaviors, esteem: "The Disciples and Blackstone Rangers were terrorizing this neighborhood. That's why it got down to be so low," Anne Boger explained. Leonard Watson was even more explicit: "People that have lived down here, they consider it was ghetto going bad. And they called it the Low End." Alexander Pratt bought a house in 1978, but the neighborhood was still too "low end" for him to move in: "Low income, very low, mostly probably public aid recipients and people who had retired with not much income. I mean it was no hope there, you know, at all." Norman Bolden put it even more bluntly: "Low rent, low life, you know," adding the counterpoint, "If you were living on high cotton, you lived on 79th Street." Julius Rhodes grew up further south, where the cotton was high, and reflected on his evaluation of places like North Kenwood–Oakland. "The Low End, from when I was a child, wasn't necessarily where you, you know, where you wanted to be." More than a geographic designation (and an historical epoch, as I am using it), the Low End marked the neighborhood's lowly status amid a class-heterogeneous Black Belt that by the 1970s stretched to the southern edge of the city and into the suburbs.[70]

"I think that was the worst time for this neighborhood," lamented Dorothy Smith, who grew up on Berkeley and relished the golden era when, so goes the lore, everyone knew each other and played together. Like so many of her neighbors, she was quick to give her theory on what went wrong: "Once the gangs became really prevalent and drugs became more common, the neighborhood started to change . . . because, well, people were afraid of their children. That's basically what it was. Adults were afraid of children. Because that's when I really, I'd say, that I recognized that children were killed during this time." Smith did not give details, but perhaps she was remembering 1968, when twelve-year-old Robert Hampton of 4310 Berkeley and ten-year-old Theophilus Hoffman of Greenwood Avenue were shot as they walked home from Price Elementary School. Or 1969, when thirteen-year-old Aliceteen Nunnley of 4305 Berkeley was shot while visiting a friend at 41st and Lake Park.[71] Or later, in the 1980s, when death seemed to grab the block. Another Berkeley resident narrated:

You know, a lot of things have happened here. Like people getting shot. [Ms. Lawrence's] son got killed. Her son got killed, Hank, on 47th. Right there at 47th, but it started on the block. Two of her boys can't come back here now because they was in a shooting right there at 43rd. They haven't been here in years. 'Cause it was a shooting and they had to get away otherwise it would have been trouble. She had nice kids [but] all of them was in the wrong crowd. She didn't raise them like that. She or her husband did not raise them like that. They were raised as good church-going kids. . . .

Because they called me when Hank died, when Hank got killed. I was still on the third floor and they called me. It had to be in '85, '86, somewhere around there, Hank died. They called my number 'bout four o'clock in the morning. The police called me and asked if Hank Lawrence's parents lived next door. [The police couldn't] get in touch with them [so they asked] would I go next door and tell them that it was a homicide. So I called my aunt, 'cause I'm nervous then. So my aunt said go on over there. And this was before I was getting ready to go to work. So I went over there and told them. I rung the bell and told them. I broke it down. . . .

And something happened to Hank, of course [his brothers and friends were] going to retaliate. They all ran around together. They all grew up on the block together and they just had the kinship about each other because they were all good friends. The other people I guess was telling them who had did it. So of course, they found out who did it, they did something. And that day they shot him down there and they got out of here and they haven't been back since.

If the Lawrence children got mixed up in the wrong crowd it was at least in part because the wrong crowd was ever more present in the neighborhood. George Wade was a teenager in the 1970s: "It was treacherous. More gangbangin', shootin', killin'. . . . The Warlords against the Disciples, the Disciples against the Stones. It was bad." Michael Dearing moved into the neighborhood in 1978: "The El Rukn street gang was right across the street on Drexel, and the Disciples were right over here. Constant gunshots, we'd get broken in on, you couldn't leave things in your yard, people walkin' up on your porch, that kind of stuff. The police response was basically zero unless somebody was down for their death. It was terrible." Maurice Finch grew up across the street from the El Rukn headquarters in the 1970s: "[They] retrofitted it for their gang use and they had drug stashes, weapon stashes, and it was nuts. It was crazy. It was crazy. They were so dug in. Like a tick or something. They were just so dug in, ready for war."[72]

Of course North Kenwood–Oakland was no worse than other neighborhoods in Chicago where gangs were (and are) integral, but often deadly, parts of the social fabric. As elsewhere, the clannish violence that seemed so painfully local was anything but. One resident who came back to the neighborhood in the late 1970s was depressed by the violence and despair that had overtaken his childhood paradise and longed to find a culprit: "Was it black people that did this? Was it a combination of people that did it? Who did this?" he asked rhetorically but with real bewilderment.

Social scientists were asking the same questions, and the comprehensive analyses of the decline of black urban neighborhoods during this period is completely applicable to North Kenwood–Oakland. At the center of this discussion is the changing labor market, including the location of jobs, their skill requirements and wages, and the ability of workers to organize. Sociologist William Julius Wilson offers statistics on all of these trends as they apply to Chicago during the period of the Low End. From 1967 to 1987, Chicago lost 60 percent of its manufacturing sector, or 520,000 jobs. During the 1970s and 1980s, good-paying manufacturing jobs moved to American suburbs and the south, and in more recent years they have moved overseas, rooting the changes in North Kenwood–Oakland firmly within a discussion of globalization. "As a result," Wilson reports, "young black males have turned increasingly to the low-wage service sector and unskilled laboring jobs for employment, or have gone jobless." Even when working, workers are less empowered, as illustrated by declining rates of union membership in Chicago. Whereas 55 percent of black men in their twenties were union members in 1969, only 35 percent of the next generation belonged to unions in 1987. Fewer jobs with lower pay and weakened bargaining power means less money with which to support families and maintain community infrastructure and institutions. It means a younger generation with less hope about its economic prospects, and thus more attraction to illegal means of making a living. These problems of "concentrated poverty," as social scientists describe it, are wrought by job loss and are confined to black neighborhoods because of the tenacity of racial segregation, what sociologists Douglas Massey and Nancy Denton call "American Apartheid."[73]

But the "disappearance" of work and its disproportionate toll on black communities is only part of the story. Beginning with President Richard Nixon's freeze on new funding for public housing and continuing through Ronald Reagan's preferences for downtown commercial investment, the federal government "completely jettisoned" urban policy through the 1970s, '80s, and early '90s. During this time, historian Raymond Mohl writes, "big-city budgets gradually were decimated as Congress and the administration further choked off the flow of federal dollars."[74] Reagan's War on Drugs, which in many respects translated into a war on African American men caught with drugs, further destabilized black neighborhoods by fueling what sociologist Loïc Wacquant has termed (following Foucault) the "carceral state."[75] Incarceration rates increased fourfold in the last quarter of the twentieth century, and African Americans are seven times as likely to be in prison as whites. All of these factors, along with others such as neglect by private investors, the

Figure 16a. 47th Street commercial district, 927 East 47th Street, May 18, 1956. Chicago History Museum, film negative ICHi-39185. Photo by Mildred Mead.

1968 riots, crack, family dissolution, and environmental racism, were felt as acutely on Berkeley Avenue as anywhere. Still, these societal-level explanations were useless in keeping grocery stores open, saving houses abandoned by their owners, supplying schools with books and teachers, or bringing back murdered sons.

The once thriving commercial districts on 43rd and 47th Streets saw early vacancies even during the golden years, and truly faded in the 1970s (see figs. 16a and b). "By the '80s, no business to be done," remembered Norman Bolden, whose father was one of the few merchants to hold on during this time. "And the few businesses that were here were fronts," he continued. "You know, the candy store that didn't sell candy. You know, a Laundromat that wasn't washing any clothes." Again, the gangs were implicated in this decline. Anne Boger left the neighborhood as an adult in the late 1960s but came back in the 1980s, only to find almost nothing of what she had cherished as a child: "The gangs ran [the businesses] away. And they set that place on fire—the department store. That's what I heard that happened." The exodus was

Figure 16b. 47th Street commercial district, 1358 East 47th Street, April 19, 1956. Chicago History Museum, film negative ICHi-39186. Photo by Mildred Mead.

palpable, almost magical in its swiftness: "All your nice stores just disappeared back then," Gladys McKinney recalled. "Then, I'm thinking in the '70s, early '70s and '70, '71, '72 Walgreens left. And we had a Jewel [grocery store], Jewels left. And you had A&P, it left. . . . Like with 47th, I think the early part of the '70s, maybe '65 or so, all your nice hotels was gone and everything." The end of the magic trick was complete desolation. "I saw it go down to nothing, really," offered Harriet Patterson. "The bottom. That means there was nothing. No stores, nothing to work with."

And nothing is what came in behind the businesses that left, leaving vacant buildings that eventually fell into disrepair and ultimately were demolished. Leroy Bowers saw the whole thing firsthand, as a boy in the late 1950s, a teenager in the 1960s, and a young man returning from military service in the late 1970s:

[The theaters] got torn down in the early '70s—late '60s or early '70s. The south side of 47th Street started coming down. . . . [Then,] when I came home from the service and I came into the neighborhood, it was all bombed out. It was like we was bombed, you know. The buildings was burned down. I remember the furniture store that was right where Mc-Donald's sit at 47th and Cottage. It had burned down and the buildings were abandoned and vacant. And it was just unbelievable. Because I remember when I delivered papers it was no vacant lots.

Bowers had been stationed in Japan and did not see actual fighting during the 1970s. The irony is that while he was safely overseas, his own neighborhood had been a combat zone. Abandoned buildings turned to vacant lots, and vacant lots collected litter, debris, and more. One resident claimed that the whole area was rodent infested due to the accumulated garbage. Fast-food chains got free advertising in North Kenwood–Oakland by having their bags and containers strewn across people's front lawns and the main thoroughfares. On Berkeley, Avis Green told the following story:

There's something about people who see a neighborhood like this with vacant lots who think that real people don't live in here, so that they drive by and throw trash in the street. You go out there, and somebody's been out there with McDonald's or Kentucky Fried or something, and boxes are all over the street and things like that. And they come down here and sit in their cars and drink.

While there are few structural explanations for shameless individual disregard for neighborhood upkeep, some of the refuse was likely dumped in the neighborhood illegally by commercial firms. The situation was exacerbated by diminished city services, which made garbage collection and street improvements less frequent.

In 1969, the United States Senate commissioned two physicians from the American Public Health Association to travel around the country to learn about the public health needs of poor communities. One of the places they visited was Kenwood-Oakland. Their assessment of the neighborhood began, "The streets of the Kenwood-Oakland community are an unforgettable profile of destitution and deprivation." Since their focus was on health, they detailed unsanitary living conditions that contributed to disease. "About half of the tenements are substandard," the doctors observed. One elementary school "had every single window broken and replaced by plywood sheets. No natural daylight entered the building." Such squalid living conditions, coupled with the fact that there were only five doctors for a community of over fifty thousand residents, created a situation in which "about 45 of every 1,000 babies in Kenwood-Oakland die in early infancy." The observers' conclusion was as disheartening as their introduction: "If someone had decided to design a system to break people's spirit, and to break them as human beings, they couldn't have done a better job."[76]

If, following the multiple metaphors implicit in the Low End label, gangs were the neighborhood's lowlife, and its streets were low on the priority list for cleaning and maintenance, and the buildings were made low by neglect and demolition, the overall population might simply be described as low income. In public housing, as Gladys McKinney, a resident of the projects herself, explains, eligibility standards were changing.[77]

> These two buildings here, this one here and the one on the corner, was a show place because the people used to actually come off of Lake Shore Drive and drive around just to see these two buildings. The two gentlemen we had—one was named Mr. Graves, he was a maintenance superintendent at 3939 [South Lake Park]. I can't think of the man who was here off the top of my head, but these were two of the [most] beautiful buildings from CHA that you would ever want to see in your life. But back then you had a different climate of residents. Back then, CHA really screened. And if you didn't pass the screen, you didn't get in. . . . The people in the building at that time worked. You had some who got assistance, but majority of the people they put up were working people. Then over the years it changed. They lost their job and so forth, and then they started getting assistance. That's when it really changed then, when they lowered the standards and everything. And then the people that was already up here started to move out.

By the 1970s and 1980s, the public housing buildings in the neighborhood were filled with poor families. In 1980, 55.8 percent of the families in the census tract that included the six high-rises had incomes below the poverty line, up from 51.2 percent in 1970. Again, North Kenwood–Oakland was not unlike other declining black neighborhoods across the country where concentrated poverty translated into crime and disorder. Although 4432 Berkeley was about a mile from the large high-rise developments, residents of the block still felt their presence. "A lot of nice people," said Berkeley resident Emmett Coleman about public housing residents. "But," he continued, "when you crowd people all up together, you know, the troublemakers get all the attention, and seem to be influential as well as intimidating every one else. So it was kind of rough, you know, around here." In addition to the public housing on Lake Park Avenue, east of Berkeley, there were also high-rise projects to the west, on Cottage Grove Avenue. Flanked by public housing, many residents of the interior streets, like Patricia Sanders, found themselves maneuvering to avoid the high-rises: "It was kinda like you was trapped in the middle. . . . So, you know, if you caught the bus you'd have to get off at a certain stop, walk down the alley, you know, 'round the corner and all of that. And that wasn't even nice. You couldn't even get to your house."

But despite having to dodge danger, Sanders stayed in North Kenwood–Oakland, and so did others.[78] People stayed for different reasons—the cheap rents, the comforts of familiarity, strong family ties, or a belief that the neighborhood would turn back around. Leola Brown stayed at 4432 Berkeley until she died in 1982. She had been a widow for over ten years and suffered from very poor health and limited mobility, which explains why there were so few stories about her among the neighbors. Because she had no children, her nephew assumed responsibility for her care, and the house passed to him and his wife when she died. Arthur and Marguerite Jones (Leola Brown's nephew and his wife) would have had a hard time selling 4432 Berkeley in the 1980s even if they wanted to. So they stayed too.

Many residents who persevered tell stories that are not nearly as bleak as the picture of the neighborhood thus far painted. They could not help but be aware of the neighborhood's flaws, but as Patricia Sanders's circuitous walk home from the bus stop illustrates, they all came up with strategies to cope and, more, to find pleasure and good times. Even if the solace ended just outside their doorstep, stayers like Vanessa Lewis concluded that the Low End wasn't all that bad.

> It was like a island too. And every now and then you had a few people that come from 43rd and a few people come on this block. But basically it was a really nice block considering what we had. Ellis was pretty bad and Lake Park was pretty bad, but this was like a little island, I guess, because of the dead end right there. So it was pretty nice—considering the surroundings.

For Lewis, Berkeley Avenue was an island in an otherwise chaotic community. But when I interviewed people who had lived on Ellis or on

Lake Park, the streets that were "pretty bad" in Lewis's eyes, they too saw their streets as safe havens. Michael Smith and his wife Sylvia grew up in the 1950s and 1960s in the Ida B. Wells housing project at the northernmost end of Oakland. Mr. Smith refuted the negativity associated with the projects and noted that everyone had friends who were gang members:

> Well, we had gangs. We had some of the oldest gangs in the city. But the thing was, we grew up in Ida B. I'm talking about the old gangs. They didn't fight [each other] much. They went to the same schools. We lived in the same neighborhood. So it wasn't a whole lot of in-fighting. They used to fight gangs at [other projects]. They used to go over there and fight gangs, you know, go over on the other side of 43rd Street. See, Ida B. Wells was a cohesive unit. And for the most part there you didn't have gang violence, you know.

As in Ms. Lewis's account, in the Smiths' view most of the violence happened elsewhere—at other projects, or south of 43rd Street, or at other schools. For people who lived in the other projects or south of 43rd Street, or who went to those other schools, all of the violence happened in Ida B. Wells, where the Smiths had lived. Despite the litany of problems that made the Low End so low, many residents envisioned zones of safety within the dangerous landscape. To persevere, they put danger at a safe distance.[79]

On the side of good there was continued organizational vitality, especially in the form of the Kenwood Oakland Community Organization (KOCO). KOCO's early organizers were first inspired in 1965, when members of the Southern Christian Leadership Conference came to Chicago in advance of Martin Luther King Jr.'s 1966 campaign against slums. KOCO quickly became a player in neighborhood and city politics, and its director, Reverend Curtis Burrell, secured the cochairmanship of the Model Cities Planning Council, appointed by Mayor Richard J. Daley in 1968. (The Model Cities board also included George Bonner of 4406 Berkeley.) But Burrell did not serve his full term as cochair because KOCO became increasingly suspicious of the designs that Daley and other city elites had for black communities. Despite its genesis, KOCO's philosophy did not follow the racial reconciliatory stance of Dr. King's movement, but instead leaned toward the community empowerment sentiments championed by the Black Power movement. Hence KOCO was skeptical of programs funded and directed by "white planners," as

Burrell often put it. Its mission was to develop indigenous black leaders who would make plans derived from widespread community participation. KOCO's motto was "Black people serious about one another."[80]

This emphasis on ideological and political independence (if not economic self-sufficiency) was highlighted in KOCO's relationship with the Community Renewal Society, a white Christian organization dedicated to improving Chicago's neighborhoods. In 1968, the Community Renewal Society made a covenant with KOCO for an experiment in community development. The Community Renewal Society would fund the endeavor for three years at $100,000 per year and provide technical assistance and research, but KOCO alone would lead the planning and implementation efforts. The covenant read: "Both parties agree that the Kenwood-Oakland Community Organization shall be self-determining and shall exercise control and direction over the operations in the community." After three years, the partnership yielded a new day care center, a leadership training program (funded by a large grant from the Rockefeller Foundation), a commitment for a new health care facility, a construction contract, planning for a new housing development, and the incorporation of an economic development arm appropriately named True People's Power Development Corporation. These early planning documents suggest that KOCO was a pioneer in envisioning the elements necessary to support and stabilize the neighborhood's low-income and working-class population.

Consonant with its belief in grassroots leadership, KOCO also formed an early alliance with the Blackstone Rangers gang. This relationship quickly went bad. KOCO invested $3,000 and many hours to help the Blackstone Rangers open a restaurant at 4651 South Woodlawn. The report to the Community Renewal Society stated that this relationship "failed completely and the policy was dramatically altered with Rev. Burrell's 'walks against fear' in the community."[81] Robert Lucas, who worked at KOCO during its formative years and later became its executive director, recounted the sequence of events.

> They believed [that KOCO] could redeem the gangs. So the Blackstone Rangers were actually part of the organizing back when I went to KOCO in 1969. Jeff Fort, the leader, was on the payroll, but he wasn't doing anything. . . . There was 11 guys on the payroll. And there was another guy on the payroll who I guess was a second-level leader. He told me he was in charge of economic development, and he pulled out a roll of money in

my face [laughter] and said this is what I make. . . . In 1970, [Reverend Burrell] put the Stones out. The Blackstone Rangers had put him under gunpoint.

Guns seemed to be the only things to which the Blackstone Rangers were irrevocably attached, and they shunned the opportunity to go legit.

KOCO's effectiveness (but not its presence) waned in the 1970s, corresponding to the general government disinterest in cities after the Great Society programs of the 1960s. KOCO secured funding from the United Way to deliver various social services, such as a food pantry and workforce development activities, but the big plans of its early years were stymied by the tight grip with which the local alderman held onto control of the neighborhood's future. Very little happened in the neighborhood to reverse its downward slide under the watch of Tim Evans, alderman from 1973 to 1991. Robert Lucas, who became chairman of KOCO's board in 1972 (and its executive director in 1975), felt that Evans was the big reason why KOCO was spinning its wheels during these years.

> There was seven or eight plans. We created three or four of those and none of them really went anywhere because of the land. It wasn't the lack of community support, it was the lack of aldermanic will. We had seen them all from 1969 until. He wouldn't support it.

The relationship between KOCO and Alderman Evans remained rocky throughout Evans's tenure, with Evans once blocking KOCO's attempt to buy tax-delinquent buildings to rehab for affordable housing.[82] Several other residents concurred with Lucas, making similar critiques of Evans as someone who guarded his command of the neighborhood by demanding little of the city's administration. Despite Evans's roadblocks, KOCO was able to make inroads in improving the neighborhood's housing stock in the 1980s using government funding for rehabilitation. The mayoral election of Harold Washington, who was a strong KOCO supporter and who Evans strongly backed, eventually helped to smooth the KOCO-Evans relationship for a handful of projects.

But while KOCO did not like Evans, many others did. On Berkeley, one resident remembered fondly, "He used to ride through the neighborhood, honey, and he would see the trees and things that need to be pruned and stuff." A small act given the disinvestment and violence that racked the neighborhood, but his presence was still worth something for residents. Also, Evans maintained strong ties with public housing residents and tried hard to protect the high-rises from demolition.

Ultimately, despite the activism of the late 1960s and the steadfastness of the stayers, North Kenwood–Oakland could not triumph over the forces that were attacking black central-city neighborhoods across the country. As the evaluators of KOCO's efforts concluded: "Bootstrap renewal of a slum community is a comforting myth, but a myth nonetheless. Most of us would like to believe that if only 'those people' would get themselves together, they could eradicate the conditions of the slum community. But the slum community is part of the larger society, and the rest of the society is deeply implicated in the slum—politically, economically, and morally."[83] The built environment, which was "steady going, just going, going, until it was all gone," as one resident put it, had its parallel in the human landscape. Between 1960 and 1980, the population of North Kenwood–Oakland dropped by more than a third, and 29 percent of the public housing units in the high-rises were vacant just before the buildings were vacated.[84] To make a final play on the neighborhood's nickname, the population in the Low End dropped even lower in 1986 with the removal of more than six hundred families living in the Lakefront Properties so that their buildings could be renovated.

Black on the Block (1988–Present)

I had decided that my next research project would be a study of North Kenwood–Oakland before I started looking for a house there. During my years as a graduate student at the University of Chicago, I had ventured onto the residential streets north of 47th Street only once, not just because of the subtle and not-so-subtle warnings from the university that it was unsafe, but because there was little reason to do so. There were no restaurants, stores, or services, and no one I knew lived there. Then I got invited to dinner at a friend of a friend's house. The host was actually a graduate student at the University of Chicago, an African American man who had recently purchased a condominium in a six-unit graystone building in North Kenwood. It was sometime around 1995, but what I remember most as we drove down Oakenwald Avenue looking for the address was rubble. The street was uneven and cracked as if there had been a rare earthquake in Chicago, there were crumbling buildings on either side, and it seemed especially dark. Surely, much of this first dismal impression was borne of unfamiliarity and negative conditioning, but those influences were at an unconscious level. Consciously, my friend and I looked at each other thinking that either we were in the wrong place or this guy had taken a big leap of faith, and was demanding that we do the same by coming over for dinner. The eeriness of it all made me intensely curious.

A few years later it was time for a new research project and I remembered that trip to North Kenwood. I read up a bit, and the contradictions and complexities were fascinating. I learned of the neighborhood's grand history and of Oakland's contemporary distinction (in 1990) as the poorest community area in the city. I read about the entrenched gangs and the rumors that a Borders Bookstore was soon to open there. I found out that a community planning process involving hundreds of residents, elite consultants, and multiple city and state agencies had resulted in a conservation-area designation and produced a conservation plan. And it was clear from feature newspaper articles that private investors also eyed the neighborhood for its redevelopment potential. Finally, I learned that black professionals (or aspiring ones) were the residential vanguard in the revival. This kind of situation, I thought, was bound to be rich with the sociological processes I was interested in—complex backstories that would illuminate the mechanics of urban politics and the functions of social capital; neighbor-versus-neighbor disputes that constitute the bases of community; lived, remembered, and fabricated histories whose simultaneous inspection might provide a fuller portrait of neighborhood change; and, most importantly, conversations among black folks about being black folks.

In April 1998, I moved into 4432 South Berkeley. The previous owner, a young African American lawyer, had bought it from Arthur and Marguerite Jones just a few years earlier. She made a pretty penny off of me—a 44 percent return on her investment in two years—not because I was foolish, but because more and more people were now home shopping in North Kenwood–Oakland and the prices reflected this increase in demand. I was drawn to the house for its rich vintage character—pocket doors, transoms above each entryway, a butler's staircase off of the kitchen, a water closet in the master bedroom, and the original skeleton keys for each bedroom door. It was in incredible shape given that it was more than a century old. When the real estate agent gave me the booklet that described its landmark history I was sold, and the house was too. Now, having uncovered the lives of its previous owners and neighbors—hearing the struggle between Mrs. Hooke and her servant Mary Hall next door; being awed by the distinguished Dr. Willoughby Walling's visits to collect the rent; imagining Mrs. Hirsch weaving Indian baskets in the front parlor; watching Roy P. Donovan sign two restrictive covenants; and soothing Leola Brown at the death of her husband—I am even more enamored and enthralled by the house. The contemporary chapter of 4432 Berkeley's long and continuing life begins in the late 1980s as more black professionals like myself move to the neighborhood. As "the black bourgeoisie meets the truly disadvantaged," an encounter I will consider in the next chapter, another journey begins to forge, fashion, and fathom the black community.

2

When Ruby Harris moved to North Kenwood in 1987, she rolled up her sleeves and got to work. Not just in her new home, which was in such disrepair that living there was dangerous, but also in her neighborhood. One of her first projects was to find a place where her daughter could play. Given the neighborhood's poverty, in terms of both income and political clout, it is not surprising that Harris found few options. "There was nothing for her to do," she remembered. "Anywhere." Down the street from their 1890s row house was a public school building. The school was built in 1960, during the neighborhood's golden era, and closed only a few decades later when the population declined. It was being rented by a social service agency that ran a program for special-needs children. Ms. Harris, who moved to the neighborhood confident that its renaissance was imminent, reasoned that all the new young families, like hers, would need some kind of recreation center. The school building seemed like a good place for it. Special-needs children were no doubt needy, but the new community would have different needs. "We're the community. We want a center," she declared. The "we" in her sentence meant the savvy, energetic newcomer parents and a dedicated group of old-timers who were eager to partner with them to get the things they had been wanting (and should have had) for a long time.[1] They held fund-raisers and garage sales for their cause. And they made their demands known to the social service agency that occupied the building, the Chicago Board of Education, which owned the building, and the Chicago Park District, which they hoped would take it over and start up activities. All of their targets were unprepared for and a bit surprised by the level of sophistication of these community activists. "Mind you, I'm talking about people who are principals," Harris offered as a signal of the professional credentials of the new community her group represented. "It makes a difference, the educational levels of the black people living here. . . . They didn't know that we were, should I say, back on the block, so to speak."

Black professionals, the black middle class, black gentrifiers, "buppies," educated blacks, the black bourgeoisie. None of these terms is exactly appropriate. When sociologist E. Franklin Frazier published *Black Bourgeoisie* in 1957 his purpose was to expose the group's "obsession with the struggle for status." Their quest for status was doomed, he surmised, because of the thin economic ground on which the black bourgeoisie stood. Frazier dismissed this black pseudo–middle class as "subsist[ing] off the crumbs of philanthropy, the salaries of public servants, and what could be squeezed from the meager earnings of Negro workers." Yet from this pitiable table of wealth, the black bourgeoisie gave the appearances of eating like kings. They created, in Frazier's words, a "world of make-believe" in which the trappings of society life mattered more than being well-read or politically aware. This is the general thrust of Frazier's arguments, but it is not the reading from which I draw my use of his term "black bourgeoisie." Buried within his full-scale attack on the attitudes and actions of the black middle class, Frazier puts forth three points that have particular utility for the study of North Kenwood–Oakland. First, he argues that the black bourgeoisie had adopted mannerisms that differentiated them from the black poor. In his words, the black bourgeoisie had been "uproot[ed] . . . from its 'racial' traditions or, more specifically, from its folk background." While "uprooted" is a bit too strong, it would be impossible to ignore the behavioral distance between the black bourgeoisie and the "folk" in North Kenwood–Oakland, and elsewhere. Lifestyle differences in the neighborhood are at the core of many conflicts, and newcomers are adamant about the need to alter the behaviors of their poor and working-class neighbors.

The other two traits Frazier highlights are interrelated and concern the political positioning of the black bourgeoisie. Frazier argues that in the world of politics middle-class blacks "serve two masters" and have a rigid "middle-class outlook." The two masters are the black constituency they must lead and the "propertied classes in the white community" they must serve. "In his role as leader," Frazier writes, "the Negro politician attempts to accommodate the demands of the Negro masses to his personal interests which are tied up with the [white] political machines." In the end, he concludes, the black bourgeoisie frequently takes on the anti-egalitarian interests of the white elites with whom it is allied. Furthermore, even when black middle-class leaders are not playing the middleman (my term) between their two masters, they promote their own class-inflected agenda, sometimes disregarding the negative impact it may have on another group of African Americans. Frazier labels this phenomenon—when "middle-class Negroes oppose the economic and social welfare of Negroes because of their own interests"—black middle-class "aggression." Frazier's themes of lifestyle distinctions, middleman politics, and particularistic middle-class interests deeply infuse the empirical material in *Black on the Block*, but I also offer strong *critiques* of Frazier's most hypercritical diatribes, especially his assertions that the black bourgeoisie "is without cultural roots" and has "rejected identification" with other blacks.[2]

To return to the opening vignette: Ruby Harris was working part-time as a salesperson when she first moved to North Kenwood–Oakland, hardly the banner black middle-class occupation. But she was moving up from pink- to white-collar employment to join her siblings who were all professionals. As Frazier illustrated (albeit with certain derision), being a member of the black bourgeoisie is almost as much a state of mind and comportment of body as it is an actual reflection of one's wallet. This recognition suggests an expanded definition of the black bourgeoisie—black professionals and other well-paid workers, plus the people who keep their company. This broad black bourgeoisie is the population that is moving to North Kenwood–Oakland. Or moving *back*, since the first group of African Americans to move into the neighborhood in the 1940s and 1950s were also black people of some means. Unlike the first black middle-class settlers, who were *racial* pioneers in an all-white neighborhood, the current generation of black bourgeoisie newcomers are *class* pioneers in a low-income neighborhood. To use the slogan of one developer, they are "re-neighboring" North Kenwood–Oakland, an ironic marketing ploy given the fact that the place already had neighbors in it. The implicit meaning of this phrase, then, relates to the absence of middle- and upper-income neighbors. While the old neighbors are not a monolith—young families and senior citizens, a majority of renters and a minority of home owners—they are disproportionately poor and working class. "You're gonna have to infiltrate at least a thousand units almost with professionals—people with jobs," remarked Lauren Lowery, a black real estate agent in the neighborhood, on the re-neighboring necessary to get the proportions back in whack. "You infuse those numbers into that community, it's gonna completely overshadow the brothers who already are still there, who are not leaving, and probably shouldn't leave."

"The brothers who already are still there" are "the truly disadvantaged," the underclass, low-income residents, poor people, "people people." Again, there is not a precise fit. When William Julius Wilson published *The Truly Disadvantaged* in 1987, his purpose was not so much to describe the disadvantaged themselves as to explain the causes of their disadvantage with "a comprehensive set of variables—including societal, demographic, and neighborhood variables."[3] Still, the power of the term "the truly disadvantaged," and its even more charged sibling "the underclass," drew attention to a group defined by what are often deemed to be bad behaviors—crime, teenage pregnancy, illegitimacy, welfare dependence, and chronic unemployment. Whereas I use the label "the truly disadvantaged" simply to convey the income poverty that existed in North Kenwood–Oakland prior to its current revitalization, it is clear in the rhetoric of the neighborhood's new residents and in the public discussion of poverty more broadly that the two meanings—one based on economic status, the other on individual behavior—are not so easily separated. Poverty is often attributed to bad behaviors. In this reductionist view, the workings of the labor market and politics are obscured, and thus absolved.

This fact could not have been more evident than in recent statements of Bill Cosby, who chided the "lower economic" class for "women having children by five, six different men," for "people getting shot in the back of the head over a piece of pound cake," for a "50 percent drop out rate," and for "five or six generations sitting in the projects" "with names like Shaniqua, Shaligua, Mohammed and all that crap, and all of them are in jail." These biting criticisms caused quite a stir, but black America did not need Bill Cosby to inflame the debate about the behaviors of low-income African Americans and the propriety of better-off blacks' saying something about those behaviors. That happens every day at grocery stores, in living rooms, at community meetings, in barbershops, and on television shows that black people patronize, inhabit, attend, frequent, and watch. It also happens in North Kenwood–Oakland.[4]

Within this range of meanings and intentions of the term "the truly disadvantaged," some portion of the North Kenwood–Oakland community qualifies, more if the criteria are simply socioeconomic (i.e., income below the poverty line, unemployed, with little education) and fewer if defined by the disparaging list of disruptive behaviors. It is noteworthy that despite her support for creating a better socioeconomic balance, Lauren Lowery, the real estate agent, felt that the people already living in the neighborhood should not have to leave. Her distaste for displacement is shared widely among other newcomers, investors, and activists. On the other side, however, North Kenwood–Oakland's poor and working-class residents do not always perceive the goodwill of the newcomers. Rather, they feel as if their days in the neighborhood are numbered. They observe the new sidewalks and spruced-up homes as pleasing but ominous improvements. Andrea Wilson was born and raised in North Kenwood, but when I interviewed her she lived in a subsidized apartment a few blocks outside of the neighborhood with her mother, brother, and young son. Her previous North Kenwood landlord had raised the rent out of her family's reach, and so they had to move. They were lucky to find a place so close to where her family had lived for generations. She was quite aware of all of the remodeling that an unidentified "they" were doing while people like "us" suffered the consequences. "It's getting more expensive to live around here. So a lot of people tend to move away. Because it's our neighborhood but they're remodeling so much and doing some condos, and our local income can't afford it." In her use of pronouns Wilson highlights the contests over ownership not just of the physical buildings and homes but also of that intangible sense of the word "home" that connotes familiarity and comfort.

The meeting of the black bourgeoisie and the truly disadvantaged is not a rare event that uniquely distinguishes North Kenwood–Oakland. Perhaps the interaction is more charged at the neighborhood level because of the high stakes riding on where we live, encompassing everything from the financial investment in a home to the psychological imperative of feeling safe. And in a neighborhood undergoing the kinds of changes that are occurring in North Kenwood–Oakland, safety is not just about crime but about being protected from the logic of a housing market that would like to turn someone's apartment into a condo, recapture someone's corner for a community garden, or convert someone's school for special-needs children into a park field house. When the black bourgeoisie meets the truly disadvantaged face to face as neighbors, the issues are as crucial as keeping a roof overhead, raising a healthy and productive child, and feeling like you belong.

Gladyse Taylor easily felt that she belonged when she bought her home in Oakland in 1989. She was literally coming back, not to the block on which she grew up, but not too far from it. She was born in the Ida B. Wells projects a stone's throw away from her new home. Her journey from the projects to a five-thousand-square-foot, three-story house was, she believed, what public housing was all about: a stepping-stone—or in her case a launching pad—on the way to success. Bringing her talents and experiences back to the block felt right, and welcomed. "I've not had any problems with people in the community. Actually, I think for the most part, they were kind of excited. Even though they realized that the gentrification was taking place, they were happy and pleased that it was someone black." Taylor has a hypothesis that when the black bourgeoisie meets the truly disadvantaged it is more amicable than an encounter between the white gentry and the black poor. An assumption underlies her statement that black gentrification is distinctive, maybe even strange, and is smoothed by the common skin color of old-timers and newcomers.

Ms. Taylor's comment suggests a set of research questions: Is "pleased" how old-timers feel about the blackness of the gentrifiers? Or is it contempt? ambivalence? appreciation? a sense of betrayal? Or does it provoke different sentiments in different contexts? When in the late 1990s Paul Knight and his family sold the home that his grandparents bought in 1949 they were worried about severing the generational legacy that the house represented. "The neighborhood is alive in some kind of way. Like this house. This house is what we wanted, and it didn't want us to leave. But now it's okay. It likes Tracey and it likes her husband." Something about the buyers calmed Mr. Knight (or the house). Maybe it was that the buyers were married, or that Tracey had helped Knight with his résumé a few years before. Or maybe it was that Tracey and her husband were black. Mr. Knight did not say specifically, but other cues—like the pride he expressed about his uncle, who was the first black graphic artist for the Chicago Police Department, or his outfit by Sean John, a popular black clothing company—made it plausible that he was more "pleased" to sell his house to a black couple than he would have been had they been white.

In a different context, Rosie Foster was bothered by a community meeting in which residents maligned public housing, of which she herself was a resident. Having heard enough in the meeting, she rose from her chair and interjected, "[It's] like you don't want the projects in this community. I thought this was a community thing? Maybe I'm getting the wrong vibe here. Some of the questions just seemed like people have a problem with things. Always acting like you don't want to live next to people in CHA." Whereas Paul Knight's soul was soothed by the blackness of the couple that bought his house, Rosie Foster got the *wrong* vibe from African American newcomers who seemed allergic to public housing and its residents. The reality is that a range of emotions and sentiments characterize the interaction in North Kenwood–Oakland as the settings change and communication styles are practiced and perfected. Exploring and analyzing the variable tenor of these exchanges provides a rich depiction of the forging of a black community, and an empirically informed theory of the intersections of race, class, and place.

The Encounter

Emmett Coleman moved to North Kenwood with his wife and daughters in 1983. He was a bit ahead of the real rush, but his boss, who was well connected with higher-ups in city planning, advised him that the move would pay off financially. "Everyone else was saying don't do it, you know. Hoodlums and thugs, you know. And dope. And it's slum and blighted." Twenty years later he concluded that his decision to buy the house was a good one. He also recognized how common it was to be torn by contradictory advice from the optimists and the naysayers. "Each buppie family that I talked with tells the same story. Their friends were apprehensive at first and then in recent years, you know, recent months [their friends ask], 'Are there any more properties around?'" Coleman also got confirmation of what he expected: all the supposed hoodlums and thugs weren't as bad as they were rumored to be. His early "encounters," like the one narrated below, went off without a hitch.

> Like I said, I was working in a corporate setting, so I had to wear a suit. So the first day I moved over here, my wife was out of town with the kids and I got off the bus at 43rd and Berkeley and all the brothers were out there. You know what I mean. There was a tavern up there, so you know. I

looked kind of conspicuous because in those days people would dress, you know, rebelliously and what not. . . . [So] I'm in a business suit and I get off the bus. And this wasn't pretended, it was just instinctive. When I got off the bus, I said, "Hey fellas! I got some time on the transfer. Anybody need a transfer?" [And they responded,] "Yeah, mellow. Thanks, man." And [I] went on down the street. And I thought about that afterwards. I said, "Hey, you fell right in.". . . And my point is, it wasn't pretended. It was just automatic. It was just, you know, it was just there.

The lilt of Coleman's voice is not perceptible on the written page, and it's hard to re-create how the word "fellas" fit into the black slang of the 1980s. When read, the exchange makes Coleman sound kind of square. But this is misleading. Coleman told this story to make a point about how he "knew something about urban problems and urban living," having grown up in Chicago's Black Belt in the 1940s. As an adult moving up the corporate ladder he lived in integrated Hyde Park, but he had not forgotten how to maneuver the social worlds of working-class and poor black neighborhoods. It was in his body. It was in his voice. "It was just there." In the conceptual framework of anthropologist John L. Jackson, it was "sincere." His performance required "trust over proof"—the trust of the "fellas" who accepted the transfer, and the trust of me and my readers (you) that it was as heartfelt and comfortable as he claimed and experienced it to be.[5]

Coleman might have exaggerated, but only a bit, in saying that his suited presence was a conspicuous anomaly in North Kenwood in the 1980s. The unemployment rate in 1980 was over 20 percent, but nearly 40 percent of those who did work worked in white-collar occupations, a broad category for sure, but one that could include workers who wear suits. He did likely catch the eye of the young men on the corner when he got home from work, but as much for his newcomer status as for his suit. And just as he naturally pulled out the appropriate words and delivery to make the interaction work, so too did the young men he greeted.

George Wade wasn't, but could have been, one of those men standing in front of the tavern as Coleman came home from work. He lived only a few blocks away from Coleman's house when he was a young teenager in the 1970s. He was not in a gang, but his older brother was and Wade remembers sneaking to watch the older guys fight, sometimes using homemade zip guns. When I met George Wade, he was unemployed and having difficulty finding work due to chronic health problems. He had moved from apartment to apartment in the neighborhood, once because the house he was living in was sold to someone who planned to convert it back into a single-family home. That experience made him acutely aware of the changes going on around him. The plan, as he saw it, was to "balance the budget. We tryin' to make the poor live with the rich. . . . The whole idea is to make the neighborhood comfortable. That's what all this is about. To make the whole neighborhood comfortable." Wade liked the idea of mixing rich and poor, and even mixing black and white. And when new people like Emmett Coleman moved in, he knew how to act. He told me, "Like me, I don't think of myself as poor, poor, poor. I see myself as a little bit above poor. And I can hang in with them and get along with them 'cause I know how to talk to people. And then I can get a good response and they get a good response. But [with] some of us, it's not that way, you know. It's just, we wanna do it the hard way." Wade welcomed the changes in the neighborhood and committed himself to holding up his part of the bargain to make the mixed-income community experiment work. But he also recognized that other longtime residents might not be so inclined and might take a different route, "the hard way." "If we live in this neighborhood together, everybody help one another, [then] I'm sayin' it's no need of me to *take* from you when I can *ask* from you." As the neighborhood changes and the new groups come in contact with one another, Wade sees the options as aggression or accommodation, crime or solicitousness, and both are possibilities.

Envision Emmett Coleman alighting from the bus, an exemplar of the black bourgeoisie with his suit and his briefcase. He meets George Wade with his truly disadvantaged friends, drinking and having a good time right where they've been drinking and having a good time since well before Coleman moved in. Coleman offers his bus transfer. Wade accepts it and adds a cordial greeting and maybe a handshake to show his appreciation. They go their separate ways with a subtle sense of accomplishment. The encounter took work on both sides. If it had not, neither man would be so cognizant of and pleased with his ability to make such interactions go smoothly. As North Kenwood–Oakland experiences the transition from being a predominantly poor neighborhood to one where rich, middle class, and poor live side by side, most (but not all) meetings fall within this type. In the public sphere tolerance is the norm.[6]

For newcomers who sociologist Japonica Brown-Saracino would call "social preservationists," socioeconomic diversity is also part of the allure of the neighborhood.[7] Reflecting on what she enjoys about North Kenwood–Oakland, resident Soeurette Hector commented:

> I like it in the sense where I'm able to touch the poor right on 43rd Street, and the store that was there, [and] the alcoholics. I like that in a sense. In a sense that as long as they don't dirty it, they don't throw their bottles and everything, it doesn't bother me. It doesn't bother me to see older fellows sitting at the corner of 43rd Street talking about old times and listening to the blues. It made me feel good. Or the older guy that sits over here and he blasts his music, his blues, and he sits there with his cane just contemplating nature, whatever, the sun. It doesn't bother me. I think it's a beautiful thing. That's me. He's not dirtying anything. He's cleaning his flowers by himself. He's sitting in his chair, nobody bothers him, he's not bugging anybody, he's not screaming, he's not yelling. He's just outside.

"The poor" that Hector likes to "touch" are a reality in the neighborhood, and both Mr. Coleman and Ms. Hector congratulate themselves on their ability to get along in such a diverse context. The brothers and alcoholics display the same ability. Both sides draw on their repertoire of experiences to communicate respectfully with one another. If this were not the case, the neighborhood would be nothing more than a boxing ring of scorn and suspicion. It is not that at all, even if such feelings and perspectives do lurk beneath the agreeable surface. The facility with which the haves and have-nots negotiate each other is based partially on having been trained in all-black settings that were also mixed-income, not necessarily by design but because of the circumstances of racial discrimination and disproportionate poverty that impact black residential America.[8]

This easygoing public face notwithstanding, the subterranean mutual critiques that stem partially from class differences are equally important for understanding the interactional milieu and the political battles in North Kenwood–Oakland. At the most basic level, the two groups just do things differently. John Mason, a bank supervisor, did not have to think long to answer my question: "Any stories to share about your neighbors?" "I guess in my upbringing we didn't have a lot of traffic through the house," he began. "They're the exact opposite. I mean it's like they have relatives, daughters and cousins, who come over every day, seven days a week. To me it'd be nauseating because there's no privacy. I mean, when do you kind of regroup to do what you need to do?" Mason's discomfort with the comings and goings of extended family next door is an example of Frazier's characterization of the black bourgeoisie as removed from the traditions of the "folk." But it's more complicated than that. The evidence shows that middle-class blacks still engage with their extended families and tend to have more contact with their mothers and siblings than middle-class whites have.[9] I doubt that the practice of visiting relatives is so foreign to Mr. Mason. Instead, Mason was commenting as much on the *performance* of the family gathering as the contact itself. It was the congestion that he would have found nerve-wracking, especially given the fact that all of his siblings were financially stable enough to own separate homes, which were scattered across the Chicago metropolitan area.

Randall Van Dyke, a lawyer, was also occasionally bewildered by the things his neighbors did:

> We didn't always see eye to eye with what our block club wanted to do. A lot of the members of the block club were the—I shouldn't say the older residents 'cause some of 'em are probably no older than I am—it's probably 50-50, new residents versus residents who have been here prior to the "gentrification."... One of the residents wanted to get the block club behind him to allow him to run his own car wash down the street here. He lost my interest right away because, you know, I'm like, I would have moved next to a car wash if that's what I was wanting to do. You know, we have zoning laws for a reason. And all the older residents were on his bandwagon. And when I would sit there silent in the meetings they just couldn't understand. [They would think] what is wrong with him? I just had no interest in it whatsoever, or things like that.

The block club is supposed to be a mechanism for bridging differences, but in this instance, and many others like it, it only made more glaring the lifestyle clashes that occur in a changing neighborhood.

Of course, the puzzlement goes both ways. Just as Van Dyke could not relate to his neighbor's plan to run a car wash on the street, some poor and working-class residents find the ideas of their middle-class neighbors curious. At a community meeting, the owners of a local gas station presented remodeling plans that called for the removal of the pay phones. This decision was based on more than aesthetic considerations; the owners had been advised by community leaders (most of whom are middle-class home owners) that pay phones create a security problem. Basically, drug dealers use pay phones. One resident protested, "So everybody has a cell phone now? What's up with the people? So say you're just lost and you just need directions. For people people!" This resident argued that all pay phone users are not up to no good. There are *people* people—as opposed to *cell phone* people or *drug dealing* people—who still need the convenience of public phones. She was astonished at how the people making the decisions—who were apparently all cell phone people—were oblivious to this fact.

Anne Boger is a bit less critical of the actions of the more affluent newcomers. This is perhaps because she is not a member of the truly disadvantaged, even though she grew up in the neighborhood and lived through its hard times. Because of this experience, she sees herself as apart from the middle-class blacks now moving in. But she appreciates their sense of style, the fact that "people [are] renovating, remodeling inside, a kitchen or a bath or something. You know, I think bit by bit people are trying to put, you know, wrought iron fences on the front. The windows, there were people doing things like leaving the curtains open more now. I would just love to just have mine open because I like that look." If there ever was doubt that people are acute readers of social class, Anne Boger's attention to the positioning of curtains should erase it. It only makes sense to keep the curtains open if you have something worth showing off, especially given the oversize picture windows that adorn many of the houses in North Kenwood–Oakland. In homes where the drapes are elegantly pulled back, they often frame things like a piano, an ornate flower arrangement, a piece of stained glass, or a decorative vase. Pulling the curtains back is a way to display and convey material wealth. Boger did not have any of these showpieces and thus viewed the practice with a mix of envy and admiration, imbuing it with a bit of mystique.

A most straightforward display of difference exists in the juxtaposition of the neighborhood's two grocery stores (see fig. 17). One Stop Foods has been in operation since 1928, and at its current location at 43rd and Lake Park Avenue, on the border between North Kenwood and Oakland, since 1978. It was just a few blocks west before that. On its facade are the mottos "Buy the Can, Buy the Case" and "From Our Trucks to Your Shopping Carts." The messages: bulk buying is more economical, and there's no point in paying for frills. One Stop's market

Figure 17. Co-op Markets and One Stop Foods, two grocery stores in North Kenwood–Oakland that cater to distinct clienteles, 2005. Photos by author.

is the shopper with a larger family and a tight budget, and the store passes on to its customers the money it saves by keeping things simple. Four blocks south is the Co-op Market, which opened in 1999 in a new mini-mall at 47th and Lake Park, at the southeastern corner of North Kenwood and closer to racially integrated Hyde Park. It was the third store location of the Hyde Park Co-op, a cooperative grocery store that opened in 1933 and has served Hyde Park ever since. This store displays the motto "A Love Affair with Wonderful Foods" and offers such items as exotic fruits and vegetables, a fresh salad bar, and live lobster. The two places are like night and day. "The Co-op is for people that have money," felt Emma McDaniel whose part-time salary did not land her in that category. "If you go down there and catch their sales, you got something. But other than that, honey, that's not the place for me." Mc-Daniel's MBA neighbor had exactly the opposite orientation. "Every now and then I'd go to One Stop, like if I needed, whatever, some collard greens or something. Not very often, because the brands that they have there aren't ones that I necessarily like. But there's some stuff that I would go and get there. Like if I need to get some, whatever, neck bones, stuff like that. But I would not do general shopping at One Stop." Each store had its niche and exploited it. The Co-op carried high-end brands and a wide selection of fresh foods, and One Stop stocked basic canned and boxed goods along with black ethnic food staples. As a resident my-self, and a black bourgeoisie newcomer, I've been in One Stop no more than three times and then mostly for research purposes.[10]

This all seems harmless enough. The market efficiently allows for two grocery stores to serve distinct market segments, and residents look across the class divide with a bit of wonderment or confusion. But such observations of difference often morph into a rhetoric of condescension, which when empowered can turn into exclusion. "The biggest problem in the Co-op was the people working and the people shopping," explained Kirk Clemons, who should know a little something about groceries since he has worked as a brand manager for a major food manufacturer. "They wanted community hiring, but these folks wasn't ready to be the may-I-help-you type of people. . . . Oftentimes they'd engage a conversation within themselves. Some of the language wasn't becoming of a professional environment. I'm a customer—if I want to cuss, I can cuss. You're getting paid—you have to say, 'Yes, sir. No, sir.' " Clemons grew even more agitated when talking later about various social programs, like the ones that placed these purportedly unpolished workers in their jobs in the first place. His next target: indigent sick people who use free health clinics. "If you're going to go to the doctor, you go to the doctor. Why do they have to put a clinic there for you?" he asked, referring specifically to a new health clinic in the neighborhood that took clients of all economic means. I answered, "Because you don't have health insurance." Not a good enough answer for Clemons, who had a logical free-market solution to everything: "[Then] why are you living over here? You need to downgrade the living, take the profits, and buy you some health insurance. If you're sitting on a property and let's say you're an indigenous resident—and this may be a totally vain thing— you got your house paid for. You might have bought it for $10,000 or $20,000. You got an opportunity to turn around and sell this house for $180,000. I'm sorry—it's not for me to put a social net for you. You sell your home, you downgrade." Ironically, when I interviewed Clemons, he no longer lived in the neighborhood, having cashed out for a cheaper house in the suburbs when it made financial sense for him. He was not being callous, but rather articulating principles that he too lived by.

The issue of the safety net is at the center of many of the more consequential debates in the neighborhood. While there are occasional references to racism, an inhospitable labor market, or a crumbling educational system as the causes behind an array of behaviors that the middle class finds objectionable, most explanations instead focus on the deficient internal states of the families that haven't been able to make it out of public housing, into steady full-time work, or on to college. The culprits are "questionable values," "not being responsible," an insufficient "work ethic," "welfare recipients and other kinds of recipients that couldn't really do without someone assisting them," as one resident put it, echoing Kirk Clemons's reluctance to assist those who cannot solve their problems through personal initiative. But while I found few hard-line structuralists among North Kenwood–Oakland's middle class, there were many environmentalists. Individuals are products of their environments, this perspective holds. People's immediate surroundings have a greater impact on their lives than the more distant notions of a capitalist economy that feeds on inequality, or of racist whites with their foot on the necks of black folks.[11]

Given the primacy that residents attribute to the environment, of which the neighborhood is a key part, the task of the black bourgeoisie has always been to model a different set of behaviors and provide a new spate of resources to create a different environment. The return to North Kenwood–Oakland is as much about reclaiming a poor black neighborhood with the flag of middle-class behaviors as it is about striking it rich with a smart financial investment. In this regard, the arguments in *The Truly Disadvantaged* resonate with the beliefs of North Kenwood–Oakland's newcomers. As if using Wilson's book as his text,

Robert Blackwell lectured, "If you look at the '70s, I'd say in the '70s and '80s, blacks wanted to be out of black neighborhoods. I mean, so there's a flight from black neighborhoods. There has not been a major flight into [black neighborhoods]. I don't think blacks who I have seen anyway would look at somebody poor, a poor black person, and say, I am somehow very connected to that person. I need to make sure that this group is protected." In *The Truly Disadvantaged*, William Julius Wilson emphasizes the spatial and thus social out-migration of the black middle class. Other public intellectuals like Henry Louis Gates also promulgate this notion of racial detachment, going so far as to say that black America is divided into "two nations"—what author Michael Eric Dyson has critiqued as gross divisions into an Afristocracy and Ghettocracy. From Gates's position as a Harvard professor, one black man he encountered on the other side of the class divide "seemed like a Martian."[12] Is the gulf that wide?

Mr. Blackwell makes a point that sounds something like Gates's—"I don't think blacks who I have seen anyway would look at . . . a poor black person, and say, I am somehow very connected to that person"—but his behavior charts a different direction, and thus critiques the position staked out by Gates, and by Frazier before him. The black middle class is *not* without cultural roots, is *not* mired in racial self-hatred, and (despite the drama of this chapter's title) is *not* so detached from the black poor that the latter seems to be from an alien world. Blackwell's move to North Kenwood–Oakland *contradicts* contemporary arguments that there are two nations within black America by refusing to allow such a development. And Robert Blackwell is not alone. His emphasis on the individual ("*I* need to make sure that this group is protected") is contradicted both by the swell of returners like himself and by the social science research.

William Julius Wilson's theories about out-migration seem to have made a greater mark on everyday rhetoric in the black community than those of other researchers who find actual connections between poor and nonpoor black folks, and a widespread sense of group identification and responsibility among blacks. My own research with colleague Colleen Heflin shows that just over 40 percent of middle-class blacks have a poor sibling (compared to 16 percent of similar whites), and a third of middle-class blacks grew up poor themselves. As John L. Jackson writes in his ethnography of Harlem, "The black people I met in Harlem have lives that shoot through overly rigid, static, either-or designations of class." This familiarity with poverty is unlikely to support the contention that there are "two nations." It might also explain why, as political scientist Michael Dawson shows, two-thirds of blacks believe that their fate is linked to that of other black people. And Dawson finds that this is even *more* true among better educated African Americans.

Measuring the propensity of middle-class blacks to, as Blackwell put it, "protect" poor blacks is trickier. On the one hand, blacks with higher incomes (but not those with more education) are more likely to *oppose* policies aimed at economic redistribution, the safety net of which Kirk Clemons was so critical. On the other hand, more middle-class blacks than poor blacks think that the black middle class has an *obligation* to help the black poor. That is, middle-class blacks feel even *more* responsible than poor blacks think they should feel. Hence, if protection means calling for government funds to help black families in need, then Blackwell is right that black professionals are more likely to shun such advocacy. But if protection is more straightforwardly measured as personal obligation, then he is readily joined by other professional African Americans like himself. [13]

Given the prevalence of belief in the "linked fate" of African Americans across the class spectrum, the emphasis that middle-class African Americans put on the "environment" makes sense. The neighborhood, the schools, and the symbolic "black community" are all parts of the environment and are places in which individual middle-class blacks can actually make a difference. It takes concerted and collective action to redirect the economy or politics at the local or national level, whereas it only takes parking your BMW in front of your house to be an example of financial success for your less well-off neighbors. When Oakland resident Sharon Liberty's neighbors played their music too loudly or trampled her lawn or double-parked too many cars, she would politely go outside and say something. After a while, her concern for neighborhood decorum was taken up by the same people who used to violate it.

For some of the neighbors that have been here for years, it's just that they haven't had the same exposure. They're still people. If they had the same exposure they would do the same. And to show the value [of exposure]: these neighbors that live on our street, all of their friends would come over and they visited in the street. It's the craziest thing. People don't come in their house. They have cars around and all that kind of stuff. But now you don't hear them out in the street any more. The street is quiet. Because there was a time when I'd get up in the morning and the street was like a graveyard. When I come home at night they'd get it perked up. And when it was time for me to go to sleep they were full scale. But now you don't hear that. And what was so amazing, one night I was just sitting here getting in bed 'cause I sleep in this front bedroom. And I won't use her vernacular, but one of the persons that you always knew [was] out there, [whose] voice was very prominent, I heard her tell 'em, "Don't bring that stuff over on Ellis, now take that stuff over where you live. Don't come over here with that."

When her neighbors took responsibility for policing themselves and each other, Ms. Liberty felt that her work was done, that she had successfully exposed them to what a block *should* look and sound like.

There is also a notion among newcomers about what the vanguard of neighborhood activism should look and sound like. It is commonly assumed that because poor residents, and public housing tenants in particular, have lacked exposure to good schools and orderly civic engagement, they are often not the best representatives of neighborhood demands. "We were at the Chicago Planning Commission discussing why these projects are a problem and why, you know, [residents] have this type of mentality," said Ruby Harris, explaining the fight she and many others waged to lessen the concentration of public housing in North Kenwood–Oakland. Zeroing in on the importance of environment, she continued, "We're not fighting the fact that the people have this mentality. The fact is that a lot of times it has been because of their surroundings. We understand what environment is, you know. It's 50 percent of who you are." In other conversations, Harris made it clear that many public housing residents go on to be highly successful, but here she emphasized that too many are left behind. The latter category was a sobering reminder of the incomplete project of black advancement. When public housing residents spoke up in meetings, she wanted to "get up under a chair somewhere, you know, the lowest point that I could, and just try and hide, you know." Long-term residents of the projects, who had proven unable to use public housing as the temporary support it was meant to be, were for that reason neither suitable nor effective representatives of this changing black neighborhood. I pushed Harris on her desire to have her poor neighbors take a backseat in community leadership, to disappear to ease her discomfort.

"But she represents a real population," I interjected about one woman who Harris thought was particularly outspoken but not well spoken.

"Yes, she does," Harris agreed.

"And she should have a voice," I added, making my ideological position clear.

"They have had too much voice" was her even clearer response.

When the black bourgeoisie moves back on the block, they mean business.

It must be emphasized that Ruby Harris's comments addressed the *voice* of public housing residents, not necessarily their presence. With a few exceptions (as in Kirk Clemons's advice that poor home owners should cash out of the neighborhood to be able to afford health care), new residents to North Kenwood–Oakland do not *want* to displace anybody. If all the poor people moved out, there would be no one who needed role modeling, no destitute neighborhood to reclaim, nobody to "protect." Julius Rhodes, for example, worried that school improvements would come only after existing residents had been moved out. "I would hate to think that the reason that they became successful schools is because the neighborhood changed and, as a result, there was a recognition that those schools needed to be able to do more. They need to be able to do more now." Norman Bolden had the same critique of the multimillion-dollar renovation of the local high school. "King High School should have been revamped fifteen years ago," he said, implying that the poor children who attended the school in the past had been ignored by the Chicago Public Schools. He used the high school example to express an even larger point: "Let me be real clear about my perception of success. Who were they developing King for? When four years ago you stopped accepting students and flushed them out, that's no success. I can't think of the words but I can clearly tell you that that was not a success. All that's being done is not being done with the intent to serve the existing community. That's urban planning." As discussed further in the next chapter, the newcomers want the old-timers to benefit from the investments in the neighborhood stimulated by their presence. Yet for all their good intentions, some of the strategies used to improve the neighborhood have exclusionary results. As Carolyn Hobbs commented with sadness about the prospects for young people who could not qualify for the new high school: "We just gotta kinda deal with some of the realities, you know, that this place is changing. And if you can't change with it then they're not looking to accommodate you."

Hence, when members of the black bourgeoisie meet the truly disadvantaged, the former hold two simultaneous convictions about their roles in the neighborhood: First, they intend to serve as both behavioral models and resource magnets to alter the environment of their less fortunate neighbors. Second, their efforts presume the superiority of their behaviors and resources. The assumption is not wholly unreasonable given the prevalence of hardships among old-timers and poor residents and the elation that many of them express now that things are turning around, but neither is it uncontested.

These debates—over how to be black and what black people need to do to prosper—are what binds the black community into one nation, rather than two.[14] When those debates subside—when Bill Cosby no longer cares about or comments on the family choices of poor blacks, and when the next generation of Robert Blackwells decides not to move into black neighborhoods—then the black community is no more. For despite Ruby Harris's trenchant critique of black public housing residents, the general gist of her argument was strongly problack. The point she wanted to convey to any public official who would listen was that in building and then neglecting public housing, "you're creating an environment that is destroying our people. And we're very serious about that." However obnoxious her words may have sounded, the public housing residents in whom she was so disappointed were but flesh and blood examples of such racist destruction. Harris's approach required the concerned participation of middle-class blacks who would stop city bureaucrats from foisting bad policies on the black community, and who would then become leaders in the quest for community control. Control, in this framework, is not a possession that can be evenly divided among the residents of North Kenwood–Oakland—or, to broaden the analogy, among the national black community. Instead, it should be wielded by those best equipped, most qualified, most able to wield it: the black middle class.

This is not, of course, a new insight. It summons DuBois's "talented tenth," Frazier's black politicians with a "middle-class outlook," and the racial uplift ideologues who believed strongly that overshadowing what was seen as a more embarrassing contingent of black folks would prove to whites the fitness of all blacks for full citizenship. This historical backdrop helps to frame the cross-class encounter in North Kenwood–Oakland.

Responsibility and Respectability

The black middle class is frequently chided for forsaking the black poor, but as previewed above, there is little empirical evidence that such abandonment has actually taken place in terms of identity, ideology, politics, or residence. On identity, David Demo and Michael Hughes find that blacks with more education and more prestigious jobs feel less close to but more positive about African Americans as a group. These plus and minus feelings toward the race no more support the notion that the black middle class lacks a black identity than they suggest that poor blacks do. Michael Dawson finds that middle-class blacks (usually defined by education, not income or occupation) are more likely to believe that their fate is linked with that of other African Americans. Dawson finds further that blacks with more income and education are no less likely than poor blacks to support black autonomy, through, for example, the establishment of all-black male academies. Blacks with higher incomes are more likely to think it is important to shop in black-owned stores and to have control over economic institutions in the black community.[15]

Middle-class blacks also perceive racial discrimination more acutely than do poor blacks. Jennifer Hochschild finds that, compared to poor blacks, middle-class blacks are less likely to think that blacks have the same chance of getting ahead as whites, are less likely to think that opportunities to get ahead will improve in the future, are less likely to think that the public education system is adequately serving poor and minority children, and are less likely than poor blacks to blame blacks themselves for the problems plaguing black America. These strong perceptions of racial bias frustrate members of the black middle class— Hochschild characterizes them as "succeeding more and enjoying it less." Middle-class blacks have not left poor blacks for a land of color blindness and other rosy ideals. Rather, they are even more convinced of the disadvantages of being black and even more fed up with the slow pace of racial progress. And when middle-class blacks get together, they spread the bad news. Claudine Gay finds that African Americans who live and engage in neighborhoods with more well-educated blacks are more likely to perceive racial discrimination to be a problem. This means that more than just an individual's own education is involved. Being around other well-educated blacks heightens one's perception of the effects of being black on important arenas of life. While there are areas in which middle-class blacks pull away from poor blacks—expressing less support for redistributive policies, less support for racial preferences in hiring, more support for interracial marriages—the preponderance of evidence shows that in their ideological and political beliefs middle-class blacks still see themselves as connected to their poor race-mates and see both of their fates as being negatively affected by being black.[16]

Middle-class blacks' sense of collective fate translates into action.

This was the hope of W. E. B. DuBois, who saw racial uplift as the duty of the "talented tenth." Juan Battle and Earl Wright II use national data to ask the question: Has the talented tenth heeded DuBois's call to "sacrifice their personal interests and endeavors in favor of community leadership activities designed to improve the social, economic and political condition of the race"? The answer, they find, is yes. Battle and Wright find that college-educated blacks are more likely to participate in politics and local community activism than blacks without a college degree. Cathy Cohen and Michael Dawson produce similar results for the city of Detroit, where more educated African Americans are more likely to be church members, belong to a group (not necessarily a black group), and to attend a meeting about community issues. Dawson also finds that blacks with higher incomes are more likely to be linked to black information sources, reading books by black authors, for instance, or listening to black radio. Ironically, however, despite their greater level of participation, well-educated blacks still think that the black middle class is shirking on its responsibilities. Battle and Wright find that members of the talented tenth are significantly less likely than nonmembers to agree with the statement "Black people who have made it are doing a lot to improve the social and economic position of poor blacks."[17]

I offer two interpretations of these findings that differ from the authors' conclusions. One possibility is that the discrepancy noted by Battle and Wright between the objective measures of college-educated blacks' activism and their subjective evaluation of the adequacy of black middle-class helping behaviors is a reflection of the *intensity* of their sense of responsibility. A powerful sense of responsibility makes them feel like they could and should be doing more. Middle-class blacks strongly believe that whites don't care about blacks, and hence they must abide by the aphorism "I am my brother's keeper." In similar research Jennifer Hochschild finds that 79 percent of middle-class blacks think that the black middle class has an obligation to help poorer blacks, yet only 17 percent of them think that middle-class blacks "do as much as they should to help improve the condition of poorer blacks." This is a trenchant self-critique, and an indication that, while middle-class blacks have taken on the burden of improving the condition of poor blacks, they perceive that their efforts are never enough to make much of a difference. The persistence of black poverty and suffering is their proof. I see these findings as suggestive that college-educated blacks feel *guilt* about the apparent ineffectiveness of their own hard work.

Indeed, Hochschild finds that middle-class blacks are more critical of themselves than poor blacks are of them.[18]

Another possible interpretation lies in the distinction between individual middle-class blacks and "the black middle class" as a category. Each middle-class black person is aware of his or her own commitment to and actions on behalf of the larger black community, which includes poor blacks. He knows that he gives money to the United Negro College Fund, she tutors a student failing in school, and he serves on the board of a program for ex-offenders. While he could be doing more, he is satisfied that he's doing something. But because there is still so much more to be done, it must be those *other* middle-class blacks—"the black middle class" as a disembodied construct—who are shirking. The blame is displaced onto a label that has no actual people in it, since many individual members of the black middle class seem to be quite actively engaged. This second possible interpretation, like the first, rests on a sense of collective responsibility that is overwhelmed by the enormity of the problem. Middle-class blacks *cannot* on their own ameliorate the woes of unemployment, overaggressive policing, underfunded schools, disparities in access to health care and in health outcomes, or inadequate housing. Their inevitable failure leads to guilt both internalized and projected onto the category of middle-class blacks. No doubt, some choose withdrawal as a palliative for that guilt, but the research suggests that such desertion is not widespread.

If abandonment of the symbolic or political black community by middle-class blacks is rare, escape from the physical black community, or the black neighborhood, is only slightly more common. William Julius Wilson's proposition that "today's black middle-class professionals no longer tend to live in ghetto neighborhoods and have increasingly moved into mainstream occupations outside the black community" raised the possibility that middle-class blacks were leaving black neighborhoods and becoming more integrated with whites. While it is true across the country that middle-class blacks (variously defined) are slightly less segregated from whites than are poor blacks, segregation of middle-class blacks from whites remains high. As I have argued elsewhere, the black middle class did leave the segregated black neighborhoods where they lived in the 1940s and 1950s, but they didn't get very far, moving into areas on the periphery of these initial settlements both within and outside of the city. Those peripheral areas were quickly reabsorbed into the black ghetto.[19]

Based on their experiences in neighborhoods, at workplaces, and in public settings, middle-class blacks continue to see themselves as fellow travelers with poor blacks in a racialized world. Both the feelings and realities of connectedness translate into a sense of responsibility on the part of middle-class blacks not only to share their success with the less fortunate of the race, but, as DuBois admonished them, to "become leaders in order to guide and conduct them out of their condition of semi-slavery."[20]

But how to lead? Where to lead? And with what particular tools? While the middle class cleaves to the black poor in the broad realm of politics and ideology, it is in the process of leading—and indeed in the assumption that poor blacks *need* leading—that cleavages hewn by class identity become apparent. Recall, for example, the survey discussed above that found that poor blacks are *less* critical of the amount of help middle-class blacks give than are middle-class blacks themselves. Another survey posed the issue differently. It asked respondents to rate their agreement with the following statement: "Blacks who have achieved middle-class status [tend] to be less understanding about the lot of less privileged blacks." On this question middle-class blacks were more confident of their empathic sensibilities, whereas poor blacks were more skeptical. On the issue of *understanding* the situation of the less privileged, poor blacks gave the black middle class relatively low marks. It is difficult to lead without understanding. And those designated as followers are unlikely, if misunderstood, to follow.[21]

Despite the ongoing resistance by less-advantaged blacks to having their agendas defined for them—as elaborated, for example, in the work of historian Robin Kelley on black working-class politics—the black middle class defends its claim on leadership through an emphasis on "respectability."[22] Kevin Gaines's thorough history of early-twentieth-century racial uplift ideology captures the complex interactions between race and class in shaping the content of black middle-class activism. "Believing that the improvement of African Americans' material and moral condition through self-help would diminish white racism," writes Gaines, "[black elites] sought to rehabilitate the race's image by embodying respectability, enacted through an ethos of service to the masses." The black middle class was the race's best foot forward, and could serve as a positive image of blacks who were not far removed from the ugliness of slavery. Embodying respectability meant modeling sexual conservatism, patriarchal family relations, financial sobriety, reserved comportment, and intellectual achievement. Not only did the poor fall outside the bounds of righteousness, but so too did loose women, practitioners of ecstatic religions, gays and lesbians, figures from the criminal underworld, and any manner of blacks who did not adhere to the most puritanical of strictures. The upright character of some middle-class blacks was a sign to whites of blacks' readiness for full citizenship and all of the benefits that entailed. Respectability proved that racism and racial discrimination were unfounded. Therefore, the best of the race, the talented tenth, the black middle class, the black elite, the black bourgeoisie must stand in front as the example of and beacon toward racial progress. To echo the language of the realtor in North Kenwood–Oakland, quoted earlier in this chapter, the respectable behaviors of the black elite would hopefully "overshadow" those of the baser elements in the black community, who collectively represented "the Negro problem."

The virtuous behavior of the black middle class required the depravity of the black poor as its counterpoint. In disparaging the speech, family life, and leisure tastes of the black working class and poor, black elites participated in the dissemination and legitimization of "dehumanizing stereotypes" of the black poor. Even more seriously, black uplift ideologues bought into a culturalist logic that laid blame for poverty in the conduct and mores of the poor themselves. Gaines writes, "Accordingly, black ministers, reformers, and educators, increasingly dependent on white philanthropists, generally sided with economic and political elites against organized labor and the unemployed poor."

When Evelyn Brooks Higginbotham introduced the concept of the "politics of respectability" in her study of black women in the Baptist church at the turn of the twentieth century she noted that respectability could take both radical and conservative forms. Her historical subjects "revealed their conservatism when they attributed institutional racism to the 'negative' public behaviors of their people—as if rejection of 'gaudy' colors in dress, snuff dipping, baseball games on Sunday, and other forms of 'improper' decorum could eradicate the pervasive racial barriers that surrounded black Americans." Such a formulation avoids an attack on the root causes in favor of rebuking the victims for their backward ways.

Uncovering the pejorative biases of the politics of respectability raises harsh criticisms of some of black America's most venerated leaders, past and present. Political scientist Cathy Cohen argues that contemporary black political projects are often shaped by heterosexist, male, and middle-class biases. The plight of black drug users and dealers, prostitutes, welfare mothers, and AIDS patients have often been seen as falling outside of the realm of proper battles to fight in the name of the black community. Nonetheless, the commitment and strongly anti-racist *intent* of black leadership, then and now, is not in question. As Gaines argues, "blacks believed they were opposing racism by emphasizing class differences." Thus it is the method and goals of leadership, not its well-meaning commitment, that require analysis and critique.[23] The decisions about who to put forth and in what direction to lead are manifest in North Kenwood–Oakland in rhetoric about the benefits of *mixed-income communities*, which offer the respectable tastes and behaviors of middle-class residents as a counterweight to the so-labeled disreputable carryings-on of the poor.

A Nonstructural Remedy for Urban Poverty

The saving graces of the middle class constitute the link that brings together two otherwise disparate literatures, one on black politics and leadership and the other on the theories behind and practices of addressing urban poverty. In the former, as discussed above, the role of the black middle class has been subjected to considerable scholarly scrutiny, which has focused on its participation, however unwitting, in the marginalization, if not the subjugation, of poor blacks. In the world of urban policy, such a critique is lacking. The middle class continues to be lionized for its generative capacities, not only for the material resources its members bring to struggling cities and neighborhoods, but also for their enactment and modeling of proper ways to live as neighbors, in other words, their respectability. This class bias fuels urban renewal's emphasis on attracting the middle class back to the city.

The importance of the middle class for neighborhoods was emphasized in *The Truly Disadvantaged*. Positing that high levels of neighborhood poverty had negative consequences for residents above and beyond their individual poverty, Wilson and others initiated a research industry to uncover and describe what were called "concentration effects."[24] The truly disadvantaged were *truly* so because concentrated neighborhood poverty compounded the disadvantages they already experienced as poor individuals and families. Part of the reason for the concentration of poverty in black neighborhoods was the flight of nonpoor blacks from previously mixed-income neighborhoods. As a result, Wilson argued, "the declining presence of working- and middle-class blacks also deprives ghetto neighborhoods of key resources, including structural resources (such as residents with income to sustain neighborhood services) and cultural resources (such as conventional role models for neighborhood children)." The "conventions" proffered by the middle class set the normative standard. While Wilson lobbied most forcefully for labor market and safety net reforms, he made brief mention of "the reintegration of the neighborhood with working and middle-class blacks and black professionals" as a possible strategy for strengthening poor neighborhoods. However, Wilson was not at all hopeful about "the so-called self-help programs to revitalize the inner city" and was surprised that they "received so much serious attention from the media and policymakers."[25] Given Wilson's own distancing from such a strategy, it is curious that policy makers have latched on to his research as the scientific basis for policies that emphasize class integration.

On second inspection, however, the embrace of the mixed-income route makes sense because it is consonant with urban elites' interests in recapturing the middle class for the city's tax base, whereas Wilson's other proposals—creating a tight labor market, extensive (and expensive) job training, more generous and universal welfare benefits, and pro-union legislation—are not. Mixed-income communities as cures to urban poverty represent a decidedly nonstructural policy intervention, relying on the prospect of cross-class affiliation to combat the existing forces of systemic stratification. The increased municipal revenue that comes with the influx of middle-class residents could in theory equalize the structural landscape by funding things like high-quality public preschools, wage increases for civil service workers, or investments in public transportation. But in practice such a redistribution of resources often takes a backseat to feeding the demands of the new gentry for more public art, smoother streets, and support for more high-end housing, recreational, and commercial activity.

Because both the public sector and the private market cater to the coveted middle-class citizen-consumer, the underlying structures of inequality are left intact. If gentrification is the point at which mixed-income communities tip upward, then whatever structural reforms had been enacted—better schools, more jobs, cleaner environment—now disproportionately benefit the incoming gentry rather than the outgoing poor residents. "Gentrification," geographer Neil Smith writes, "is a consummate example of neoliberal urbanism. It mobilizes individual property claims via a market lubricated by state donations." In this formulation, gentrification—and the mixed-income communities that precede it—is not simply nonstructural in its ideological foundations, but antistructural, reinforcing and replicating a system of haves and have nots with government support.[26]

The substantial boon that such policies portend for builders, businesses, and bureaucrats, as opposed to poor city dwellers, *has* garnered critical analysis. The sociological literature on "growth machines" offers the critique of elite hegemony that is missing from the policy agenda being enacted across the country. This research emphasizes coalitions of political officials and business, institutional, and philanthropic elites that work toward the goal of maximizing private profits and public revenues, often using rhetoric that emphasizes the supposed returns to residents. Along with attracting private industries/firms and corporate conventions/events, capturing middle-class residents and the commercial ventures that follow them is a central goal of growth machines.

The particular alliance between middle-class *black* elected officials and their private-sector partners is discussed both in the classic regime formulation by Clarence Stone and, with refinements, in Adolph Reed's designation of a "black urban regime." Together, black politicos and white capitalists devise policies and undertake projects that disempower and disadvantage poor and working-class African Americans, despite the fact that it was through their electoral support that these black officials came to political power in the first place. In a torrid critique often reminiscent of E. Franklin Frazier's writing, Reed coins a host of terms— black public officialdom, brokerage style politics, the custodial approach, demobilization—to characterize the co-opting of black middle-class leaders by white business interests and the subsequent *mis-leadership* of their black constituency. Reed writes: "Like Milton's Lucifer, many middle-class blacks are finding it more desirable to reign in the Bantustan than to be dissed outside." In making this pact with the devil, Reed continues, the functional role of the black middle class becomes the "official management and administration of inequality."[27]

My analysis of the open invitation that city officials have sent out to middle-class blacks to move to North Kenwood–Oakland, to be followed by their assumption of leadership roles, both draws on and qualifies this line of urban theorizing on a micro scale. The resources brokered by newcomers are in fact enjoyed by and sometimes purposefully directed toward the neighborhood's poor residents. These are attempts to mitigate inequality, not to administer it. Black professionals' arrival back on the block has good motives and highlights the role of racial identity in unifying this otherwise disjointed neighborhood. This is the basis upon which I build my argument about the racial "we-ness" of North Kenwood–Oakland. It is also a faithful depiction of the empirical reality. On other issues, however, the consonance between the visions of new black residents and private and public capital works *against* poor residents. This is what the urban elite expect will be the case, and this is exactly why mixed-income strategies win out over more ambitious and radical attacks on root causes.[28]

Mark Joseph and his colleagues highlight four mechanisms suggested in the relevant literatures by which mixed-income communities are theorized to combat both urban poverty itself and the associated disadvantages for families: (1) through the establishment of social networks that link poor individuals to middle-class residents who might have information about jobs, schooling, and other important resources; (2) through the improvement of social control, whereby middle-income residents, as home owners and members of organizations, act as purveyors of order and strong management, thereby increasing accountability, conformity, and eventually overall safety and quality of life; (3) through the modeling of upward mobility, which poor residents may then aspire to; and (4) through the increased political and economic attention that middle-class residents command, which benefits their poor neighbors as well. All of these uplift themes are present in the rhetoric of black middle-class newcomers to North Kenwood–Oakland, and all are similarly espoused by policy makers.

Poor residents, on the other hand, both favor income mixing and desire more low-income rental housing; they don't like the vacant lots but worry about getting pushed out once those lots are all filled up, and they have mixed opinions on the question of having neighbors with lifestyles similar to their own.[29] These ambivalent and sometimes conflicting views on mixed-income communities may signal poor residents' realization of the risks that such a strategy poses for them.[30] Moreover, the transformative possibilities that are hypothesized to flow from mixed-income communities are premised on a framing of inequality in which poor people's economic poverty is assumed to reflect or lead to moral, social, political, and cultural poverty as well. Indeed, historical studies by Michael Katz, Herbert Gans, Frances Fox Piven, and Alice O'Connor confirm the devaluation of the poor in the policies that are devised to assist them.[31]

Hence, the most radical critique of these four mechanisms goes as follows: In various ways, they discount poor residents' rich web of social relationships (the best social networks must include middle-class people), denigrate their leisure patterns and use of space (rules are necessary to prescribe public behavior and social interaction), simplify and obfuscate the structural causes of poverty (just following the model of middle-class neighbors will beget middle-class status), and sanction the political and economic disregard that poor communities have suffered (middle-class residents are necessary to draw the investments to which all communities should be entitled).

While fully acknowledging the positive changes that accompany new middle-class residents, this book also presents a counternarrative to the faith placed in them as saviors of poor neighborhoods. It is a rebuttal based first in the conviction that bringing middle-class households to a neighborhood is insufficient to combat the systemic causes of poor health, joblessness, crime, and poverty in general. The structural reforms in the labor market and welfare state that Wilson and so many others propose are still more important than shuffling households in hopes that they will get along and be pulled along. Second, the stories of negotiation, conflict, resistance, and resolution in North Kenwood–Oakland illuminate the middle-class biases inherent in mixed-income policies, which deny the possessions, rights, and humanity of poor residents. This is a common feature of modern "statecraft" more generally. In reviewing an incredible range of interventions by governments into the lives of their citizens, political scientist James C. Scott concludes that in many instances "visionary intellectuals and planners behind them were guilty of hubris, of forgetting that they were mortals and acting as if they were gods." Their "fatal flaw," despite their obviously good intentions, was to dismiss the importance of local know-how and experience, seeing themselves "as far smarter and farseeing than they really were and, at the same tie, regard[ing] their subjects as far more stupid and incompetent than they really were."[32] Even when poor residents of North Kenwood–Oakland are not displaced, and when they are given a new grocery store at which to shop, a new bank in which to begin saving, and a safer street on which to walk, the new community is not always a friendly place to them—a place that values and incorporates their perspectives. It is with good reason that they worry about when their luck in maintaining residence in the neighborhood will run out.

3

In everyday slang, there is the littleman and the middleman, and at the top is just "the man."[1] For African Americans, "the Man" is usually white. "Every city has its police department," wrote Eldridge Cleaver in 1968, when Los Angeles's police department was still overwhelmingly white. "No city would be complete without one. It would be sheer madness to try operating an American city without the heat, the fuzz, *the man*."[2] The littleman, on the other hand, is not always so racialized. He can be the worker in a big firm, the disaffected citizen who doesn't vote because politicians never listen, or the shortest kid in the class. Civil rights lawyer and later Supreme Court justice Thurgood Marshall was known as "the little man's lawyer." The man and the littleman flank the middleman. This chapter is about that man or woman in the middle. The person in the middle, if she's good, speaks at least two languages in order to translate, has two sets of credentials for legitimacy, and juggles a double-booked calendar to keep all the relationships cordial, memberships current, and constituencies appeased.

The classic middleman in today's metropolis is the immigrant store owner in the black community, selling to the littleman goods and services provided and financed by the man. Most of the time this arrangement runs smoothly, but misinterpretations (e.g., over prices or policies) and unmet reciprocal obligations (e.g., hiring local residents, supporting local institutions) can be damaging. The system can be volatile, as evidenced by riots in black communities that target immigrant businesses.[3] The situation in North Kenwood–Oakland is similarly precarious as black middlemen work to combat the racism that has created a neighborhood as poor and neglected as North Kenwood–Oakland, but do so by making alliances with the descendants of the original perpetrators. "The master's tools will never dismantle the master's house," admonished scholar and poet Audre Lorde.[4] This is the frustrating dilemma of the black middleman filled with good racial uplift intentions but bound within a system of strategies that sometimes work in the opposite direction.

There are many similar formulations of this middleman concept. Sociologist Robert Park coined the term "marginal man" to describe immigrants, people of mixed race, and—for him the archetypal marginal man—Jews. Racial, ethnic, and cultural domination, mixture, or contact create marginal men, Park argued, who experience a "sense of moral dichotomy and conflict . . . when old habits are being discarded and new habits are not yet formed." Anthropologist Victor Turner called it "liminality," or the state of those who are "betwixt and between." In immigration studies, especially those focusing on Mexico and Central America, a whole literature has been developed out of the multiple metaphors of borders/*fronteras*. Mexican migrants, for example, cross not only national borders but also linguistic, cultural, racial, economic, and political ones. The richness of this literature comes not from studying either what life was like for migrants in their home countries or what it is like in the host country, but in exploring the border itself, the line between being Mexican and being American, between speaking English and speaking Spanish, the line where immigrants perform old traditions with new materials and in new places. These halfway states are the domain of middlemen. Mexican migrants bring their labor power to "the man" and transport earnings, goods, and new skills back home to the littleman. Sociologist Ronald Burt calls this phenomenon, when it occurs in the world of business and industry, filling "structural holes," or operating in the space "between people who vary in their behavior and opinions." These brokers, or "information arbiters," are adept at "translating" ideas and best practices across different segments of the firm and thus are better positioned to identify and take advantage of opportunities.[5]

W. E. B. DuBois characterized the middle somewhat differently for

African Americans. "One ever feels his two-ness," DuBois wrote of the black experience: "an American, a Negro; two souls, two thoughts, two unreconciled strivings; two warring ideals in one dark body, whose dogged strength alone keeps it from being torn asunder."[6] DuBois posited a *double* consciousness rather than a *split* consciousness. He did not argue that a black person would be one person at one minute and another person at the next, with the latter person having little awareness of the former. DuBois's formulation is about, not liminality, but simultaneity. The black experience is not half of this plus half of that, but a full part of each; not this or that, but both. There is no middle in this formulation—no transitional point in a journey of migration, hybridization, and later-generation assimilation; no central actor linking organizational nodes; no entrepreneurs shuttling goods from profiteering corporations to paycheck-to-paycheck consumers. African Americans are not somewhere *between* being Negroes and being Americans; they are both, bonded and wrapped in "one dark body." It is DuBois's double consciousness, on the one hand, and theories of boundaries and boundary spanning, on the other, that I am trying to join in this exploration of black middlemen.

"Dark bodies" now meet a different reception in America than they did when DuBois wrote *The Souls of Black Folk*. In DuBois's time, the standing of Negroes as Americans was still under debate in many institutions, in many laws, and surely in the minds of many whites. That DuBois saw citizenship as one part of the tension of black identity was as much an aspiration as it was a statement about day-to-day reality. Today, the Americanness of African Americans is not so much at issue. To be sure, dark bodies do not go unnoticed or unchecked, and they are not immune to the "amused contempt and pity" that DuBois witnessed and experienced. But some are given a pass, if not into complete unhyphenated Americanness, as Stanley Lieberson and Mary Waters have observed in the case of white ethnics, then at least into well-paying jobs, elected offices, positions of authority, and, sometimes, into nonblack "American" families.[7]

The fact that some African Americans are given entrée into these worlds while others are not makes it clear that dark bodies are *differentiated*. DuBois's notion of double consciousness examined the souls of black folk with few qualifiers. His focus was on the one adjective "black." To the contrary, the current direction of African American studies scholarship is to explore all of the qualifying adjectives: the souls of *rich* black folk, *gay* black folk, *light-skinned* black folk, *rural* black folk, *imprisoned* black folk. These distinctions create the possibilities for some African Americans to rise over others, not morally or in terms of their humanity, but through framing and propaganda that privilege one way of being black over another. When the index of differentiation is class, the defining criteria become what one owns, what additional resources one can commandeer, and what authority is gained through one's possessions or reputation. While economic capital and its related benefits might be a narrow measure of self-worth, they are no less consequential for securing a comfortable, safe, and healthy life.[8] For this reason, it is reasonable to hold out middle class-ness as a valued and favored status.

But attaining that status is only possible because of the ability of some dark bodies to reap the benefits of being Americans. Such benefits may come in limited doses, to be sure—one may be admitted to law school but not the country club, or be accepted as mayor but not as neighbor, as CEO but not as wife—but they are benefits nonetheless. Claiming these American opportunities might require learning new interactional styles, wearing different clothes, or being bused to a new school, all of which modify the experience of being black and temper discomfort outside of the black community. These are the border crossings that create black middlemen, *both* black and American, but now also situated *between* powerlessness and power, poverty and wealth, ignorance and access, complete exclusion and full membership.

I am arguing that the complementary notions of double and middle (or liminal, or on the boundary) have distinct utility in characterizing the black experience. Double consciousness remains apparent in the term of identification itself—African American. This two-word label literally represents the "double" metaphor, neither word being sufficient on its own to convey the fullness of the experience. Increasing use of the label African American is evidence of the greater opportunities to claim, and insistence on claiming, Americanness. For example, Toni Morrison argues vehemently that black people's writing is so fully American that the notion of "American literature" would not be possible without it.[9] On the other hand, the persistence of the term "black" underscores the unifying force of the dark body. When compared to people of African descent in Latin America, for example, African Americans' inability to (or aversion to, or lack of license to) embrace an *unconditional* American identity proves the continuing two-ness that blacks in the United States experience. Afro-Cubans, Afro-Brazilians, and Afro-Dominicans are almost always Cuban, Brazilian, and Dominican first. African ancestry is not a necessary modifier of their national pride.[10] In contrast, for most black Americans the simultaneity of a racial otherness within an American nationality persists, proving the impressive longevity of DuBois's double consciousness construct.

The extent or degree of that otherness, however, is captured in the black middleman concept. The black middleman occupies a classic liminal position. Much of life is lived *on the border* rather than fully in the worlds on either side: in the car between a predominantly white workplace and a predominantly black neighborhood, in a sentence that uses "ain't" but crisply pronounces all of the "-ing" endings, walking across the stage to receive a bachelor's degree to give to mom, who dropped out of high school. Straddling these two worlds, black middlemen take up new positions within the black community and vis-à-vis the man. When directed upward, they can be either supplicants or claimants, and when looking downward, they may be suppliers or enforcers. They are brokers of a wide variety of resources. As in double consciousness they exemplify a blackness not erased by being American, and an Americanness marked by racial flourishes. And as in *fronteras* they are forever using their varied training to translate the interests, demands, and perspectives of the man to the littleman, and vice versa.

My typology of the roles and actions available to middlemen rests on three concessions. First, the presence of a middleman assumes at least a tripartite system of relationships. It requires that there be both some person or group with more power or resources and another person or group with less. In a bilateral arrangement, on the other hand, the middleman becomes the littleman vis-à-vis the man, or the man vis-à-vis the littleman. Second, microsettings have their own status hierarchies, which may differ from those that rule relationships on the macro level. Elijah Anderson and Mitchell Duneier both studied small group cultures of black men who could demand little from their workplaces or from city government, but who enjoyed the honor and deference of their peers; within his own neighborhood, family, bar, workplace, or church, in other words, the littleman was transformed into the man.[11] The criteria by which people are evaluated within their small groups may be economic, as when a group of poor girls elevate one of their number who carries a designer handbag, but such judgments may also be based on verbal skills, height, athletic talent, toughness, beauty, or any number of other characteristics. One of the consolations of the human tendency toward rankings is that almost everybody can come out on top in some clique and relative to some particular measuring stick. The third and final concession is related to the second. Even at the macro level, where people are stratified based on their possession of resources or talents, the littleman is not always powerless and the man is not forever powerful. "Them that's got shall get," Billie Holiday sang. "Them that's not shall lose." But history has shown that it is possible to triumph over such tyranny. While poor or otherwise disadvantaged groups may not have money, wealth, educational credentials, the right skin color, or prestigious jobs, they can have charisma, moral capital, creativity, determination, or just sheer numbers. These resources have been harnessed, heroically, in anticolonial struggles and labor movements, gender revolutions and squatter settlements. Unfortunately, even the gains from these upheavals seem over time to be recalibrated to keep the man on top.

Choosing Sides

There is considerable complexity in the middleman role due to the permutations of allegiances and alliances that he or she might forge. These relationships are "variables" in the most literal sense, since the nature of the middleman is the ability to assume different stances in dealing with the constituents above and below her. As one such broker in Chicago's Latino community remarked, "There are no permanent friends and no permanent enemies."[12] This vacillation is not necessarily a strategic or instrumental maneuver. On the contrary, because they have been shaped by many worlds, middlemen have sincere interests that coincide with the groups on either side of themselves, and can genuinely make bargains with each. Taking different sides in different contexts is in fact how they maintain legitimacy. At times middlemen may act strategically, taking a particular side solely to garner favor or obtain rewards, but such internal states are mostly hidden and not discernible by my ethnographic eye. Hence, this analysis is not concerned with the credibility of middlemen, or with the ethics behind the positions that they take.

Despite the fluid and dynamic tenor of middlemen's negotiations, a broad typology is possible. When middlemen are upwardly aligned, when they side with "the man," their duties toward the littleman are often coercive and exclusive. In the realm of community development, the upwardly aligned middleman might be the spokesperson for a city agency charged with communicating to neighborhood residents the city's plans for, say, a new professional sports arena that will be placed in the neighborhood and cause significant displacement. She might be the head of a community organization that gets a large foundation grant, which requires that her organization implement a vision of community improvement emphasizing home ownership over affordable rental housing, even though most of her constituents are not prepared to buy a house. She may speak in a language that intimidates and confuses community members who have little exposure to city bureaucracy. He might be a resident who works to rid the main street of businesses that have not maintained their awnings or signs in favor of newer chain stores that offer premier services at prices that are prohibitive for families on fixed or assisted incomes. The upwardly aligned middleman acts opportunistically, using "the master's tools" either because she herself stands to gain by doing so or because he has been employed or co-opted to do so. All of these approaches move toward more exclusive community institutions rather than inclusive ones, and are implemented more by fiat than by participatory debate and negotiation.

On the other hand, middlemen can side with the littleman and confront the man. In the 1960s, when African and Caribbean states were gaining their independence, theorist Frantz Fanon wrote the following about the black middlemen in these new countries: "In an underdeveloped country an authentic national middle class ought to consider as its bounden duty to betray the calling fate has marked out for it, and to put itself to school with the people: in other words to put at the people's disposal the intellectual and technical capital that it has snatched when going through the colonial universities."[13]

The biggest challenge for such downwardly aligned middlemen is substantive inclusion. The expertise attributed to planners, social service administrators, philanthropists, some community leaders, and, indeed, researchers, based on their credentials and titles, can smother or ignore the concerns, ideas, and testimonies of those whose educations have been life itself. Hence, when the middleman is downwardly aligned he must first establish genuine respect for the experiences and preferences of the littleman, fighting the urge and the pressure to act as if he knows what's best for struggling community residents—the unemployed or marginally employed, the homeless, public housing residents, youth. She might head a nonprofit organization that emphasizes community empowerment and involves residents in naming the organization's priorities and charting its strategies. Because her nonprofit must interface with philanthropic and governmental agencies in order to stay afloat financially, she must be steadfast in maintaining control of the direction of her organization when communicating with those who hold the purse strings. He might be a banker who volunteers at his church to give classes on saving for home ownership, avoiding predatory loans, or taking advantage of special programs for first-time home buyers. Instead of hoarding the benefits of a good education and important job, he funnels those skills and relevant information to members of the community without similar access. She might be an elected official who invites communication within her community (through such practices as keeping open office hours), respects the insights and judgments of her less fortunate constituents, and follows through by making specific demands of the city bureaucracy and more senior politicians to meet their needs. Sometimes those demands may be large, expensive, or radical—a moratorium on arrests of nonviolent neighborhood youth, for instance, or more jobs for black workers on a construction site. Heeding the wishes of the littleman requires setting aside arrogance and at times her own best interest: her belligerence and doggedness may not always be appreciated by her colleagues or superiors.

More often, though, the role of the middleman emphasizes balance, compromise, negotiation, and cunning. If the hypothetical elected official above pledges full allegiance to the interests of the littleman, her ties to other decision-making bodies become strained. If those ties are severed, she loses her fragile purchase on the resources she channels downward and is no longer an effective middleman. She cannot deliver. Therefore, she carefully manages her stances and requests so as not to become alienated from the man. Such management requires that she sometimes tell her disadvantaged constituents that she cannot advocate for something they desire, or that she must yield when continued advocacy would imperil her access. But neither can a middleman be aligned exclusively with the man. If he was, he would have no legitimacy with the grass roots. A black bureaucrat who comes to community meetings only to do his boss's bidding is not a middleman in the sense that I am employing the word, but rather a puppet, a mouthpiece whose rewards flow so unilaterally from above that he has no motivation to serve the masses. He is not acting as translator or as emissary, and has no intentions of taking community sentiment back to his boss. Audre Lorde noted that the revolutionary act of doing away with the master's tools altogether "is only threatening to those [people] who still define the master's house as their only source of support."[14]

Instead of being firmly aligned in either direction, the men and women who successfully occupy the middle are *brokers*. They put people together, they negotiate subsidies and concessions, they run interference, they relay information, and they mediate disputes. As brokers, they also take a cut, which may come in the form of a consulting fee, a salary, a program grant, a board appointment, votes, verbal accolades, or, if they are also residents, a share in the benefits that flow from the local investments they have brokered.[15]

Having set up the ideal types and discarded them for a more moderate amalgam, it is now necessary to eschew the pure middle middleman as an abstract construction as well. The notion of a perfectly flexible and fair middleman suggests a measure of neutrality that does not accurately portray the black middlemen operating in North Kenwood–Oakland. As I have argued, one of the defining characteristics of black middlemen is that they have walked through (or pushed open) the doors of opportunity, reaped the benefits therein, and built boundary-spanning networks that keep them engaged with both the littleman—here the collective poor and working-class black community—and the man: white corporations, government bureaucracies, and civic leadership. In their ascent (for those who started from humbler beginnings), they have been transformed.

The *Chicago Reporter*, an investigative magazine with a focus on race and poverty, once did a feature story on African American pastors who received monies from Mayor Richard M. Daley's administration in order to build housing and provide social services in the black community. The *Reporter* generated considerable controversy and dismay when it asked if these clergy were "prophets or puppets" for participating in such partnerships. These character poles may be a bit extreme, but it is impossible to become engaged in a new world and not take on some of its dominant opinions and perspectives.[16] Given the relatively privileged positions of North Kenwood–Oakland's black middlemen, they share significant interests with the man. Their gaze and aspirations are directed upwards. The reality of their blackness in a black milieu—the power of the collective "dark body"—makes unavoidable a certain allegiance to African Americans with fewer means, but the expression of that allegiance now operates through certain filters. Their advanced educations have given them new theories, their cocktail conversations have given them new interpretive schema, and their broad exposures have erased the limits of action. As a result, they sometimes tackle the problems of housing, education, business development, and job creation differently than would the people who are in need of an affordable apartment, functional schools, goods and services, and decent employment. In addition, their tastes and tolerances—for fresh food or fast food, rap or jazz, air conditioning or a summer breeze on the porch, a laundromat or a dry cleaner, extended or nuclear families— have been shaped and altered by their relative riches. The black middlemen in North Kenwood–Oakland are not simply unbiased brokers able to mediate without self-interest. They have glimpsed, and sometimes even attained, the comforts of money and prestige, and they do not plan to give those up. If it is not too taxing, they hope to pass some of those goodies on to less fortunate black kin and neighbors, but their methods occasionally require breaking racial ranks.

In terms of theories of black collective action and politics, then, the black middleman elaborates on the notion of *linked fate* elaborated in the previous chapter. Blacks' shared history of slavery and postslavery oppression, their continuing experience of racist acts, and their observation of persistent racial inequalities contribute to a collective ethos. In particular, the notion of linked fate holds that if individual welfare is tied to the well-being of the group, then blacks can use what is best for the group as a proxy for what is best for themselves as individuals. Self-interest comes to be determined by group interest. Black middlemen capitalize on linked-fate sentiments within the black community. Their dark bodies invoke collective dispositions and can successfully cloak otherwise repudiated (gay, Republican), unappreciated (young, renter), or dubious (suburban, biracial) identities.[17] When they present plans, convey rules, or announce new programs, many of which have been formulated in downtown offices with few blacks, they employ linked-fate language, noting the group benefits of the proposal and the racial progress that will be made as a result. Even when the pill is clearly going to be a hard swallow, black middlemen are given a fair hearing, definitely fairer than if the messenger were an outsider. Political scientist Adolph Reed argues critically that the use of black middlemen as spokespeople explains how policies that are horrendously bad for the black community at large, but good for black elites, garner mass black endorsement. Through the magic of linked fate, the good fortune that will come to black elites, "when filtered through the discourse of symbolic racial collectivism, [becomes] a proxy for broader racial redistribution."[18] Linked fate, then, operates to suppress, at least initially, objections to what black middlemen have to say, and to grant them a more favorable reception than if they were not black.

Linked fate does not, however, completely mute discussion and debate since the view that "what is good for the black community will be good for me" also works in the reverse: what is *bad* for black people will be bad for me. Bad political agendas are just as consequential as good ones. Linked fate only means that there might be a pause before the challenge if the messenger is black. The assumption is that if a black protagonist similarly believes that her fate is linked to that of other African Americans, then she would not put forth an idea that will be harmful to the race.[19] Once the collective rightness of a plan, a goal, or a direction is considered, debates may ensue. Black middlemen participate in these debates, in which they often have the upper hand by dint of authority, title, and, sometimes, no small amount of perks to distribute to those who join their camp.

Brokering Capital

The most obvious resource that black middlemen have secured for North Kenwood–Oakland is mortgage capital. In 1989, Oakland ranked seventy-seventh out of Chicago's seventy-seven community areas in mortgage dollars received. Total lending in the neighborhood amounted to a paltry $224,000 dollars, compared to $33 million in Hyde Park and $258 million in Chicago's predominantly white Lincoln Park neighborhood. By 2000, Oakland had moved up to number fifty-two, garnering over $3 million dollars in mortgage financing, and by 2003, total lending amounted to over $24 million dollars, more than one hundred times the amount invested in the neighborhood in 1989.[20]

North Kenwood–Oakland's newcomers created a housing market where none existed. First they focused the attention of the city and other institutions, and then they became the demand side of the classic economic principle, thereby jump-starting a supply of investments that had long been withheld. And *demand* is quite literally what they had to do. The middle and upper incomes of NKO's new black residents were not enough to convince banks and other lenders to take a fresh look at the neighborhood. Instead, newcomers devised a variety of strategies to buy homes. They made creative arrangements with sellers, they paid in full and rehabbed gradually using their salaries, and they pulled equity out of other homes to finance the new ones. Most consequentially, though, they were insistent that traditional banks support their decision to move into North Kenwood–Oakland, and they worked their networks and social clout to get mortgages.

Explicit and purposeful neglect of black central-city neighborhoods like NKO ultimately made them high-risk lending areas, which in turn solidified and justified their economic unviability. This was the investment vacuum that newcomers were challenged to fill. Many NKO residents could tell this story of disinvestment from black communities as well as any social scientist. Emmett Coleman, who moved from Hyde Park to North Kenwood in 1983, gave a concise but thorough account of why North Kenwood was in some of its darkest days when he first moved in. "What happened during the '60s, [the neighborhood] was split up," began the history lesson Coleman thought important to understanding NKO's contemporary reality. He continued:

> The dividing line was at 47th Street. So you had South Kenwood from 51st to 47th, and 47th to 39th was considered North Kenwood. Unfortunately, following the split, there was evidence of redlining. And by that I mean banks would not lend money. The city was more negligent toward that area. And the problem was compounded because during the '60s and the '70s, there were a lot of federal funds that were going into neighborhoods. And the majority of this money was targeted to the area of South Kenwood. And I don't know whether they had in mind that this would be a buffer, but North Kenwood suffered because of this.

The neighborhood suffered the redlining to which Coleman refers for almost sixty years, running nearly unabated from as early as the 1930s into the early 1990s.[21] Home maintenance is the first thing to suffer when mortgage monies are scarce. With lower appraised values, home owners lack the financial equity to reinvest in infrastructural and cosmetic upkeep, not to mention the inability to take out loans to finance college, start new businesses, or smooth income insecurities that result from unemployment, retirement, or poor health. Some home owners are just stuck in redlined neighborhoods, unable to sell their homes or buy another home elsewhere in any financially prudent manner. As the surroundings deteriorate physically and socially others make the deci-

sion to rent out their houses, cutting them up into apartments to provide income to finance a new home in another neighborhood. This was
the housing market that greeted Emmett Coleman and others as they
looked to move into NKO in the 1980s and 1990s.

Gayle Peters first moved to North Kenwood as a renter, but soon
after decided to buy a house. I asked her about the daunting task of buying a three-flat building and rehabbing it all on her own. "Oh, God!"
she answered. "Oh, my God. [Getting financing] was horrible. You know
they say redlining doesn't exist, but that's a complete lie." Getting a
mortgage was obviously an obstacle for Peters, one that would have
been impossible to endure and ultimately overcome without both her
exposure to the world of home finance and her ability to make a per-
suasive and documented argument to potential lenders. She told the
following flustering story:

> Ten years ago when I was trying to get financing—I'll never forget—
> when I applied for my first loan with them, they just flat out denied me.
> Now, I worked in this field for years. You know, I audited credit unions
> and I looked at loan files. So I know what the guidelines are. So I know
> I qualified. So I said, okay, I'm writing letters and, you know, going back
> and forth with them. The same bank denied me three times before they
> approved me. . . . So I finally got them to do the deal. But they wouldn't
> loan me the money for the rehab. . . . I had to end up writing letters about
> the area and the changes that were coming up, put in newspaper clip-
> pings. I went through this whole thing about what this area was going to
> become. Because they did not believe that the money that I was asking
> for—that the house was ever gonna appraise out at that. And they basi-
> cally told me that. "This house would never appraise out at this. You put-
> ting too much money into this.". . . I knew what the plan was for the area
> so I knew that eventually, hey, it's gonna be worth a lot more than I'm
> even asking for. I didn't think that actually it would be where it is today,
> though. I really didn't. I didn't see that.

Peters was not the first applicant to be denied a mortgage in North
Kenwood–Oakland for reasons that seemed unrelated to her ability to
pay. But how many denied mortgage seekers would be able to mount
as feisty a campaign as she did? Would most people even have had sufficient experience to smell something fishy? Or would they, instead,
accept the rejection with dejection, never questioning how the bankers

arrived at their conclusion? Gladyse Taylor, who was looking to buy a house in Oakland in the late 1980s, remembered going into a bank to apply for a home loan. "I was very excited, and before I sat down in the chair they said no." Most rejections probably weren't this dramatic, and were no doubt curtly conveyed in a form letter: "Your application for a mortgage has been denied." NKO's older working-class residents would not have been savvy enough to test what seemed to be a done deal. While a portion of them would have had middle-class credentials (some college or white-collar jobs), most were handicapped by a lack of education, older age, or few other assets, which together put their applications in the marginal category. More importantly, many of the older residents had bought their homes before thirty-year fixed-rate private mortgages were the norm, so they had limited knowledge of the opaque evaluation procedure that spits out acceptance or rejection letters.

Gayle Peters, on the other hand, was able to broker her mortgage and rehab loans because of the human and cultural capital at her disposal. College educated and entrepreneurial, Peters had worked both in state government and as an independent auditor, giving her familiarity with fair housing and lending guidelines and considerable exposure to the mortgage market. She had the education and the resources to write numerous letters in a language and style that ultimately resonated with the lenders. In practice, this means that she had full command of the lending lexicon and could communicate with data that they understood—*Chicago Tribune* articles that heralded the transformation of North Kenwood–Oakland, plans for new housing announced at the meetings of the Conservation Community Council, neighborhood projections done by the Chicago Department of Planning and Development. She delivered her arguments in typewritten letters that indicated her level of professionalism, subtly conveying to the bank that she may have the right contacts to make an even bigger issue out of this.

When Michael and Sylvia Smith were beset with similar frustrations in financing their home purchase in Oakland, they did exactly that—made a big legal fuss. "Our credit was A1," Mrs. Smith said proudly, but somewhat bitterly given that it seemed inconsequential when they struggled with four different banks in order to get a mortgage in 1992. "One bank we wound up suing because they made us wait for the appraisal." The kind of subterfuge that the Smiths experienced in the mortgage market exemplifies the discrimination uncovered in numerous studies of housing and lending discrimination.[22] It is never

blatant, but neither is it something that African Americans are searching out to make a quick dollar through a lawsuit, catching racists in the
act. In fact, Mr. Smith was initially incredulous: "I didn't think it was
gonna be an issue. I really didn't." But when the couple did suspect discrimination they were prepared to follow through. Mr. Smith continued his story about the bank's refusal to give him and his wife a copy
of the appraisal.

> That caught me too. 'Cause I called just figuring out, well, how long it
> would take to get [the appraisal]. You know, two, three days, weeks? And
> that was my only concern. He said, "We don't do that." And I said, "I beg
> your pardon. You don't do that? I thought I paid for it." And I said, "Well,
> didn't I pay for it? Then I'm entitled to a copy. You know if I paid for it,
> this is America." He said, "No, that's not our policy." I said, "That's not
> your policy?" I called the state's attorney's office to make sure I wasn't,
> you know, I wasn't going crazy and I didn't assume anything. I mean,
> I had never seen it legally written. I was always of the understanding
> over the years that's how business was done. So we went out there and
> sued 'em. The judge settled it on our behalf 'cause they never showed up.
> Twenty thousand dollars. But they filed bankruptcy.

Hiding behind the official but vacuous language of a "policy," the bank
did not likely expect the boldness with which the Smiths pursued this
act of discrimination. Or the certitude with which they acted to claim
their entitlements of citizenship, that part of DuBois's double consciousness that is not always granted. "This is America," Mr. Smith proclaimed, with the unvocalized subtext being "And I am an American."
To fully realize this assertion required the activation of skills and capacities rooted in Mr. Smith's middle-class status. He had to know or be
able to find out what government office could correctly inform him of
his rights. He needed a telephone to call them and needed not to be worried about the cost of making multiple phone calls, not a given in poor
and working-class households. He also had to be financially and intellectually able to mount a credible legal case against the bank.

Jacqueline Callery also had a problem with her appraisal. She didn't
sue, nor did she acquiesce. She was just insistent. "I had to redo the
appraisal and tell the man from the bank what number I expected,"
she said with no hint of sarcasm. She and her husband did not have
problems with their initial financing because they used a bank where

a close friend worked, a classic brokering maneuver to achieve some ends that are unlikely to be realized without such a productive network tie. But when it came time to get a home improvement loan to insulate the walls in their hundred-year-old home, they were met with skepticism. Unlike the cloud of mystery surrounding the Smiths' appraisal, the appraiser for the Callerys' bank did not hesitate to make comments about the negative effect of nearby public housing on the value of their home. Taking this as a sign of bias, Mrs. Callery, a professor at a Chicago business college, decided there was a minimum value she would accept. When the appraisal came back below that, she protested. "At a minimum," she declared, "I was going to get credit for my third floor. So I looked up the standards. I looked up the code. I looked up how much height you had to have, and I used my six-foot-three husband and had him stand up and I said, 'Can you look at how much height there is above his head. That is a usable floor.' And so mainly, I made it justified based on floor space. I can't fight the subjective subtracting, the arbitrary subtracting." Resigned to the unfair fact that her house would be devalued because it was on the wrong side of 47th Street, she disputed the more objective factors, ones that required her to research obscure building and appraising methods and make a compelling case based on them. "And I rewrote it," she said about the appraisal, which ended her saga with the banks and their delegates in her favor. Using social, human, and cultural capital, the Smiths, Gayle Peters, Mrs. Callery, and others like them forced the otherwise impersonal banking institutions, which had for years summarily dismissed the investment potential of North Kenwood–Oakland, to be responsive to their desires to put roots in the neighborhood.

Community organizations like the Kenwood Oakland Community Organization (KOCO) were also instrumental in convincing investors to put their money in NKO. KOCO had both social and financial goals in mind when it got involved in rehabilitating apartment buildings to improve housing options in the neighborhood. Its leadership wanted both to provide decent housing to low-income residents, and to support social programming, such as after-school tutoring, food pantries, and employment services, through the monies generated by management fees. The benefits would be dispersed not simply among the new tenants and recipients of KOCO's services, but also among neighbors more broadly, who would be rid of the dilapidated, dangerous large apartment buildings, eyesores that fostered feelings of unsafety. Organizations like KOCO worked outside of the traditional mortgage market, instead using financial tools designed to create affordable housing, most notably the Low Income Housing Tax Credit program, a Reagan-era invention that gave private investors tax incentives for their investment in affordable housing. Buildings built or rehabbed with tax-credit dollars primarily serve working households rather than the lowest income households.[23] KOCO was the lead organization for developing over three hundred units of tax-credit housing in NKO. While it did not prove to be an income-generating venture for KOCO, it did begin the transformation of NKO's physical landscape. People driving by inspecting the neighborhood as a possible place to move now saw the early signs of improvement: new windows, tuck-pointed brick, and budding flowers.

KOCO's work also illustrated that successful resource brokerage is as much about teaching the man something as it is about serving the little-man. In 1998, Vice President Al Gore visited North Kenwood–Oakland touting President Clinton's increased commitment to affordable housing construction. The *Chicago Tribune* reported:

In 1987, Kenwood community leaders would hardly have believed that the new yet obscure federal financing tool they used to help build the neighborhood's first new housing in 40 years would set the stage for one of the country's most dramatic turnarounds for an inner-city community. Yet, because of additional housing and development that sprouted as a result of that decision, Vice President Al Gore came to Kenwood Tuesday to announce that the Clinton administration's proposed federal budget would include a dramatic increase in the program responsible for the change. Under the proposed 1999 fiscal year budget, federal tax credits designed to encourage construction or renovation of low-income housing would be expanded by 40 percent over the next five years.[24]

Similarly, a director of the private asset-management company that partnered with KOCO recognized the organization's role in opening the eyes of private investors:

But what they did do was demonstrate in a sort of bizarre way that it could be done. By this I mean they demonstrated to the private developer that neighborhoods were worth investing in. That you could turn them around. That you could make them viable places again in which to live. And certainly Kenwood has proven that. And so that was a very important contribution. In fact, I used to always tell the not-for-profits: you ought to really see your job as demonstrating in the short run what

...uld be done. Private developers having seen that, they're willing then to come in. And then let them do so, [and] you go on to something else that you're better at.

The middleman role that black middle-class newcomers and organizational leaders played in NKO in obliging private lenders to pay attention to them as a growing market is akin to that played by the entrepreneurial immigrant middleman. Ethnic entrepreneurs use assets accumulated in their home countries, coethnic credit associations, and a collective positive reputation established with private lenders to convince banks to capitalize their endeavors in areas where the local population does not have the same clout and that larger enterprises avoid.[25] These immigrant middlemen are the conduits of capital and goods from "the man" to the littleman. Black middle-class potential home buyers similarly use their reputations, connections, incomes, and wealth to funnel dollars from private lenders to the neighborhood. The motivation of these middlemen is different, however, from that of immigrant entrepreneurs, whose primary reward is a comfortable livelihood for themselves. While black middle-class brokers in NKO definitely have their self-interests served by securing financing to invest in a home, they also express a mission to reestablish a thriving black neighborhood. They see themselves as caring for the vintage houses, filling in the spaces where houses were destroyed, bringing back black (and other) businesses, and reinvigorating the (black) organizational and institutional life. Whether they are coming back or not, they emphasize their "blackness" on the block as a strategy of racial uplift.

Paula Butler grew up in an all-white neighborhood in Columbia, Missouri. As a professional black woman in her new big city, she was explicitly looking for an all-black experience. "An attorney friend of mine told me this is going to be a nice black middle-class community," she said of the advice she was given about North Kenwood–Oakland when she was house hunting. "But," she continued, "now I'm worried that's not going to be the case when I look at the prices of some of the things going up"—out of the range of other middle-class blacks. The possibility that African Americans would be priced out of the neighborhood concerned Butler, who pined for a black (middle-class) paradise.

The Smiths also had racial solidarity and preservation on their minds when they moved into Oakland.[26] Both grew up in the neighborhood, moved out for years, and came back to participate in its renaissance.

Mrs. Smith recalled, "We were always told by our parents that this area was gonna be revitalized and come back. And that the housing market down here would be a housing market that, you know, would be expensive. And we were always told to come back because if we don't go back we won't get a chance because the neighborhood was going to be sold back [to whites]." Black middlemen in NKO are consciously bringing their good credit ratings, tidy savings, and refusal to take no as an answer from lenders in order to repossess and elevate a poor black neighborhood. They intend to make money flow into the black community, with their working-class and poor neighbors as cobeneficiaries.

Randall Van Dyke, another North Kenwood newcomer, told the following story about what has happened since he and other middle-class blacks moved into new homes built in the neighborhood. "There's a gentleman who lives down the block who said he'd lived in his home since the late '40s. In the '60s, when the neighborhood changed, he said he couldn't give it away. And he said today now it's worth over $300,000 again. And he sits on his porch, he waves to me every morning and every afternoon." Van Dyke's neighbor, a longtime NKO resident, is no longer stuck. He could sell his home for a near windfall in favor of a smaller but brand-new one-bedroom condo just around the corner, or could move in with a family member, move to Florida, or stay right where he is and allow his children to decide what to do with the sizable inheritance his house has become. His neighbor now has choices that he did not have before, and that makes Van Dyke feel good.

Where then are the allegiances of the black middlemen who created the demand that made the supply of mortgage dollars flow? They are clearly with the littleman, who has lived in NKO for years and weathered the storms of disregard. The new arrivals are also betting that they will get rich in the process of igniting the North Kenwood–Oakland housing market, and the banks that were brought in kicking and screaming also stand to make a lot of money. So while this is not a case of pure altruism, it nonetheless highlights the impact of black middle-class middlemen in funneling resources from the man to the littleman.

From Redlined to Red Hot

In a perfectly functioning housing market, the rising demand for homes in NKO, the infusion of capital, and the higher home appraisals would be an unequivocally and all-around good thing. Yet this logic holds only for owners, be they middle class or not, and most longtime NKO residents are not owners. Moreover, there are risks associated with rising values for home owners who do not want to follow the efficiency rules of the market and cash out for more reasonably priced housing elsewhere. The biggest costs of staying are the rising property taxes, assessed on the rising property values. Smaller costs may include compliance with landmark guidelines, new block-club dues, and social pressure to make costly cosmetic improvements, such as installing wrought-iron fencing, sandblasting stone exteriors, or sprucing up the yard. Aggressive mortgage marketing poses another threat to low-income home owners in the neighborhood, who are more easily fooled by promises of cash that have severe hidden strings attached. Subprime lending is growing in Chicago, and increased foreclosures follow close behind.[27] As the houses in North Kenwood–Oakland grow more valuable, predatory lenders have an even greater incentive to target the neighborhood.

When the middlemen who came to NKO as conveyors of mortgage capital transform into the engines of the growth machine, interested in ever-rising property values, they give up their downward (or neutral) alignment. Driven by the self-interest of protecting and growing their housing investment, they begin to do the bidding of larger outside developers and the city, which always looks to fatten its tax coffers. The growth machine concept suggests the upward alignment of North Kenwood–Oakland's black middle class with civic, business, and elected elites to achieve growth goals in those segments' interests. The families who can persevere as prices rise stand to benefit handsomely from this growth logic, but fewer and fewer of those stayers will be littlemen.

Kirk Clemons and his wife approached the notion of buying a house in North Kenwood with none of the problack sentimentalism that suffused the moving stories of the Smiths and Paula Butler. Instead, they constructed a decision matrix. "Coming back [to Chicago], we were surprised to find the amount of redevelopment in the city and basically we did a decision matrix on Excel. Put the MBA to work," crowed Mr. Clemons. The Clemonses were considering two other homes, one a bit cheaper and one a bit more expensive, each with unique amenities and things lacking. They assigned weights to each of the things they wanted in a home, with the highest priority put on "opportunity for appreciation." People buy houses for many reasons, but few of them disregard the question of value trajectories, and some of them, like the Clemonses, deem financial returns as the most important variable. Kirk

Clemons, then, represents a kind of middleman different than those discussed above. Perhaps, more precisely, he represents a different *stage* of black middleman activism (or a second wave of black middlemen), since many newcomers who fought for mortgage capital in order to build a black residential Eden also desire Eden to be lucrative. In order to insure rising property values, residents make clear their preferences for bigger and more swankily appointed housing units that command higher "price points." In this instance, they are not brokering goods that will be passed through to working and poor families in NKO, but rather aligning with the man's desire to maximize profits and revenue, which manifests favorably for them as rising home equity.

Black middle-class brokers justify this intervention to their poorer neighbors by preaching the need to bring in higher-income neighbors in order to create the ripple effect of better supported schools, a greater variety of businesses, and infrastructural improvements. "You need some high-end stuff here, guys, sorry," said Jacqueline Callery when community leaders were deciding what kind of housing they should invite through a request for proposals to developers. Elaborating on the premise that wealthier residents make the city bureaucracy more responsive, she continued, "Because you need some money. You need taxes. Because then you can demand the city make changes. You can demand more lighting in your alley, you can demand better [trash] pickup, you can demand the street cleaners make it over here as often as they do in Hyde Park. You know, stuff like that." Spinning high-end housing as a broad community good, Callery's logic challenges my characterization of middleman growth machine politics as self-serving and upwardly aligned, placing it instead in the same light as brokering mortgage capital, which redounds to low-income owners as well. While intent may be focused downward, however, results are not assured in that direction. Callery's logic benefits low-income residents *only if* they are still in the neighborhood by the time public agencies start responding to their higher-income neighbors' muscle flexing. The research on gentrification challenges the notion of widespread displacement, but it does find the gradual replacement of poor households with nonpoor ones.[28] When brokers encourage private builders and investors to take *full* advantage of this new market, it leaves some people behind.

The price trajectory in North Kenwood–Oakland has clearly been upward. Since 1998, when I began my research, prices for homes and condominiums have increased from just under $100 per square foot to more than $200 per square foot (or $300,000 for a fifteen-hundred-square-foot condominium/home). The city planner assigned to the neighborhood often reminded the community that prices for vacant land had doubled during his five years of service to the neighborhood, and had increased fivefold from 1994—when the first new batch of single-family homes was constructed—to 2004, from $6 per square foot to over $30 per square foot. "Land prices have shot through the roof in this area," he commented to the Conservation Community Council. "In many ways, you are a victim of your own success." But many council members did not see it this way. Increasing land value was not an evil, and thus they were not victims of it. What they *were* victims of was discrimination that kept land prices artificially *lower* on the black South Side. "How much is [vacant] land in Lakeview?" one council member inquired of the city planner, with subtle ulterior motives. The answer: "$100 per square foot, and some people say maybe as high as $350." The point was made. Lakeview—a North Side lakefront neighborhood with a black presence of under 5 percent—was *really* the proverbial roof, and NKO's land prices, roughly one-third to one-tenth of those in Lakeview, were no where near shooting through it. This meant there was still lots of room for growth in North Kenwood–Oakland real estate prices. Council members frequently pushed developers to realize that growth, or cheered them when they did it on their own. Alderman Toni Preckwinkle once reported to the council:

> You all should know that your influence is quite important here because the developers did not think they could make their price points for their development. The developer was initially very resistant to the suggestions made by the community that would increase the price of the condos, but now they are happy they were forced to make those changes.

City officials encouraged residents to encourage developers to aim high, and developers were encouraged by buyers who responded positively.

Housing prices in NKO were negotiated in a gyrating tango in which developers, council members and city officials alternated as lead dancers. One developer, aware of the fact that he was pushing the pricing envelope, spoke of his "target price" for units in the four-story building he was converting into condominiums. "I believe $320,000 is *reachable* in this neighborhood," he told the council optimistically, hoping that he would not get any skeptical looks. And he didn't. In another instance, the developers were proposing loft condominiums at $200 per square foot. A wary council member asked, "Your plans seem to be crossing a price point that we haven't seen before in this community. Can you tell us how you came to this?" Without any marketing surveys or comparison figures, the council member was adequately soothed by the developer's report that his real estate agent had determined these to be the going prices for newly constructed condominium units in the neighborhood. As a home owner, the council member was surprised, but in a pleasant way. Still another developer approached the council with a warning—"There might be a little sticker shock with these prices"—as he proposed his $350,000-plus single-family homes. He assured council members that he planned to use the highest quality materials and demand superior workmanship, and that was why his proposed houses were so expensive. To relieve some of the developer's apprehension, one community member called out from the audience: "That's alright. I own something here. So I wanna see the . . ." and she finished her sentence with her hands pushing toward the ceiling. Developers put their foot out there on the first beat of the tango, and residents followed.

City representatives from the alderman's office, the Department of Planning, and the mayor's office also took their turn at lead. Like the newcomer residents who had to prove to mortgage lenders that NKO was a safe bet, the city too had to lure new investors through incentives. The City of Chicago was a major landowner in the neighborhood, and wanted to unload its holdings in order to return the land to revenue-producing private hands. In the beginning, the land was cheap and so there was a built-in incentive for people to buy it. But the city also discounted large plots of land in order to encourage comprehensive plans. For individual residents, the city was almost giving away land. If you lived next door to a vacant piece of land owned by the city, you could buy it for $1 and use it to expand your yard or build a garage. This kind of investment paid off royally when land prices increased. The owners could reap the full profit from having doubled the square footage they owned. This also made sense from the city's perspective since it hadn't been getting anything out of the land as owner, while selling it meant it could be assessed for property taxes.

By the late 1990s, all of this changed. The city's approach to land sales in NKO took a turn. "With the development in the conservation area, at this point everything is for sale," announced the city representative when a home owner wanted to buy the city-owned lot next door through the $1 program. A few months later, when explaining why a home owner would have to pay full price (rather than the "open space" appraisal price) for land she wanted to buy to expand her yard, the city representative tersely confirmed the paradigm shift amongst his superiors in the Department of Planning, "Right now they want the most they can get for everything." Same tango, different lead.

Sometimes, residents had to inspire cautious developers with their vision of high-end homes for high-end buyers. There was one corner in the neighborhood that had scared off more than one investor because developers did not think they could sell what residents wanted built there. On the west side of the 4400 block of South Greenwood Avenue sat four mansions and one big vacant lot. Council members wanted mansions to finish off the block, but developers weren't buying it because they didn't think buyers would. To continue the dance metaphor, residents thought the timid developers were missing the beat. In response to one developer's proposal to build two-story, twenty-four-hundred-square-foot townhomes on the land, a council member who lived across the street commented with some disdain: "Most of the [existing] buildings on that street are three stories. What they are proposing is really not a mansion compared to the houses nearby." Trying to be responsive but betraying his doubts, the developer responded: "If the market is there for something larger, and we will be able to tell from what we sell, then we will definitely push up the square footage." Council members were unconvinced, and when the developer returned a few months later with what council members again deemed to be puny designs, he was met with the same disapproval. Someone at the meeting added that not only were his proposed "mansions" not mansions, but the corner was in the heart of the landmark district and would thus receive the highest scrutiny from the landmarks commission. Unlike the times when developers yielded to council members' persistence and followed their lead, this time the developer quit the dance altogether. Sure that he could not sell a mansion in North Kenwood, he backed out of the deal altogether. While the dance did not work with this particular partner, council members later got their wishes for that corner in the form of designs for seven-thousand-square-foot mansions, the neighborhood's first million-dollar homes.

Resident investors in NKO approach housing with such passion—"They'd be making a great financial investment. I've been *evangelistic* in terms of living here," trumpeted one resident—that there have been cases where their coconspirators have intervened to temper residents' growth machine impulses. "Why would somebody get something for one dollar, even if it is a community center?" asked Gayle Peters about the city's plan to sell a building it owned to the Abraham Lincoln Center, a social service center that had been in the neighborhood for over thirty years. The city proceeded with its beneficence despite this market-driven objection. In another example a council member asked what would happen to a swath of land on which a church-based developer was supposed to build homes for working families. After many years the land still sat vacant, raising doubts that the church would be able to complete the job. "Why not put this land back into the larger kitty of land available for [private] development?" asked Peter Braxton. "This is now primo lakefront land. It wasn't five years ago," he argued, making clear that he thought the city could now fetch a higher price for the land and the community could get a fancier development. Again, the city representative adhered to the initial plans and reiterated its commitment to provide affordable housing in the neighborhood.

Alderman Toni Preckwinkle has been a prominent activist for increasing the supply of affordable housing in the city and has worked with developers in her ward to do the same. She introduced legislation into the Chicago City Council that would require developers to set aside 15 percent of their newly constructed or rehabbed units for affordable housing. It is rare that city representatives promote less profitable deals, such as those that include affordable housing or require city subsidies over more profitable, market-rate ones, and Preckwinkle's affordable housing bill was not passed by the city council. But this is also what distinguishes the goals of black middlemen from the more single-minded goals of growth machines. The middleman is the pivot man, and on these occasions the African American city representatives were looking out for the littleman.

Just as the city occasionally eschewed the most profitable use for a piece of land in order to attain a social good, some developers too have underscored their desires to build affordable housing. One developer had a favorite refrain. He wanted to build housing so that people in the neighborhood could "move up without moving out." In 2000, he partnered with the Chicago Department of Housing to build single-family homes for $240,000. This price brought unexpected scrutiny because it was low in comparison to other homes of similar sizes being sold in the neighborhood. "Why not charge more and get less exterior maintenance by making the house full masonry?" asked a council member who had computed the price per square foot at a deflated $100, and wondered why the developer wouldn't add the premier finishes and raise the asking price. Two city representatives intervened: "This program is not looking to compete with all of the high-end products," clarified a Department of Housing official. In an even more concerned tone, a Department of Planning employee added, "I'm a little worried that $240,000 is deemed an 'affordable' product when this house is fully within the design guidelines of the conservation area." A similar exchange occurred regarding another plan to build housing for working families. When a council member objected to a developer building affordable housing on "one of the primest lots in the city," a city representative answered, "This is one way to put the parcel back in development in a sensitive way, to get more affordable housing done, to take some of the control out of the developers' hands, capture some of the resources, and spin on developments." These were moments when toes were mashed, the dance lost its synergy, and it was unclear just who was supposed to be leading the dance toward higher housing profits.

Why is the participation of black middlemen in growth machine politics upwardly aligned? To analyze the character of black middleman activism, one must ask: Who is the primary beneficiary? In the first example of black middlemen using their social and human capital to entice mortgage capital, the first winner is the black newcomers themselves, followed by long-term owners who can access funds that were not previously available to renovate, upgrade, or, if they wish, sell their homes and buildings. All existing residents get to enjoy improved upkeep of the neighborhood's housing stock. Similarly, the first winners in black middlemen's efforts to increase property values are, again, black middlemen themselves. But low- and moderate-income NKO residents are not the secondary beneficiaries in a growth regime because their tenure in the neighborhood is threatened by growth. They are targeted by investors who hassle unsuspecting home owners to sell at low prices; they are victimized by subprime lenders who see the potential profits when someone forecloses; and they are subject to the higher property tax levy, which is especially onerous for residents with fixed and/or low incomes.

Home owner Emma McDaniel was worried about losing her home to a bank with which she had taken out a loan on the house that had been in her family since the 1940s. "I have to scuffle to pay $1,100 a month. It's a lot, honey, and right now my behind is dragging. And by us being off work, I'm sitting here now waiting on unemployment. So, now I'm behind and they're on my behind right now." McDaniel's story was heartbreaking. She pointed admiringly but a bit shamefully to the picture of her mother on the wall above us and told me how her mother never had to take out a loan on the house. "Mama had some money," she said wistfully. "That was a lady, God knows. I pray all the time I wished I was like my mother. Looked like she just pulled money out the woodwork. Mama always had her nest egg where she could fall back on." Without such savings, McDaniel turned to the mortgage market, and the story only got worse from there:

> I had my first loan and I got behind. I called, I told them and I was try-ing to catch up. And at the time I was only $1,500 behind because my mortgage wasn't but $435. So, I just knew that I could catch that up. And do you know I couldn't get this $1,500 from anybody. And so they said, "Okay. We'll foreclose." So I had to go into temporary bankruptcy until this shyster mortgage company put it through this bank and now it's $1,100 a month. And you know, that's a big jump from $435 to $1,100 a month. And honey there's a few people on my job that I talk to and I was telling them. They said that's just too darn much money. And I've been looking in the paper where they said that a lot of loan companies have taken people. And I've been looking for the name of these people, because, honey, this man, I know he got way more money than I did. And he keeps making money because you got to pay $1,100 a month, and he's taking lots of that.

Approaching seventy years old, McDaniel was still working as a bus driver, when she could get the hours and against the advice of her doc-tor, whom she begged to give her clearance on the employment physical. Ms. McDaniel was "panicked," near ready to give up, having recently applied to get federal rental assistance to move into an apartment. "I said if they take my house, I've got to have someplace to go. If I can't get ahold of the money that I owe these people, then, bye, see ya." The most painful part of it all for McDaniel was the memory of her mother. "Honey, it's not a good feeling. It's not a good feeling. And then I feel bad because that was her request. Keep the house. That was my mom's request of me. Would you please keep the house." McDaniel's story does not have a happy ending. I tried to help, making referrals to agencies that dealt with unscrupulous lenders. But it must have been too late because when I went to recontact Ms. McDaniel a few years later, she was gone, her house sold by a bank to a young professional African American couple.

McDaniel's story is not unique. I found out that Mr. Porter, another elderly man I had interviewed, had also lost his house when a newcomer to the neighborhood gave his new address. It was Porter's old address. The newcomer had bought the house from a bank that had foreclosed on him. "Do you know what happened to Mr. Porter?" I asked. "You know I don't. I've heard numerous stories. Someone said he was out in Maywood with family. Someone else said he had gone back to the south with family. And still another group of individuals said they'd seen him in the neighborhood recently."

There are similar stories on the renter's side. George Wade told me, "I had to move because I was in a rush. I needed to move quick because they were sellin' out." Wade was not given any notice by his landlords that they were selling the three-unit building in which he rented an apartment. Instead, he found out from a tenant down the street, who told him nonchalantly one day, "He say, y'all building is on the Internet." This was not a case of rising rents but the more common occurrence of de-conversion, or changing a single-family home *back* into a single-family home after it has been cut up into apartments for many years. Wade moved to an apartment a few blocks away in the subdivided home of an elderly woman, but he was not too optimistic about that situation either. "I believe my landlord will sell out. I believe she's gonna sell. Not now. But she will sell eventually."[29]

Even if poor households do not move out of gentrifying neighborhoods any more than they move out of other kinds of neighborhoods, as the displacement literature finds, when they do move they are replaced by higher-income households, taking that apartment or home off of the market of affordable apartments or homes. Working- and lower-middle-class families who were able to move into NKO in the early years of its renewal are also priced out by rising property values. That is, NKO is essentially off limits to littlemen from outside of the neighborhood who are looking to buy a house. Instead, the big winners are opportunistic mortgage companies, developers who convert apartments into condominiums and whose incomes grow with the sales prices, and the city, for which more high-priced houses translate into more parks, more tourists, more roads, and more incentives to businesses. In sum, then, the role of black professional newcomers to North Kenwood–Oakland as middlemen in the real estate process is a mixed blessing for the neighborhood's littlemen. It brings much needed capital to a neighborhood that had long been neglected, but this renewed attention also spells danger for home owners and renters who are overrun by more savvy investors.

Middleman Me

I have given over fifty presentations on my research in North Kenwood–Oakland. Many of them were in Chicago, many of them to organizations and groups that oversaw, advocated, or protested the changes occurring in North Kenwood–Oakland. Some days I donned a suit (or something close) to attend downtown briefings on public housing policy, and other days I dressed casually to interview residents of public housing. At Conservation Community Council meetings, I listened like a student to the perplexing definition and purpose of a tax increment financing (TIF) district; the next day I went to my office to do my own research on TIFs, and by the next week I was using it as an example to undergraduates in an Intro to Urban Sociology class. When I worked with a bank to buy a house in North Kenwood in 1998 (at a price that contributed to the rising housing costs), I felt like I was experiencing racial discrimination. I was so angry that I wrote a complaint to the vice president of my university, who managed the relationship with the bank. I ultimately got the financing, but not without some strong diplomacy. I am a newcomer to North Kenwood (and Chicago); I bring a laptop to CCC meetings to take notes; I am funded by the MacArthur Foundation; my friends have moved into NKO after me; and with my Ivy League BA and University of Chicago PhD, I am no littleman in the neighborhood. I am a middleman.

Just as other black brokers exploit their own professional talents—bankers bring money, educators fix schools, architects monitor aesthetics, city workers get the streets fixed—I trade on my ability to "profess." Doing this research, I have had access to many audiences and been involved in diverse forums. In some I am the expert and in others I am an untutored neophyte, but in all of them I am a *participant* observer and it is my voice that is requested and respected. Being a "professor" in this somewhat altered sense of the word is not a straightforward task when it comes to the changes in North Kenwood–Oakland because the purpose of my research has been to uncover the multiple voices within and thus visions for the neighborhood. My representation of these perspectives requires conscious decisions and interpretations. The result is not always coherent. The schizophrenic "case for/case against" chapters of this book illustrate this complexity, as do the examples below. My professions are, however, always informed by some piece of local insight, no doubt refracted through and by me, but no less informed. I broker knowledge, tastes, and fears by speaking up in community meetings with the words given to me by interviewees who never attend CCC meetings but are residents nonetheless, or by conveying information from one community meeting to another, or by lecturing to foundation program officers on the racism that affects middle-class blacks, or by writing this book.

Let me give an example of the kind of "information arbitrage," as sociologist Ronald Burt has called it, in which I have engaged during my research. In 2002, at a downtown meeting on the status of the Chicago Housing Authority's Plan for Transformation, I asked a question about the income mix of the new development that was replacing the demolished Lakefront Properties public housing project and was told, rather flippantly, by a CHA official that the information I had stated in my question was incorrect. When someone else asked for further clarification, the official, whom I will call Mr. Holmes, referred to me as "this lady," as in "I'm not sure where *this lady* is getting her information, but there is no income tiering in the new CHA developments." In fact, however, there is income tiering at the two developments being built in Oakland. The court-issued "revitalizing area" order that allowed new public housing to be built in Oakland (see chapter 5) read in part: "One-half of the public housing units developed pursuant to subparagraphs (a) and (b) above shall be occupied by families whose incomes are in the range of 50–80% of the median income in the Chicago Metropolitan Area."[30] The city's directions to developers wanting to build the mixed-income developments repeated that stipulation: "Half of the public housing units on the site must be reserved for public housing-eligible families with incomes below 50% of the area median income ('AMI'). The remaining half of the public housing units on the site must be reserved for public housing eligible-families with incomes between 50% and 80% of AMI."[31] Having dug up these facts, I wrote an e-mail later that day in which I reported these guidelines to Mr. Holmes, cited the sources, and name-dropped the people who confirmed my information. "Please excuse my obsession with the particularities of Lake Park Crescent and Jazz on the Boulevard," I wrote, "but I have much interest in having my facts right. I am a resident of North Kenwood–Oakland (NKO), a member of the North Kenwood–Oakland Conservation Community Council (CCC), and an academic researcher studying the processes of change in the area. Hence, I die by the details." Holmes, who had been in his job for only eight months, sent me an e-mail back with one line of gratitude.

This exchange is noteworthy not primarily for the specific information at issue. The condition that half of the public housing units be reserved for working- and middle-class families (50–80% of the median family income in the Chicago metro area is roughly $35,000–$55,000 in 2004 dollars) was in response to the demands of North Kenwood Oakland's middle-class newcomers. But being their mouthpiece was not my intent in setting the CHA official straight. Instead, I was inspired to write because of a comment made by Terry Peterson, CEO of the Chicago Housing Authority, earlier in the same meeting. His remarks subtly belittled the suspicions that public housing residents held about the Plan for Transformation. My e-mail to Holmes also conveyed this point:

> I feel much relieved about getting to the bottom of this. . . . But, it is also a lesson learned. Terry Peterson spoke in the meeting about always having to "combat the misinformation," most of which we assume to be on the side of the CHA residents. But sometimes, we "residents" are right, or at least we have been told what we think we know by actual spokespeople for the redevelopment process. And hence, we must remember to respect the knowledge that all parties have, and hopefully get to the bottom of all disagreements.

In this example, I was only bringing to light details that were already in the possession of the CHA staff, and that were indeed a part of their own negotiations. I was neither translating nor relaying an opposing viewpoint or community sentiment. Yet I still intended to empower public housing residents by my actions because for a moment I was a littleman, dismissed as an uninformed agitator. I was a downwardly aligned middleman using my access to court documents, lawyers on the case, and a computer with e-mail to hopefully broker some appreciation for the claims of public housing residents. And I forwarded my letter to six other people to increase the impact.

My allegiances were not always with the littleman, however. As a member of the Conservation Community Council for the second half of this study I have not been allowed to simply record and interpret the activities in North Kenwood–Oakland. I've had to cast my vote. The CCC is the forum in which all proposed developments are presented. One such proposal was for a land swap between the City of Chicago and the Chicago Housing Authority. The city wanted land owned by the CHA in the North Lawndale neighborhood as the site for a residential campus for people with HIV/AIDS. The CHA wanted land owned by the city in Oakland to complete the redevelopment of the Ida B. Wells public housing project. At issue for the CCC was whether the CHA should be allowed to acquire more (property-tax exempt) land than it already owned in the North Kenwood–Oakland Conservation Area.

When it was my turn to ask a question, I raised a concern that had been initiated several years earlier by black middle-class newcomers to the neighborhood. At the time, these gentrifiers had argued passionately that black neighborhoods were overburdened with public housing while white neighborhoods seemed spared this civic charge. As I discuss in chapter 5, not only was this the argument of middle-class blacks in this neighborhood, but it is also a robust finding in the social science literature that middle-class blacks live with and near more poor families than similar whites. I reasoned that transferring more land in North Kenwood–Oakland to the CHA would only perpetuate these racial inequalities. "Given that the CHA is having so many problems developing public housing in other parts of the city, namely white neighborhoods, why wouldn't the CHA swap for city-owned land in those parts of the city?" I asked the CHA representative. Alderman Preckwinkle gave the answer: To her disappointment, no alderman in a predominantly white ward (or a predominantly black middle-class ward) would agree to swap city land for CHA land. That is, all of the other aldermen were exercising their "not in my back yard" prerogative when it came to public housing. "We need to distribute new units around the city, and the mayor needs to take leadership on this issue," asserted the alderman, indicating that she agreed that black neighborhoods alone shouldered the responsibility of supplying public housing but also that she was powerless to change the fact. This proved my point. In voting to approve the land swap, we yielded to the doggedness with which those other politicians continued to thwart court-ordered desegregation goals for public housing.

I ultimately abstained on the motion. I did not want to signal any lack of support for the public housing redevelopment within North Kenwood–Oakland with a negative vote, and I also wanted to support the city's efforts to build an HIV/AIDS residential community. But I needed to register the voices of black middle-class home owners concerned both about the suppression of their own personal property values and the discriminatory constriction of black wealth more generally. Here I used my voice to express allegiance with other middlemen in NKO, who were still treated as littlemen in the racial hierarchy through the systematic oppression of black neighborhoods because they are black.

Finally, I have at times acted against the interests of the littleman. While I love urban living, I also love my car, and I like to be able to drive it without being snarled in traffic. This means that I have preferences against high densities. The conservation plan to which the CCC adheres puts limits on the number of housing units that can be built on the various plots of vacant land in the neighborhood. But those constraints have made it increasingly impossible for developers to make a profit because land prices have risen so dramatically. Because prices do not increase in a linear fashion with dwelling sizes, developers can make considerably more money by selling twenty one-thousand-square-foot condos than they can by selling ten two-thousand-square-foot condos. To pay for the land, then, developers need to sell more units. The only way to keep new investments flowing is to increase density. Or so we CCC members are told by the developers and the city representatives.

But density has two faces. In addition to ensuring developer profits, it also allows for more affordable housing. Indeed, municipalities that expressly do not want affordable housing within their boundaries use density restrictions as tools for keeping it out. Fitting smaller units tightly onto less land translates into lower prices for buyers. This would benefit the littleman (or at least men and women with lower salaries than my own). Therefore, when I raise objections to developers who present proposals before the CCC to build at higher densities, which I frequently do, I am pushing them to build fewer bigger units instead. My aversion to high densities drives up the prices of new homes, contributing to the gentrification of the neighborhood. In such instances, I have aligned with the man.

Can a middleman be bought? There is no question that where my allegiances lie as a middleman could be related to the funding of my research. The MacArthur Foundation gave me $150,000 to conduct the research in North Kenwood–Oakland. All of that money did not go directly to me. Some of it paid college and graduate research assistants, some bought computers, software, books, and other materials, some of it sent me to conferences to present my findings, and some of it went to the people I interviewed in the neighborhood, each of whom received $25 as a gesture of appreciation for sharing their stories with me. Northwestern University got 10 percent of it for what is called "overhead," the time I spent in my office with the lights on and air conditioner running, using their Internet connection, and working at a desk supplied by the university.

My relationship with the MacArthur Foundation was first and foremost self-interested. Middle-class brokers do the work of translation, negotiation, and the delivery of goods, but rarely without some form of compensation. Mine came in the form of extra salary during the summer and funds to have someone else transcribe the interviews, dig in the library for obscure newspaper articles on microfilm, and research the intricacies of the Housing Act of 1998. This financial arrangement clearly aligned me with the man. To be sure, MacArthur Foundation staff never asked me to change anything I wrote or to "profess" some point that my research did not support. On the contrary, they were completely hands-off when it came to my research. Still, I cannot help but be influenced by them. In its community development ideology, the MacArthur Foundation strongly supports mixed-income strategies that valorize middle-class residents, especially in the transformation of public housing.[32] In that respect, the foundation is, however unwittingly, a party to the dispossession and shuffling of poor families around the city in order to make way for gentrifiers. By requesting and accepting their sponsorship, I am also implicated in this philosophy.

As I have argued, the mixed-income approach overlooks the deeper problems of skyrocketing inequalities between corporate owners and workers (which yield the kind of wealth that the foundation now redistributes) or the meager government funding for the basic human need of shelter and other social welfare provisions. Addressing these societal injustices is not within the scope of work defined by the foundation. Nor is it within the scope of the City of Chicago or of the Conservation Community Council. Each of these players, like many of us, continues to toil diligently and sometimes admirably in the constricted space of local remedies, representing the littleman, the middleman, or the man.

In North Kenwood–Oakland black middle-class brokers—who mean well in their valiant efforts to bring resources and services to a poor black neighborhood—traverse the space between the often unharnessed power of poor and working-class black old-timers and the highly organized machine, or "white power," of elected officials, philanthropists, businessmen, and developers. I am caught in that middle as well, alternately refusing, fumbling with, and wielding the master's tools.

4

When the North Kenwood–Oakland Conservation Plan was approved in 1992, there were three operating public elementary schools and one public high school in the neighborhood, all with abysmal records. When Mayor Richard M. Daley took control of the schools in 1995, the four-year graduation rate at the high school was only 58 percent. Twenty-three percent of the students there were chronically truant. In 1995, at Price Elementary School in North Kenwood fewer than 10 percent of the students were performing at or above national norms in reading and math. The students at Robinson, the elementary school in Oakland, performed only marginally better. The third elementary school was closed for low enrollment. It is no secret that high on the list of the things that people think about when choosing a neighborhood is schools. The schools in North Kenwood–Oakland in the early days of its revitalization were hardly attractive choices. What could be done?

The public discourse of school reform always emphasizes improving educational options for all families, including low-income residents. The available reform tools, however—schools with selective enrollment criteria, charter schools, small schools—make school reform more exclusive than its rhetoric suggests. Though none of these strategies "privatizes" public education, as critics often assert, each of the options available to North Kenwood–Oakland activists puts limits on the ability of neighborhood families to take advantage of the new schools. This is the power structure under which black brokers must operate. These were the "master's tools" with which newcomer brokers tried to dismantle years of educational violence against North Kenwood–Oakland's children.[1]

The framework I employ here extends the middleman concept and adds to it a discussion of the contemporary emphasis in urban governance on "choice" and the personal initiative of residents, who must choose from the array of resources available from the state. The model has changed from one in which cities "deliver" public services like education, health care, and protection from crime, to one in which residents "shop for" these goods in a service landscape that includes more nongovernmental, private subcontractors. An informant in Eric Klinenberg's analysis of the 1995 heat wave in Chicago, in which over seven hundred people died, said that the tragedy was an example of "murder by public policy." The public policies that this informant indicted, like those indicted in the aftermath of Hurricane Katrina ten years later, were characteristic of an era of "reinvented government, administered with techniques and system values honed in the private sector and recently adapted to public institutions." Klinenberg refers to this new approach to urban service provision as the "entrepreneurial state," but in its general (and more global) guise it is referred to as "neoliberalism," or the promotion of unfettered free markets. "The embrace of public-private partnerships, deregulation, fiscal austerity, cross-subsidies, and market solutions have been characterized as a form of urban neoliberalism," writes geographer Nicholas Blomley. Political scientists Neil Brenner and Nik Theodore make the case that neoliberal ideologies can only be understood by investigating their local manifestations, where reliance on the market interacts with particular national, state, or municipal policy regimes, personalities, and histories.

Going back to the local, to what Brenner and Theodore call "actually existing neoliberalism," is what Klinenberg did to explain the extreme death toll of the heat wave in Chicago, and what other scholars have done in analyzing urban labor markets, governance structures, gentrification, and school reform. For example, in line with the thrust of this chapter, Arlene Dávila's study of the gentrification of Spanish Harlem tracks the debates over the opening of a charter school that would be managed by a private, for-profit corporation, Edison Schools, Inc. The proposal, despite its failure, was illustrative of the neoliberal belief that the private sector can offer a product that is superior to what is available in the public sector because it is less encumbered by legislative regulations, union contracts, and requirements for local participation.[2]

The critique of this new direction in urban governance and service provision focuses on the inequalities that often accompany such an approach. While regulations may constrain the flexibility that actors desire in order to experiment with best practices, they also exist to forestall dangerous experimentation or to make sure that the least powerful constituents are not left behind. Labor agreements may keep some workers on the job whose performance is less than stellar, but they also ensure decent pay and benefits, reasonable work hours and environments, and protection for workers from capricious hiring and firing decisions. And lay stakeholders may be unruly or simply a pain, but they represent an indispensable knowledge base in any effort aimed at improving their lives.

The particular inequality-producing properties of neoliberalism on which I focus in this chapter are those based on various levels of exclusion, often of people who are most in need of inclusion. As Klinenberg writes, the neoliberal managerial strategy "disproportionately empowers residents who are already endowed with the forms of social and cultural capital necessary to navigate through bureaucratic systems while in effect . . . punishing people who are least likely to have the social skills and resources necessary to obtain goods and services that they are most likely to need." In North Kenwood–Oakland, it is the middle- and upper-income newcomers who are best positioned to take advantage of new schools envisioned under the rubric of the entrepreneurial state. This explains why they utilize their brokerage positions to foster such innovations in the neighborhood, energized by the overly optimistic expectation that their less-advantaged neighbors will be similarly equipped to get with the new program. The intentions are benign, and in many respects the routes taken by middle-class school brokers in North Kenwood–Oakland are the only ones possible as the city, state, and federal governments imagine a public school system in which involving private-sector partners improves the choices that parents have. Still, the limitations of such an approach exacerbate and reproduce already existing class inequalities in access to quality educations.

Education professor Pauline Lipman, who studies the reform of Chicago's schools, similarly acknowledges the laudable goals of all those involved, despite gravely unequal results:

Current CPS policies represent a convergence of interests of financial elites and the city's political regime. But they are supported and accomplished by well-meaning educators at all levels of the school system, as well as many Chicagoans, operating out of a shared common sense that the policies will improve schools. This common sense is constructed out of real hopes and frustrations. It is bolstered by CPS's rhetoric of equity and resoluteness and the pragmatic logic of a quick fix through the blunt force of sanctions and punishment. Unequal educational experiences are rendered less visible by establishing standards and tests that promise equal treatment and rigor. Although new advanced academic programs involve a very small percentage of students, their well-advertised initiation serves to legitimate the current policy regime even as it helps to develop the city as a concentrated expression of new global inequalities.[3]

There is no question that something had to be done to remedy the disgraceful state of the schools in North Kenwood–Oakland. There is also no question that the activists who put in the hard work to make a difference wanted to improve the educational options available to parents. But the philosophies of reform rested on the logic of options rather than uniform excellence, on choice rather than universal provision, and on parents' ability to shop rather than the public sector's responsibility to deliver.

New Schools for All . . . Who Can Get In

The efforts in North Kenwood–Oakland were but one part of widespread changes in public school administration in the city of Chicago overall, sparked by the 1995 mayoral "takeover" of the public schools. With bipartisan support in the state legislature, Mayor Richard M. Daley won the right to independently manage the Chicago Public Schools (CPS), to decrease the size of the Chicago Board of Education, and to name both its members and the Chief Executive Officer of Schools. The change in the top school administrator's title, from superintendent to CEO, is a powerful symbolic indication of the new market model in which educational performance and accountability are grounded.

The educational initiatives in NKO happened in tandem with, and in many ways were reflections of, reforms at the city and state level, and were not completely restricted to the arena of schools. The consolidation of power under Mayor Daley meant that the same city leadership that was transforming public housing and enabling the resurgence of home buying and building in NKO was also addressing the poorly performing schools. All three endeavors were in the service of making Chicago an attractive place to live and work, and especially attractive to the middle class. In the cases of public housing and school reform the strategies were basically the same: clear the high-rises of their residents and the poorly performing schools of their students and then start from scratch. The infusion of middle-income families and children into the replacement buildings and schools would then encourage, pull up, support, or "overshadow" those poor neighbors and classmates who were able to return.

Like the mayor's administration, the alderman and the Conservation Community Council in North Kenwood–Oakland knew that good schools were crucial for attracting higher-income home buyers. As a result, efforts coalesced around the transformation of two existing schools: the closing of Shakespeare Elementary School, to be reopened as two separate schools—Ariel Community Academy and the North Kenwood/Oakland Charter School—and the closure of Martin Luther King Jr. High School, to be reopened as Martin Luther King Jr. College Prep High School. The three resulting schools are essentially brand new, with completely new student bodies and rehabilitated buildings. Two other elementary schools in the neighborhood—Price and Robinson—have been the target of small-scale improvement efforts but remain neighborhood schools with general admissions, and high school students who cannot gain admission to King College Prep are sent to a nearby (low-performing) high school that has general admissions. After giving the histories of each of these efforts, I discuss the importance of black middle-class brokers to their implementation and examine how each reform strategy featured some level of exclusion. The stories illustrate the policy constraints within which brokers and their allies must operate, and how those constraints can create a gulf between intent and result, in this case in the form of limits on the scope of beneficiaries.

Ariel Community Academy is named after the first black-owned money-management firm in the country, Ariel Capital Management. Ariel's headquarters are in Chicago, and its founder and board chairman, John Rogers Jr., comes from a prestigious black Chicago family. In 1991, the Ariel Foundation established the I Have a Dream Program, which adopted the sixth-grade class at Shakespeare Elementary School in North Kenwood and committed to seeing its students through college, promising college scholarships as an incentive.[4] Two years after the program's inception, in the students' eighth-grade year, the Chicago Public Schools closed Shakespeare because of low enrollment. I Have a Dream staffers scrambled to find school placements for the nearly forty eighth graders that would further support their college-bound aspirations. Given the poor quality of the city's public schools, they ended up placing nearly all of their students in Catholic schools. "We were just looking for anything above what I considered educational malpractice," remembered Sarah Duncan, the program's director. "Most of the Catholic schools represented at least one step above that." While they got good "bulk" deals on tuition at the Catholic schools, it was a frustrating expenditure of resources and a sobering recognition that there were no free, public schools of high quality available to the students in their program.

The experience stirred the idea among Ariel Foundation employees of opening a school of their own. The Dreamers, as the students were called, would not directly benefit from a new school, but the Ariel staff was just as concerned about the next generation of neighborhood youth. When the group got a generous gift from an anonymous donor, staff from the Ariel Foundation and other volunteers began hammering out concrete plans for opening a new school. Things moved quickly, and reforms at the city level created opportunities for outside organizations to run public schools under a program called the small schools initiative. By 1995 they were submitting an application to CPS for a small school in North Kenwood, and they were open for business by the 1996–1997 school year. At that time, the "small schools" movement was just beginning and the definition of the concept was still evolving. In the early years, there were no caps on class size or total enrollment. Also, small schools were not defined by local attendance boundaries and were required to accept students citywide, but now schools like Ariel can use "neighborhood preferences" in admissions.[5]

This is but a skeletal sketch of the complex web of interactions, friendships, and influence that was necessary to open Ariel Community Academy in North Kenwood. Within these efficacious networks were black middlemen of considerable accomplishment. Given his financial, political, and civic stature, it would be disrespectful to label John Rogers Jr. as a middleman. The son of Jewel LaFontant—a prominent Chicago lawyer and presidential appointee in the Eisenhower, Nixon, and George H. W. Bush administrations—and Judge John Rogers Sr., he is much closer to, if not a part of, the central coalition of business and civic elites than most middlemen in NKO. But this too is part of the story of racial politics in contemporary Chicago, as a second and third genera-tion of African American professionals are becoming as entrenched as the dynasties of white ethnic power brokers before them. They are no longer a new hue on the political landscape, and they have been raised with the privileges of elite schools and lucrative contacts. Their names invoke lineages of engagement and activism that comprise an inner circle of black Chicagoans past and present who have been deal makers across the racial divide.[6] These are brokers who do not need to make re-quests of a (white) superior in order to deliver. The decision rests with them. For example, when Ariel had no building in which to open the new school, John Rogers Jr., then chairman of the Chicago Park District, facilitated the use of the Kennicott Park building in North Kenwood until the Shakespeare building could be renovated.

Because he himself has no immediate ties to the neighborhood, John Rogers Jr.'s involvement in North Kenwood–Oakland is not too unlike most relatively impersonal corporate philanthropy. He did not appear at local meetings as plans for the school were being presented and ham-mered out. He did not deliver any passionate speeches to the first fami-lies who enrolled. He was a stealth patron, lending his name, his con-tacts, his staff, and his influence when it was necessary. In an interesting flip of racial positioning, the only familiar faces of Ariel's involvement in the neighborhood were Sarah and Arne Duncan, a white brother and sister duo from neighboring Hyde Park. The Duncan siblings spent much of their childhood at a church in North Kenwood where their mother, Sue Duncan, had run an after-school program since 1961, and so they felt a commitment to education in the neighborhood.[7] When the siblings came back to Chicago after graduating from Harvard Uni-versity, they took up positions with the Ariel Foundation, including running the I Have a Dream Program, and when it came time to adopt a class, they chose the sixth graders from the school with which their mother had so long been involved. Sarah and Arne Duncan's partici-pation was key since the program's anonymous donor had previously been a benefactor of their mother's tutoring program.

The I Have a Dream program also tapped the expertise and commit-ment of several black professionals who worked for the Ariel Founda-tion or served as mentors for the program's students. The Duncan sib-lings were the ironic "local" faces (although neither lived in NKO), but there was also a group of dedicated black professional women who were equally instrumental in putting together the proposal for the new school. All of these players represent crisscrossing associations formed at the University of Chicago Lab School and Princeton and Harvard Universities, on basketball courts, in childhood neighborhoods, and through marriages and family relations, producing an interracial cadre of energetic, twenty-something do-gooders with the financial backing to make something happen. "As young, naïve people we thought: this is ridiculous, anybody can do better than this," summed up Sarah Duncan, capturing their acute disappointment with the public school system and their bold and optimistic plan to make a difference. In the creation of Ariel Community Academy, there was not one middleman. Instead, the unofficial collaboration of black John Rogers Jr.'s philanthropy and white Sue Duncan's community involvement provided an umbrella under which the school could be born. Black professionals affiliated with the Ariel Foundation were key participants in the germination and implementation of ideas for changing the educational landscape of NKO. "It was very impressive people that were around the table," remarked Ruanda Garth, the Ariel School community liaison, about the lively planning process. This seat at the table is part of the job description of the middleman, and it explains how such people could broker new resources for the neighborhood from a public school system that was then in the midst of a takeover by the mayor's office.

The second educational initiative in NKO was the University of Chicago's North Kenwood/Oakland Charter School. The university had long been involved in after-school tutoring in and around Hyde Park through the Neighborhood Schools Program. In 1988, it got more actively involved in teaching and curricular issues through the Center for School Improvement. The center focused on teacher-training programs and on developing educational models that could reform whole schools. Yet even given the university's world-class reputation, few local schools were willing to turn over the administrative reigns to the center for its educational experiments. Like the Ariel school concept, the university charter school notion was born of frustration with what could be accomplished within the existing public school mold. And again like Ariel, changes afoot at the city and state levels offered new public education possibilities. In 1996, the state of Illinois passed the Charter Schools Law to "create a legitimate avenue for parents, teachers, and community members to take responsible risks and create new, innovative, and more flexible ways of educating children within the public school system." Later legislation authorized sixty charters across the state (in the early years an organization could open more than one school under a single charter), with no more than thirty to be granted in Chicago. *Charter schools are public schools,* "open to any pupil who resides within the geographic boundaries of the area served by the local school board." They cannot charge tuition or set admissions criteria. But they are governed independently by the board of directors of the entity that runs them, as opposed to being managed and overseen by the local school board.[8]

The university turned to this legislation as an avenue to open a new school in which it could set the curriculum, hire the teachers, and put together the various reform pieces that were then scattered across the seven separate schools with which its staff worked. The university was already affiliated with a private school, the University of Chicago Lab School, but in this undertaking was explicitly interested in developing high-quality *public* education that would benefit students in the nearby low-performing schools in an inclusive manner.[9] This foray into the schools followed similar ventures by the university in community planning and crime and safety, as discussed elsewhere in this book.

Alderman Toni Preckwinkle, a University of Chicago alumna, was influential in offering North Kenwood–Oakland as a possible site for the university's new public school. Shakespeare Elementary had just closed, so an empty school building sat waiting for an infusion of ideas and resources. And the Conservation Community Council gave the community's unanimous blessing to the university's designs.[10] In this case, black elected officials and community leaders in North Kenwood–Oakland clearly brokered the institutional interest of the University of Chicago in addressing failing public schools by steering that interest to their neighborhood, but all were constrained to work with the particular tool available. The university's vision required substantial autonomy, which was possible under the charter school legislation. What was not possible at the time, however, was making the school a *local* school. The initial charter school legislation did not allow for neighborhood preferences but required that schools be open to students from across the city. This stipulation was conceived to thwart the ability of elite neighborhoods to create their own little school havens, but the effect for charter schools in poor neighborhoods was the possibility that they would be overrun by outside, nonpoor families enthusiastic to have a decent public school option for their children. If that were to happen, the local benefits would be significantly diluted.

When the North Kenwood/Oakland Charter School first opened, roughly 60 percent of the student body came from outside the neighborhood. The school's directors tried hard to keep it as local as possible. They got permission not to provide bus service, so as to discourage outsiders, and they only recruited in the immediate area. Still, an "amazing underground" of information about educational options got the word out beyond the neighborhood's borders, prompting the school to have to be even more "aggressive" in marketing to local parents.[11]

Since new housing and new schools were indelibly intertwined, the new schools got some help in their marketing campaign from the builders of new homes. As if the construction sites and the smell of new lumber were not enough to signal the rebuilding of NKO, the private developers of nearly a hundred new homes and condominiums across the street from Shakespeare School, recognizing the synergy of homes and schools, posted a banner on the abandoned school building that read "Future Home of North Kenwood/Oakland Charter School." "I'll tell you what the developers did around here," reported one of the charter school's early staff members. "They put a big sign up on this building before we even moved in here. They did that. We didn't do it. They did it because that was the appeal." School revitalization and housing construction were mutually reinforcing signs of neighborhood change. One seemed impossible without the other. At the same time, people who could afford the expensive homes that were being built would never send their children to the unreformed local public schools, but they would love not to have to pay private school tuition. Banker Shannon Howard looked cautiously into the future of her child's education. "We'll see what happens once my kid gets to be school age. At this point, I kind of think he's going to private school, but it would be nice to not have to foot that bill. But it just depends. You can't really take a chance on education today." Residents like Mrs. Howard would have to be convinced of the excellence of the local public schools before they sent their children there, and the University of Chicago believed it could bring about that change of heart.

The final NKO school intervention was the conversion of King High School to King College Prep, a magnet high school for high-achieving students, officially known as a "selective enrollment school." King actually underwent two reforms. First, in 1997, King High School was "reconstituted," which in Chicago school reform parlance was the most drastic intervention possible. For King, it meant that half of its teachers were replaced and a completely new administration installed. The impetus for these actions was King's chronic poor performance. For the 1996–1997 school year, daily school attendance was at 70 percent, total student enrollment was less than half of the building's capacity, fewer than 60 percent of the students graduated in four years, and only 7 percent of students met state testing standards in reading. Post-reconstitution indicators showed very slow improvement in test scores and a steady decline in enrollment. This prompted a second intervention. In his announcement of the plans to turn King into a magnet high school, Chicago school board president Gery Chico remarked, "We're frustrated with King's failures. This is our way of getting some value out of the school."[12]

The name change and accompanying shift from a general education curriculum to a college preparatory curriculum might entice one to see this conversion as an unambiguously positive step. But King's conversion was even more drastic. Beginning in the fall of 1999, the school stopped accepting freshman. As the 1971 modernist building gradually emptied, construction crews moved in for a complete multimillion-dollar renovation. King reopened in the fall of 2002 with two hundred freshman, selected from a pool of more than a thousand applicants, all with above-average standardized tests scores. Unlike the two new elementary schools, the new King College Prep was unabashedly "selective."

Could local students meet King College Prep's new, higher admissions standards? When the school reopened in 2002, the first hurdle for admission was scoring at or above the national average on the Iowa Test of Basic Skills in both reading and math—a minimum of 229 in reading and 231 in math. At Price Elementary School, which shared a campus with King, the average standardized test score for seventh graders was 225 in both areas:. fewer than half of the Price students could even apply for King. Mean test scores at two other nearby elementary schools were similarly below the application threshold.[13] Qualifying to apply is only the first step in an admissions process that also requires a separate entrance exam, seventh-grade report cards, and attendance records. King College Prep—where each classroom was wired with a bank of new computers, and the recreational facilities included gymnastics equipment and a newly refurbished swimming pool—was essentially closed to more than half of North Kenwood–Oakland's local students. And then only one out of seven students who were qualified to apply got in. In its first freshman class, 13 percent of the students were from elementary schools in Hyde Park and Kenwood (including three students from the North Kenwood/Oakland Charter School), and 24 percent were from the Bronzeville area, the black communities to the west of North Kenwood–Oakland.[14]

The conversion of King High School was not a top-down affair. North Kenwood–Oakland had a well-placed ally in the CPS bureaucracy. Arne Duncan, who was already fully involved in education in the neighborhood through the I Have a Dream program and the Ariel Community Academy, became the project manager for magnet schools in 1998 and deputy chief of staff at Chicago Public Schools in 1999. As Alderman Preckwinkle and members of the CCC "were beginning to have real issues and concerns with regard to attracting home buyers to the area who had teenage young people, and where they would go to school" they began discussions with Duncan "with regard to creating a desirable high school for the area."[15] NKO's rebirth was synchronous with Mayor Daley's educational overhaul, which included a new magnet school for each of the city's six educational regions. Given Daley's plans, a magnet school was the most feasible means by which to achieve the end of improving King High School.

Whereas brokers in North Kenwood–Oakland saw themselves as forward-looking in considering the high school needs of newcomers, area real estate agents reported that most of their business came from young singles, childless couples, and younger families. Thus few newcomers had kids in King, and most were unaffected when it stopped being a local school. This explained the eerie silence as King died and was reborn. With no stake in its present and unanimous disapproval of its past, newcomers could more easily support a plan that would clean it out, commencing a new history for the high school as a school of choice. Alderman Preckwinkle remarked at the school's rededication ceremony that King had been "an embarrassment to me because in performance it was always near the bottom in the state and high school rankings. If we do not have quality public schools, we'll lose the working and middle-class families who are the backbone of the city."[16] While the alderman hid nothing in her explanation of why King needed so badly to be transformed, the problem facing Preckwinkle and officials citywide was not so much *losing* working- and middle-class families as *attracting* and *accommodating* them.

Overall, the changes at King High School, as well as the creation of Ariel Community Academy and the North Kenwood/Oakland Charter School, show a community wrestling with the realities that, while the existing schools were not justly serving the children in the neighborhood, the tools available for reforming them were also limited in their ability to deliver decent education in an equitable manner. Both the University of Chicago and the Ariel Foundation expressed a fervent desire to serve the low-income students who lived in North Kenwood–Oakland. The leadership of both schools has commented in hindsight that they did not anticipate how rapidly the neighborhood would change, and how much they would be unintentionally complicit in urging it on. When North Kenwood/Oakland Charter School came close to having half of its students *not* eligible for free and reduced lunches (that is, *not* low-income), the administration got worried. "A lot of schools would welcome what we're trying to avoid," remarked the charter school's director about its becoming attractive to middle-income parents.[17] But the designers of the university's charter school were not so excited, since their goal was to show success at a public school that looked like any other in Chicago, where 85 percent of the students are low-income. Hence, in this brief overview of the three new schools in the neighborhood, the contradictions between goals and results are already evident. In some cases, reformers were cognizant of the fact that the masters' tools—charter schools, small schools, and magnet schools—were exclusionary on some levels. Yet the imperatives of gentrification demanded some good schools *now*, even if only for a few, rather than good schools later for all.

The Local Debates against School Reform

In the overarching formulation of this book, one resident's anticipation is another's suspicion. All three of the new school proposals were questioned and contested by neighborhood residents, and each school evoked a unique objection: Ariel was the harbinger of gentrification, the charter school was another example of university experimentation on poor black communities, and King represented exclusionary upgrading. All three schools required the help of black middle-class brokers and their white allies to smooth the way. All three schools ultimately require that parents have the wherewithal to find out about and "choose" the superior options they offer. All three controversies root the local experiences of school reform within a larger discussion of the responsibilities of the state to provide for its citizens, and the balance between public sector delivery and individual responsibility.

Ariel Community Academy was the first of the new schools to open, and as a result it was at the center of what the coordinator of I Have a Dream remembers as a "really harrowing fight." The bulk of the battle involved turf issues over the use of Kennicott Park facilities for the school. As Ariel added a new class every year, it took over more and more space for classrooms and recreation, limiting the time available for general community use and closing off access to parts of the park entirely. This sparked considerable anger. The conflagration over space in the park typifies the battles over space that ensue when outside organizations come into the neighborhood with flashy plans to elevate its residents' quality of life. The fear of displacement at the park proper was one component of the fear of displacement from the neighborhood more generally. Each new proposal, program, and Parade of Homes, as the first new market-rate housing showcase was called, requires a place to put it. But space is a finite resource. Since there are already schools and homes and parks and people in North Kenwood–Oakland, either some people will be squeezed out to make room, or everyone will have to live, learn, and play just a bit more snugly. Usually, as was the case with Kennicott Park, a bit of both happens. While Ariel's daytime use of classrooms squeezed out community groups that would otherwise have used them, the money that Ariel brought in for after-school programs helped support existing park activities and the two after-school programs essentially merged (snugging up).

In retrospect, Ruanda Garth, the community liaison for Ariel School, saw clearly the roots of the community's reservations about the new school. "We had to get past the [Park] Advisory Board and the CCC," she remembers, and these were not easy feats:

> The Advisory Board was just not trusting of the school. They basically saw what is now happening in the community. We were one of the first waves of that. I was saying, what's wrong? When I went there, there's nothing but empty lots. Shakespeare's closed, everything that is now a townhouse was a burned-out lot. And I'm thinking, why wouldn't you want something? But they knew what was coming, and I was naïve in saying why wouldn't you want a school. I'd go to the meetings and they were just so contentious. And everything they said they were worried about, happened.

As a graduate student at the University of Chicago, Garth was a black middleman-in-training. While she was a racial insider, she was a reputational outsider. She had just recently moved to Chicago and had no experience in North Kenwood–Oakland aside from being an I Have a Dream mentor. Despite this, she represented the confidence with which black middlemen approach their projects. Having diagnosed the neighborhood with a closed school and vacant land, the school she touted was clearly part of the cure. Looking back, she recognizes that her eyes were bright and clouded at the same time. She was filled with the enthusiasm of making a difference in a neighborhood that needed a lot of differences but blind to a future in which some people would not fit after the change. Her reflections draw attention to the knowledge-base of the littleman, which is often disregarded by middlemen. This is not to say that Ariel Community Academy has not done good work in the neighborhood. It definitely has. But along with the other schools and the rash of high-end development it has fueled a revitalization that has no brakes. This is what opponents foresaw when all Garth saw was burned-out lots in need of improvement.

Garth also recognizes that she lacked community legitimacy. The primary asset of a successful black middleman is his or her legitimacy. The Ariel initiative had a hard time identifying a spokesperson who could garner residents' trust. None of the primary planners lived or had lived in NKO. None had gone to Chicago Public Schools. While their symbolic sponsor, John Rogers Jr., was black, the school was clearly an interracial effort. The black team members had racial legitimacy, and because of that they were dispatched to community meetings as the face of Ariel Community Academy. But they were not indigenous. And they were clearly not littlemen. "Kendall and I are not of them," Garth said, explaining why neither she nor another black woman who was centrally involved in the initiative could be an effective broker. "Kendall is Ms. Princeton Grad and so they looked at her as the token [black person] sent to the meeting." The black community is not blind in its racial loyalty, and dark bodies alone do not command approval. Black middlemen have to bring something else to the table: community credentials, family affiliations, a familiar performance, something. Without that proficiency, community littlemen see right through it.

Sarah and Arne Duncan did have something else to bring to the table, namely their family's thirty-plus years of educational service in North Kenwood–Oakland. Their commitment was unquestionable, and they were well integrated into the neighborhood fabric. But they were white, and thus their motives were never above scrutiny. Their white bodies often served as apparitions of the impending gentrification. Who could represent the new school as in the best interests of NKO? Who could invoke residents' proclivity to believe in a racial "linked fate"? The Ariel planning group had not included such a person in its brainstorming process. When it presented the new school idea to the North Kenwood–Oakland community at the park advisory council meetings described above, the plan seemed foreign to most residents. It appeared to be a done deal. Done by outsiders. Done by whites and their black cronies. Done in central CPS offices. Done *to* North Kenwood–Oakland residents, rather than with, for, or by them. Again, Garth laments this reality, saying, "Well, I just think we did that very poorly. I think in hindsight it was, we should have involved [the community] more in the process. They felt very threatened by us. It got pretty ugly."

The ultimate black brokers were the people who had the final say in the matter.[18] The Conservation Community Council did not officially vote on the school, but it also did not express objections. Alderman Preckwinkle strongly supported the new school, working tirelessly to secure funding to renovate Shakespeare School and insisting, despite some opposition, that it would add value to the community (see fig. 18). With regard to temporary space, John Rogers Jr., as chairman of the park district, could exercise his influence to place the school at Kennicott Park. It was the clout of all of these actors, and the credentials of the contingent of young black and white professionals who did the planning legwork, that got the final approval and funding from the Chicago Public Schools. CPS would not have okayed just any upstart bunch of citizens who thought they could do public education better. Success required the myriad forms of capital that these middlemen possessed, including their close association with important power brokers. More importantly, they played within the rules. They represented the kind of "public-private" partnerships so coveted by officials of the new "entrepreneurial state." Urban boosters Paul Grogan and Tony Proscio write in their "blueprint" for city leaders trying to revitalize neighborhoods that "the deepest effect of opening a market to competition is that it engages the energies of people and institutions outside the monopoly—people who previously used their gifts elsewhere."[19] The players involved in creating Ariel were exactly the kind of energetic, gifted educational outsiders to whom city politicians were looking to hand the public-service reins.

Figure 18. Shakespeare School building in 1998 and 2000, before and after its renovation to house Ariel Community Academy and North Kenwood/Oakland Charter School. Photos by author.

Ariel made it through the process, and when it opened it quickly accumulated a long list of students waiting to get in. By their eagerness to attend, local parents signaled their acceptance of this new school option. But the battles that preceded its opening highlight the discerning nature of the black political public, which will not allow itself to be completely duped by strategically placed black spokespersons and liberal white activists, no matter their tenure. Many NKO residents maintained their skepticism and ultimately were proven right about the impending gentrification and the role of the school in making the neighborhood an attractive place for higher-income newcomers. At some level Sarah Duncan wished they had heeded the knowledge that community members possessed, the warnings of the littleman. "I don't think we realized how much it was gentrifying or how fast," she said, registering a disbelief similar to Ruanda Garth's. "It's hard to envision that kind of thing. That Parade of Homes happened, but it was just one street. And everything else was still a lot of empty lots, poor people's housing. I think had we known, we probably would have gone to a school twenty blocks west, you know. Our mission is to serve traditionally underserved people."

It was not the intent of the Ariel school's founders to usher in the neighborhood's revitalization or, for that matter, to educate the children of the revitalizers. But it was an unintended consequence. Many children from poor and working-class families who lived in the neighborhood before its revitalization do attend Ariel Community Academy, but more of them are at the nonreformed local public schools. As with the charter and magnet schools, the strategy of school reform took on a life of its own because it was enacted within a urban renewal context that was working to attract middle- and upper-income residents. In the midst of community development, new schools operated by such middle-class brokers—Ivy League–educated and successful in business—grease the wheels that sometimes ride over the truly disadvantaged who those brokers wanted to serve.

The Ariel controversy in many ways smoothed the way for the two other new schools in North Kenwood–Oakland, each of which sparked less controversy. Also, by 1998, when the North Kenwood/Oakland Charter School opened in a local church, more new houses had gone up, the public housing high-rises were scheduled to come down, and even more new people had moved in. While not everyone was completely resigned to the neighborhood's future, that future was now much closer, and opposing another new school was not going to stem the tide of change.

The protagonist in the charter school venture, however, provoked a different kind of resistance. The University of Chicago had a reputation in these parts, and it was not a good one. The new charter school was the topic of conversation at a block club meeting one night. Mrs. Lawrence, a longtime resident of the block, brought back news from another community meeting where charter school staff were trying to get the community's support for the school. Although she herself supported the new school idea (she even agreed to distribute school literature to her neighbors), she reported that the reception by other residents was not that good. Community residents were suspicious because the university was primarily known for "their surveys and so on" and for "doing studies in inner-city neighborhoods." "People were thinking this was another attempt to get these kids in there so they could study 'em," Lawrence explained about the negative reception. Fitting scattered facts into this framework, she also reported that community skepticism resulted in lower enrollment than the university had expected in the school's first year of operation. "So that's why they had to open up city-wide, 'cause they couldn't get enough kids from around here. And so they had funding and so they had to fill it up. But it was a matter of mistrust." Although this was not the truth in an objective sense—the school was required by state law to have citywide admissions and in its first year of operation it had twice as many applications as slots—Mrs. Lawrence's story suggested tempered community enthusiasm for the school, a truth also recognized by the charter school administration, which was disappointed with the proportion of local students.

Unlike the cadre of black and white middlemen that opened Ariel school, the University of Chicago was most definitely "the man." It was, in both lay and official community histories, responsible for the 47th Street boundary that so drastically split North Kenwood from South Kenwood, sucking all public and private monies to the southern side of the line. The university frequently reappeared in the surrounding neighborhoods in the form professors, graduate students, statisticians, social workers, and former graduate students (myself included) who used places like North Kenwood–Oakland as their research playground and the residents as their subjects and respondents. The list of studies from the university's sociology department alone in the 1980s and 1990s gives justification to community wariness: the Urban Poverty and Family Life Study, the North Kenwood–Oakland and Woodlawn Community Survey (which included a community resource inventory and focus groups), and the Project on Human Development in

Chicago Neighborhoods. On top of the University of Chicago studies was research conducted by other universities: the University of Illinois at Chicago's study of commercial and housing priorities, Northwestern University's study of Lake Parc Place, a Loyola graduate student's dissertation on Lake Parc Place, a University of Pennsylvania student's BA thesis on gentrification, the MacArthur Foundation's survey of community capacity, and, of course, my own study of community change.[20] Few local residents can tell the universities or researchers apart, so many residents attributed it all to the closest and most usual suspect, the University of Chicago. To be sure, some of these studies were commissioned by local (or semilocal) groups and were meant to provide information that would be helpful in pinpointing local needs. But no one interviewee would know this background when they got the phone call asking them to answer survey questions, and very few residents ever saw the final research reports. Though the studies were not as nefarious as the infamous Tuskegee syphilis study, North Kenwood–Oakland residents nonetheless felt poked and prodded on the examining table.

Perhaps feeding residents' skepticism, North Kenwood/Oakland Charter School is actually a *proud* laboratory for research and training. "As a school development center," its Web site announces, "NKO provides a meeting place and demonstration center for the Center for School Improvement school network. Teachers from Network schools visit the site for residencies and workshops to observe the practices they are attempting to implement in their own schools." University of Chicago president Don Randel echoed these sentiments, placing the charter school within the university's "tradition of applying the best thinking to the hardest problems and then contributing the fruits of that thinking to bettering the lives of real people." This entails "sending out [social work] graduates armed with the ideas (and, yes, the commitment) that it takes to make a difference in what have often seemed intractable circumstances."[21] Given the fact that the charter school always has more applicants than it can serve, many parents gladly submit their children to the inquiries of University of Chicago researchers, and get out of it a better education than is available at the average Chicago Public School.

In order to overcome the university's dubious history, key community leaders were involved in the planning of the charter school before it was presented to the neighborhood. The alderman shepherded the school into the neighborhood; Shirley Newsome, chairman of the Conservation Community Council, was included as a member of the school's first board of directors; and Sara Spurlark, a longtime and highly regarded educator in Hyde Park–Kenwood, was often the passionate and pleasant (and African American) community face of the university's charter school. The university had also begun to illustrate its desire to work collaboratively with North Kenwood–Oakland. Henry Webber, vice president of community affairs, said that the university aimed to be "the partner but not quite a senior partner" on housing, commercial development, and safety issues. All of these overtures constituted a concerted effort to rebuild a more positive reputation.

Moreover, for newcomers to NKO, the university did not have to try so hard to improve its image. Many of them were not reared in the shadow of the university's urban renewal projects and therefore were not so distrustful of its designs. Many of them had gone to predominantly white universities not unlike the University of Chicago, so it was not the menacing behemoth that it was to those familiar only with its aggressions. In general the opening of the charter school was uneventful, compared to the controversy stirred by Ariel, because key local black middlemen were enlisted early in the process and owned the project from the beginning. The charter school proposal was well received by the Chicago Public Schools system, because, after all, it came from the most prestigious university in the city, one with considerable resources to infuse into the cash-strapped public education world.

The transformation of King High School came last. In 1998, the year after the University of Chicago opened its charter school, King stopped accepting freshmen and began the plan to reopen as a college preparatory school. It was surprising how relatively faint the outcry was at the meetings discussing King's conversion from an open enrollment school to a selective college prep. Just a few years earlier, there had been vigorous debate over the King-Price campus, a plan to connect King High School to Price Elementary School, a block away, with a collection of landscaped walkways, practice fields, a playground, an amphitheater, and a parking lot. The design required that CPS acquire private land and demolish some privately owned buildings. In that case, residents had protested the wanton incursion of CPS and the city into the lives and homes of local residents.[22] But whereas those debates, concerned with land, solicited months of participation, petitions, letters to city agencies, and a threat of legal action, the King conversion and the future of the community's high schoolers was discussed among a group of about fifty residents who showed up in 2000 for a presentation by Chicago

Public Schools CEO Paul Vallas. By the time Vallas appeared in North Kenwood–Oakland, the transition process for the school had already begun. The first group of prospective King freshman had been shuffled off to other nearby high schools to begin the flushing out process. King's glory days had been defined, not by classroom achievements, but by the three state basketball championships it had won. These accomplishments receded into the past, and in 2001 its revered coach, Landon Cox, called it quits after twenty years at King.[23] All that was left, then, was a dwindling number of students and, according to Vallas at the informational meeting, only 25 percent of those students were from the community. "This school has not been the school of choice for many residents," the CEO said bluntly, reiterating the neoliberal theme of increasing choices for citizen-consumers, "so let's not fool ourselves and say that many residents are choosing King."[24]

Yet the crowd that listened to Vallas was not completely acquiescent either. They pushed the schools CEO, especially on the issues of inclusion and equity, cleverly invoking the school's namesake. "It would do injustice to the legacy of Dr. King, who argued that no one should be excluded," commented a man at the meeting. Other similar questions followed. "Nobody has any objection to a quality school, we just want a quality school that everybody can get into," asserted one woman. "My kids aren't at the sixth stanine, and I want good schools for my kids too," added another mother, referring to the standardized test score bar (roughly the top 40 percent) used to determine eligibility for King. Another woman who elaborated on these themes received hardy applause for her comments:

> It makes me wonder what's going on in the elementary schools. If these students are brought up, there wouldn't be any need for magnet schools. You're separating kids. You're making some kids feel like they're on top of the world and other kids feel like don't nobody give a damn about me so why should I try. It's just like Beasley [a magnet elementary school in another poor black neighborhood], where they don't even want to take kids from right across the street.

While attendance at the meeting was moderate, the objections voiced above were supported in several of my interviews. Avis Green—who was born in the Ida B. Wells projects, moved out of the neighborhood, and moved back to North Kenwood in 1982 with a nursing degree and a good job—gave an extensive analysis in response to my question "Have you heard about changes planned for King High School?"

Oh, my God, yes! My idea behind public education is, again, it is public, public, public, public. If something is public, then ain't I the public? Aren't these kids who are being put out of King High School and going over there to Dyett [High School], [which is like] a factory, aren't they part of the public? How can you have a public school and then say that everybody in the public can't go to it? That's what I think. It's a bunch of hogwash. A magnet school allows the fifth floor down at City Hall, or whomever he selects, to make decisions about my neighborhood. Now, mind you, there are kids in this neighborhood that will be bused or shipped out of their neighborhood in order to turn King into a magnet school. That's not right. If education is to be improved, it's to be improved for everybody. One of the things that's happening in the school system that I don't like is the fact that the kids are being tested. First, they're being screwed around. They're being given poor education. They're coming from families where the needs are not being met in the home, and then they're shipped to these schools where the teachers don't know how to teach. They're screwed around. But somebody makes their basic living off of these poor little souls. Then they get to third grade, and they're tested. That allows you to put them in a specific slot, you see. They can't go to the magnet school. They go somewhere else where somebody else keeps them in the dark and makes their living off of them, drives all sorts of Cadillacs and wears all sorts of ugly clothes and does all that sort of stuff, you see. And then they're slotted for west hell at the age of 21. . . . These magnet schools should be outlawed, but nobody's taking up on that. You don't make no magnet school with my money. I did not tell you to do that, and I don't want King to be a private school in my neighborhood. If it's public, I want you to do the best that the public can get right over there for the people in this community.

While most responses to my question were not nearly so detailed, many people raised similar issues concerning the definition of "public" schools that are not completely open to the public, making them in some ways like private schools. Others restated the central concern raised when Ariel was being planned. King's conversion, they estimated, was in service of gentrification, not quality education. A parent of a King High School senior asked: "Twenty million dollars—where was all this money when my son enrolled four years ago?" The desperate tenor of this question exemplifies how protests over King's transformation sputtered before they even began. Residents would not *turn away* a multimillion-dollar renovation plan that finally brought highly qualified teachers and a commitment to college preparation into their back yard.[25] But they were deeply disappointed and resentful that such a transformation happened only after hundreds of new, expensive housing units had been built. Even more, residents worried about the two layers of exclusion that King now represents: it accepts only the most gifted students, and it accepts them from across the city, with no preference for local high schoolers. Pauline Lipman refers to the magnet system as a "*separate* high-status-knowledge program," and computed that in the 1999–2000 academic year, only 6 percent of Chicago Public Schools students attended such schools. From this, she concluded that "the regional magnet high schools provide little additional access to challenging academic courses of study for the majority of students."[26]

Yet in the ideology of the neoliberal transformation of cities and their distribution of public goods, King is the reward for families who take on the responsibility of canvassing the public educational landscape and preparing their children to take advantage of opportunities when they are available. Seen this way, King represents a new, high-quality choice for children who have proven themselves in elementary schools and parents who submit their children's applications, get them tested, and gather all of the other information required to be considered for admission. These are families who might otherwise move out of the city in search of a better public school system, and hence this strategy, however exclusive, benefits the city by hanging on to them, their tax dollars, and their disposable income.

A few years into King's new incarnation as a selective enrollment school, local school reformers, disgruntled parents, and groups that advocate on behalf of low-income families all began to recognize how selection excluded many neighborhood kids. In 2005, a new community development corporation stated as one of its goals to "advocate for local attendance areas for charter schools, magnet schools and other new schools." The organization aimed to "assure that neighborhood children who meet academic requirements for King College Preparatory High School can bypass the lottery system and attend the school." This attention to broadening the class of beneficiaries of King's transformation is a move away from exclusivity. The fact that the proposal has come from some of the same players who initially advocated for the magnet school illustrates the frustrations that resource brokers have with the reform tools available. Being firmly ensconced in the neoliberal state predetermines and constrains strategies of action that disproportionately advantage the already advantaged. But black middlemen, while players in that milieu, are simultaneously compelled by a sense of racial responsibility, an obligation to the littleman. Such allegiances can occasionally motivate brokers to push against the strictures of neoliberal policies and to think creatively about how to make reforms more equitable. By 2006, the push-back against King's exclusivity had grown even more egalitarian and now implored CPS officials to add to the King campus a nonselective component that would exist alongside the magnet school but admit local students regardless of ability.[27]

New Schools Deliver

The enthusiasm with which each of these three schools has been greeted affirms the reality that they provide quality options where none had previously existed. Both of the elementary schools have waiting lists, and King College Prep receives at least seven applications for each student opening. At Ariel, for example, the principal explained that the admissions process, though ostensibly open regardless of students' abilities or where they live, has become competitive. It starts with a preference for siblings and family members of current students. "Most of the families, when they have younger children, they come here. If they have a cousin, a brother, a sister that moves in the neighborhood and has children, they come here." By the time family members are taken care of, there isn't much room left for unrelated community children, and even less for children from outside the neighborhood. Because they must stick to enrollment limits, part of their definition as a "small school," they routinely turn interested students away.

Such demand is not an indication of protest and withdrawal, but rather of approval and participation. This story is not unlike black middlemen's stimulation of mortgage capital: North Kenwood–Oakland gained resources that it did not have before, this time in the form of new schools. As public schools, they do not discriminate by income and they are, in principle, open to any family that is interested. The new schools were the result of the social and political clout that newcomers represented in North Kenwood–Oakland, just as the mixed-income model

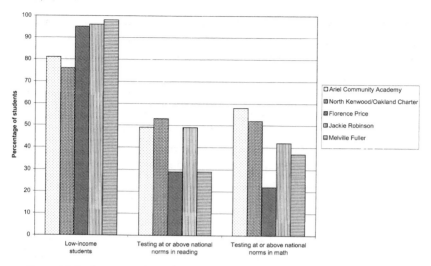

Figure 19. Performance of North Kenwood–Oakland area elementary schools, 2004–2005. Chicago Public Schools, "School Test Score and Demographic Reports," http://research.cps.k12.il.us/ (accessed December 1, 2005); Illinois State Board of Education, "eReport Card Public Site," http://webprod1.isbe.net/ereportcard/ publicsite/getSearchCriteria.aspx (accessed December 1, 2005).

predicts. Even when new residents were not visibly organized, their presence, and the desire to maintain the flow of new gentrifiers, motivated elected officials and members of the Conservation Community Council to push for what the neighborhood would surely need—good schools. With history as proof, the working-class and poor residents of NKO could not have done this on their own. It took the confluence of available policies, political greasing, and connected and—here is the critique of the mixed-income paradigm—*respected* people to get what every neighborhood and all citizens should receive, access to quality schools. The results are in the data.

Figure 19 shows data from the 2004–2005 academic year for the two new elementary schools (Ariel Community Academy and North Kenwood/Oakland Charter School), the two previously existing elementary schools in the neighborhood (Price and Robinson), and Fuller Elementary School, which is not in NKO proper but is the local school for students at the northern end of the neighborhood. All of the schools are over 90 percent African American. On the issue of socioeconomic composition, the two new schools are predominantly low-income: 81 percent of the students at Ariel come from low-income families, as do 76 percent of the students at North Kenwood/Oakland Charter School.[28] Given these figures, these schools have been able to follow their original missions of educating disadvantaged students. However, these proportions are lower than the proportions of low-income students in the regular public schools in the neighborhood, which range from 95 percent to 98 percent, and lower than the citywide figure: overall, 85 percent of Chicago students come from low-income families. That is, Ariel and the NKO Charter School are more utilized by the neighborhood's (or the city's) nonpoor parents than are the regular schools, evidence of some measure of selection into these schools. As the principal at Ariel described it, "Initially, we started and they were about 96 percent [low-income] and it's dropping as the community gentrifies."

The lower proportion of low-income children at the new schools is also evidence of the capital necessary to secure a space for one's child in these schools. Middle-income families with more education and white-collar jobs are embedded in networks that discuss and access information about innovative and decent public schools, and they have the wherewithal to maneuver the sometimes complex procedures for applying and enrolling in them. You can contact Ariel to get an application and have it submitted by January, but you're unlikely to make it in before the siblings and other family members of current students. The charter school's application can be downloaded from its Web site or retrieved at the school, and must be submitted by March. The three-page form includes general family information, plus questions about the student's needs and talents. The application must be completed, signed, dated, and accompanied by the child's birth certificate to be considered for admission. But, the Web site notes, there are almost no slots available for grade schoolers. "Since siblings have priority for enrollment, we do not expect any openings in the other grades," the site explains.[29] The process for admission to King College Prep is considerably more arduous. It begins in November or December with an application that can only be obtained from a school counselor and which requires a letter from the counselor, test scores, attendance records, and additional student information. Students who qualify must then sit for a separate test. It is more like applying to college or graduate school than to high school.

Do the new schools, after all this, produce better student performance? Both new elementary schools have a greater proportion of their students testing at or above national norms in reading and math than

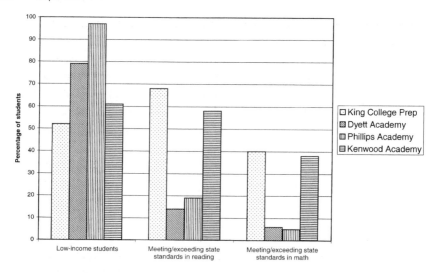

Figure 20. Performance of North Kenwood–Oakland area high schools, 2004–2005. Chicago Public Schools, "School Test Score and Demographic Reports," http://research.cps.k12.il.us/ (accessed December 1, 2005); Illinois State Board of Education, "eReport Card Public Site," http://webprod1.isbe.net/ereportcard/publicsite/getSearchCriteria.aspx (accessed December 1, 2005).

their neighborhood school peers, although Robinson's scores in reading are comparable. Ariel and the charter school also beat out Chicago elementary schools overall in standardized test scores. The differences are not enormous, but they are notable, reaching as high as a 36 percentage-point difference between Ariel and Price in math. Moreover, Price Elementary School, the school with the lowest performance outcomes, also has the highest enrollment.

Figure 20 presents data for King College Prep and three other public high schools. Dyett Academy High School is the local high school designated for most of North Kenwood–Oakland's teenagers now that King is a selective enrollment school, while Phillips Academy High School serves students in the northern third of the neighborhood. The figure also includes data for Kenwood Academy, which is located in the South Kenwood neighborhood and serves Hyde Park–South Kenwood students; it has a magnet component into which high-achieving students from across the city can be accepted. It has traditionally been one of the city's better public high schools, although not as good as the separate selective enrollment schools. At over fifteen hundred students it is at capacity and thus not an option for high schoolers from North

Kenwood–Oakland who cannot test into King. I include it here because it illustrates the stark division between North and South Kenwood. A school named Kenwood is not open to North Kenwood students, even though it is closer to many residents and clearly a better educational option than either Dyett or Phillips. The mobility rates at Dyett and Phillips (data not shown) suggest that these schools do not provide a curriculum that attracts and keeps students; 32 percent of the students at Dyett and 37 percent of those at Phillips enter or leave those schools *during the school year,* indicating a high degree of instability in the student populations. The mobility rate at King is only 4 percent.

The performance differences at the high school level are even more stark than among the elementary schools. King College Prep is doing exactly what city officials hoped it would do, attracting students from middle-income families. (Unlike some of the city's other magnet schools, King mostly attracts middle-income African American families.) Barely over 50 percent of King's students are low-income, compared to 79 percent of the students at Dyett and 97 percent of the students at Phillips. And while King still has plenty room for improvement in performance, especially in math, its students do dramatically better on standardized tests than students at the nearby general admissions high schools, where fewer than 20 percent meet or exceed state standards in reading, and fewer than 10 percent do so in math. It is no surprise that King so roundly outperforms its competitors since it picked its students based on test scores. The point of this exercise, however, is to illustrate the severe *lack of choice* for North Kenwood–Oakland students who cannot enroll in King.

Conclusion

Local leaders and educational activists can take pride in their role in convincing city and Chicago Public Schools officials that North Kenwood–Oakland needs and deserves good schools. The choices that exist in Ariel, the NKO Charter School, and King College Prep represent opportunities for an increasingly solid public education in the neighborhood. Yet subjecting this issue to critical analysis raises concerns about the origins of educational reform, the ideological frameworks guiding reform, and the practical implementation. Ariel staff member Ruanda Garth remembered what protestors wanted instead of the new school that she was trying to sell. "Their point was to improve Price, improve

Robinson. Don't add something else and then you're going to take the more able kids away from them." At community meetings, and in my interviews, numerous residents voiced this same critique of the approach to improving NKO's schools. But reform in the neighborhood went in the other direction.

Each intervention signaled profound pessimism about the hope for the existing schools' restoration, and instead skirted or dismantled them. The school reforms executed the visions of the state politicians, who enacted the charter school legislation, and the mayor, who took control of the public schools and offered selective enrollment schools and small schools as solutions to low performance. Not only were these the only tools *available,* they were also the explicit tools *utilized.* In the Ariel and charter school cases, each group of school leaders opted out of the regular local public school mold because of their experience of working within an entrenched system of failure. They desired the flexibility and autonomy that new school management opportunities offered, but in buying into these new strategies they also participated in some of the more exclusionary features of the new school types, such as forgoing local attendance boundaries and limiting enrollment. Along with the creation of King College Prep, the tools of the new entrepreneurial state created a tiered educational universe that put the onus on parents and students to choose their way into the best school options. While Chicago Public Schools officials claim that the regular (unreformed, neighborhood, general admission) public schools will eventually receive similar attention and resources, it is not always apparent how investments will trickle down to them when the more prestigious schools, like the magnet schools, have at times received nearly half of CPS's construction and renovation funds.[30]

In addition, a main tenet of this market approach to public goods is that competition will eventually lead to the total failure of some schools, just as some commercial ventures are run out of business by competition from better firms. In the end, this competitive weeding process will lead to improvement in the overall selection of schools. Paul Grogan and Tony Proscio take the philosophy to its Darwinian extreme, writing: "And finally, of course, it offers extinction to anyone unwilling to compete."[31] The political and ethical question is if we are prepared to slate some children—most likely the poor and minority ones—and the schools that educate them for extinction. Moreover, is it *just* to pit citizens with different abilities and unequal access to information against each other in competition for public goods?

Before the advent of school reform in North Kenwood–Oakland, parents who lived near Price, Robinson, and the old King, could do nothing, and on the first day of school in September they would still be sure that their child would have a desk in a classroom. The education they received once seated was subpar, to be sure; open access alone does not satisfy the state's duty to provide decent educations to its citizenry. In the neoliberal model, the attitude is that some of that burden should be passed on and shouldered by citizens themselves. Applications with due dates, waiting lists that must be checked, online distribution of forms and information, mandatory orientation sessions, test score reporting, additional testing—all these things require an informed and efficacious parent with considerable time to spend on researching school options and admissions procedures, not to mention Internet access.[32] As Klinenberg states, there is an expectation that residents "will be active consumers of public goods, expert 'customers' of city services made available in the market rather than 'citizens' entitled to social protection. This market model of governance creates a systemic *service mismatch*, whereby people having the weakest capabilities and greatest needs are the least likely to get them."[33]

The story of school reform falls squarely in this new model of service delivery, in which parents have to "shop for" schools. The relative underrepresentation of poor students at the three new schools is one indication that those with the greatest need for good schools—that is, those for whom good schools could contribute to intergenerational mobility—are less likely to be in them. Public goods are no longer broadly and equitably available, but instead constituents must be well-informed, industrious, and "entrepreneurial" enough to demand and search out the best public services. All others are consigned to languishing in bad public schools (and dilapidated housing and infirm public health facilities). As players in this new regime, black middlemen in North Kenwood–Oakland deliver a valuable commodity but on terms that overlook the preferences, talents, and limitations of indigenous working-class and poor families. Black professionals have the information and the networks to navigate a stratified public service infrastructure, and hence charter schools, small schools, and selective enrollment schools seem like unproblematic great ideas to them. But the error in this perspective (one that is now being recognized in calls for unfettered local access), and in the choice-based model that underlies many similar urban reforms, is that they expect the same of their less-advantaged neighbors.

The Case against Public Housing

In 1967, Judge Richard Austin summarized the core allegation in the now-landmark lawsuit *Gautreaux v. Chicago Housing Authority:*

> Plaintiffs, all Negroes and either tenants in or applicants for public housing . . . allege that since 1950, the CHA has selected sites, deliberately or otherwise, for public housing projects almost exclusively within neighborhoods the racial composition of which was all or substantially all Negro at the time the sites were acquired, for the purpose of, or with the result of, maintaining existing patterns of urban residential segregation by race in violation of the Fourteenth Amendment.[1]

Nearly thirty years later, in 1996, Linda McGill, a black resident of North Kenwood, filed an affidavit with the *Gautreaux* court, which continues to oversee public housing matters in Chicago. The letter shared her perspective on why she opposed plans to build new public housing in her neighborhood.

> Greater than 90 percent of new publicly funded CHA properties have been placed in minority neighborhoods. Until each and every other Chicago area community has an equal number, no additional publicly funded housing should be placed within the North Kenwood/Oakland community. . . . We can't take any more![2]

McGill's plea for relief was repeated in various ways in affidavits by seven other home owners and supported by a petition with over 350 signatories. Each expressed the same complaint that was initially made in 1966 on behalf of Dorothy Gautreaux and other black public housing residents: Public housing in Chicago, in which the vast majority of residents were and are black, was and is intentionally and disproportionately placed in black neighborhoods. The courts found the Chicago Housing Authority (CHA) and the U.S. Department of Housing and Urban Development (HUD) guilty of such racial discrimination in 1969, and North Kenwood–Oakland residents argued that not much had changed since then.

The case against public housing foregrounds the racial consciousness of North Kenwood–Oakland's middlemen and women and amplifies the muted historical racist undertones of the public housing issue. When debates about public housing arise in places like North Kenwood–Oakland, it is easy to attribute the causes of such debates to class-based rather than race-based animosities because, after all, everyone in the neighborhood is black. But even though the debates over public housing have seemed to be more about class than race, this is only true because of the genius of systemic racism. Past racism has so distorted the functioning of institutions and markets—here the housing market—that overt racism is no longer even necessary to ensure inequality, and the discriminatory racial history is no longer visible. The legacy of past racism sustains and reproduces contemporary racial disparities without even having to mention race. The current intraracial character of the conflicts does not absolve whites or governments of this culpability.

The case against public housing in North Kenwood–Oakland is also built on the sociological finding that racial segregation creates negative outcomes for African Americans primarily because it leads to reduced political clout, the concentration of poverty, and related disadvantages. For middle-class blacks, racial segregation means an inability to translate their middle-class resources into neighborhood amenities and securities, and it means that they and their children fall behind similar middle-class whites. Reporting a finding quite common in this body of literature, sociologists Robert Sampson and William Julius Wilson write: "The worst urban contexts in which whites reside are considerably better than the average context of black communities." In a series of studies on this topic, sociologists have found time and time again that affluent African Americans live in neighborhoods with higher poverty rates, higher crime rates, fewer college graduates, higher unemployment rates, and more vacant housing than *poor* whites.[3] These inequalities all begin with racial residential segregation, the centerpiece of the original *Gautreaux* lawsuit and the linchpin for North Kenwood–Oakland activists like Linda McGill.

McGill's desperate coda—"We can't take any more"—emphasizes the negative *economic toll* that concentrated and segregated public housing has had on places like North Kenwood–Oakland. She and other middlemen construed themselves as racial littlemen who would forever be doomed to a lowly economic status if such racist acts were not stopped. As sociologists Douglas Massey and Shawn Kanaiaupuni state bluntly, "The presence of public housing in a segregated [black] tract takes a bad situation and makes it worse, producing an isolated social environment where poverty is not only common, but the norm." When public housing projects and their poor black residents are sited, indeed, concentrated, in black neighborhoods under a segregationist regime, those neighborhoods and their residents collectively suffer the consequences of constrained property wealth, limited commercial investment, scarce amenities, and overburdened schools and social welfare institutions. They are losers in what Xavier de Souza Briggs calls "the geography of opportunity."[4] This would be the result, argued some residents, if new public housing were built in North Kenwood–Oakland, and just at the time that they were struggling to *reverse* years of disinvestment, depopulation, and decay.

It is all too easy to group the actions of North Kenwood–Oakland residents with countless related episodes of home-owner opposition to the nearby settlement of stigmatized groups or facilities. From mental health facilities to waste treatment plants to HIV care centers to public housing projects, home owners often resist and reject what they see as incursions and threats. Protests against these kinds of uses are generically referred to as the Not in My Back Yard syndrome, or NIMBY. To some observers, North Kenwood–Oakland is just NIMBY-ism in blackface. About black home owners' fight against public housing, one journalist editorialized:

> Sounds familiar enough. But this time the setting is not a largely white city neighborhood or suburb fending off the construction of public housing, which in Chicago mainly serves low-income blacks. This particular fight, in the North Kenwood–Oakland area on the South Side, involves

mostly middle-class blacks who have the same fears: falling property values and neighborhood decline.[5]

Juxtaposing the protests of middle-class blacks and whites and reducing the former's rationale to narrow concerns for property values obscures the racial logic that permeates decisions about public housing. On the surface, the sight of NKO's middle-class blacks in conflict with poor black public housing residents suggests localized antagonisms between black people of different social classes. To the contrary, I argue that, appearances aside, the relevant framework for analyzing the case against public housing in North Kenwood–Oakland is historical, structural, and *interracial, rather than intraracial.* The most important details exist primarily in the *antecedents* to current events in North Kenwood–Oakland. Racist decisions made in the 1950s and 1960s charted a course of systematic black disadvantage into the future, but their fading from historical memory allows contemporary elites to see their actions in nonracial terms.

Sociologist Lawrence Bobo defines this regime of inequality as "laissez-faire racism," a decidedly hands-off approach in which "modern racial inequality relies on the market and informal racial bias to re-create, and in some instances sharply worsen, structured racial inequality."[6] One such market force that perpetuates racial inequality in Chicago's housing market and ensures the placement of public housing in poor or working-class minority neighborhoods is land prices. Given the limited federal funding available for constructing new public housing, it is economically impossible to build it in Chicago's white neighborhoods because of their high land costs. The inflated price of land in white neighborhoods is, in turn, a reflection of the effects of racial segregation, whereby predominantly white areas enjoy a price premium. Therefore, the exclusion of public housing from some places concentrates it in others and racially segregates its predominantly black clientele.[7] In this chapter, I add another institution that is enlisted to indirectly maintain racial inequality—the courts.

Revitalizing Areas

A significant turning point in the *Gautreaux* lawsuit came in 1981, when the judge issued a consent decree that, even in his estimation, stood "in sharp contrast to the 1969 judgment order entered against

CHA."[8] The original order took an unequivocal desegregationist stance,[9] requiring the CHA and HUD to stop and undo the segregation it had created and severely limiting the amount of new public housing that could be built in black neighborhoods. The 1981 consent decree, however, retreated from this hard line. Under the "revitalizing area" provisions of this consent decree, public housing could be built in "areas which have substantial minority population and are undergoing sufficient redevelopment to justify the assumption that these areas will become more integrated in a relatively short time."[10]

The revitalizing area concept was significant in two ways. First, it traded a loss on one front for a win on another: the plaintiffs' lawyers ceded in part the issue of creating desegregated public housing options in Chicago in return for getting decent new housing built for their clients. For years, the City of Chicago and the Chicago Housing Authority had resisted the desegregation mandates through their "slow progress in complying with the 1969 judgment order," which meant they built no new public housing. The CHA's recalcitrance frustrated the plaintiffs into compromise.[11] Second, it shifted the focus from racial integration to class integration as the curative for the poor state of public housing in Chicago. The original *Gautreaux* ruling divided Cook County (which includes Chicago) into two kinds of areas: "General Areas" that were less than 30 percent black, in which the CHA was ordered to build new "scattered-site" public housing, and "Limited Areas" that were more than 30 percent black, in which new public housing construction was, as the term implies, "limited." These categories illustrate the clear intent of the court to have new public housing built in a dispersed way in predominantly white neighborhoods. Not rich neighborhoods, not suburban neighborhoods, not good neighborhoods, not redeveloping neighborhoods. *White* neighborhoods. Still, despite very little progress toward providing desegregated housing opportunities to public housing residents (only a few hundred units had been built in predominantly white areas prior to the 1981 order), and thus very little progress in spreading the responsibility of housing the black poor across Chicago's nonblack neighborhoods, the revitalizing area notion reopened black neighborhoods to new public housing.

This was not the first time that the initial 1969 ruling had been softened because of CHA's inaction. In May 1979 the court, acting on a joint motion of the *Gautreaux* lawyers and the CHA, altered the previous requirement that CHA build three units in white neighborhoods for every one unit built in black neighborhoods, lowering the ratio to one-to-one.[12] The effects of this more lenient standard were exacerbated by the 1981 ruling, which did not require any commensurate public housing units to be built in predominantly white areas to match new units in revitalizing areas. The 1981 language thus further deemphasized the *racial* wrong in *Gautreaux* and was a step toward eviscerating the racial remedy.

On rhetorically and pragmatically vague grounds, the revitalizing area concept allowed more public housing to be built in black communities if there was an "assumption" that they would become "more integrated" in an unspecified but "relatively short time." The 1969 court had found that the CHA was guilty of systematic racial segregation and that consequently race must be the key consideration in formulating a remedy. The 1981 concession all but erased this recognition of the centrality of race. These new quasi-colorblind operating rules would be crucial in North Kenwood–Oakland. By the time NKO became a battle-ground in the ongoing *Gautreaux* case, the court was guided by the revitalizing area provisions in the 1981 consent decree. As a result, it could only rule on the specific question before it regarding the definition and determination of "revitalizing areas." I argue that the precedent set in the 1981 consent degree, which the court was now bound to follow, disallowed challenges based on historical racism. As emphasis on the initial racial harm receded, past wrongs were allowed to be recommitted. Charting this systemic (or laissez-faire) racist logic through the history of public housing in Chicago allows it to be reasserted in the debate about public housing in North Kenwood–Oakland.

Placing Public and Affordable Housing

Without ignoring the strong progressive intentions of its designers and the "Good Times" that have been had in it, public housing has been a failure in the United States and particularly in Chicago. This is not the fault of the residents, many of whom have shown heroism in rising above formidable obstacles. "Poor people help poor people," one resident told sociologist Sudhir Venkatesh. "They have no one else, so they know how to help each other get by." Instead, as historian Lawrence Vale points out, public housing failed because of America's "collective ambivalence," "collective discomfort," and "cultural unease" with providing housing for people whose poverty is taken as "evidence of personal irresponsibility."[13] Chicago public housing is notorious for its concentration, its poor design and construction, its horrendous management, its violence, and not least of all its racially discriminatory siting and tenanting, as exposed by the *Gautreaux* lawsuit.[14] Chicago is not alone in its isolation of black public housing tenants in black parts of the city. The pattern is repeated across the country and is most acute in other large public housing authorities. According to HUD, 64 percent of black public housing residents nationally live in majority black neighborhoods, and 51 percent of black residents live in neighborhoods with poverty rates over 40 percent, compared to 13 percent of white public housing residents.[15]

At the center of the racial segregation of Chicago public housing were the 1948 Chicago City Council resolution and 1949 Illinois state law that gave local aldermen veto power over public housing sites proposed by the Chicago Housing Authority. Prior to these decisions, the CHA was not subject to the oversight of the Chicago City Council and was able to act autonomously.[16] During its time of relative autonomy, the CHA followed the practices of the federal Public Works Administration, which built the first public housing projects in Chicago and around the country. During the late 1930s and early 1940s, both agencies operated under the "neighborhood composition rule," which meant they matched the demographics of a new public housing development to the demographics of the surrounding community. Given Chicago's racial landscape, this usually meant segregated housing projects, but racial quotas were used in the few integrated neighborhoods to create the desired racial balance. Some of these earlier housing projects, such as the Cabrini, Dearborn, and Addams Homes were racially integrated through the 1950s. Other projects, such as the Ida B. Wells Homes, which sat partially in Oakland, and Lathrop Homes on the northwest side, were all-black or all-white according to the prevailing segregated landscape. Quotas in the integrated projects were difficult to maintain, however, because there was disproportionate need for subsidized housing among Chicago's growing black population and because whites were fast being pushed and pulled to the suburbs, leaving once integrated areas all-black.[17]

During World War II, the overwhelming need for housing for blacks and veterans (some of whom were black) required the CHA to experiment with integrated projects located *not* in integrated neighborhoods but in white neighborhoods. This brought the CHA under intense fire.

Mobs of whites in the hundreds and thousands attacked the new black residents of integrated public housing. In the city council chambers the reaction was equally virulent. With an impending expansion of federal housing funding, the council fretted about its ability to maintain Chicago's rigid color line if the CHA was allowed to continue on its integrationist path. Council members called for the dismissal of the executive secretary of the CHA, Elizabeth Wood. Historian Arnold Hirsch writes, "The personification of the CHA's nondiscriminatory postwar policies, [Wood's] removal marked a turning point in the process in which the housing authority was first subdued and then *enlisted* in the struggle to maintain the racial status quo."[18]

The subjugation of the Chicago Housing Authority to the will of the city council solidified the segregationist regime in Chicago. Aldermen from white neighborhoods summarily dismissed CHA proposals to site new public housing in their wards, knowing that the tenants would likely be black. Conversely, proposals for sites in black neighborhoods, even those requiring substantial demolition, were approved by black leadership, whose constituents were desperate for decent and affordable housing. The CHA built over twenty thousand units of family housing in the 1950s and 1960s, and nearly all were located in black communities. In the first *Gautreaux* ruling in 1969, Judge Austin wrote in his opinion:

> Therefore, given the trend of Negro population movement, 99½% of CHA family units are located in areas which are or soon will be substantially all Negro. It is incredible that this dismal prospect of an all Negro public housing system in all Negro areas came about without the persistent application of a deliberate policy to confine public housing to all Negro or immediately adjacent changing areas.[19]

There was no gray area in the intent of Chicago's white leadership to keep blacks out of white neighborhoods, and Austin ruled strongly in favor of the plaintiffs.

One thousand miles east of Chicago, in 1971, two years after the first *Gautreaux* ruling, another landmark housing case commenced, one that would similarly proceed over several decades and affect housing policy beyond the then-small suburb where it was filed. The lawsuit was brought by black residents of Mount Laurel, New Jersey, some of whose families had lived in the once-rural town since the seventeenth century. Despite their tenure, when upscale, suburban-type housing came to Mount Laurel they were told by the new white mayor, "If you people can't afford to live in our town, then you'll just have to leave."[20] The *Mount Laurel* cases centered on municipalities' use of zoning laws to exclude affordable housing, by, for example, requiring developers to buy and build on large plots of land or to build only large houses, so that the final price of the houses would be too high for low- or moderate-income families. The legal challenge was thus grounded in class, not race, and concerned affordable housing, not public housing. But the plaintiffs were all black; hence, as in NKO and many other examples of fair housing litigation, race and class were inextricable. Moreover, the amorphous category of "affordable housing" to many people's ears simply translates into "housing for the poor." The fact that this fight was not in fact about public housing did not make the resistance any less vehement or the necessary remedies any less intense.[21] The case worked its way to the New Jersey Supreme Court, where the judges ruled in favor of the plaintiffs. The ruling established the obligation of municipalities to craft zoning laws that allow for affordable housing. It also stated that each jurisdiction should have an affordable housing supply equal to its *fair share* of the regional need.

The relevance of the *Mount Laurel* cases to the story of public housing in North Kenwood–Oakland lies in its popularization of "fair share" rhetoric and the underlying idea that affordable (and public) housing should be equitably distributed across a metropolitan region, avoiding the kind of racial and economic concentration that characterized Chicago's public housing. While achieving fair distributions has been exceedingly difficult, the *Mount Laurel* decisions lend a framework for evaluating the placement of public and affordable housing. As will be clear, the residents of North Kenwood–Oakland sang a "fair share" battle cry. They highlighted the dearth, if not absence, of public housing in other parts of the city and the abundance of it in their black neighborhood. To be sure, North Kenwood–Oakland's home owners were not above challenging public housing residents' worthiness to live in a neighborhood that poor families could not afford on their own, echoing the comments of Mount Laurel's mayor. But the *root* of the antagonisms in NKO was the racist legwork done by previous Chicago mayors and aldermen who had created such long-lasting systemic inequalities.

Concerted tactics of delay and avoidance on the part of public officials in Chicago meant that for many years public housing was nearly unaffected by the *Gautreaux* ruling and remedy. As law professor Leonard Rubinowitz writes:

> Implementation of the "scattered site" program was virtually non-existent for the next five years. . . . The obstacles to implementation were numerous and varied. First, local officials, including the CHA itself, the mayor, and the Chicago City Council opposed the program. They used a variety of means to thwart it, including refusals to identify potential sites for public housing or provide necessary approvals for sites that were proposed. Each of these actions—or inactions—necessitated returns to the district court for additional orders, with the inevitable delays involved in hearings and appeals.

The courtroom dramas and stubborn resistance dragged on for years. Alexander Polikoff, lead attorney for the *Gautreaux* plaintiffs, writes in 2006 that he is still "waiting for *Gautreaux*."[22]

The public executives who blocked the desegregation of public housing were only responding to ordinary white citizens who "flooded elected officials with demands that [Judge Austin's] orders be resisted."[23] Even if white Chicagoans, the CHA, the aldermen, and the mayor had been willing to build new public housing outside of black neighborhoods, land prices had become prohibitive. That land is more expensive in white areas than in black ones is obviously a result of the same racial segregation that the *Gautreaux* ruling aimed to remedy. This illustrates precisely the circle of disadvantage in which acts of racial discrimination erect auxiliary hurdles that proscribe efforts to right the initial wrong. In this case—a perfect example of the laissez-faire racism discussed above—the high price of land in white neighborhoods is proffered as a market barrier to desegregation, not a racial one, and thus is difficult for civil rights lawyers to challenge.

With no land to build it on, no will to build it, and—after Richard Nixon's 1974 public housing moratorium and a housing bill that shifted federal monies from construction to rent subsidies—no money to build it with, new public housing built in a desegregated manner became an unrealizable fantasy in Chicago. Black neighborhoods and all of the public housing placed in them persisted in their near complete separation from white neighborhoods. By the time the story begins in North Kenwood–Oakland in the mid-1990s, middle-class and poor blacks were duking it out over public housing because white Chicago had scored successive KOs in the previous *interracial* bouts. Legally, the *Gautreaux* plaintiffs had won, but substantively "very little had been accomplished."[24] When middle-class blacks in North Kenwood–Oakland suggested that new public housing not be built in their neighborhood but rather in Chicago's white neighborhoods, they were invoking the ghost of the original *Gautreaux* ruling. Their argument appeared harsh, surely snobby, and perhaps even racist. But it was, instead, an attempt to recapture their place as *co-victims* of racism, along with black public housing residents, not to become *purveyors* of it.

The *Gautreaux* "Victims"

The stance of middle-class blacks *against* the opportunities of poor blacks to have decent low-cost housing presents complicated interpretive dilemmas. How do we discern the moral high ground in this debate when both sides claim to be victims? How do we evaluate the varied attitudes toward public housing when both sides have lived in it and around it, argued for it and against it? How do we disentangle the respective political interests when both sides belong to a group—"the black community"—that is often assumed to be a political monolith? These difficult questions stem from a particular ambiguity in the *Gautreaux* lawsuit, and by extension in the NKO conflict: Did Dorothy Gautreaux and the six other named plaintiffs represent a class of public housing residents who were black, or a class of blacks who were public housing residents? Put another way, is *Gautreaux* about the rights of public housing residents, or about the rights of blacks living in public housing in segregated black communities? The easy answer is that the plaintiffs represented both identities, but the framing of the violation and the content of the remedy leave room for multiple interpretations in the courtroom and even more in the neighborhoods in which the saga is ultimately played out.

Ruling in favor of the *Gautreaux* plaintiffs, Judge Richard Austin found that the Chicago Housing Authority exhibited a "purpose to perpetuate racial separation" by limiting the number of black occupants in the few public housing projects in white neighborhoods and actively locating the majority of public housing projects in black neighborhoods.[25] While the decision affirmed the unconstitutionality (under the Fourteenth Amendment) and illegality (under Title VI of the Civil Rights Act of 1964) of such practices, it left open the question of why racial segregation in public housing was so bad in the first place. Who was the victim?

The court's ruling and remedy focused on the rights of black public housing residents, as participants in a federally funded housing program, to have the opportunity to move to nonblack areas. Black public housing residents were the victims of CHA's discriminatory siting policies that disallowed such a possibility. Referring to the City of Chicago's eager use of federal monies to provide free breakfast to black children but its unwillingness to provide desegregated housing, Judge Austin quipped, "You're telling me it's better for a child to have breakfast than to have the opportunity to move out of the ghetto. Let them have cake, but don't let them move to the [predominantly white] Northwest side or the Southwest side."[26] One apparent priority for the judge, then, was to ensure the unconstrained residential choices of black participants in a federal housing program.

But outside of the courtroom and in the wake of *Brown v. Board of Education* the emphasis was squarely on the negative impact that racial segregation had on blacks as a group, since separate almost never meant equal. In this larger context of legislative and judicial developments and social science argumentation,[27] the victims of CHA's discriminatory policies extended beyond black public housing residents alone to encompass entire black communities, the manifestations of concerted efforts to separate the races. To combat this larger evil, the *Gautreaux* order was written with activist and ambitious language and took a strong integrationist stance. Judge Austin wrote: "Existing patterns of racial separation must be reversed if there is to be a chance of averting the desperately intensifying division of Whites and Negroes in Chicago."[28] This summary finding against the Chicago Housing Authority did not specify the public housing context of the case but rather took all of Chicago as its sphere. This illustrates the subtle oscillation between a focus on black public housing residents *as public housing residents* subjected to the racism of the CHA and HUD, and black public housing residents *as blacks* subjected to the racism of institutions and individuals more generally.

This confusion has its analogue in the North Kenwood–Oakland controversy. Residents like Linda McGill, quoted at the chapter's outset, latched on to the generalized racial wrong suggested by the *Gautreaux* decision. As a black Chicagoan, she too is a victim. This construction overlooks the specificity of the lawsuit as a case about the racial segregation of public housing residents. But it is an interpretation that the court has at times shared. For the plaintiff class, the two are inseparable—their blackness and their residence in public housing. But for the various factions and legal entrepreneurs who have been involved in the case, there is sufficient ambiguity to allow the foregrounding of one or the other of those statuses. The specific history of public housing in North Kenwood–Oakland is illustrative of this confusion.

The Projects and the Conservation Plan

In 1953 and 1956, the two buildings comprising the Victor A. Olander Homes (named after the secretary of the Illinois Federation of Labor) opened, the first of North Kenwood–Oakland's "Lakefront Properties," as the public housing high-rises came to be known. A decade later, in 1962 and 1963, there were two additions—the Washington Park Homes (one building) and the Lake Michigan Homes (three buildings). Together these developments comprised six fifteen- and sixteen-story buildings and roughly nine hundred public housing units. Like much of the other public housing in Chicago's Black Belt, the projects were heralded as signs of progress and promise by some, but feared by others as "calculated to continue the ghetto."[29] "When they first went up I saw these big, mountainous buildings going up in the neighborhood," recalled longtime resident Leroy Bowers. "And I went to my dad and I say, 'Dad, I just went over to the new buildings over there and they are fantastic. They got new tile floors, new refrigerators. You could see the lake. We oughta move over there.' And my daddy almost tore my head off. He said, 'Boy, we not movin' over there.' But I didn't understand, you know."

The now-familiar story of poor management by the CHA, structural decay, declining maintenance funds, and general neglect would seem to vindicate Bowers's father's skepticism. By the time they were a mere twenty and thirty years old, the Lakefront Properties were in serious need of repair. In 1985, residents found out from a newspaper leak that their buildings were slated for rehabilitation and that they would all be relocated. Fearful of permanent displacement, the residents organized into the Lakefront Community Organization (LCO) and negotiated a deal with the Chicago Housing Authority—a "memorandum of accord"—guaranteeing their right to return to the Lakefront Properties once they were rehabbed. Despite announcements of an eighteen-month construction schedule, the years passed. A decade elapsed.

As I chronicle in chapter 6, the CHA began to retreat from its plan to rehabilitate the buildings in the face of challenges by the *Gautreaux* plaintiffs, the burgeoning activism of middle-class newcomers to North Kenwood–Oakland, and the backroom deliberations of powerful actors and institutions. In 1995, the CHA brokered a Revised Agreement with former residents of the projects that allowed for the demolition of four of the high-rises (the original Olander Homes buildings were rehabbed in 1991). Among other things, the new contract called for 241 replacement public housing units to be built within North Kenwood–Oakland. One hundred of these new units would be built on the lakefront where the high-rises then stood, 50 would be located on the site of a public housing high-rise on Drexel Boulevard that had already been demolished, and 91 would be scattered throughout the community. The official parties to this agreement were the Chicago Housing Authority and the Lakefront Community Organization. The next task was to sell this plan to the larger North Kenwood–Oakland community, which would be the most immediate receiver of the new public housing units.

As the public housing residents were organizing to protect their interests, so too were the home owners in the neighborhood, culminating in the conservation area. On the issue of the Lakefront Properties, numerous planning documents recommended that the buildings be demolished, either entirely or in part, with total replacement or with none. According to the report of the two-hundred-member Neighborhood Planning Committee:

> The presence of the Chicago Housing Authority (CHA) Lakefront Properties and the negative image of public housing deters investment in the community both by existing homeowners who are reluctant to maintain their property and by outside developers who are reluctant to invest in new development.

Reflecting a growing consensus in favor of demolition—which did not, of course, include the leadership of the Lakefront Community Organization—the Neighborhood Planning Committee gave its final recommendation regarding the high-rises in an eerily passive voice: *"In the event CHA property became available,* new construction should be limited to three stories."[30]

There was no explicit reference to the Lakefront Properties in the 1992 North Kenwood–Oakland Conservation Plan approved by the

Chicago City Council. However, the sentiment that public housing was a deterrent to investment continuously underlay the deliberations of the Conservation Community Council (CCC). Such was the case when the executive director of the CHA, Joseph Shuldiner, came to the CCC in the Fall of 1995 to present to the community the Revised Agreement made between the CHA and the Lakefront Community Organization to demolish the high-rises and build 241 replacement units throughout North Kenwood–Oakland. The reception was not a warm one. One observer recalled:

> People were just extremely angry at him for being the person who was bringing public housing to their neighborhood. And they felt he should go out and build public housing in other neighborhoods where white people lived. And stay away from their neighborhoods and stop destroying their neighborhood, and he was the destroyer of their neighborhood. He was the personification of destruction in the neighborhood. And they were trying very hard to build and rebuild the neighborhood and were doing a good job at it, and he was screwing it. I don't know whether they called him the devil incarnate or what they said, but he didn't have any trouble figuring out that he shouldn't take this personally.

The passion with which North Kenwood–Oakland residents defended their neighborhood was obvious. For some activists, defending the neighborhood was synonymous with defending the race, even if it simultaneously defended *against* members of the race. As the controversy proceeded, it became clear, however, that none of the arguments about racism that residents put forth were relevant.

The Case against Public Housing in North Kenwood–Oakland

Residents for the Responsible Redevelopment of North Kenwood–Oakland (RRR), the organization opposing new public housing in North Kenwood–Oakland, was organized primarily by newcomer home owners, black middle-class brokers poised to use their intellectual and political capital to protect their new neighborhood from further racist aggression. Of the eight home owners who filed affidavits with the court, six had moved into the neighborhood after the Lakefront Properties were emptied in 1986, and three had lived in the neighborhood for less than a year. Although the organization's most active members were relative newcomers, RRR was backed by a petition with over 350 signatures, including residents of varying tenure. The neighborhood's new home owners felt that they had been led to believe that the high-rises were coming down and that the community would thereafter be left alone. "That was the main issue," recalled one CCC member, "because, you know, once the CHA was imploded I guess the community felt that was the end of it. That it would never come back." The CHA's Joseph Shuldiner abruptly disabused residents of this assumption. Demolition of the high-rises would come at the price of replacement units. It was in opposition to this prospect that RRR organized its campaign against public housing in the community. The content of its case and the responses by the CHA, the City of Chicago, and the court illustrate the challenges of waging a battle against structural racism when the antecedent discriminatory processes have receded from official memory.

RRR's crusade was waged in the courtroom because construction of new public housing requires the approval of the *Gautreaux* court. The North Kenwood–Oakland neighborhood presented a particular quandary for the court because the neighborhood was majority black, and the *Gautreaux* lawsuit had been won by proving that the Chicago Housing Authority purposefully and illegally relegated public housing to majority black neighborhoods. Nonetheless, the 1981 consent decree opened the possibility that more public housing could be built in such neighborhoods, as long as they were "revitalizing." Hence, the issue confronting the *Gautreaux* court in May 1996, when oral arguments were heard before Judge Marvin Aspen, was the establishment of North Kenwood–Oakland as a revitalizing area. If the judge entered a revitalizing area order, the CHA (through the court-appointed receiver, the Habitat Company) could build scattered-site public housing in NKO to replace what would be lost when the Lakefront Properties were demolished. New public housing could be built even though NKO was 99 percent African American, and with no requirement that the CHA build offsetting units in white neighborhoods.

To what extent was North Kenwood–Oakland revitalizing? The conservation plan had been accepted by the community and the city in 1992, but as is often the case with development, actual building was transpiring slowly. Rehabilitation of apartment buildings for low-income tenants had preceded the conservation plan, but the "Parade of Homes" in 1994 marked the first new construction of single-family homes in NKO in decades. It featured over twenty new homes, priced in the $200,000 range, which brought in new middle-class black families who saw themselves as pioneers. The Parade of Homes was followed by more plans for new construction, but by 1996, when the stage and character of revitalization was being evaluated by the court, none of these relatively small-scale projects had altered the vistas of empty commercial strips, boarded-up buildings, and crumbling streets.

The only true legal parties to the revitalizing area question were the *Gautreaux* plaintiffs, whose lead legal representation was Alexander Polikoff, and the defendants, the Chicago Housing Authority and the federal Department of Housing and Urban Development. Yet, many other players were involved in the deliberations over how to define North Kenwood–Oakland, including

- the *Lakefront Community Organization,* the organization of residents displaced from the Lakefront Properties;
- *Habitat Company,* which in response to CHA inaction was appointed by the court in 1987 to take over CHA's charge to build scattered-site public housing units;
- *Alderman Toni Preckwinkle,* who was elected after the high-rises had been emptied, and who was committed both to seeing them demolished and to building some replacement units;
- the *City of Chicago,* through its *Department of Planning and Development,* which was responsible for the creation and administration of the conservation plan;
- the *Conservation Community Council,* the body of city-approved neighborhood residents that held monthly community meetings and carried out the conservation plan;
- the *Fund for Community Development and Revitalization,* an organization backed by the University of Chicago and the MacArthur Foundation that was involved in affordable housing and commercial development in North Kenwood–Oakland; and
- *Residents for Responsible Redevelopment,* the impromptu group formed to argue against new public housing in the neighborhood.

RRR's position was an unenviable one, both because of the harsh and public position it took against the already disinherited former Lakefront Properties' residents and because of the internecine nature of the conflict, with one group of African Americans opposing the claims of another. Not being a legal party to the case, RRR moved to file an amicus curiae, or friend of the court, brief in opposition to the proposed revitalizing area designation. The judge denied this motion, but he allowed RRR's lawyer to present oral arguments and submit supporting materials and testimonies that the judge could consider.

RRR's argument was threefold: (1) NKO had more than its fair share of public and other subsidized housing (i.e., *concentration*), (2) the neighborhood suffered unfair concentration *because* it was African American (i.e., *racial harm*), and (3) replacing the demolished high-rises would doom NKO's fledgling revitalization efforts (i.e., *economic harm*). RRR's position raised the simultaneous realities of racial and economic segregation, and the impact that the court's decision would have on both racial and economic progress.

While not explicitly invoking the *Mount Laurel* decisions, RRR's use of "fair share" rhetoric subtly alluded to the landmark case but reversed its argument, claiming that NKO, unlike the town of Mount Laurel, was already fulfilling its obligation to provide housing for poor families. Had members of RRR been actual litigants in the *Gautreaux* case, their claims would have required an official examination of the need for affordable housing across the Chicago region compared to the supply located in North Kenwood–Oakland. They incorporated this quantitative evidence into their documentation for the court and used statistics to demonstrate the excessive supply of public and affordable housing in their neighborhood. These efforts were intended to counteract the elaborate presentations by the City, Habitat, and the Fund for Community Development and Revitalization, which described how "right along the border [of North Kenwood] you've seen development creeping and, in fact, over the last several years entering into the neighborhood."[31] That is, while the CHA and its allies were making the case that the neighborhood was revitalizing, RRR was building the case that it was not (but that it could if left alone).

RRR entered into the record tables with neighborhood tallies of total CHA units (1,691), Section 8 units (1,603), and total subsidized and public housing units (3,858). According to the 1990 census, the total number of housing units of any type in North Kenwood–Oakland was 7,350. Given RRR's tabulations, then, subsidized and public housing constituted over half of all housing units in the community. But the group's tally of public housing units included the 600 apartments in the Lakefront Properties, which of course would be demolished if the revitalizing area motion was successful. RRR also included Section 8 units in *South* Kenwood, which was outside of the relevant planning area, rather than only those in *North* Kenwood and Oakland. Desperation led to overstatement. Still, other sources lent support to RRR's general argument that NKO had an abundance of low-income housing. During the planning for the conservation area, multiple city agencies had issued reports on NKO's housing stock. One survey by the city's Department of Housing stated that 39.85 percent of the housing units in NKO were "owned and operated by the Chicago Housing Authority." Even after subtracting the Lakefront Properties and other vacant public housing units from the Department of Housing's tally, 19 percent of NKO's housing stock was public housing, and these figures did not include other kinds of subsidized housing for low-income families. Another report, by a group of outside planners, academics, and architects convened at the request of the Chicago Department of Planning, stated: "The planning area has a very large concentration of public housing and subsidized housing units. The greatest concentration of public housing units is in census tract 3604—approximately 1,193." Whatever the exact numbers, nearly every planning document ever created for North Kenwood–Oakland commented on the concentration of public housing in the neighborhood.[32]

More powerful than the numbers, however, were the tools most readily available to RRR members, their eyes. In their affidavits arguing that public and other kinds of subsidized housing was disproportionately concentrated in North Kenwood–Oakland, residents wrote vivid descriptions like the following:

My home is located in the 3601 census tract which is the northern boundary of the North Kenwood Oakland Conservation Area. North of my house is a housing complex called Lake Grove Village. This complex was built with HUD funding in 1973 for low-income residents. There are over 400 units of housing located in a one block radius. To the east of my home is the Lake Park Manor, a twelve story building which was also built with HUD funding for low-income families in 1974. This building has 164 section 8 renters. There are only 6 single family homes and one six flat unit on the 3600 block of Lake Park Avenue with this 162 unit building. Half of the west side of the block is vacant land. One block west of my home from 36th and Ellis to 39th and Ellis there are approximately twelve (12) homes, three abandoned structures and 396 CHA units (lowrise and high rise) located at 38th and Ellis called Madden Park Homes.

Additionally, there are 12 units of CHA extensions at the northeast and northwest corners of 37th and Ellis. Two thirds of the land is vacant between 36th and Ellis and 37th and Ellis.[33]

In many of the affidavits and in the minutes of the relevant CCC meetings, other residents listed the low-income housing around their homes, while also citing the abundance of vacant land, the lack of commercial development, the struggle of the area schools, and the eyesores of abandoned buildings.

To the numbers and the visual tours, residents added words of desperation that went beyond a fair-share claim. Many felt overburdened, besieged: "The Oakland community is a very poor African-American neighborhood," stated one resident, "CHA's proposal of mixed-income housing, i.e. housing for low income and very low income, would only increase the present depressing statistics and reconcentrate poor people." Another resident concluded, "In closing, I would like to reiterate that according to their proposal to the Court [sic] they are attempting to reconcentrate public housing in the Oakland community. This is not a revitalizing area as described by them and if it were, the public housing outweighs the private housing." Still another wrote, "Presently, there are less than 40 new homes in North Kenwood–Oakland. If the court allows Chicago Housing Authority to build 241 units of public housing in North Kenwood–Oakland, that would be a ratio of 6 public units to every 1 of market price unit. Statistically and in reality that would permanently devastate the development of North Kenwood–Oakland. . . . Finally, in my twelve years of being a real estate broker and developer, no one has ever called our office and asked to live next door to public housing."[34]

Implicit in residents' statements about the existing concentration and possible *reconcentration* of racially segregated public housing is a reference to other areas that had not taken on their fair share. Since "fair share," as defined by the *Mount Laurel* court, represents an even distribution of public or affordable housing as determined by the need for such housing across the metropolitan area, a concentration of public housing in NKO necessarily means a shortage or complete absence of it in some other area. By calling for the replacement units to be built somewhere else, namely in white areas of the city, NKO residents connected their claim of concentration to the specific *racial* harm that they argued would be caused by the revitalizing area designation.

One RRR leader made a presentation to the Conservation Community Council entitled "Making the Second Ghetto," intentionally borrowing from the social science research on racial segregation in Chicago public housing, specifically historian Arnold Hirsch's book of the same name. However, most residents of NKO did not need to refer to academic research to understand acutely the history and contemporary realities of racial segregation and discrimination. To counterbalance what seemed to be a collective amnesia on the part of the court and the *Gautreaux* lawyers, RRR and its members emphasized the antidiscrimination purpose of *Gautreaux* and demanded that it not be skirted. "Instead of these parties offering a remedy for past federal violations and discriminatory practices to the North Kenwood–Oakland community," wrote Sandra Chapman in her affidavit, putting the spotlight back on the *defendants* before the court, "the community must now prove its burden." Chapman is precise in her wording. She reminds the court that a racial harm was done *specifically to North Kenwood–Oakland*, not just to public housing residents across Chicago. The second set of buildings comprising the Lakefront Properties was erected during the most segregationist era of public housing construction in Chicago. Thus, she argued that *the neighborhood itself* should be seen as part of the plaintiff class.

In his oral arguments before the judge, RRR's lawyer, Benjamin Starks, also raised the primacy of race in *Gautreaux:*

> They are not concerned about our community because they know that Gautreaux says, do not build more than 15 percent publicly-assisted housing in one census tract where the majority of the people are black. They are just overlooking that. If they can get waivers on top of waiver, they will nullify Gautreaux; Gautreaux means nothing.

In his closing remarks, Starks drove home RRR's theme of racial subjugation. The speech was oratorically clumsy but symbolically poignant:

> Now they talk about the Parade [of Homes] on the other side, near Ellis, 40th and Ellis or 42nd and Ellis, somewhere in there. But we're saying, how can 40 or 50 homes offset 241 units? And if the people find out that these [new CHA units] are going up, they're not going to come in there. They are not going to even buy those Parades, and we're going to be stuck in the same mud that we've been stuck in since the Emancipation

Proclamation. And we are asking you, your Honor, to not grant them their motion to go forward. Thank you.[35]

RRR argued that the racial harm that would be done by a revitalizing area order was a *continuation* of the purposeful relegation of black public housing residents to all-black neighborhoods, repeating the original wrong in the *Gautreaux* case. This particular occurrence of discriminatory behavior, argued Starks, existed in a series of offenses perpetrated against African Americans from slavery through emancipation to the present.

To summarize RRR's argument to this point: Placing new public housing in North Kenwood–Oakland would both worsen the concentration of poverty—since it would add new poor families to a neighborhood with an already very high poverty rate—and continue racial segregation, since nearly all Chicago public housing residents are black. The final piece of RRR's opposition to the revitalizing area designation was that new public housing would retard private, and perhaps even public, investment. "We need *Gautreaux* now more than ever" was resident Linda McGill's emphatic message to the court. Struggling to get back on its feet, residents saw the protection of the courts against discrimination as crucial to this black neighborhood's future. The social science literature on how racial segregation and concentrated poverty lead to various forms of immiseration, political disenfranchisement, municipal and state neglect, and private sector abandonment could have been helpful here. But again residents did not need it, because it was their reality.[36] Having lived the disadvantages of racial and class exclusion, NKO's residents were not buying the story that revitalization would continue unabated even with the modest number of proposed public housing units.

Still, a certain irony is immediately apparent. Many of RRR's leaders were newcomers to the neighborhood who deemed the neighborhood fiscally promising enough to invest upwards of $200,000 in purchasing or rehabbing a home. It is unlikely that they would have made such an investment if they did not see evidence that the neighborhood was "revitalizing," exactly the designation they were now disputing. Perhaps aware of the conundrum, they did not completely deny the harbingers of change but asserted that such change was fragile and in its germination stage. Moreover, they argued, they had made their investments under the assumption that the high-rises would be demolished and not replaced. In one CCC meeting "several residents from the Parade of

Homes stated that they were deceived about the cities [*sic*] plans regarding public housing in this area." At another meeting, "Leroy Williams stated that the people who purchased homes on Oakenwald [Avenue] would not have bought them, if they knew of the proposed 241 units of CHA to be built in the community."[37] What these statements reveal is that RRR's concern with the negative impact that public housing would have on revitalization was as much about protecting *individual* investments as about collective racial and/or economic well-being.

The new residents who had bought homes in North Kenwood–Oakland were concerned about what all home owners are concerned about—property values. Robert Blackwell, a leader in RRR and newcomer to the neighborhood, remembered:

> When they started announcing the plans for CHA development there was kinda, I would say, widespread panic among people who had bought homes. And at that time they were really in the minority. So that's kinda how that started, primarily the people that were on Oakenwald. But, it came out of the, I'd say, nervousness of people who had just bought homes and then they're talking about building CHA, which you can feel the impact of the CHA in that neighborhood. You know, people who had just bought their homes were worried about their investments.

Who were these newcomers to NKO? Some were as well off as Blackwell, who by his midthirties owned a very successful business. Some were lawyers and doctors and other well-paid professionals. And still others were civil servants, teachers, and lower-level administrators. On the whole, few could be cavalier about the money they had invested in their homes and the neighborhood, which they thought was imperiled by the possibility of more public housing.

Clearly, one salient identity of the opponents of public housing was "home owner," and by extension, "investor." But an equally important aspect was their strong racial identification, rooted in their commitment to the symbolic and literal black community. Most NKO residents—newcomers and, obviously, old-timers—had been reared in black neighborhoods, black schools (in some cases through college), black churches, and black friendship networks, mostly in Chicago but also across the country. This collective biography is important for understanding their opposition to public housing. Their position did not stem from a lack of experience with public housing but rather from a profound *familiarity* with it. Many of the residents spoke from their experiences in other black neighborhoods similarly saturated with public housing, or from their own experience growing up in public housing. Gladyse Taylor's justification for why she opposed new public housing illustrates this familiarity.

In closing, Judge Aspen, I live in this community and I am committed to its revitalization and growth. I am also not opposed to publicly assisted housing; but I strongly feel that it should be properly placed. My husband and I both were raised in publicly assisted housing. He was raised in Cabrini-Green with his single parent mother and six siblings. I was born in Ida B. Wells Public Housing project, lived with my single parent mother and four siblings on a Section 8 certificate until I was 12 and until I left home after college lived in a Federally subsidized home in Harvey, Ill. We also know Judge Aspen that we are the exceptions. 3 of our siblings are incarcerated, 5 of them are drug addicts, 3 of us have college degrees, the remaining 9 have a high school education or less. I saw my community, Harvey, Illinois go from a racial mix of 70% Caucasian, 30% other ethnic groups to 85% African American. I saw the businesses leave the community with the over saturation of Section 8 Certificates and publicly assisted housing that was built in Harvey, Illinois between 1963 and the present. I saw the major grocery chain leave the community and in 30 years not be replaced. Harvey is currently one of the 5 worst socially and economically depressed communities within the State of Illinois. My husband and I have worked hard to overcome the social and economic barriers to which we were born. We do not support CHA, HUD's, Habitat's plan with the support of the City of Chicago to "revitalize North Kenwood–Oakland" by inundating the community with public or federally assisted housing. This will only magnify and prolong the damage already done over the past fifty years.

Draped in this family and personal history, many residents of North Kenwood–Oakland feared the effect of new public housing just as the neighborhood was attempting to rise from the shadows of the deserted high-rises (see fig. 21). And a dark shadow it was. "We're here as property owners having our insurances go up by the day because we've got all this vacant stuff around," Shirley Newsome recounted. "Bad enough with these vacant houses being set afire and all of that. I mean, the stench on a warm day, [and] the whole area was rodent infested." Prop-

Figure 21. Empty Lakefront Properties high-rise casts shadow over nineteenth-century Oakland homes, 1998. Photo by author.

erty values, insurance premiums, the ability to attract new residential and commercial investments, clean and safe streets were all, in opponents' minds, jeopardized by the possibility of new public housing. Sure, the neighborhood was turning the corner. RRR granted that. But the momentum was faint and could be reversed by the slightest roadblock. Stymieing the efforts of black residents in North Kenwood–Oakland to better their neighborhood by burdening it with more public housing represented for RRR the continuance of the cycle of racial discrimination, with all of its economic repercussions.

RRR versus LCO

Neither Residents for Responsible Redevelopment nor the Lakefront Community Organization, which represented the displaced public housing residents, were parties to the *Gautreaux* lawsuit. The case of public housing nonetheless put them in opposition. Exploring the experience of these interlocutors—middle-class black home owners on one side vehemently opposing poor black renters on the other—highlights the processes of construction and negotiation that create "the black community." The intraracial character of the controversy in North Kenwood–Oakland fostered both ambivalence and agony. In my interviews with former RRR members nearly seven years after these matters were debated, some disowned the intensity of the original dispute with LCO. Alexander Pratt, a former RRR participant, said that his group and Izora Davis, one of the LCO leaders, "never really had a real problem." He elaborated, "As I said, we felt that basically people should have some place to stay and we didn't have no problem with it. We just wanted it controlled and wanted the replacement piece to conform to what we thought the community was becoming." Pratt suggests a mutuality between RRR and LCO, a notion that he quickly contradicts when he recognizes that RRR wanted new public housing "controlled." In the documents RRR filed with the court, such control meant to "oppose any diminutive [sic] of the Gautreaux Consent Decree." RRR argued further that "the Gautreaux Limited Areas guidelines should not be waived so that HUD and CHA can fulfill obligations they have to the Lakefront Community Organization."[38] This is pretty clear and total opposition to any new construction of public housing. Contrary to Pratt's more sanguine version, RRR was at the time of the proceedings quite explicitly against the position staked out by LCO because satisfying LCO's claims to housing in NKO would repeat the segregation that the *Gautreaux* rulings were established to eliminate.

While retrospective softening is not surprising given the passage of time, it also illustrates the complex rationalizations involved in putting forth a race-conscious argument that can easily appear racist on its face. RRR imagined itself to be protecting the interests of African Americans against the segregative impulses of the Chicago Housing Authority. But what often came across, especially in the media, was that middle- and upper-income African Americans did not want poor blacks in their neighborhood. In Chicago, the latter formulation resonated strongly with the resistance by whites in the 1950s and 1960s to the residential settlement of African Americans, whether in public or private housing.

The seemingly intraracial conflict was also aggravated by the involvement of white intermediaries—including the executive director of the CHA, the judge, the lawyers for the *Gautreaux* plaintiffs, and some representatives from the City of Chicago—in negotiating and deciding the final resolution. A resident at one CCC meeting "stated that he had a problem with the fact that the people making the decision regarding this issue tonight did not look like him."[39] The speaker's sentiments, coded but not disguised, reveal the irony that for all of the contentious and contemptuous racial in-fighting, many of the decision makers were white.

Resident Gayle Peters had a similar interpretation: "That whole battle was just insane. And I think there was a lot of the system against the common people. And when I say system—the city and their workers fueled a battle between the CHA residents and the residents who were saying, 'Hey we don't want these public housing units here.'" Peters accomplishes an interesting analytical transformation. In her version, middle-class and poor blacks *together* make up the "us," the common people, the littlemen, covictims of a divide-and-conquer strategy waged by the racially unspecified "them," the system, the city, the man. RRR's lawyer Benjamin Starks made a similar point in his arguments to the court during the official proceedings. "We're not against poor people," he said, referring explicitly to class but implicitly to the blackness of the poor people in question. He continued, "We're poor. Every one of us are poor. We're against our neighborhood being inundated with subsidized housing, causing us to continue to be poor and our descendants to be poor. *They* don't care about that. It's a money-making scheme for them. Make money now."[40] The comments of the resident at the CCC meeting and of Gayle Peters and Benjamin Starks are all consonant with the broader intentions of RRR, namely to emphasize the *interracial* political struggle being waged within the context of an all-black neighborhood. In such a homogeneously black milieu, RRR maintained, the power of whites may be hidden, but it is nonetheless deeply implicated, in the historical constitution of patterns of racial segregation and in white's present roles as municipal and judicial arbiters.

Yet for all of RRR's attempts to reframe the issue and redraw the lines of debate, this did nothing to diminish the hurt experienced by LCO's leadership. "The truth came out when it came to build the replacement housing," said Izora Davis, head of the Lakefront Community Organization, going on to describe the controversy:

After we got the Revised Agreement signed, they really looked at us like we were lower than dust. . . . It hurted me so bad because I never would think that our own people would feel that way. You know you look for different races to feel that way but not your own people. And I mean it was just something. I mean, it was just, I've never seen anything like it before in my life, not amongst our own people anyway. It was horrible.

> And I took my daughter with me because I told her, I said, "I want you to understand and see for yourself exactly how your own people will treat you when it comes to certain things." And I told her, I say, "especially when they feel that they are above you." And I took her with me so she could see and hear things for herself.

Davis's comments demonstrate the tenuous and fractured alliance that constitutes the "we" of the black community. Her frequent references to "our own people" bespeaks her unwavering belief in a collective black identity; like the RRR members quoted previously, she saw the black/white divide as fundamental. Yet it is precisely because she believes that African Americans should always be on the same team that her experience in fighting for replacement public housing in NKO was so painfully bewildering. Her distress over blacks that "feel that they are above you" challenges Gayle Peters's depiction of the situation, which portrayed all of NKO's black residents as "common people" up against a more powerful (white) "system." While the rhetoric on both sides may highlight fissures within black identity, it never fully discards a belief in racial solidarity. And thus the pain. The strong commitment to the notion of "the black community," even in the face of discordant ideals and practices, magnifies the grief of having one's "own people" as adversaries. Ultimately, however, the black-on-black RRR versus LCO fight was just an undercard to the main event, which itself was not much of a fight since the plaintiffs and defendants were of one accord.

Erasing Race

Because RRR was not a party to the *Gautreaux* lawsuit, neither the plaintiffs (the *Gautreaux* families) nor the defendants (CHA and HUD) were obliged to respond to its position. And with the exception of plaintiffs' counsel's brief rebuttal during oral arguments, neither the plaintiffs nor the defendants substantively engaged the points made by RRR. The two sides' lawyers did, however, in the original joint motion asking the court to designate NKO as a revitalizing area, state why they deemed such a designation appropriate. Their motion can be put in dialogue with RRR's oral testimony and written briefs.

The case for a revitalizing area designation presented jointly by the attorneys for the *Gautreaux* plaintiffs and the attorneys for the Chicago Housing Authority and HUD rested on (1) the signed Revised Agreement between LCO and the CHA, in which LCO agreed to the demolition of the high-rises in exchange for a promise of replacement units, (2) the claim that, even with the construction of new scattered-site CHA units, the total number of public housing units in NKO would be *reduced,* and (3) the signs of revitalization. The motion acknowledged that "the community is divided respecting the development of new public housing in the area, with some residents in support and many others opposed." But because all of the other relevant actors were on board, the two sides moved forward with their request to the court.[41]

The joint motion recognized the Revised Agreement between the LCO and the CHA as the document guiding the request for revitalizing area status. "The replacement housing provisions in the Revised Accord," the movants wrote, "are appropriate and desirable."[42] The Revised Agreement not only bolstered the legal case for building replacement units, but also raised a moral argument: displaced public housing residents *should* receive their due. A promise had been made to the residents of the Lakefront Properties, who were now dispersed across the city and beyond, that they could move back to rehabilitated public housing on the lakefront in Oakland. Although the current proposal offered much less than what LCO members had originally been promised, it was an effort to finally make good on this ten-year-old promise. These evaluative terms signaled the plaintiffs' and defendants' belief that respecting LCO's rights outweighed RRR's opposition.

The second response to RRR's opposition was more technical than normative. At issue was the definition of public housing units, and thus the number of such units in the neighborhood, and the definition, and thus the extent, of revitalization. The joint movants stated that after the demolition of the high-rises and construction of the proposed new public housing units, "The number of family public housing units in the Revitalizing Area would be reduced by approximately 50% from 1986 levels, i.e., from 1,066 to 538."[43] These numbers differ greatly from those presented by RRR and point to the centrality of definitions to legal proceedings. The original *Gautreaux* order sets the following exact definition of public housing:

> "Dwelling Unit" shall mean an apartment or single family residence which is to be initially made available to and occupied by a low-income, non-elderly family, subsequent to the date hereof, directly or indirectly by or through CHA, whether in a structure owned in whole or in part by CHA (whether or not newly constructed) or to be otherwise made available for occupancy by or through CHA to such a family.[44]

This definition erases the 300 units of senior public housing that RRR included in its tally, all of the nearly 750 units subsidized by state low-income housing tax credits, the over 1,000 project-based Section 8, Section 236, and Section 223 units, and any other developments that took advantage of the nearly twenty federal programs used to fund low-income housing in NKO.

I argue, however, that the issue is neither who was right about the number of public housing units nor what is the appropriate definition of low-income housing. Instead, I argue that the genius of systemic racism is that such technicalities were the only allowable terms of debate in these court proceedings. RRR was unable to make a comprehensive argument about the relationship between race and the concentration of poverty because housing units *not* funded or managed by the Chicago Housing Authority were excluded from discussion. The high proportion of *subsidized* housing in the neighborhood was part of the same racism that concentrated *public* housing there. While this fact may be substantively important, it was legally irrelevant. The court could consider only non-elderly public housing units run by the Chicago Housing Authority in applying the general formula used to decide if the CHA could build more public housing in an area.

But the revitalizing area precedent goes even further toward erasing the context and history of racial politics and prejudice in Chicago. As *Gautreaux* attorney Alexander Polikoff reminded the court in his oral remarks, the number of public housing units in North Kenwood–Oakland was irrelevant to the limited question under consideration:

> It's also correct, as I'm sure your Honor knows, that the 15 percent limitation for census tract applies only to public housing, not to other forms of subsidized housing. And the figure that Mr. Starks mentioned is not a public housing figure. He mentioned, I believe, it was 70 percent. *But even that figure goes by the boards in a waiver, or revitalizing area context, as your Honor well knows.*[45]

Polikoff was correct. The issue of existing public housing is not a consideration in determining revitalizing areas. Thus, despite RRR's plan to interject issues of a fair distribution of public and other subsidized housing across the city, its unfair concentration in black neighborhoods, and the impact of that discrimination on efforts to rebuild such areas, the only question facing the court in these proceedings was Is North Kenwood–Oakland a revitalizing area?

Hence, the third and most important part of the arguments presented by the plaintiffs, CHA, and HUD was that North Kenwood–Oakland qualified for this designation. The court defined the term in the following way:

> An area may be designated as a Revitalizing Area if it is: 1) undergoing visible redevelopment or evidences impending construction; 2) located along the lakefront; 3) scheduled to receive Community Development Block Grant Funds; 4) accessible to good transportation; 5) an area with a significant number of buildings already up to code standards; 6) accessible to good shopping; 7) located near attractive features, such as the lake or downtown; 8) free of an excessive concentration of assisted housing; 9) located in an area which is not entirely or predominantly in a minority area and 10) not densely populated.[46]

Because the neighborhood unambiguously met some of these criteria—it sits along Lake Michigan, is ten minutes by car from downtown, has good public transportation and two entrances to a highway, and is not densely populated—the proponents of the designation worked to convince the court that the neighborhood also met the more subjective criteria. On the question of whether there was visible redevelopment in NKO, the RRR members were themselves ironic exemplars of this criterion. They were well-dressed, well-spoken, capable home owners. Clearly the neighborhood must be revitalizing if it could attract such newcomers. Other evidence marshaled by the movants included plans by the Chicago Department of Planning and Development and private firms to build new single-family homes, plans for a new shopping center developed by the Fund for Community Development and Revitalization, the location of a major bank branch at the edge of North Kenwood, investment of funds by the MacArthur Foundation in community improvement, and the planned opening of two new schools in the neighborhood. RRR countered that the neighborhood's failure to satisfy criteria eight (no excessive assisted housing concentration) and nine (not predominantly minority) should decisively militate against the requested designation. The joint movants conceded the presence of public and other subsidized housing in NKO. "Suffice to say," argued the city's representative, "there is a fair amount of assisted housing in the area."[47] But the larger point was that its presence had not deterred the redevelopment efforts underway.

On the question of race, however, the plaintiffs and defendants were glaringly silent. In the oral arguments, the first mention of North Kenwood–Oakland's all-black racial composition was made by the lawyer for RRR. This followed elaborate presentations by various witnesses sympathetic to the revitalizing area designation, none of whom even mentioned racial considerations. Even in response to RRR's plea to the judge not to "nullify *Gautreaux*" by allowing new public housing to be built in a black neighborhood, Polikoff avoided racial language, stating simply: "But this, as we believe, is a good revitalizing area, it's a good place for Gautreaux families generally to live."[48] The terrain of *Gautreaux* had so clearly and thoroughly drifted away from race under the revitalizing area regime that the standard for relief for Gautreaux families was reduced to the nebulous "goodness" of a neighborhood.

Without question, the new paradigm was provoked by CHA's resistance to building racially desegregated public housing and the desire of the *Gautreaux* counsel to get some, any, new housing for its clients. But in this turn of events, racial composition, once the dominant consideration in the *Gautreaux* order, was diminished to just one of ten criteria the judge might use in evaluating the appropriateness of opening a neighborhood to new public housing. Alexander Polikoff, himself one of the architects of this shift, assesses it with much ambivalence, writing: "In the important redevelopment context, our racial desegregation case had now been transmuted, with the judge's blessing, into a mixed-income, economic integration vehicle. Whether or not this was a cause for celebration is a good question."[49]

At this point, it is relevant to refer to another set of legal proceedings in the *Gautreaux* case regarding the same question but in a different neighborhood. In considering the very first revitalizing area motion by the plaintiffs and defendants for the redevelopment of the Henry Horner projects on Chicago's Near West Side, Judge Marvin Aspen took the "risk of being characterized as one of those dreaded activist judges" and offered his very telling musings on the state of race and public housing in Chicago.

> There's no question that Gautreaux initially was a lawsuit and the consent decree was a relief in response to a segregated city. And I—and perhaps I'm being sanguine again—see the changes in the city. I think that economically people of all races can live where they want to in the city, and that's an important step. I think in spite of many problems that we have to deal with, just as we have made progress significantly in terms of

urban integration or urban—or relief from urban segregation, the problems of urban housing, putting aside racial problems, have, if anything,
in my view become worse by both neglect and also because of the unfortunate monetary crunch that all federal and local governments are under
these days.

To me, your proposal is one that addresses a 21st century view of the
City of Chicago and its housing problems as opposed to the 1966 view
that was properly the view at the time of the filing of the Gautreaux litigation. . . .

Although this project does not directly impact on the goals of racial
integration that the Gautreaux consent decree was designed primarily
to address, it does have an impact in the broad sense of doing something
about the ghettoes of the City of Chicago, which I think are the source
of obviously [sic] misery for those people who live in them and social
excuses for others to live in a community where people of differing back-
grounds, economic, social, racial and culturally, can live together. As I said
before, I think it's really a 21st Century view of what Gautreaux ought to
be about.[50]

The judge's enthusiasm for the new direction of public housing remedi-
ation—away from race and toward class—clearly contradicts his reluctance to be seen as an activist judge in the area of housing. He voiced the
same aversion to activism in evaluating the North Kenwood–Oakland
motion. But as legal scholar Abram Chayes writes, it is impossible for
judges in public law litigation *not* to be an active force in creating policy
and precedent. Instead, judges are "thrust . . . into an active role in shaping, organizing and facilitating the litigation."[51]

Furthermore, Judge Aspen's appraisal of appreciable progress in over-
coming racial segregation in Chicago—to the extent that "people of all
races can live where they want to"—is patently wrong. Using standard
social science measures, racial segregation in Chicago inched down from
92.6 in 1960 to 88.8 in 1970, went back up to 90.6 in 1980, and dipped
to 87.4 in 1990, five years prior to Judge Aspen's statement. Practically,
this index means that 87.4 percent of Chicago's white population would
have had to move to a black neighborhood (or vice versa) to make each
neighborhood in the city mirror the city's overall black/white demographic composition—that is, to perfectly integrate blacks and whites
in Chicago. While the statistics do establish a pattern of decline in racial
segregation, it is understood that anything over 60 is a "high" degree

of segregation. Chicago has been well over this mark for decades, and remains so. In 2000, Chicago ranked as the fifth most segregated city in the nation.[52] These realities strongly contradict Judge Aspen's wistful depiction of Chicago's racial geography.

Given the sentiments expressed in the Henry Horner deliberations, it is not surprising that Judge Aspen ultimately ordered North Kenwood–Oakland designated as a revitalizing area. In this case, his oral meditations symbolize the narrow jurisdiction of the court once previous decisions had been rendered.

> So what we have here is a unique situation: A plaintiff, the federal authorities, the local authorities, the Receiver and people in the community, for the most part, working together to do what they can to implement the 1996 [sic] Gautreaux decree. It is not surprising—and I would be shocked if it were otherwise—that people generally do not want scattered site housing in their communities, and with good motives on their part. People who have worked hard all their lives and invested most of their money—and indeed, their entire estate probably is the equity that they have in a home—whether they are black or white, do not want that equity or home, their nest egg, to be deteriorated or obliterated by mindless planning that will affect the value of their property and ruin their neighborhood and ruin the lifestyle that they have worked very hard to create for themselves. And as I say, significantly people complain in African American communities that, look, we have got enough public housing in our area; put it elsewhere. You try to put a handful of units in a predominately white area and the people in that community claim that they can't even handle a handful of units. The reality is that publicly-assisted housing is not popular in any area with the people in that area. The bottom line is, though, that this is not a decision for me to make. I've said on many times that I don't sit as the housing czar for the City of Chicago. It's a job that I don't want; it's not a part of my job title. It's not part of my obligations in the Gautreaux case and it's a job that I wouldn't accept, in any event. I'm not competent to handle that job. I don't delude myself that I am. From time to time lawyers come before me, the plaintiff comes before me or one of the other parties in this lawsuit, with a motion. Sometimes, like the motion today, it's a motion that is agreed upon. Sometimes it's not agreed upon. Sometimes it's a motion which the consent degree requires them to make in order for me to implement part of the consent decree. Sometimes it's a motion to vary some specific

restrictions in the consent decree in order to go along with the broad-based philosophy and spirit of the consent decree. And I rule on those motions and I rule on them as a matter of law.[53]

The racial wrong that the court initially established in the 1969 *Gautreaux* order had now receded into years of legal machinations in response to CHA inaction. Only such erasure could allow the judge to abdicate his role as Chicago's "housing czar" on matters of race and public housing, and to instead narrowly construe his role as ruling on motions. The racial logic inheres in the history of racial antipathy and segregation, creating black neighborhoods disproportionately burdened with public housing, which in turn occasioned municipal neglect of and private disinvestment from those neighborhoods. The institutional amnesia displayed in the events chronicled here portends the vicious, but this time unspoken, repetition of that cycle, a possibility that NKO's new black middlemen tried to fight.

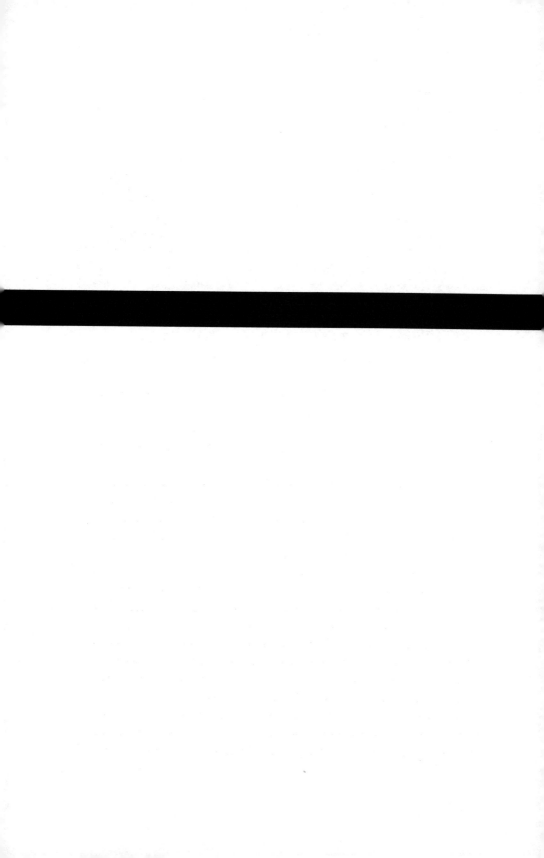

6

"Sure I'm paranoid. But am I paranoid *enough?*" This quip is often delivered with a self-deprecating chuckle, but feelings and accusations of paranoia have been no laughing matter in North Kenwood–Oakland. The decades-long fight by public housing residents to maintain a presence on Chicago's lakefront is filled with anxious fears about a dark plot against them. These fears are contradicted, denied, and dismissed by public officials as premature, unfounded, and outlandish. But frequent regime and administrative change allows for institutional unaccountability, backtracking, and amnesia. In the end, the residents' seemingly paranoid fears come to pass just as they predicted. It is difficult to uncover mal-intent on the part of those in power who make, break, and revise promises to residents. Instead, urban bureaucrats, elected officials, and civic visionaries characterize their actions as being good for public housing residents and for the city, and in line with market principles of land use (i.e., higher land prices mean better use) and resource distribution (i.e., middle-income taxpayers can demand and attract more services and commercial outlets). It is a perfect example of what political theorist James C. Scott describes as a "hegemonic planning mentality that excludes the necessary role of local knowledge and know-how."[1] This chapter argues the rational basis for the paranoia of the public housing resident leadership. The politics of the promises made to public housing residents exemplify their littleman status, well outside of the networks of power. In the course of their struggles, they have been pushed beyond strategic skepticism and sometimes to the limits of sanity, to the point where the question "Am I paranoid *enough?*" makes perfect sense.

Urban Renewal I and II

A brief history of the Lakefront Properties is crucial to understanding the fears that public housing residents felt when their apartments were slated for "renovation" in 1985. Parts of this history have been told in earlier chapters. The focus here is on the particular *actors* involved in the municipal building efforts that lead to the erection of the projects in North Kenwood–Oakland.

The need for public housing in Oakland in the 1950s and 1960s was generated by urban renewal projects underway in the Douglas neighborhood, immediately to the north and west (see frontispiece map). Douglas was the heart of the Black Belt, just south of where the Illinois Central Railroad spilled out carloads of black passengers coming up from the South during the first and second Great Migrations. "Men in worn, outmoded suits carrying battered luggage and women clutching ragged, barefooted children crowded into the Illinois Central station on Twelfth Street looking hopefully for a familiar face," writes historian Allan Spear.[2] Douglas was home to nearly all of the major black ventures—the funeral parlors, newspapers, insurance companies, and banks—that made the Black Belt a city unto itself. As sociologists St. Clair Drake and Horace Cayton characterize it, it was "Black Metropolis."

But stuck within the growing Black Metropolis were predominantly white institutions established in the previous century, namely the Illinois Institute of Technology (IIT) and Michael Reese and Mercy Hospitals. Historian Arnold Hirsch writes, "Whereas the Loop was cut off from its customers by a ring of 'slums,' Michael Reese Hospital and IIT existed in their midst." These places, while prominent citywide, were so socially isolated from and irrelevant to the growing black community that they received no index entries in Drake and Cayton's *Black Metropolis* or James Grossman's study of the Great Migration, *Land of Hope*, and only very minor mentions in the Black Belt histories by Allan Spear and Dempsey Travis.[3] That these places were geographically embedded in the Black Belt yet so socially apart is indicative of the limits of northern integration.

Because of their isolation, these institutions were looking for ways to either leave the area or insulate themselves from the ghetto around them. In the mid-1940s, a powerful coalition of downtown business interests and real estate developers—of particular note was Ferdinand (Ferd) Kramer—teamed up with these establishments to invent and implement a redevelopment scheme that would serve all of their respective interests. Their plan was to stop the growth of the poor and working-class black community by building a racially integrated middle-class community in its place. This in turn would attract students and professors to the university and doctors, nurses, and paying patients to the hospitals, all of whom would shop, bank, and be entertained downtown—and all of which would be a windfall for real estate investors. By the end of the 1940s, these investors were supported by federal and state legislation that financed "slum clearance," fostering the transformation of urban areas across the country.[4]

The first of these joint endeavors was the Lake Meadows housing development. Hirsch has thoroughly and richly chronicled the story of Lake Meadows, with its menagerie of political and financial players and strategic legislative lobbying. The part of Lake Meadows's story that is relevant to North Kenwood–Oakland is that it was constructed not on vacant land but in a densely populated Douglas neighborhood. One prominent real estate agent "knew that 15,000 blacks lived on the Lake Meadows site and that redevelopment plans accommodated but 5,000. 'Where,' he asked the Chicago Plan Commission, 'will these people go?'"[5] Building Lake Meadows required substantial land clearance and assembly, which translated into thousands of displaced people who spilled south and east. Some of those "cleared" from the Lake Meadows area in the years from roughly 1948 to 1952 braved the hostile terrain of nearby white neighborhoods with their racial restrictive covenants—now legally worthless but still symbolically potent—and threat of physical violence. Newly built public housing was the option for others. Of course, public housing construction also required land clearance, further exacerbating an already critical housing shortage in the black community. This pressure from blacks for housing was felt in the communities that bordered the traditional Black Belt, including Oakland and Kenwood, Hyde Park, Washington Park, and others. In this era—the 1940s through the 1960s—the Black Belt more than doubled in size and even began to push into the suburbs. Indeed, the real estate agent's question, "Where will these people go?," reflected a fear of just this expansion. He worked in a white neighborhood ten miles south of the Black Belt, where his clients dreaded the influx of blacks displaced by the Lake Meadows redevelopment project.

David Wallace, a PhD student in planning at Harvard in 1953, analyzed the data on families moved from the Lake Meadows site. He found that 27 displaced families bought homes in Oakland (of 235 families who bought homes overall). And although exact data on North Kenwood was not reported, Wallace's maps plotting the location of homes purchased show that at least 15 families bought homes there. Looking at the entire sample of displaced families, not just the home buyers, Wallace noted further that "single-person families, as might be expected, clustered around the original site and moved in large numbers to Oakland and north Kenwood, where rooming houses predominate." A quarter of the families moved into public housing, with the nearby and new Victor Olander Homes a likely destination. Wallace concluded that the Lake Meadows project directly contributed to the rapid racial transition of white neighborhoods like Oakland and North Kenwood that bordered the Black Belt.[6]

The public housing projects in Oakland were built in response to both the pressures from urban renewal in Douglas and overcrowding within the neighborhood itself. Oakland's population was at its all-time high in 1950 (see fig. 6), with nearly twenty-five thousand residents in an area of barely more than one square mile. The design solution to the pressing housing needs of blacks in cities across the country, observed Jane Jacobs, had become "a routine matter of plunking down ever higher towers in ever more vacuous settings." This was indeed the approach taken in Oakland on a half-mile strip of land fronting Lake Michigan, part of which was vacant and the rest of which was cleared to make way for the six high-rises that would become the Lakefront Properties.[7]

This history of how the Lakefront Properties came to be *built* is meant to foreshadow the story of how they came to be *torn down*. By the 1980s, having completed Lake Meadows and a series of other new developments, many of the same players, including Ferd Kramer, turned their eyes to North Kenwood–Oakland. The public housing built as part of urban renewal in the 1940s and 1950s now became the target for urban renewal itself. Like Douglas, the Oakland neighborhood was poor and black. As was the case with Lake Meadows, there were nearby institutions—some of them the same ones—that stood to gain from the racial and class transformation of the area. Once again, the necessary coalitions were formed between private interests and public agencies. People would have to be moved and buildings demolished. And as in the earlier undertakings, the residents who would be most affected were hardly consulted, their relocation was shabbily planned, their outcomes were poorly monitored, and their "rights" were questioned and debated. In this case, only the persistence of the public housing resident leadership prevented their complete erasure from the planning process and from the community itself. Nonetheless, the record of victories and concessions at the Lakefront Properties is reminiscent of the cycle begun at Lake Meadows: many people are moved out, few original residents get to move back, and other neighborhoods feel the reverberations. Meanwhile, elite investors, institutions, and city bureaucrats smile at a job well done. As Larry Keating observes in a similar history in Atlanta, the story of the Lakefront Properties involves "relearning urban renewal's immutable lessons."[8]

The Renovation Promise

In February 1985, the Chicago Housing Authority (CHA) submitted a preliminary application to the U.S. Department of Housing and Urban Development (HUD) for funds from the Comprehensive Improvement Assistance Program to renovate nearly forty thousand units of public housing at a cost of almost $750 million. The massive size of this request is evidence that nearly all of CHA's units were in need of some rehabilitation. After reviewing the application and visiting every CHA development, HUD determined that "because of the high concentration and critical need, the greatest impact could be made by comprehensively rehabilitating the properties on the Lakefront." In response to HUD's assessment, the CHA requested $14 million specifically for the Lakefront Properties, and HUD granted that request in September 1985.[9] The story hit the newspapers soon after CHA was awarded the money but *before* the agency had informed the residents that the renovation would require relocation. The residents learned about that with the rest of the city from the daily newspapers: The *Chicago Tribune* headline read, "CHA Work to Empty 6 Buildings." The *Sun-Times* was equally clear: "700 Families Face Move in Renovation Plan at CHA."[10] While most residents agreed that the buildings were in bad physical shape, they were not pleased with the surprise announcement that they would be moved to other CHA developments, most of which they perceived as more dangerous.

From the very first, residents had their suspicions. "Once they relocate us and renovate the buildings they'll raise the rents and we won't be able to afford to move back in," one speculated. "They also expressed concern," wrote one reporter, "that the CHA was vacating and renovating the buildings to sell them to private interests."[11] Moreover, residents worried about how long the renovation would take, whether they would have first priority to move back, and whether they would be able to reclaim their same apartments. The CHA responded in all the right ways, denying that CHA property would ever be sold to private developers, assuring residents that they could return—and could even reserve their specific apartments—and pledging that rents would not be raised. These promises and agreements were short-lived.

Residents raised their voices and demanded inclusion in the planning for the rehabilitation. In October 1985, soon after the first announcement, they organized into the Lakefront Community Organization (LCO). Representatives of the group met with CHA executive director Zirl Smith and CHA board chairman Renault Robinson, and the agency promised to consider alternatives to mass relocation. One possibility was to phase the construction work by moving families into vacant apartments within the building while their own units were being worked on. This way residents would not have to leave the Lakefront community. A task force was convened to go over all of the options. It included Lakefront residents, heads of community organizations, CHA staff, elected officials, planning consultants, and citywide civic leaders. They were charged with collecting feedback from residents about their preferences and consulting with planners and builders about feasible rehabilitation and relocation schedules that would cause "the least possible discomfort and inconvenience for residents."[12]

Desiring an objective method of gauging resident sentiment, the task force distributed a survey. However, based on an assessment of the scale of work and the contingencies of HUD funding, it had already decided that "entire buildings must be vacated" and "an individual resident's option to remain in the building during construction could not be considered."[13] As a result, the survey made no provision for residents to protest relocation outright. They could only choose *which relocation program* they preferred. They could opt to receive a Section 8 voucher, to be moved to another CHA building, to move into private housing with no public assistance, or to receive down payment assistance for a home purchase.

It is no surprise, then, given the forced choice, that the results of the survey suggested widespread support for relocation. While 568 households (84 percent of the total) completed the survey, only seven wrote in that they did not want to move at all. All of the others chose one of the four options. However, 113 residents, including some who had ostensibly signaled support for relocation in responding to the survey, also signed a resident petition that protested mass relocation. This opposition group was ultimately unsuccessful. The task force forwarded its recommendation for full relocation to the CHA in June 1986.

Concurrent with the work of the task force, the Lakefront Community Organization was negotiating an agreement that would govern the relocation and rehabilitation process. On May 27, 1986, the LCO, the presidents of each building, the CHA, and the respective lawyers signed an agreement entitled the "Memorandum of Accord Regarding Relocation of Residents from the Lakefront Properties Pursuant to the CIAP Rehabilitation Project." The Memorandum of Accord outlined several points of agreement between the residents and the CHA about how renovation would proceed. First, LCO acknowledged that residents would have to be relocated. The memorandum then set out priority criteria for residents' return to rehabbed units, affirmatively recognized residents' demands for additional security personnel as buildings were emptied, specified relocation benefits, and guaranteed jobs for residents on the rehab work. Perhaps most importantly, it established the official "right to return as a tenant in the Lakefront Properties after the rehabilitation is completed."[14]

Sanctioned by both the Memorandum of Accord and the task force recommendations, relocation began in earnest in the summer of 1986. All of the buildings were emptied save one, which was occupied by about thirty tenant leaders determined to monitor and enforce the memorandum on-site. LCO's initial push to secure the memorandum and its stubborn presence in buildings that over time became almost uninhabitable demonstrate that its members did not fully trust the CHA to honor its contract. They knew that vigilance was a necessity. Carlos Roberts, a leader of the Lakefront Community Organization, conveyed this resolve: "Just because we're poor and living in public housing doesn't mean we'll allow ourselves to be taken advantage of. We'll do whatever

Figure 22. Lakefront Properties high-rises sit vacant, 1998. Photo by author.

is necessary to ensure that we remain where we're at."[15] Some of them stayed for nearly five years. But nothing happened. No repairs, no construction, no security. Nothing except the slow and severe deterioration of these abandoned steel and concrete behemoths (see fig. 22).

As a result of constant turnover at the Chicago Housing Authority, the rehabilitation of the vacant Lakefront Properties was continually delayed. Between 1986 and 1988, the CHA had four different executive directors, each of whom made promises at occasional meetings with the Lakefront Community Organization that rehabilitation was imminent. Outside interest in the land on which the vacant public housing high-rises stood grew during this period of CHA inactivity. In the late 1980s, developers, the City of Chicago, nearby institutions, home owners, and community groups began to imagine North Kenwood–Oakland's future, culminating in the conservation area designation in 1990. Almost all of the plans envisioned the demolition, not the rehabilitation, of the Lakefront Properties.

The saga of the Lakefront Properties' transformation will ultimately span three decades. In some ways, it is foolish to assume that promises made in the 1980s would be honored by contemporary administrations, especially when so many hands have stirred the pot over the years. Given the indignities that the onetime residents of the Lakefront Properties have suffered, the case *for* public housing in NKO rests on the rights of and responsibility to the tenants who were told in 1986 that their buildings would be renovated and that they would be able to return in a matter of months. This was not the case. Instead four of the six buildings have been demolished. The road from renovation to demolition illustrates the immense power differential between public housing residents on the one side and city officials and private investors on the other, with NKO's black gentrifiers occasionally mediating and brokering. Public housing residents did not have access to powerful networks. They were unable to hold institutions accountable. They could not define the terms of the debate. And because of their poverty, their claim on cultural, moral, or civic legitimacy was constantly called into question. These dimensions constitute a contentious politics of promises in North Kenwood–Oakland and provide a sense of how things get done in cities more broadly.

The Kramer Plan

The years from 1985, when it was announced that the Lakefront Properties would be renovated, to 1998, when four of the high-rises were demolished, were characterized by residents asking skeptical questions, the CHA making firm assurances, and then nothing happening. The CHA's complete flip-flop on the issue of demolition is perhaps the most blatant example of institutional disingenuousness. Meetings between the two parties would go something like the following, as reported in the *Chicago Tribune:*

> Local and federal housing officials Thursday assured current and former Chicago Housing Authority residents who were forced to move nearly two years ago for building renovations that the work would begin in the spring—almost a year behind schedule.
>
> The meeting between representatives from the CHA, U.S. Department of Housing and Urban Development and the Lakefront Community Organization, composed of the remaining and relocated tenants of the six South Side buildings slated for renovation, was the first since residents learned that they would have to move.
>
> Concerns expressed by many of the roughly 75 tenants at the meeting reflected the 2-year lapse in communication. Much of the evening

was devoted to dispelling suggestions that the six buildings would be razed or that they would not be made available for poor tenants upon completion.[16]

The displaced residents of the Lakefront Properties received numerous guarantees from countless housing officials. CHA and HUD representatives spent much energy "dispelling" rumors of a nefarious plot to rid the lakefront of public housing and its residents to make way for the wealthy. But if CHA and HUD officials were unaware of such a plan, then what was the genesis of the demolition notion?

The first public suggestion of demolishing the Lakefront Properties came from real estate mogul Ferd Kramer (see fig. 23). Draper and Kramer, the real estate services company started by Ferd Kramer's father, Adolph, and his partner Arthur Draper in 1893, is one of the most prominent in Chicago. Although Draper and Kramer made its fortune constructing and managing downtown and suburban office and residential buildings, Ferd Kramer never forgot where he came from, so to speak. He was born on the near South Side of Chicago and first lived in a mansion on Prairie Avenue, the posh area south of downtown and north of Oakland where Marshall Field, Philip Armour, and others of Chicago's most prominent families lived. Kramer's family later moved further south. Historian Lois Wille writes: "When Prairie Avenue deteriorated and the great stone houses were chopped into tiny flats, the Kramers moved south to the Hyde Park community surrounding the university. Watching Prairie Avenue crumble ignited an abiding passion in young Ferd: He resolved that the South Side would rise again."[17] Further solidifying Kramer's South Side attachment, he graduated from the University of Chicago in 1922, lived in the South Kenwood neighborhood for many years, and went on to become a lifetime trustee of the university. His connection to the university would prove helpful in his efforts to get things done in North Kenwood–Oakland.

By the time Kramer turned his attention to the Lakefront Properties in 1987, he had already spearheaded two massive redevelopment projects on the mid- and near-South Side—Lake Meadows in the Douglas neighborhood, which was discussed earlier, and Dearborn Park, just south of downtown Chicago. These endeavors were all interconnected. The year of the groundbreaking for Lake Meadows, 1952, was also the year that the first Lakefront Properties building was dedicated. Dearborn Park was completed in 1985, the same year that the CHA an-

Figure 23. Real estate developer Ferd Kramer in front of the Lakefront Properties, 1988: the Olander Homes are in the foreground, the Washington Park and Lake Michigan Homes in the background. *Chicago Tribune* photo by Ernie Cox Jr. All rights reserved. Used with permission.

nounced the Lakefront Properties renovation. These co-incidents were not simply coincidence. In the 1950s, the need for public housing was driven by the demolition to make way for Lake Meadows and other urban renewal projects. And in the 1980s the revitalization of the Lakefront Properties made sense only because Dearborn Park had proved that areas south of downtown could attract affluent newcomers. Its immense success spurred interest in the south lakefront all the way to Hyde Park. Kramer had the same laudable vision for all of these developments, including the Lakefront Properties: to build racially mixed middle-class residential neighborhoods.[18]

In Lake Meadows, the first of Kramer's large-scale undertakings, realizing his vision required removing the existing poor and working-class black residents in order to attract white and middle-class residents. Dearborn Park was quite a different scenario since the land consisted mostly of vacant rail yards with almost no residents; there the focus had been on ensuring racially sensitive and inclusive marketing strategies. The situation at the Lakefront Properties resembled the Lake Meadows project more than it did the Dearborn Park development. As with Lake Meadows, poor and working-class African Americans lived in the area Kramer hoped to transform. Achieving racial integration and middle-class predominance in all-black and predominantly poor North Kenwood–Oakland would again require both removing existing residents and attracting whites and middle-class buyers. In this case, however, the CHA had already started the job. The first and perhaps greatest hurdle, that of moving residents out of the neighborhood, had been completed when the Lakefront Properties were closed for renovation. Thus Kramer's proposal to demolish the already vacant buildings was considerably less audacious than it would have been had residents still been living there. Moreover, Kramer had significant community support, having included block club leaders and the Kenwood Oakland Community Organization (KOCO) in the creation of his plan.

The Kramer Plan, as it came to be known, called for four of the six public housing high-rises in the Lakefront Properties to be demolished.[19] It proposed one-for-one replacement of the demolished apartments in low-rise buildings to be built across North Kenwood–Oakland, as well as construction of roughly three thousand new homes, plus new businesses and parks. The *Chicago Tribune* reported on the unveiling of the plan in 1987:

> An ambitious plan to raze four 16-story public housing high-rises located on prime South Side lakefront land and replace them with low-rise housing for people of all income levels will be presented Tuesday to federal housing officials in Washington.
>
> If implemented, the proposal, conceived by Ferd Kramer, a prominent Chicago real estate developer, and backed by the Illinois Housing Development Authority, would revitalize one of the most deteriorated neighborhoods in the city and fill in one of the last underdeveloped gaps along the lakefront between the University of Chicago on the south and the middle-income Lake Meadows and Prairie Shores apartment complexes on the north.[20]

Behind its veneer of journalistic restraint and neutrality, this article contains many subtle messages that churned public housing residents' early fears of permanent displacement.

The first line of the article contains a word that would become a standard descriptor in discussions of the Lakefront Properties site: "prime." The phrase "prime real estate" commonly refers to land that is attractive to developers for a variety of reasons, in this case its proximity to both the lakefront and downtown. But "prime-ness" is a social construct like any other, historically and politically contingent. After a patrician beginning, North Kenwood–Oakland experienced a precipitous decline in desirability. In the 1950s and 1960s, when the high-rises were built, downtown was a deteriorating center of congestion and disorder and, from whites' perspective, the city was being overrun by African Americans. Whites turned their eyes toward the hinterland where, thanks to the federal government, modern, air-conditioned houses were both relatively cheap and easily accessible via smooth new roads. In that era, "prime real estate" was suburban land adjacent to highways or commuter rail lines. Neighborhoods like North Kenwood–Oakland—far from the new suburban shopping malls and entertainment centers, still the destination of black migrants from the South, and full of old, high-maintenance attached graystones with little yard space and no room for garages—held none of the charm for which buyers are today willing to pay a half-million dollars. The return of North Kenwood–Oakland to "prime" status has not been lost on public housing and other poor residents, but they interpret North Kenwood–Oakland's second dawn as signaling a dusky future for them.

There is another key word in that first sentence of the *Tribune* article: "replace." While the author is clearly referring to the replacement of high-rises with low-rises, it is but a short interpretive step to the idea of replacing one type of people, namely poor people, with another. Given the ubiquity of mixed-income language, the new type of person was unlikely to be poor. For a neighborhood in which over 60 percent of the families had incomes below the poverty line, and most others were not much better off, creating a mixed-income neighborhood meant that many poor people would have to be "replaced" by richer people, a fear echoed throughout the planning process in NKO.

The second paragraph of the news story is significant not for the use of any particular words, but for the historical networks and events it evokes. First, Ferd Kramer. As the same author noted in a later article, Kramer "had a hand in just about every other major urban renewal project undertaken in Chicago in the last 50 years."[21] This was not a distinction without its underside. The phrase on the tongues of many African Americans is "Urban renewal equals Negro removal." Some North Kenwood–Oakland residents had experienced this equivalence personally as refugees from the "renewal" of Chicago neighborhoods into developments like Kramer's Lake Meadows. Hence, Ferd Kramer's name called to mind a foreboding history for many. Mention of the University of Chicago invoked similar memories. It had been the architect of urban renewal in nearby Hyde Park, which the *Chicago Defender* officially opposed as segregationist. Observers at the time acknowledged that "it was fairly clear in the [university's] Plan proposals themselves that the effects of the Plan would be to limit the proportion of Negroes in the population."[22]

All of these references were red flags for poor and working-class African American newspaper readers, suggesting the replay of a history in which their claims to a place are denied and the future of that place taken out of their hands. Thus, public housing residents' fears of being moved out of the Lakefront Properties with little hope of return were rooted in their "reading" of the discourse about and players involved in the plans for North Kenwood–Oakland. And atop that discourse was reality. The Kramer Plan had enlisted the support of many key institutions and organizations. *For* the demolition were: the Kenwood Oakland Community Organization, the Conservation Community Council, the University of Chicago, the Illinois Housing Development Authority, the Chicago Urban League, and the legal counsel for the plaintiffs in the *Gautreaux* lawsuit.

But despite these gathering clouds, nearly every public authority who addressed the displaced public housing residents seemed to dismiss the dire scenario of demolition and permanent exile as unlikely. Indeed, many public officials opposed the Kramer Plan outright. Mayor Harold Washington's position on the Kramer Plan was: "I'm opposed to it . . . but we can't stop developers from dreaming." His successor, Eugene Sawyer, was leaning strongly against it, commenting reticently, "I'll think about it, and I'll pray." Jerome Van Gorkom, the CHA's executive director at the time of the initial announcement of the Kramer Plan, left the door ajar: "No one is going to grab that property and tear it down without CHA or HUD approval. . . . There is no danger of that until and unless the developers can supply, before they tear them down, equal or better units." But, Van Gorkom's successor, Vincent Lane, closed the door again with his opposition to demolition: "Those buildings can be rehabilitated and can be managed better than they have in the past. . . . I think we need to expand housing opportunities and not replace them one for one." Lane, an African American, had grown up in public housing and knew from his own example that it could bear positive fruit.

At the local level, Alderman Tim Evans opposed the demolition of the high-rises so strongly that he became the chief adversary of Kramer and others who endorsed the Kramer Plan. Alderman Evans's office was picketed by KOCO, which favored the Kramer Plan. And Kramer himself was so bold as to say that Evans had only "emasculated" plans for redeveloping the neighborhood. Finally, the Kramer Plan was opposed by federal HUD officials stationed in Chicago. "We simply told [the developers] there would be no recommendation from this office. . . . However, if we are asked to make one by Washington [D.C.], it will be that those high-rises not be torn down. Instead, they should be rehabilitated as originally intended and the families who were relocated should be given the opportunity to move back into them when the rehabilitation work is completed."[23]

So with the exception of the State of Illinois, as represented by the Illinois Housing Development Authority, every level of government opposed the demolition of the high-rises. Van Gorkom had allowed that it might be possible, but only if Kramer replaced every public housing unit *before* demolishing any building. This would be a serious challenge for Kramer since there was little federal money available for construction of new public housing units.[24] Most people thought that the insurmountable hurdles Kramer faced should calm residents' anxieties about being dispossessed of their public housing homes.

The most hopeful sign for former Lakefront Properties residents was that CHA director Vincent Lane began renovations of two of the six buildings. What had been the Victor Olander Homes when they were built in 1952 and 1956 were reopened in 1991 as Lake Parc Place. But while things appeared to be going their way, public housing activists still did not let down their guard. They persevered, maintaining residence in one of the deteriorating buildings as a constant reminder of their claims on the neighborhood.

Given the seemingly unanimous early commitment on the part of local and federal officials to saving the high-rises, how did it happen that in June 1996 the Chicago Housing Authority, HUD, *and* the Lakefront Community Organization went together before the federal judge in the *Gautreaux* court with a plan to demolish the four remaining empty high-rises, and with only partial replacement? There are of course as many answers to this question as there are people to answer it. There had been activity at almost every level of government, with changes in federal legislation, administration, and funding, new federal court rulings, and city and community elections that replaced mayors and the local alderman. I briefly review these shifts below and then turn to a more micro-level *sociological* story about the social relationships within which CHA officials reversed their position on demolition, and from which public housing residents were excluded as those decisions were being made.

The Road to Demolition

At the federal level, there was significant ideological change in public housing policy during the period in which the high-rises sat vacant. The mantra became mixed-income housing in low-rise settings. The notion of income mixing is not new. In its early years public housing was a mix of lower middle-class, working-class, working poor, and unemployed families. That ideal was jettisoned when funding waned, maintenance suffered, and nonpoor families moved out. Beginning in 1969 with the Brooke Amendments to the 1937 Housing Act, and through the 1980s, federal mandates required public housing authorities to give priority to only the neediest of families. Scholars of urban neighborhoods grew critical of these policies, the effects of which were to isolate poor people in high-poverty neighborhoods. Poverty concentration, scholars argued, amplified and exacerbated the social problems of poor individuals.[25]

By the late 1980s and early 1990s, the policy community caught on to this rhetoric. CHA director Vincent Lane was a pioneer when he transformed two of the Lakefront Properties into a model of mixed-income public housing. Lane lobbied the federal government to allow moderate-income working families into public housing, rather than only the poorest applicants. The program that resulted from his requests to Congress was called the Mixed Income New Communities Strategy. Lake Parc Place—the rehabbed twin buildings of the Lakefront Properties—was the only demonstration under this program that ever got off the ground (see fig. 24).[26] On the heels of the Mixed Income New Communities Strategy was the federal Urban Revitalization Demonstration Program authorized in 1992, and later renamed HOPE VI. Lane's experiment at Lake Parc Place was the forefather of HOPE VI. He was so successful in shaping national housing policy because he chaired the National Commission on Severely Distressed Public Housing, which made recommendations to HUD. The federal government's growing flexibility in reforming public housing culminated in the Quality Housing and Work Responsibility Act of 1998, which solidified

Figure 24. Cover of video promoting Lake Parc Place. Author's copy. Video produced by Ray-Roc Productions, Inc., for Lake Parc Place RMC.

earlier measures such as lowering the percentage of public housing units reserved for the poorest families and ending the rules that required public housing authorities to build one unit of housing for every one they demolished. Within this national policy context the probability of rehabbing the Lakefront Properties and returning all of its very poor residents was diminishing.

Another march toward demolition began in the courtroom. Since the original 1969 judgment, all new public housing construction in Chicago has been overseen by the *Gautreaux* court to ensure that the CHA and HUD comply with the desegregation order.[27] The lawyers for the *Gautreaux* plaintiffs, headed by Alexander Polikoff, were perhaps the most consequential *supporters* of demolition because they had the power to enlist the federal court in definitively deciding the fate of the high-rises. In 1990 and again in 1991, attorneys for the *Gautreaux* plaintiffs filed motions to block the CHA from rehabilitating the Lakefront Properties. With the exception of the activist squatters, the buildings had stood empty for four years, but there was still money available from HUD to rehabilitate them, and the CHA intended to do just that. Polikoff and his team argued that repairing structures that were found to have been built illegally in the first place would essentially redo the initial wrong. The CHA had an obligation to "affirmatively administer its public housing system to the end of disestablishing segregation." Rehabilitating the high-rises in all-black North Kenwood–Oakland went against this requirement.[28]

Furthermore, Polikoff argued, rehabilitating the roughly six hundred units of public housing in the four high-rises would "frustrate the prospect of providing hundreds of scattered-site public housing units under highly advantageous circumstances for members of the plaintiff class."[29] The preferred scattered-site units to which Polikoff referred were the ones proposed in the Kramer Plan. And the "highly advantageous circumstances" meant North Kenwood–Oakland without the high-rises, a community imagined in the Kramer Plan as racially and economically mixed. While the motion did not explicitly ask for the demolition of the high-rises, the picture that Polikoff painted rested on exactly that. The judge ultimately denied the plaintiff's motion to stop rehabilitation on the grounds that work on the high-rises was not imminent. CHA had not even secured the required funding from HUD. This, the judge concluded, left the plaintiffs ample time to negotiate with the CHA and HUD without a court order. Still the effect of these

motions by the *Gautreaux* plaintiffs' lawyers was to put CHA on notice
that they would not support the rehabilitation of the high-rises, adding
one more vote for demolition.

The Lakefront Community Organization and later the Central Advisory Council, which represented all Chicago public housing residents,
attempted to intervene in the case. They saw the plaintiffs' motion as
threatening their chance of seeing the high-rises renovated and thus
their members' ability to come back to the neighborhood. Hence, their
motion to intervene was in support of the CHA's plans to use HUD
money to rehabilitate the high-rises and *against* the *Gautreaux* plaintiffs' motions, which indirectly supported demolition.[30] These motions
and countermotions highlighted a paradox to be resolved in establishing the best interests of public housing residents. The *Gautreaux* lawyers acted as counsel for one class of public housing residents, namely
those who had charged the CHA and HUD with racial discrimination
in 1966. The "plaintiff class" it represented is more symbolic than comprised of actual public housing tenants. The lead plaintiff, Dorothy Gautreaux, died even before the first finding in 1969 that CHA and HUD
had broken the law. Meanwhile, a group of present-day public housing
residents argued that the *Gautreaux* lawyers did not represent their interests regarding the fate of the Lakefront Properties. As current public
housing residents, they favored the rehabilitation of the high-rises to
provide decent housing to needy Chicago families, no matter the racial composition of the surrounding neighborhood. The judge granted
LCO's right to intervene, giving its leadership a seat at the negotiating
table outside of the court.

Changes were also afoot at the city and local governmental levels.
Chicago had three different mayors in the years immediately following the closing of the Lakefront Properties. Harold Washington (1983–
1987) died while in office and was succeeded by acting mayor Eugene
Sawyer (1987–1989), who lost in the subsequent primary to Richard M.
Daley (1989–present). Such turnover did not bode well for maintaining a city-level commitment to the displaced Lakefront residents or, indeed, for preserving municipal memory at all. The same was true at the
community level, where in 1991 Tim Evans, alderman since 1973 and
a staunch opponent of demolition, was defeated by Toni Preckwinkle,
who publicly supported demolition. Both candidates' stances on the
high-rises had been central to their campaigns. When the high-rises
were emptied, Evans lost an important constituency. On the other hand,

as home owners in NKO became more involved and organized in the late 1980s, they began to see the looming high-rises as detrimental to their plans to revive the neighborhood, as well as to their own property values. Preckwinkle's commitment to tearing down the high-rises and building public housing in a low-rise scattered fashion appealed to their interests and won her a voter base in the neighborhood. As the community's composition changed, so too did community sentiment.

To recapitulate, federal legislation was now promoting mixed-income communities. The *Gautreaux* plaintiffs, who wanted the high-rises down, had been sent by the court to negotiate with the CHA, HUD, and the Lakefront Community Organization. The new mayor and alderman had not themselves made any promises to public housing residents and were quite open to the idea of demolition. And although the informal prodemolition coalition met considerable resistance from public housing activists, it enjoyed the visible support of NKO home owners.

Still, there were lingering questions—and one pivotal holdout, Vincent Lane. Lane became executive director of the Chicago Housing Authority in 1988 and quickly made numerous public statements opposing the prospect of demolishing the high-rises. His stance was that the stock of public housing in Chicago needed to be increased, not decreased, and he was committed to keeping the promise made to displaced tenants. He bolstered his words with actions, reapplying for federal funds to rehabilitate the six buildings and successfully completing the renovation of two of them, creating Lake Parc Place in 1991. By 1994, however, Lane was brokering a deal for the demolition he had once vociferously denounced and had often promised would never happen. Lane's turnabout was surely facilitated by changes in federal housing law, but it was also *orchestrated* through the activation of influential networks with mutual interests in North Kenwood–Oakland. As sociologist Ronald Burt notes, "Networks do not act, they are a context for action."[31] Lane's change of heart had a definite social context.

Plans, People, and Persuasion

While this is not primarily a story about the University of Chicago, the university is nonetheless a powerful institution on the South Side of Chicago and the site for the formation or crystallization of important relationships and alliances. By the 1980s the university was ready to venture beyond its most immediate neighborhoods of Hyde Park and

South Kenwood, both of which had been almost completely upgraded and redeveloped through university-directed urban conservation and renewal beginning in the 1950s.[32] The university now considered its potential impact on the adjacent communities of Woodlawn, to the south, and North Kenwood–Oakland, to the north. Both areas were predominantly black and very poor. The university first set its sights on North Kenwood–Oakland in the late 1970s in a collaborative planning process with other major South Side institutions. These early efforts failed because of intense opposition by the Kenwood Oakland Community Organization to the interference of this outside (white) institution.[33] University representatives were beaten back from North Kenwood–Oakland in their first overture, but this was not the end. By the mid- to late 1980s the university had begun to act as a kind of central but inconspicuous organizing node for the various parties interested in revitalizing NKO. Not only was the University of Chicago the largest and most powerful institution on the South Side of the city (thus everyone and everything had to go through it at some point), but many of the players had preexisting and ongoing ties to the university. This web of affiliations facilitated entrée to and cooperation with the university, and with each other.

For starters, Ferd Kramer did not have to make a cold call to university personnel to get a hearing for his plan. He was a 1922 graduate of the University of Chicago and a lifelong trustee who served on multiple committees, including the Committee on Campus Planning and the Neighborhood.[34] Hence, Kramer was, in this case, not only the petitioner but ultimately a judge since any university-backed initiatives for the surrounding community would come before the board of trustees. Jonathan Kleinbard, who was then vice president for community affairs, remembered: "Ferd Kramer called me up . . . and said, 'I was born in North Kenwood–Oakland. Now my early childhood was there and I want to see that revitalized. And I want the university to be a part of it.'" Kramer had not really been born in North Kenwood or Oakland, although he had grown up on the city's South Side. Errors of fact aside, the tenor of this exchange was clearly familiar, on a first name basis, and conducive to a positive reception.

The university had only one requirement before signing on to the Kramer Plan: Kramer had to get community leaders in North Kenwood–Oakland to buy into the plan, including the demolition of the high-rises. Kramer had already started working on that. He incorporated the block clubs and other home owners into his planning group so that they had a stake in the plan. Most importantly, Kramer had garnered the support of Robert Lucas, executive director of the Kenwood Oakland Community Organization. KOCO was in the process of expanding its activities to include rehabbing derelict apartment buildings for affordable housing. It had also undertaken some new construction along the same lines. The groundbreaking over which Mayor Harold Washington presided on the afternoon that he died was for a new development sponsored by KOCO. Given KOCO's aspirations in housing, its leadership likely saw possibilities for a financial or management role in developing some of the affordable housing that would be built under the Kramer Plan. With assurances that the local community leadership was on board, the University of Chicago became a full participant in promoting the plan.

The other key node in the dissemination of information was the Metropolitan Planning Council (MPC), "a nonprofit, nonpartisan group of business and civic leaders committed to serving the public interest through the promotion and implementation of sensible planning and development policies necessary for a world-class Chicago region."[35] MPC's history in North Kenwood–Oakland dates back to the 1940s, when it participated in the first discussions of "conservation" as a development strategy. More recently, MPC had participated in the Lakefront Properties Task Force, which developed recommendations for relocation strategies during the rehabilitation of the Lakefront Properties. Ferd Kramer was an "honorary life governor" of the Metropolitan Planning Council. So, once again, it was no cold call when he presented the Kramer Plan to MPC's executive committee in February 1988. Even more importantly, one of the members of MPC's executive committee was Vincent Lane, a successful African American developer of affordable housing, who a few months after Kramer's presentation would become executive director of the Chicago Housing Authority. Also on the executive committee was George Ranney Jr., then a partner at the law firm of Mayer, Brown, and Platt and an executive at Inland Steel Company. And here the circle begins to close: Ranney, who was a friend of Lane's through their work on the MPC executive committee, also led the team of civic leaders that chose Lane to head the CHA. Moreover, Ranney was a resident of South Kenwood and a trustee of the University of Chicago, where he served with Ferd Kramer.

Establishing these connections is the first step in understanding Vincent Lane's turn from opposing the demolition of the Lakefront Properties to supporting it. From his early years, he expressed a desire to deconcentrate public housing and build mixed-income communities. This was the rhetorical mantra that motivated Lane's lobbying for federal legislation to support his Mixed Income New Communities Strategy. In 1988, when he opened the bid process for construction firms to do the work on Lake Parc Place, Lane declared, "We're sending a message to the residents. Where we can extend the life of existing buildings, we will do that. We need to expand the housing stock."[36] His success at Lake Parc Place strengthened his resolve to improve public housing through renovation rather than demolition. "It's a myth that families with children can't live in high-rises successfully," Lane wrote in a 1994 *Policy Review* article. "When you drive along North Lake Shore Drive in Chicago, all you see are high-rises. We all know that families are raised successfully in high-rises. The problem in public housing is the concentration of poor people living there, not the buildings themselves."[37] Similarly, newspaper accounts from the early years of Lane's tenure as executive director and chairman of the CHA quote him as strongly opposing the demolition of public housing: "Vincent Lane, the private developer who has been the CHA's chairman and executive director since June, opposes any talk of demolishing high-rises, arguing that new money should be used to provide new low-income housing rather than simply pay for the replacement of existing apartments."[38]

But the Chicago newspapers are eerily silent between the 1991 opening of Lake Parc Place, when Vincent Lane was a champion of public housing, and the 1994 community meeting at which Lane asserted: "It was a major public policy mistake to build the public housing you see today. . . . If that agreement [with displaced Lakefront residents] didn't exist, I would endorse demolishing all the buildings"[39] (see fig. 25). This statement marked a major change in the Lane who time and time again said he would not demolish the Lakefront Properties.

The absence of newspaper coverage during those years is telling. The press reports on public events. What transpired between 1991 and 1994 happened "quietly." In late 1991 and early 1992 a never-named group "agreed informally to meet quietly every month" to "talk about how we could really build a healthy community both in North Kenwood and in Woodlawn"—the neighborhoods to the north and south of the University of Chicago. This working group was comprised of many of the actors introduced above: Alexander Polikoff, lead counsel for the

Figure 25. Chicago Housing Authority CEO Vincent Lane addresses displaced residents of the Lakefront Properties, 1994. *Chicago Tribune* photo by Milbert Orlando Brown. All rights reserved. Used with permission.

Gautreaux plaintiffs; George Ranney, board member of the University of Chicago, MacArthur Foundation, and Metropolitan Planning Council; University of Chicago vice president Jonathan Kleinbard; and CHA executive director Vincent Lane. There were other participants as well, such as developer Allison Davis and former gubernatorial appointee Paula Wolff, both of whom also had strong ties to the University of Chicago, foundations, and the public and private sectors.[40] The group's glue was the newly appointed commissioner of the Department of Planning and Development for the City of Chicago, Valerie Jarrett. Jarrett came from a prominent African American family in Chicago, and she grew up in South Kenwood. She was not an alumna of the University of Chicago, but she later became a member of the board of trustees because of her strong ties to and impact on the university community. Jarrett commented that the members of this working group "came without portfolio but . . . wanted to be helpful." In saying that the participants were "without portfolio," Jarrett indicates a recognition on the part of some members that they lacked grassroots legitimacy because they were not *residents* of the neighborhoods they hoped to affect. But of course these individuals had considerable experience and expertise, and could exert power far beyond that controlled by the residents. Their portfolios might not be useful at the community meetings going on in North Kenwood–Oakland as residents prepared their neighborhood's conservation plan, but they held much sway in the boardrooms where these leaders operated.[41]

The working group quickly established that the Lakefront Properties were the key X-factors in planning for a healthy community. The presence on the working group of both Polikoff, who filed the motion to stop rehabilitation of the high-rises and favored their demolition, and Lane, who wanted to convert the high-rises to another mixed-income model development, meant that some hard negotiations lay on the horizon. Conspicuously absent from this group was any representation for the Lakefront Community Organization. There was considerable reason to include the public housing residents. The federal court had granted them intervenor status, and they would ultimately have to be convinced to let CHA out of the Memorandum of Accord, the agreement that promised them rehabilitation and return. But these were considered either minor pieces of the puzzle or easily tackled hurdles. Whatever the reason, their absence is a testimony to their insignificance in the practice of urban development.

According to its brainstorming memos, the group saw the Lakefront Properties as an "obstacle to redevelopment" that required "leadership from individuals involved in the litigation and controversy over the CHA high-rises." Clearly, one of the charges of the working group was to mediate the impasse between Polikoff and Lane. Both parties had also been admonished by the federal court to hammer out their differences. The outcome of the negotiations that occurred in the monthly meetings of the informal working group was Lane's public appearance in North Kenwood–Oakland with a plan to demolish the high-rises. The first high-rise in Chicago to be demolished was the Washington Park Extension, a sixteen-story building that stood alone a few blocks west of the Lakefront Properties on Drexel Boulevard. At the January 1995 demolition Lane spoke like a zealous convert: "This is just the beginning. If there's anything whose time has come, it's the demolition of these God-awful places. We can no longer isolate the poor in those high-rise prisons."[42]

The informal working group, operating behind the scenes, had facilitated this change of direction. Surrounded by friends and associates whom he respected and who favored demolition, Lane slowly let go of his dream that public housing in Chicago could be salvaged through a concerted cooperative effort between the CHA and dedicated residents. Members of the working group remembered Lane arguing that the success of his mixed-income project at Lake Parc Place was proof that other high-rises could be made into decent housing for Chicago's poor. But Lane was clearly in the minority. Most members of this select assemblage of city officials and business leaders thought that the high-rises should come down, which is the sentiment that eventually prevailed. The movement from point A, where Lane's vision differed substantially from that of others in the group, to point B, where he advocated the high-rises' demolition, was lubricated by the mutual regard that members of the working group held for each other through their multiple and overlapping relationships and affiliations.

Returning to the urban theory that guides this book, this informal working group operated firmly within the tenets of the growth machine. Urban elites agree that the way to improve a neighborhood is to encourage the settlement of higher-income families, thereby maximizing land uses, increasing tax revenues, and creating an economic base to attract businesses and services. Poor people are a drag on such efforts, and poor people housed in conspicuous high-rises are an even greater hindrance. Lane, who grew up poor and proud and whose heart was in public housing resident empowerment, had to be convinced of this premise. "Preferences," writes political scientist Clarence Stone, "are not formed independent of social relationships."[43] Growth machines are not always characterized by unanimity on a particular issue. Instead, their success rests on their ability to reach agreement. One of the most effective avenues for doing so is by enlisting people who can use their social ties of affect and respect to persuade others. This is the power of social capital, which is the mechanism by which distinct urban players are formed into "machines." Moreover, social capital is augmented by its opposing property, elaborated below, namely the power to *exclude* people from those same social networks.

What's in an Agreement?

The plan for demolition was, of course, no easy sell to the displaced residents of the Lakefront Properties. By March 1994, when Vincent Lane came to them with his plan, they had been waiting eight years to be moved back to their neighborhood. Residents were understandably skeptical. Lane dazzled them with visions of low-rise homes with yards and garages. He made more promises, saying residents would be able to come back to an improved lakefront public housing community much better than the renovated high-rises could ever be. Residents, however, were no dupes. "I just hope it's not just for TV purposes," said Izora Davis, the leader of the Lakefront Community Organization, voicing both skepticism and optimism at the same time.[44]

With the new gospel of demolition, Lane had to renegotiate with the LCO to devise terms to replace the old Memorandum of Accord. Maintaining their fierce determination, LCO began those talks by driving a hard bargain. Bob Jones, an attorney for the *Gautreaux* plaintiffs, remembered:

> My knowledge picks up in '94 when you know there were serious and regular meetings under way. I think it would be fair to characterize the situation at that point as LCO was really sticking by their original agreement with CHA and pushing for rehabbing those buildings. And basically every other entity, you know [the City of Chicago], Habitat [which would build the scattered-site CHA housing], BPI [the *Gautreaux* lawyers], whatever, favored demolition and redevelopment in a mixed-income configuration. But obviously, you know, LCO had, was presumed to have, well, not only a significant stake in it but also legal leverage through their agreements.

The minor self-correction in Jones's last sentence is of major importance. The LCO was *presumed to have* power on the basis of the contracts it had negotiated with the Chicago Housing Authority. This presumption was later proved to be false. The sequence of activities that showed it to be false answers the question: What is the fate of an agreement made between unequals?

Finalizing any plan to demolish the high-rises required two negotiation processes, one to alter the Memorandum of Accord that the CHA signed with the Lakefront Community Organization in 1986, and the other to decide on a plan to present to the *Gautreaux* court to win approval for building replacement public housing in an all-black neighborhood. These two sets of negotiations moved on parallel tracks and included some of the same actors. Both were legal negotiations, but only the one involving the *Gautreaux* court included any oversight beyond the feuding lawyers. As a result, the discussions regarding what would be proposed to the *Gautreaux* court were more involved and thorough than the renegotiation of the Memorandum of Accord between CHA and LCO. The latter process was particularly hampered by continued administrative upheavals at the CHA. In May 1995 the U.S. Department of Housing and Urban Development took over the CHA amid findings of gross financial mismanagement and Vincent Lane resigned. A few months later, former HUD official Joseph Shuldiner took the helm of the CHA. In light of this turnover, much of the dialogue between the Chicago Housing Authority and the Lakefront Community Organization and its lawyers took place under chaotic circumstances. The flux at CHA created a lack of accountability, and ultimately another set of broken promises to the LCO.

Simultaneous to the LCO-CHA dialogue was a more participatory series of meetings about what would replace the Lakefront Properties if they were demolished. These sessions included representatives from the LCO and CHA, the *Gautreaux* plaintiff's lawyers, Shirley Newsome from the Conservation Community Council, Alderman Toni Preckwinkle, and Valerie Jarrett, who during these meetings switched hats from representing the City of Chicago to representing the Habitat Company. Habitat is a curious player in these discussions because it is a private firm charged with providing a public good, public housing. In 1987, the *Gautreaux* judge appointed Habitat as the "Receiver" for the Chicago Housing Authority because the CHA was doing such a poor job of building public housing in a desegregated fashion. As punishment for its intransigence, the CHA lost control over the ability to build new public housing. That responsibility now fell to the Habitat Company, which worked in collaboration with the CHA.

In these meetings, the Lakefront Community Organization was not altogether opposed to the notion of replacing the high-rises with low-rise mixed-income housing. Izora Davis felt that LCO entered the negotiations with a receptive attitude:

> We understood the big picture more so than what they thought we understood it. And that we were not trying to, you know, congest the community again with a lot of public housing or whatnot. We were trying, especially with residents, to spread out, you know. . . . People, they *wanted* the front doors and the back doors. They wanted a town house and a row house and stuff. I mean, they were elated about it, you know. And we were too. Because we felt like well we, the residents, we doin' good. We takin' care of our people, you know. We had a good working re-

lationship with CHA, Habitat, and HUD at that particular time because, I mean, I think we all were on the same level and we were about taking care of the business.

Whereas negotiations started off cordial, wrangling over the number of units to be replaced if LCO agreed to demolition of the high-rises was more complicated. Here Davis became more stern:

Well it was interesting. I had some of 'em think that I was a lawyer. It was interesting because I would not [back] down. I stayed on 'em. They tried to convince me that, you know, the residents don't wanna come back. So the negotiations—it was pretty long and hard. But I held my ground and the [LCO] board members hung in there with me as well. [The other members of the group] couldn't figure out how many units that they would have to build. And I told them this. I say, "Well, this is what you need to do. Because when you're talking about unit for unit, you can only replace unit for unit what you have." And I said, "Therefore, the number of units that we have standing already is the number of units you have to replace, plus the number of units that you've used in [Lake Parc Place] for the 50 to 50 median income [referring to the half of the units in the rehabbed buildings that were now reserved for moderate-income families]." So they looked and they thought about it. I said, "That way you don't wind up with a [law]suit." And they hadn't thought about that.

Others in the working group similarly felt the tension as the group tried to come up with the number of units to replace the 607 apartments in the four high-rises. *Gautreaux* attorney Bob Jones saw Davis as a particular challenge.

You know, Izora is a very strong and very insistent woman. And Izora's negotiating approach and demeanor was not, you know, hey let's work this out, you know, I'm sure there's some middle ground we can find, etc. Izora was just adamant: Hey, we have an agreement. It entitles us to X number of units. You know, I'm just not going to agree to this other stuff. There was a lot of no, no, no and suspicion and mistrust from Izora. And they were very difficult discussions. I mean, I think everybody else in the room could, you know—there just weren't fundamental disagreements among the people at the table about what should be done or needed to be done there in a general way. Except with Izora, you know. I mean, I think the atmosphere was really—I don't want to say everybody against Izora. But, you know, the question was always will Izora ever agree to anything. And is there any way we can find a way to get Izora to buy into something. And that's not to say that everybody else at the table had sort of worked out and agreed on every detail of anything. But we all knew that we could. But Izora just constantly threatened to go to court to enforce her agreement.

Izora Davis and Bob Jones both agree that Davis was a force to be reckoned with at the bargaining table. Davis saw herself as balancing her resolute demeanor with an openness to various plans that included demolition. She was not, however, amenable to reducing the amount of housing available for poor families, be they former residents of the Lakefront Properties or not. Her steadfastness was interpreted by some members of the group as unproductive obstinacy, but Davis feared that bending was but a short step from being broken. This was the paranoia of which public housing residents were often accused.

Yet Davis did ultimately compromise. She agreed to not having all 607 replacement units concentrated in North Kenwood–Oakland. "Well, how did she get moved," I asked Bob Jones, "because clearly at the end she made concessions?" Jones responded: "I think there might have been an element of, you know, Izora just getting worn down." Whereas the hard negotiations that took place in the informal working group relied heavily on persuasion, the tactic in this case was closer to pressure or coercion. Ultimately, though, Davis's flexibility (or batteredness) went unrewarded.

These negotiations demonstrate that Izora Davis was not a party to the trust that inheres in the social networks of urban elites. That trust and mutual regard assures machine members that an acceptable agreement can be reached in most circumstances. As Jones saw it, everyone else at the table had not reached an agreeable solution, "but we all knew that we could." Davis, however, was not operating with these assurances. Quite the opposite, she stood on the outside, apart from the contingent of power brokers, because she was on the wrong side of the economic engines of the growth machine. Her activism for poor people's housing was anathema to the investors who now saw this neighborhood as prime real estate. Had Davis bought into the scheme of reducing the number of public housing units to make way for housing for middle- and upper-income newcomers, then she would have likely been welcomed into the inner circle with open arms. Indeed, she would probably have become the face of the redevelopment plans, their most legitimate and authentic sponsor. But she was not convinced and instead held on to the dream that revitalization could include public housing, and lots of it. Not being a member of the power brokers' circle of trust, she always had to keep in play the threat that she would take her case, her group's prior agreements with the CHA, to court. Davis presumed that in the halls of justice her lack of education, poverty, blackness, and reliance on governmental provisions would not count against her. But she soon learned that even the courts would not support her if she tried to stop the master plan to transform the lakefront.

Two documents—the Revised Agreement and the "revitalizing area order"—emerged from the two years of meetings about the Lakefront Properties' future. The separate legal nature and purview of these documents allowed for the strategic disavowal of some of the promises made to public housing residents. The "Revised Agreement Regarding Former Residents of the Lakefront Properties and the Future Use of Those Properties," signed by the LCO and CHA in September 1995, supplanted the earlier Memorandum of Accord and contained a new set of promises to displaced public housing residents. Joseph Shuldiner represented the Chicago Housing Authority, but he was only an interim executive during this period of federal management of the CHA.

The Revised Agreement included nineteen points of agreement, beginning with the linchpin compromise allowing the CHA to demolish the remaining four lakefront high-rises. LCO approval of demolition was tied to certain stipulations about the planning for and timing of replacement units. To compensate for the 607 public housing apartments to be demolished, the agreement stipulated that 241 units would be built in North Kenwood–Oakland, 200 public housing units would be built elsewhere in the city, and 302 Section 8 vouchers would be distributed to public housing families. Moreover, the high-rises could be demolished only after the CHA had secured HUD funding to build the replacement units, had secured land in North Kenwood–Oakland for the 241 units to be built there, and had gotten approval to build them from the *Gautreaux* court. The agreement also established that the replacement units were to be developed by the CHA and the *Gautreaux* court-appointed receiver, the Habitat Company, and that former residents would be given priority in filling the new units (subject to screening for income eligibility, prior evictions from public housing, felonies, rent arrearage, and other criteria).[45]

Curiously, the Chicago Housing Authority submitted an application

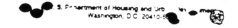

S. P͢ artment of Housing and Urb   n   meg.
Washington, D.C. 20410-5

OFFICE OF THE ASSISTANT SECRETARY
FOR PUBLIC AND INDIAN HOUSING

Mr. Joseph Shuldiner
Executive Director
Chicago Housing Authority
626 West Jackson Boulevard
Chicago, IL 60661

Distribution: 10/10/95 dist (✓ if applicable)	
✓ J. Shuldiner	✓ A. Rochgue
❏ Dr C. Adams	✓ G. Russ
❏ H. Holton	❏ S. Rutyna
❏ G. Murray	✓ S. Onakhi
✓ M. F. Johnson	✓ A. Vargas
❏ T. Lipo	✓ B. Prescott
✓ R. Monocchio	❏ Prob/Owe
✓ J. Nelson	

Dear Mr. Shuldiner:

SUBJECT: Approval of the Chicago Housing Authority (CHA) Request
          for the Demolition of 607 Units at Developments
          IL06P002034, Washington Park Homes, and IL06P002041,
          Lake Michigan Homes know as Lake Front Properties

     The Department has reviewed the above-subject application
dated July 26, 1995, which was received in the Demolition
Processing Control point, August 2, 1995.

     I am pleased to inform you that your request to demolish
607 units in the four buildings at Washington Park Homes and Lake
Michigan Homes (identified below) is approved.

LAKE FRONT PROPERTIES DEMOLITION APPROVAL						
Project Number	Address	1-BDR	2-BDR	3-BDR	4-BDR	TOTAL
IL06P002034	4040 S. Okenwald Ave	2	28	90	30	150
IL06P002041	4155 S. Lake Park	3	28	90	30	151
IL06P002041	1130 E. 41st Street	4	28	90	31	153
IL06P002041	1132 E. 42nd Street	4	28	90	31	153
TOTAL		13	112	360	122	607

     Approval of your application is based on the Department's
understanding of your application as outlined in the enclosed
memorandum from me to the Illinois State Office.

Figure 26. Letter from the U.S. Department of Housing and Urban Development
authorizing the demolition of the Lakefront Properties, 1996. *Gautreaux v. Chicago
Housing Authority* files, United States District Court, Northern District of Illinois.

to HUD requesting permission to demolish the four buildings in August 1995, a month *before* the Revised Agreement was signed (see fig.
26). This preemptive request illustrates the speed with which plans for
demolition proceeded.

The second document produced during these negotiations was the
joint motion of the CHA and the *Gautreaux* plaintiffs to the *Gautreaux*
court requesting that North Kenwood–Oakland be deemed a revitalizing area. A revitalizing area order from the judge would legally en-
able the CHA, through the Habitat Company, to construct replacement

public housing units in this predominantly black neighborhood (see chapter 5). Although the LCO was not a party to this action, the motion includes in its argument the process that yielded the Revised Agreement and asserts that "the replacement housing provisions in the Revised Accord are appropriate and desirable." The motion also confirms support for building replacement units on the part of the Habitat Company and the City of Chicago.[46] The precise purpose of this motion was to authorize, not demolition, but the construction of replacement public housing. The judge granted the motion in June 1996. Tailoring his order to the question before him, Judge Aspen granted only that North Kenwood–Oakland was a revitalizing area in which 241 public housing units could be built. His order did not comment on or recognize the various stipulations in the LCO-CHA Revised Agreement that ostensibly allowed the Lakefront Community Organization to stop demolition.

In November 1998, less than a month before the scheduled demolition of the four high-rises, the Lakefront Community Organization filed a motion with the *Gautreaux* court to stop the demolition. The LCO argued that too few replacement apartments had been built—just 111 of the 441 total promised units—and that the CHA did not have full funding commitments from HUD for the remaining replacement units.[47] The judge denied the motion on the primary grounds that it was "untimely." Too much time, work, and money had gone into preparing the buildings for demolition to delay the event any longer. In his decision, the judge wrote: "Both of [LCO's] motions stem from a 1995 agreement between the [Lakefront Community] Organization and the CHA which *appears* to prohibit the CHA from demolishing those buildings before it satisfies certain conditions." With one word, "appears," Judge Aspen's order called into question the enforceability of the Revised Agreement between the LCO and the CHA.[48] It was not so consequential at the time because the judge's basis for allowing the demolition to go forward was the last-minute nature, not the actual legal grounds, of LCO's protests. But it portended difficulties in the next battle. On December 12, 1998, the Lakefront Properties were demolished as planned in a spectacular implosion that took only a matter of seconds and drew hundreds of spectators (see fig. 27).

LCO did not go away just because the buildings were gone. The organization filed numerous further appeals with the *Gautreaux* court to try to force the CHA to hurry the building of replacement housing, to accept relocated Lakefront residents into the housing that had been built, and to support LCO's efforts at finding displaced residents. All of

Figure 27. Demolition of the Lakefront Properties, December 12, 1998. Photo by author.

these appeals were also unsuccessful. Each time, the judge returned to the point he had made when disallowing LCO's motion to stop the demolition, namely, the flimsiness of the Revised Agreement. Clarifying his position, Judge Aspen emphasized that it was the job of the Habitat Company, not the CHA, to develop new public housing. In May 1999, the judge ruled plainly:

> The problem is that the requested relief must come from the Receiver, and the Receiver was not a signatory to the deal. Or, to put it differently, because of the Receivership Order the CHA did not have the authority to enter into a contract concerning the development of non-elderly public housing—the Receiver's domain—and it did not have the authority to contract on the Receiver's behalf. . . . Those parts of the contract [i.e., the Revised Agreement] concerning the development of non-elderly public housing are unenforceable, so to allow LCO to intervene to attempt to enforce them would have been a waste of time.[49]

In contrast to the ambiguity of Judge Aspen's initial description of the Revised Agreement as appearing to prohibit certain courses of action, in this ruling he stated unequivocally that what "appeared" to protect LCO's interest in actuality could not. The Revised Agreement refers to the "the *Gautreaux*-appointed Receiver" seven times in its text, acknowledging the Habitat Company's responsibility as receiver to build replacement public housing. But since the receiver, i.e., Habitat, did not sign the Revised Agreement, none of those references meant a thing.

Unrelenting, the LCO tried again to introduce its motion to push the CHA and Habitat to action, this time adding "equitable and promissory estoppel" claims. These legal doctrines would hold Habitat to promises made in the Revised Agreement even though the firm did not sign it. LCO tried to make the case that Habitat was well aware of the content of the promises included in the Revised Agreement and that an injustice was done to LCO because of its reliance on those promises. In its motion, LCO presented various pieces of evidence that suggested Habitat's complicity in the Revised Agreement. For example, Habitat had supported the revitalization area motion to the *Gautreaux* court. That motion included the replacement housing provisions that had been negotiated for the Revised Agreement and in fact included the Revised Agreement itself, with its various stipulations, as an attachment. Also, Habitat had begun building replacement housing in North Kenwood–Oakland in accordance with the terms specified in the Revised Agreement, which suggested that it was responding to those terms. And Habitat participated in the years-long negotiations at which the Revised Agreement was repeatedly referenced.

Perhaps LCO's most compelling documentary evidence was a letter to LCO's lawyer that stated the following: "1) The Receiver will use its best efforts to achieve the development of market rate as well as public housing on both the Lakefront and Drexel corridor sites which have been the subject of discussion among us; and 2) In the event that community representatives or former Lakefront Properties tenants become dissatisfied with the pace of progress in developing either form of housing, *Gautreaux* plaintiffs' counsel and the Receiver will support the request of either or both groups for a hearing on that issue before the *Gautreaux* presiding judge."[50] This letter was signed by the chairman of the Habitat Company and the lead attorney for the *Gautreaux* plaintiffs. Even though this letter refers specifically to the replacement units to be built within North Kenwood–Oakland, which were the subject of both the revitalizing area order and the Revised Agreement, the judge did not see this statement as a blanket endorsement by Habitat of the LCO-CHA Revised Agreement. He ruled again that the "intervention was pointless because the LCO could not prevail on its contract claim."[51]

The point of this history is not to challenge the expertise and authority of the *Gautreaux* court, which ruled that parts of the Revised Agreement, perhaps the most important parts covering the pace and tenanting of replacement units, were unenforceable. The legal rightness or wrongness of that ruling is inconsequential to the fact that again promises were broken. Perhaps this is the most egregious case of broken promises because unlike impromptu proclamations made at community meetings and in ongoing negotiations, even when captured in the newspapers, the Revised Agreement was a seemingly more binding document. Drafting it required nearly two years of emotional discussions and debates and the participation of countless lawyers and other professionals. It was a contract, with all of the idealized lay understandings that are attached to such a document.

When LCO relentlessly pressed its claims to enforce the agreement, the CHA's general counsel wrote the following to LCO's lawyers:

> In your letter you allege that CHA has violated substantive provisions of the Revised Agreement. . . . In partial response to those allegations we are enclosing copies of Orders entered by Judge Aspen in the matter of *Gautreaux vs. CHA*, Case No. 66C 1459, dated 5/6/99 and 7/1/99, respectively. These orders, in effect hold that all parts of the Revised Agreement dealing with redevelopment of the Lakefront properties are unenforceable, as said Revised Agreement was not entered into with the necessary party—The Habitat Company ("Habitat")—which as you know, is the Receiver for all development of CHA properties since 1987. In effect, the *Gautreaux* Court held that CHA was not an authorized party, nor did the CHA have authority to enter into the re-development parts of the Revised Agreement without Habitat.[52]

The letter's use of the passive voice ("said Revised Agreement was not entered into with the necessary party") and third person ("CHA was not an authorized party") powerfully exemplifies the lack of accountability that characterized the long history of the Lakefront Properties. When this letter was penned, the CHA was on its ninth executive director in the sixteen years since the 1985 surprise announcement that the buildings would be closed for renovations.[53] Even when CHA was stripped by the federal court of its ability to develop new public housing, and denied sovereignty by the HUD takeover, it continued to strike deals like the Revised Agreement with public housing residents across the city. When public housing residents really needed to rely on those agreements they learned they were worth no more than the paper on which they were written. And then the CHA extricated itself from those broken promises using subtly condescending language. The CHA lawyers wrote that Habitat, "*as you know*, is the Receiver for all development of CHA properties since 1987." That the CHA now saw this point as so obvious begs the question of whether it intentionally entered into the Revised Agreement without the participation of the Habitat Company, knowing that Habitat's absence would void the agreement and the CHA would not have to live up to its promises. Only the actual officials involved know if true mal-intent played a role here, but the malevolence of CHA's cavalier dismissal is beyond question.

The Politics of Promises

The story of the Lakefront Properties is dizzying in its twists, turns, flip-flops, and reversals. Ten years after plans were announced to renovate the Lakefront Properties a deal was struck to demolish them instead. The Lakefront Community Organization had been deserted by its most powerful ally, Vincent Lane, weakened by the scattering of its constituents across the city and beyond, and increasingly isolated by the transformation of North Kenwood–Oakland into prime real estate. Other, more normal transitions also occurred over the course of the Lakefront Properties battles. The city elected new mayors, the ward got a new alderman, and the North Kenwood–Oakland community created a conservation plan. Like earthquakes, the upheavals created mounds of debris. Both the Memorandum of Accord and the Revised Agreement wound up in that debris, along with many other contradictory claims and empty assurances. In each case, what was regarded as paranoia on the part of public housing residents was actually keen foresight. There are many examples of their fears becoming reality:

- When residents protested that they did not want to move during the renovation of the buildings, the CHA chairman responded, "The board of commissioners has heard the voices of angry tenants. . . . It is our decision today to put to rest the notion that the residents will have to move. It's a dead issue."[54] Less than a year later all of the residents were being moved out.
- Residents feared a plot to dispossess poor Chicagoans of prime lakefront land. Lake Park Crescent, the new community rising on

the site of the fallen Lakefront Properties, will include nearly 500 homes, apartments, and condominiums, including 120 public housing units (see fig. 28). But poor families are excluded from half of the public housing units simply because they are poor; those apartments are reserved for families with incomes between 50 and 80 percent of the median family income for the Chicago metropolitan area—roughly $37,000–$58,000 in 2005 dollars.[55]

- Residents expressed concern that the buildings would be sold to private interests. While some of the land remains in the ownership of the Chicago Housing Authority, Lake Park Crescent is privately managed, with the homes and condominiums, along with the land under them, sold to individual buyers. As if to tie up all the loose ends, Lake Park Crescent was initially contracted to be built by Draper and Kramer, the firm headed by Ferd Kramer, who first envisioned demolishing the high-rises.

- The most important component of the Memorandum of Accord and the Revised Agreement ensured residents' right to return to the redeveloped lakefront. But the screening criteria eventually adopted for Lake Park Crescent go well beyond those allowed for in the agreements bartered by LCO. Thirty-hour-per-week work requirements, bankruptcy prohibitions, housekeeping inspections, ten-year criminal background checks, and drug tests, along with other restrictions, will surely exclude former Lakefront Properties residents and many other poor and even nonpoor families.[56]

During the period of bitter court battles, relations soured between LCO and almost every other group or agency involved in the redevelopment of the land where the high-rises once stood. In 2003, at the groundbreaking ceremony to officially commence construction of Lake Park Crescent, representation from the Lakefront Community Organization was conspicuously absent.

No simple reconciliation of the cases for and against public housing in North Kenwood–Oakland is possible, and the aim of these twin chapters has not been to propose one. Instead, the complex stories were meant to raise both substantive and theoretical issues that are often lost in the commotion of court battles and community meetings. The first point is about the existence of multiple victims. Middle-class African Americans in North Kenwood–Oakland emphasized the racial

of the history and present-day reality of the significantly constrained residential opportunities available to African Americans. Middle-class and poor blacks fight over small territory while some whites oversee the brawl and others excuse themselves from participation by moving ever further from areas of significant racial and/or economic diversity.

7

In 2004, when housing construction was in full stride across North Kenwood–Oakland, a new task force of residents was convened to begin a second stage of planning. The bricks and mortar had been set. Now, the mission, as one task force subcommittee worded it, was to create "a safe and harmonious mixed-income community with affordable housing for all families and an aesthetic and functional physical environment."[1] Rolled up into this one sentence were concerns about housing, social integration and interaction, crime and safety, infrastructure, and arts and landscaping. At one subcommittee meeting, a resident suggested that the group focus on one of the area's main thoroughfares, Drexel Boulevard. The boulevards in Chicago were a key part of Daniel Burnham's vision to ring the city with parks and landscaped promenades. Drexel Boulevard is a two-way street divided by a wide green parkway that runs along the western end of North Kenwood–Oakland. It is flanked by a mixture of four-story graystone mansions and ornate and imposing apartment buildings. Like the rest of the neighborhood, Drexel Boulevard has seen better days.

As the idea of focusing on Drexel took off, task force members began to imagine an inviting, active space. They would add decorative benches, garbage cans, and flowerpots and repave the cracked and buckled path that wound through the parkway. They would invite proposals from

Figure 29. Drexel Boulevard with its center parkway and walking paths, 1893. Chicago History Museum, film negative ICHi-04213. Photo by Gravere.

artists for sculptures and other installations in the parkway. In essence, they would return Drexel Boulevard to the grandeur it enjoyed in the late nineteenth century when it "was one of the preeminent addresses in the old suburb of Hyde Park" (see fig. 29).[2]

Into this discussion, a local police officer, a member of the task force who represented the emphasis on a "safe" community, interjected the following:

> When we're thinking about working on Drexel Boulevard, we should really think about discouraging some of the current uses there because people are out there barbecuing and setting up tents, selling snow cones, and drinking, and just doing all kinds of things. People seem to think of it as a *park*, and they just come out and plant themselves. I would like to see a larger contingent of residents use the parkway. I've heard complaints from many people that they are afraid to go out and use it because of some of the people there. So we want to think about that as we plan.

Figure 30. Birthday barbecue on Drexel Boulevard parkway, 2005. Photos by author.

A number of suggestions were made in support of this comment, such as making the benches uncomfortable, issuing citations for unlicensed vendors, or designating a specific area for barbecuing (see fig. 30).

I was a member of this task force and raised the concern that these ideas might contradict our second stated goal: to create a "harmonious" community. But, I was told, the parkway was *not* harmonious. Only a "small minority" of residents used it, and in ways that precluded its use by other residents. "Is barbecuing there illegal?" I asked. The police officer said that it was not but frequently referred to the residents' behavior as "loitering," suggesting a violation of the law. In fact, though, leisurely strolls and long rests are what the parkway was meant for.

I did not want to make my point too forcefully. I thought that we should respect the residents who currently frequented the parkway, but I also sensed that I was outnumbered. So I sat quietly after my initial caution. I had participated, now it was time to observe. I observed as the conversation drifted toward turning the Drexel Boulevard parkway into a completely passive decorative space with large flower arrangements and sculptures, and no walkway or benches. I also observed that none of the people whose use of the parkway was being scorned seemed to be members of the task force. As with much of the community organizing in the neighborhood, the task force was dominated by home owners and newcomers. Home owners have yards or decks on which to socialize and barbecue. They don't need Drexel Boulevard for such purposes and are content with admiring the parkway from their car windows.[3]

This exercise in managing public space in a changing neighborhood may seem to touch only slightly on the topic of crime. However, in this chapter I show how the definitions of crime and danger in North Kenwood–Oakland ultimately migrated from concerns about violent interpersonal and property crimes toward the manipulation and control of modes of being and interacting in the neighborhood. As the focus shifted to policing behavior, the disciplinary approach did not strongly distinguish one end of the behavioral spectrum from the other. That is, the affront of barbecuing on Drexel was attacked with as much passion as were drug dealing, robberies, muggings, and homicides. Despite the fact that the broken-windows theory—the notion that disorder leads to crime—is all but discredited, the concept has thoroughly permeated lay perspectives on crime.[4] Many residents are convinced that there is a slippery slope from loitering to assaults, from barbecuing to theft. And when the worry is not about disorganization's links to serious crime, it is about the effects that indecorous acts may have on property values. The thread of attention to respectability and middle-class propriety first introduced in chapter 2 weaves its way through the discussion of crime and deviance as well.

Crime and Gentrification

In 2002, two men were beaten to death by a large crowd after their van careened out of control and killed two young women sitting on the porch of a home in Oakland. It was an immense tragedy. While the city mourned and debated the incident, North Kenwood–Oakland's alderman, Toni Preckwinkle, joined the dialogue by emphasizing that this violent event would not stand in the way of the neighborhood's revitalization (see fig. 31). "The redevelopment of North Kenwood/Oakland and the transformation of public housing projects will continue to move forward," she wrote in an op-ed article for the local newspaper. "Within days of the incident," she reported, "my office received calls from people eager to move into the proposed Lake Park Crescent development. Bond counsel/underwriters for the development coincidentally arrived in Chicago a day or two after the incident, toured the site and community and left feeling more enthusiastic than ever about the project and its potential impact. Recent events, tragic as they are, will not impede the redevelopment of the lakefront."

Preckwinkle's comments illustrate the centrality of crime to neighborhood change. This is true of both upward and downward change. High crime can doom a neighborhood and low crime can help a neighborhood get back on its feet. In this instance, the alderman's words were meant to soothe the worries of residents that their anticrime efforts had failed. She assured them that the developers were not scared off, the banks were still on board, people were still eager to buy, and the revitalization would proceed as planned.

Geographer Neil Smith argues that contemporary gentrification has taken on the character of the French "revanchist city" of the late nine-

page 4 lakefront outlook, august 14, 2002

Mob murders won't impede redevelopment

by Ald. Toni Preckwinkle (4th)

Last Saturday, my daughter and a friend asked me to take them swimming. We usually go to 57th Street beach several evenings a week after work, but the recent turmoil had taken up most of my evenings and kept us away.

The water was wonderful and the kids had a great time. As I watched them, I was struck yet again by the beauty and serenity of the waterfront. The lakefront is a great gift to us all.

Sitting on the beach, the tragedy at 40th and Lake Park that continues to unfold seemed very far away, yet only two miles separate them.

Readers of this column know that the tragedy of 40th/Lake Park is not really about the North Kenwood/Oakland neighborhood. Sadly, this could have happened in many places around the city or country. I am still struggling with the horror of the incident, as I'm sure you are.

Over the past two weeks, I have heard many theories about why this tragedy took place ranging from distrust of police and the criminal justice system (the police aren't going to show up, so we better do something

ourselves), to tensions between the new and older residents of North Kenwood/Oakland, to the advocacy of "beating down" someone in rap and hip-hop music and to our culture's increasing numbness to violence.

While any one of these factors may have played a part, at an elemental level, this was a criminal act, plain and simple. Beating people to death is murder, and I hope and expect that the perpetrators will be brought to justice. Seven men are in custody, and I understand that more suspects are being sought.

I want to commend Commander Adrienne Stanley and the officers and detectives of the 21st Police District for their exemplary work in this case. The calls for assistance (20 or more) were responded to promptly. The first officers were on the scene four minutes after the first call was received. The commander herself, nearby responding to a constituent complaint, was on the scene shortly there-

after. The detectives were thorough and respectful in their investigation. Twice, they visited every single apartment in the high-rise across the street to find witnesses. On behalf of all my constituents, I want to thank them for their good work.

Thanks are also due to all the neighbors and witnesses who called the police when the tragedy occurred and cooperated with the subsequent investigation. Early media reports characterized the community as uncooperative, and it should be clear that no suspects would be in custody without the help of community residents. We are all indebted to those who have had the courage to come forward and assist in the investigation.

The redevelopment of North Kenwood/Oakland and the transformation of our public housing projects will continue to move forward. Within days of the incident,

my office received calls from people eager to move into the proposed Lake Park Crescent development. Bond counsel/underwriters for the development coincidentally arrived in Chicago a day or two after the incident, toured the site and community and left feeling more enthusiastic than ever about the project and its potential impact. Recent events, tragic as they are, will not impede the

> Within days of the incident, my office received calls from people eager to move into the proposed Lake Park Crescent development

redevelopment of the lakefront. North Kenwood/Oakland is a strong and vibrant community. We will grieve together, and in time, heal together.

Figure 31. Alderman Toni Preckwinkle's op-ed trying to quell fears that violence will hamper revitalization. *Lakefront Outlook,* August 14, 2002. Used with permission.

teenth century. *Revanche* means revenge, and in its historic context it represented the Parisian elite's vilification of the French working class. Smith contends that the same sentiment characterizes modern U.S. attempts at urban revitalization. Racially, economically, sexually, or otherwise marginalized groups are blamed for the decadence and decline of not only the American *city*, but of American *society* more generally. On a nightly basis, television newscasts, with their disproportionate coverage of crime and violence, reinforce the notion of the loss of the city to people of color, often poor and more often menacing. The response to this takeover by social undesirables is a stream of regressive, if not punitive, welfare, immigration, housing, and crime policies. Smith asserts that the revanchism of gentrification "represents a reaction against the supposed 'theft' of the city, a desperate defense of a challenged phalanx of privileges, cloaked in the populist language of civic morality, family values, and neighborhood security."[5]

In North Kenwood–Oakland revenge against gang members and drug dealers—the most frequently named perpetrators of neighborhood violence—is achieved through increased police action, falling right in line with the tough-on-crime approach at the national level. But there are two important extensions of this vigilance that have been underexplored in the literature on gentrification and on communities and crime. First, there is an easy slippage from criminalizing individuals to indicting the physical landscape believed to spawn such bad individuals, frequently the public housing project. In North Kenwood–Oakland, revenge is taken on public housing both rhetorically, through "othering" and maligning, and violently, through demolition. A second area of slippage is in the progressive criminalization of "quality of life issues," as illustrated in the opening vignette. On the national scene, the best-publicized quality-of-life policing effort was New York City mayor Rudolph Giuliani's crusade against squeegee-men, who were said to epitomize the assault on New Yorkers' enjoyment of their city. Whereas activism, whether in New York or North Kenwood–Oakland, is initially focused on lowering the incidence of serious violent or property crimes, attention soon moves to curtailing activities that straddle the line between licit and illicit, or simply fall into the category of objectionable (to some) but legal behaviors.

Working-class, poor, and old-timer residents' leisure tastes and use of public and private space differ from those of their newcomer professional neighbors. Their actions and activities are sometimes expe-

rienced by newcomers as offensive or alarming behaviors that should
be controlled. The response of the home-owning, *civil*, middle-class recent arrivals to neighbors who play their music loudly, teenagers who
travel in packs, and people who barbecue in public is both rhetorically
disdainful and substantively hostile. Moreover, some poor residents,
because of their reliance on publicly subsidized housing, are more easily subjected to regulation. Hence, the focus of this chapter is on the bidirectionality of violence, both symbolic and literal, in North Kenwood–
Oakland.

Surprisingly, only three studies have examined the empirical relationship between gentrification and crime, and their findings are contradictory. Scott McDonald, studying gentrifying neighborhoods in
five cities, finds a decrease in personal crime and no change in property
crime. Two studies by Ralph Taylor and Jeanette Covington on changing neighborhoods in Baltimore find an increase in personal crime and
a decrease in property crime. This is not a sufficient body of research
from which to draw conclusions, and in all of these studies it is difficult
to isolate "gentrification" as the cause of any of the changes.[6] But while
there are few firm answers to the question of whether crime goes up or
down when neighborhoods gentrify, there are myriad empirical elabo-
rations in the literature on the reaction of gentrifiers to urban crime and
what they consider to be signs of disorder. These responses range from
the aggressive criminalization of homelessness and transient housing
to the demonization of black and Latino men to the somewhat less volatile disputes over how fast people drive in the alley.[7]

Crime reduction is one of the foremost concerns of North Kenwood–
Oakland's returning middle class. Of course, newcomers are not the
only ones concerned about crime. Long-term residents—the group that
Elijah Anderson might call "decent" or the "old heads"—put in many
years working toward a safer neighborhood. Yet, for a variety of reasons—their inability to get the ear of the police and city government,
their fear that police brutality might accompany police protection, their
embeddedness in networks that relied on some illegal activities, and a
sense of overwhelmed resignation during the most perilous periods—
they made little progress.[8] These old-timers were initially beneficiaries
of the successful war against crime waged by a more boisterous and
commanding gentrifying black middle class. But over time, many of
these residents, who weathered the neighborhood's worst storms, and
even more so their children, have become the *victims* of crime-fighting

successes. The campaign has broadened beyond shootings, muggings, and break-ins, which the old-timers equally abhorred, to encompass habits and routines in which some young and old old-timers regularly engage, like public drinking or informal economies. There have also emerged movements that vilify public housing, which some residents see as the physical representation of crime and disorder, and to intensify the regulation of all manner of behaviors, especially those of public housing residents. I argue that there is a turning point in neighborhood revitalization efforts where the benefits of anticrime efforts are no longer equally distributed and poorer residents, many of whom have lived in the neighborhood for years, suffer as their lifestyles are delimited by the desires of middle-class newcomers.

Crime Trends in North Kenwood–Oakland

Alderman Preckwinkle's mantra, repeated at nearly all of her public appearances, is that in order to attract new residents, North Kenwood–Oakland must be a safe neighborhood with good schools. On the safety issue, the alderman, the Conservation Community Council, and other residents have been vigilant in demanding service and results from the Chicago Police Department. These activists also convinced the University of Chicago to extend its police services to the area. How has the neighborhood changed as a result of these efforts?

At the subjective level, residents are nearly unanimous in their assessment that the neighborhood is getting progressively safer. "I have seen changes. I definitely have," one resident testified, using the fact that we were enjoying the summer afternoon on her back porch as her proof. "Because I wondered if I would actually want to sit back here maybe ten years ago. I don't think I would have trusted sitting back here." Another resident commented succinctly, "The most dramatic change for me is not hearing gunfire. That was, that was bothersome." And still another offered: "Forty-third and Greenwood was like the dope den, if you will. I mean you stood around and sold drugs on the corner unmolested. Winos and, I mean, liquor bottles all over the neighborhood. It was awful. Terrible. It has improved like 100 percent almost." A real estate agent in the area made a seamless connection between the issue of safety and marketing the neighborhood to middle- and upper-income buyers. She described a steady and nearly complete evolution toward being a place where her clientele would feel comfortable.

We want to focus on that area because we think it's an area where professionals—young black professionals as well as white professionals—they want to come and raise their families, and be there for the next thirty years, and have their properties increase in value, to continue to have that feeling of safety, to continue to feel like you can have your kids run around and not be killed, you know, that kind of thing. But, you know, there are pockets there [where] you probably still wouldn't want to have your kids there. But, you know, we see that transforming itself. By the time Thrush opens up their Drexel Development, Draper and Kramer opens up their Lake Park [Crescent] development, there won't be a hint of unsafety there. I believe that wholeheartedly.

Ironically, while residents who had a long historical view perceived a dramatic change in crime, one developer did not see it that way. Brad Welch's observation was that the neighborhood still had a ways to go, and that the progress was slow:

Initially I thought that there was a powerful movement for fast growth in the area, and what I saw after spending more time there is that there are some serious social issues that need to be dealt with in order to encourage that. . . . I mean, you walk a block away and it is incomprehensible to me how the city and the alderman and the federal government can expect all these initiatives to happen when they won't support a community at the base level and clear out the drug dealers and the negative influences that scare away your solid citizens. . . . Why can't something be done? I've been at 44th Street in that area now five years. We have been assaulted there, physically. My people have been assaulted when we've been constructing. We've been told time and time again that our presence in the neighborhood is very inconvenient and if we don't take our business elsewhere that certainly there's going to be a penalty for that. . . . I think until somebody can get their arms around those issues, growth is going to be slow and it's going to be block by block, inch by inch, lot by lot.

Welch ignored the risks and continued to work in North Kenwood–Oakland because, he said, he was "stubborn." The abundance of cement trucks and work crews in the neighborhood suggests that there are other developers who are equally headstrong. More important is Welch's perspective on crime as an outside white developer with no indigenous ties to the neighborhood. First, as a resident of an affluent, predominantly white suburb, he had a distinct comparison point for open air drug sales. Where he saw unacceptably rampant drug selling in North Kenwood–Oakland, local people saw unequivocally radical declines. Second, Welch's story documents the acts of resistance to gentrification waged by existing residents. Roughing up construction workers is a criminal act without question, but one that is not directed at neighbors, and one rooted in a shrewd but impotent sense of the possible negative outcomes of neighborhood change.

Brad Welch was a conscious agent of change, hoping that through his development he "could maybe get the critical mass necessary to bring in enough people to drive that out"—"that" meaning the class of residents responsible for the drug dealing and violent acts against his workers. Many existing and new residents enthusiastically share this goal and are prepared to answer literal violence with the symbolic violence of displacement. To be clear, I am not arguing that violence or street-corner drug selling should be tolerated or accommodated. Rather, I am illustrating, as I have tried to do throughout the book, the narrow and punitive strategies used in response to drugs and crime, which are but symptoms of society-level social and economic ailments. Instead of addressing the issues of employment, drug treatment, and gun control, the quick fix at the neighborhood level is to drive out what is seen as the offending class. The city supports this approach in hopes that perhaps the bad apples will be driven beyond the city limits and become the headaches of some other municipality.

Brad Welch's impressions notwithstanding, local residents' perceptions of decreasing crime rates are confirmed by official crime statistics (see figs. 32 and 33). Following a citywide pattern, data for the Chicago Police Department's 21st district, which includes North Kenwood–Oakland, show that the number of both index crimes and homicides dropped by 57 percent from 1990 to 2005, while the populations of both the district and the city increased. The decline in crime was greater in the 21st district than in the city as a whole, where crime declined by 46 percent. Non-index crimes like drug possession and vandalism showed similarly steep declines in the 21st district. Chicago police districts are further divided into beats, and North Kenwood–Oakland (plus small parts of nearby neighborhoods) falls within beats 2122 and 2123. In 1991, there were thirteen homicides in these two beats; in 2004 there were none. Finally, in 2002, a University of Chicago organization began tracking crime specifically for the North Kenwood–Oakland Conserva-

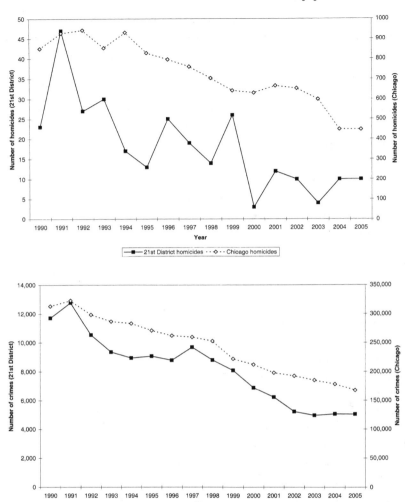

Figure 32. Homicides for Chicago and 21st police district, 1990–2005. Chicago Police Department (for detailed information see note 9, p. 345).

Figure 33. Index Crimes for Chicago and 21st police district, 1990–2005. Chicago Police Department (for detailed information see note 9, p. 345).

tion Area. Violent crime in the conservation area was down 11 percent from 2002 to 2005, and property crime declined by 8 percent.[9]

Of course there are many things that get conflated in these downward crime trends, making it difficult to attribute them to the anticrime mobilization that accompanied the neighborhood's revitalization.

Crime has been declining across the country since the early 1990s, co-inciding with improvements in the economy, the declining use of crack cocaine, the mass incarceration of young men, the changing age distribution, and more aggressive policing tactics nationwide.[10] Disentangling these various realities is beyond the scope of this chapter, as they are outside of the control of gentrifiers concerned with what they can do to improve safety on the ground in North Kenwood–Oakland. Their strategies are intensely local and personal. At one community meeting a resident urged attendees to step up their use of the local park. If the "right people" were more visible in the parks, she argued, their presence would discourage use by the wrong people, such as groups of young men who "terrorize" nearby churchgoers with their cursing and loud talking. Many residents have few qualms with replacing criminals with noncriminals and, in turn, neighbors who exhibit "bad" behaviors with those who enact "respectable" ones.

Danger

Anthropologist Sally Engle Merry argues that the cognitive experience of danger in urban neighborhoods is primarily a reaction to that which is unknown. "Danger," she writes, "is fear of the stranger, the person who is potentially harmful, but whose behavior seems unpredictable and beyond control."[11] This definition explains the fear of and aggression toward the construction workers, who represented an alien presence in the neighborhood. Likewise, it makes sense that incoming gentrifiers would feel considerable danger simply because their new neighbors are unknown to them, and thus their behavior is unpredictable. It is from this notion of the seeming danger of the new that we derive the label "urban pioneers," people who brave the uncertainties, and indeed dangers, of an untamed urban landscape. This terminology also assumes a reassertion of control, or *revanche,* by gentrifiers, who embark on a mission not of exploration but of settlement.

Newcomers make clear in their retrospective accounts that they initially perceived and experienced North Kenwood–Oakland as a dangerous space. Soeurette Hector, who moved to North Kenwood in 1992, remembered:

> The day I came home and I heard shooting, I was like totally devastated. I didn't know whether to come out of the house or stay. And I'm like, "I grew up in a regular residence in New York." And I'm like, "I've never

seen this in my life. I'm going to die in here of bullet shots." I thought, "I have to get out of here. I want to be a pioneer, but I don't want to be dead."

Along with their early experiences of hearing gunshots, witnessing drug sales, seeing drug addicts, and being burglarized, many newcomers remember their friends thinking they were crazy for moving into the neighborhood. Janice Black recalled her real estate agent telling her about a house. "You probably won't want it," the agent began, as she described a house she had for sale in North Kenwood for $25,000 in 1982. Thinking the price very attractive, Black went to see the house. "It was really raunchy. And everybody was saying to me don't go down there, don't go down there, don't go down, oh my goodness, don't buy that. Don't go down there. My friends were having a fit."

Some residents who defied their friends' warnings and bought anyway spent their early years in relative isolation. "I was really embarrassed," reflected Shirley Newsome. "I didn't have company, I think, the first three years I was here. It was horrible." And it wasn't just friends who wouldn't come. "You couldn't even get nobody to come up here and do work, you know, for repairs on your house. They didn't want to come up in here," remembered one resident. "We eventually convinced Nicky's to come [to deliver food] and a couple of restaurants," added another. "Years ago, I [couldn't] convince them it was okay to deliver in this area." With very few exceptions, established and newer residents share these recollections of danger, or of the repercussions of the neighborhood's reputation as dangerous. These narratives recall the neighborhood's "very turbulent" years, when, as one local pastor summed it up, "some people, they were intimidated, so much so that they moved."

Experiences of danger are particularly connected to the built environment. Perhaps most emblematic of the historical dangers that existed in the neighborhood was the headquarters of the El Rukn gang. The Fort—or the Grand Temple as it was also called—stood at 3947 South Drexel Boulevard. The gang bought the former Oakland Square Theater in 1978, but the El Rukns had a presence in the neighborhood and elsewhere on the South Side dating to the 1960s. The Fort, as its name implies, was a formidable presence in the neighborhood. The *Chicago Tribune* offered a particularly brooding and sensational description of the neighborhood in 1988, focusing on the presence of the Fort. "Residents say there are only two thriving businesses in Oakland," the article began. The first was a grocery store and the second, the Fort, where, "federal investigators claim, the gang's most powerful leaders gather to plot strategy and coordinate illegal activities such as narcotics sales and acts of violence against those who defy them."[12]

For many residents at that time, the Fort, like "the projects," was a physical incarnation of the neighborhood's ills. But as with public housing, there were good times and fond memories associated with the Fort and its leadership as well. Residents' perceptions of the Fort and the El Rukns as dangerous turned on how familiar or unfamiliar they were with its headquarters and its members. For example, as Emma McDaniel got more acquainted with events at the Fort, she became less fearful. She narrated:

> They didn't bother us, honey. I mean everybody knew that they went down there and they had their meetings. And then I'll tell you what they did. They start having a get-together on Saturday for dances and things. And all of our kids would go down there and nobody would get hurt. No they would not. . . . And, honey, I was leery at first, you know. Because, doggone, my kids are like, "Can we go down to the El Rukn party?" [I would say,] "Oh no," you know. But they said, "Mom, it's not like that." And after they went one time, oh well, we knew every weekend that's where they was going. And they would go down there and dance and get together and come back and everything was okay.

Similarly, Michelle Campbell corrected me when I framed for her my understanding of the 1970s as a very scary time. Wasn't she afraid with the gangs so prevalent and the Fort nearby, I asked. She replied:

> It wasn't like that. I mean, I will be honest with you. Being here all my life when the El Rukns was here, the El Rukns kept it more safer so far as keeping drugs out of the neighborhood. You know, they sold, I think they allowed for them to sell marijuana, but it wasn't cocaine. It wasn't crack cocaine in the neighborhood. Heroin wasn't sold freely. Basically it was when those leaders were taken away that you went into your violence here. It was not like that before. . . . I think it was like the mid '80s when they started arresting all these people. Then you had all these—as far as I saw—gang factions that broke up. Everybody wanted to be the leader. . . . Back then, like I say, by being more controlled, if you knew somebody that was in it, or you knew a gang leader or something like that, you told 'em, "Hey, my child isn't gonna be in a gang." [And] they didn't bother

your child. And I only had one son. I wasn't gonna lose my son to no gang violence and I wasn't gonna see him join a gang.

In Campbell's estimation, the El Rukn leadership provided protection against the wholesale ravages of drugs, respected her wishes that her son not join a gang, and were admirably loyal, qualities that distinguished them from contemporary gangs. While she stops short of longing for those days, she definitely has positive memories of the role played by the El Rukns in the neighborhood.

Other residents, however, had profoundly negative experiences with the El Rukns. Jerome Green commented on the effect the gangs had on the neighborhood:

> They [the El Rukns] would actually break into people's apartments and beat up on them and things of that nature. And I remember one of my uncles was living with my grandfather at that point in one of the apartments in that particular complex and they broke in and beat them up. So, things were getting a little bit hot around here in this particular neighborhood at that point. My parents had always wanted a house and at that point we decided to move to the southwest side, where they still live. But I moved back over [here] because I began to see the potential.

Green's comments include many important components of North Kenwood–Oakland's history and present transformation as it relates to crime. He vividly recounts the heightened danger in the 1970s due specifically to the presence of the El Rukns and his own family's experience with neighborhood violence. The fear of violence, combined with his family's aspirations to home ownership, pushed them out of North Kenwood–Oakland into a more middle-class area further south.[13] Green's return in 1995 places him among the newcomers who in many ways are not newcomers at all, but rather returned children of the neighborhood who have been enticed by its redevelopment and greater safety. Jerome Green has literally come back to the blocks on which he played as a child, beckoned by the upscale changes. The building he lived in as a boy has been converted to condominiums, and the Fort, which was across the street, is gone.

The El Rukn headquarters was ceremoniously demolished in June 1990. "Spectators rushed to collect pieces of the building as souvenirs, and police officers and prosecutors posed for pictures in front of the wreckage," reported the *Chicago Tribune*.[14] One of the police officers watched the demolition with excitement. He had been investigating and fighting the gang since 1964. "This building has never been good for anything," he said. "There was nothing here but narcotics, extortion and recruitment." His statement contradicts the memories of Emma Mc-Daniel, Michelle Campbell, and others who recall the parties thrown at the Fort and the El Rukns' management of the drug trade. It illustrates the broad vilification by some factions of the community of places that other residents have experienced as more nuanced. The assertion that the Fort "has never been good for anything" also betrays a short historical memory. The Oakland Square Theater was once a popular legitimate entertainment venue, a history that is lost on those obsessed with the neighborhood's debasement.

The reporting on the demolition of the Fort at times uncannily parallels coverage of public housing in NKO, which became public enemy number one after the Fort was demolished. Another police officer who watched the wrecking ball slog through the bricks of the Fort commented, "It doesn't happen in one fell swoop. It would have been nice if they used dynamite."[15] Eight years later and less than four blocks away, dynamite *was* brought in for the spectacular implosion of the Lakefront Properties. The ceremony marking the demolition of the projects was accompanied by the same kind of demonizing rhetoric employed at the Fort's demolition. Also characteristic of both ceremonies were the metaphors of rebirth. When the Fort was first seized by the Chicago Police Department in 1989, one reporter interviewed people who lived near the gang headquarters and captured this quaint exchange between a landlord, Vernie Jess, and a potential renter.

A former resident of one of the apartments arrived on his bicycle Sunday to inquire about renting once again.

"Do you have a job?" snapped Jess.

"Sure," the man responded.

"Where and for how long?" Jess continued as he screened the potential resident.

"I was here for five years, Vernie, you know me. I had a real nice place," responded the man.

"Well, it's not going to be as cheap as it was before," Jess said as he broke into a broad smile. "The neighborhood's coming up, you know. We don't have the El Rukns here no more."[16]

The razing of the Fort allowed for the raising of nearby rents. The eradication from the landscape of these brick and mortar emblems of deviance opens up doors for new development and new faces.

While residents had a complex set of feelings about and memories of the Fort, its onetime identity as the headquarters of an organization whose members were ultimately prosecuted and jailed on charges ranging from drugs to murder to terrorism justifies some targeting of it as a dangerous space. Public housing, by contrast—the residence of thousands of law-abiding citizens—cannot be summarily defined in terms of criminality. Nonetheless, it is. Specifying the locus of crime in public housing was a recurring theme among residents who found it difficult to extricate the public housing *structures* from the criminal minority that resided within them.

Residents posited a range of theories about the causal relationship between public housing and crime. One theory, explicitly propounded by Verdell Wade and shared by many others, is that the buildings' physical form engenders bad behavior. Wade had lived across the street from the Lakefront Properties for forty years and once had a bullet shot from the projects shatter her window and lodge into her bedpost. She concluded, "It's not that I don't like poor folks. It's just that you can't stack 'em up like that and expect them to act decent. It's not right."[17]

Another theory is evident in the words of Jackie Sanders, a middle-class woman who moved to the neighborhood in 1989. "With the dismantling of the high-rises," she opined, "some of [the gang activity] has left, but then some of it has returned because they're trying to place the residents." Sanders reasons that the bad behaviors inhere in the residents themselves. Hence, the neighborhood was relatively serene when the projects stood empty, but when public housing residents were brought back to the neighborhood—even when placed in new low-rise buildings—the problems with crime and violence reemerged. Her theory is on the opposite end of the structure-culture (or nurture-nature) continuum from Verdell Wade's. Whereas Wade blames crime on the environment or on policy makers' bad decisions to build such atrocious buildings (structure/nurture), Sanders implicates the moral makeup of public housing residents themselves (culture/nature), no matter their physical surroundings.

Finally, there are anthropomorphic theories that attribute bad things to the high-rises themselves. When causal explanations do not include people at all, it is as if the buildings were the actual perpetrators. "What was before the biggest minus to me," commented Sadiya Glass, "was it just would be a lot of shooting, you know. I would hear shooting 'cause the projects used to be over there." Lindsey Beck similarly exonerated possible human actors and equated the unsettling gun shots she heard with the public housing buildings: "Because when I bought [my house], the high-rises were still there and there was still gunfire in the neighborhood." Finally, the principal of King College Prep hypothesized that public housing was part of the reason why "nonminority" parents did not enroll their kids in the school. "They just finished demolishing that last high-rise over there on 44th and Cottage Grove. Before that maybe they felt that the area was not safe, you know." Unlike the arguments that the dense and towering architecture of public housing breeds bad behavior by residents, or the notion that the people in the projects are incorrigible, this last theory posits a direct causal correspondence between the buildings and crime, as if the buildings themselves acted dangerously.

Whatever the theoretical explanation, and residents do have their strong theories, there is near consensus among newcomers and old-timers who did not live in public housing that the high-rises epitomized the demise of the neighborhood. The aggressive, perhaps even vengeful, response to what some perceive as the physical manifestation of crime and disorder—those buildings, which sent some residents running to other parts of the city, bottomed out the property values of those who remained, curtailed residents' daily routines, and raised the cost of home insurance—is no less than demolition. If public housing has to remain, one resident suggested boldly, residents should be compensated for their willingness to live near it. "[For] people like me," she argued, "there should be some people who are paid to stay in war-torn areas. Yeah, in order to maintain some semblance of humanity in there. Other than that, it would just go into the jungle." Given such sentiments, the fervor with which anticrime activists focus on public housing is more comprehensible.

Activism

Anticrime activism takes myriad forms in North Kenwood–Oakland, and the various types of activism have both internal and external roots. At the most immediate level, local crime motivated residents and block clubs to request increased police services, lodge complaints about bad landlords, and, perhaps most proactively, confront offenders (drug dealers, loiterers, etc.) face-to-face. There were also developments at the city level that supported local efforts, especially the Chicago Alternative Policing Strategy, which began citywide in 1993 and emphasized citizen-police collaboration in identifying high-crime areas and devising strategies to reduce crime.[18] Here I chronicle three particular areas of anticrime activism in North Kenwood–Oakland: (1) the public safety–related campaign to demolish the public housing high-rises, (2) the emphasis on tenant screening in private and public rental housing, and (3) the invitation to the University of Chicago police to patrol NKO.

The Menace of Public Housing

Given the venomous language directed at public housing, it is not surprising that getting rid of the high-rises was seen as a top priority for improving safety in the neighborhood. The city's daily newspapers were particularly "incite"-ful in the tenor of their reporting about the high-rises. "They're breeding places for all kinds of crime, drugs and rape and what have you," the *Chicago Tribune* quoted one resident as saying. Taking liberties with these sentiments, one *Tribune* editorial writer offered this prescription: "Chicago's decision-makers should realize why the depopulation of CHA family high-rise projects will continue. Their families are terrorized, night and day, by lawless invaders, gangs and drug peddlers." And finally, an article foregrounding the newspaper's role as real estate booster asserted that, given NKO's location, "an easy walk to the lakefront, the neighborhood could have been—and still could be—one of the most desirable in the city. But prior to 1986, when the CHA emptied the high-rises for an overhaul, home owners lived in constant fear of the gang-banging and drug-dealing that swirled around the projects."[19]

Residents saw demolition of the high-rises as the prerequisite to increasing neighborhood safety. Michelle Campbell summed up many non–public housing residents' feelings when she commented that "the best thing in the neighborhood that happened is when they tore down the projects." This before-and-after logic is also apparent in the stories that Patricia Sanders told:

You know they had the projects on Lake Park that they blew up. And when they had them there you couldn't even walk down the street. Those people were shootin', throwin' urine and bowel movements out the window. You know you couldn't even walk to [the grocery store]. . . .

And then they used to have another little project right there. It was one right here on Cottage Grove and, what was that, 41st [or] 40th. Now they, they was rough too. . . . But now since both of 'em are gone, it's a lot better around here.

Concurring, resident Sadiya Glass added, "Sometimes the guys used to just hang out all times of the night and wild and everything. [Now], they changed and rehabbed and everything, trying to make it better." No community should be racked by such peril. There is growing evidence that such assaults on people's sense of safety have negative effects on both physical and mental health.[20] In this respect, taking action toward alleviating the fear that residents endured is an obvious good. But what sort of action should be taken? In North Kenwood–Oakland (and indeed nationally), the target of such action—public housing—is once again only a surface manifestation of the underlying causes of crime like poor education, unemployment, and the availability of drugs and weapons. Demolishing public housing in favor of mixed-income communities does little to address these issues.

While disdain for the projects was widespread, home owners were at the vanguard of the fight for demolition. In addition to their belief that the projects were themselves criminogenic, they were concerned with the secondary effects of crime on financial investments in the neighborhood. The Residents for Responsible Redevelopment, the home-owner group most active in lobbying for demolition and fighting against new public housing construction, made this point explicitly in documents filed in the legal battle over the Lakefront Properties. One resident wrote in the affidavit she submitted to the *Gautreaux* court:

In April 1996 we completed 4420 Oakenwald, the construction of the largest single family home in North Kenwood–Oakland. Hyde Park Bank financed the construction loan and was supposed to provide permanent financing too. When it came time to appraise the house for the permanent loan, the vice-president of Hyde Park Bank indicated that no house in North Kenwood–Oakland could be worth more than $250,000. When asked how he came to this conclusion, the response was, the development in North Kenwood–Oakland depends on what they do with the public housing. This scenario is of particular interest to me because this is my PERSONAL home.[21]

This reasoning was commonplace among the first wave of middle-class newcomers, who moved in when the public housing high-rises were still standing. It expresses the final point in the connection between the criminalization of public housing and the desire for its removal. The presence of public housing—as a den of crime, as housing for the poor, as the emblem of all things bad—impedes the investment goals of gentrifiers. The Lakefront Properties were ultimately demolished. But the community had to agree to accept new public housing units to replace some of those that would be lost. This stipulation opened another chapter in NKO anticrime activism, one that focused on tenant selection as a preventive crime-reduction strategy.

Apartments for Rent, Selectively

What kind of public housing residents would be *allowed* back into North Kenwood–Oakland once new replacement housing was built? The answers lie in the creation of and adherence to rigorous screening criteria deemed necessary for the success of mixed-income projects. Support for screening applicants for public and private apartment buildings was widespread among North Kenwood–Oakland residents, including those people who themselves lived or had lived in public or subsidized housing. Prudence Stagg, a resident of subsidized housing since 1977, remarked, "I would screen like they did when we moved in. I would check with your landlord to make sure that you wasn't in fact the person that let the kids tear the place up." Emma McDaniel had a similarly nostalgic perspective on her time in public housing and how she had to be squeaky clean to qualify: "I mean they screened us from the time we were born. They did, baby. I said, 'Doggone, I'll never get into housing.' Because these people, honey, they want to know almost why did your mother have you." As the fond memories of these older residents suggest, screening public housing tenants is not a new idea.

Longtime public housing resident Gladys McKinney looked back wistfully to the time when most of her neighbors were working families. "But then," she remembered, "during the urban renewal a real change [happened]. They say that people had to have some place to stay." Beginning in the late 1960s, new federal regulations made public housing the shelter of last resort for the poorest and hardest to house families. Now the pendulum is swinging back toward a stricter regime.

In choosing the firms that would build the mixed-income communities to replace the high-rises in North Kenwood–Oakland, community leaders paid close attention to bidders' screening and tenant management plans. In their fancy PowerPoint presentations, development teams addressed the issue of screening early and explicitly. "How can we work within the context of this development to make sure that the rental and CHA component, everyone in there, can grow with this community?" asked one team competing for the community's blessing to develop the mixed-income community on Drexel Boulevard. "The answer is blended management, screening and assessment up front, coupled with social services for residents. . . . As manager of the rental units, we will also be a part of the home owners' association and will help residents comply with the rules of the home owners' association." Similar issues were raised in the community meetings to choose the developer for the mixed-income community to be built on the lakefront. When a community resident worried that the apartments that were open to disabled people would actually house former drug addicts who qualified as disabled under federal housing law, the developer responded with an emphasis on tenant selection: "What we have to do is attack any problems in our screening process. And we will do considerable background checks and screen out any problems, social problems." Another development team vying for the same contract promised to go a step further by creating covenants with residents regarding their self-improvement plans: "So, for example, if people are interested in a GED or other training we will have people sign agreements that they are working towards that. We think that will make sure we have a committed resident." This second presenter also planned to check the school attendance records of the children of potential residents, upping the ante for eligibility and ultimately winning the majority vote of the Conservation Community Council members.

The firmer the selection plan the more pleased were residents who attended these meetings. The final tenant selection plans for the new mixed-income communities included, among other things, credit and bankruptcy checks, housekeeping inspections, ten-year criminal background checks, and drug tests.[22] All renters, including those who receive no public monies, are subject to this review. These thresholds are more stringent than the Chicago Housing Authority's requirements overall, and each new mixed-income development gets to develop its own "site-specific criteria."

Driving home the point about the zealousness with which screening is advocated, some community leaders in North Kenwood–Oakland suggested that managers go a step further and administer drug tests to *the youth* as well as the adults in a household seeking residence in one of the new communities. It was argued that such checks would be, after all, for their own good. I asked Lawrence Grisham, who works for the company that manages public housing construction in Chicago, how he thought the rigorous selection criteria would affect the ability of public housing residents to move into the new mixed-income communities. His answer:

> I hope it will affect it positively. And I hope that families take it as an op-portunity to get some things done that need to get done. I think the key thing is to make sure that the stuff is in place to help. And this is going to be a long, drawn-out process. It's going to take time to get families ready, but I think you have to have that goal in front of them and that expecta-tion in front of them. These are families that are isolated families. They are out of the mainstream, and you've got to bring them to the middle. You've got to give them that. Nobody gives them any—the only thing they expect out of them is failure. So we've got to give an expectation that there's something that will help them get through. So I'd like the idea of site-specifics as long as we make sure that we work with the fami-lies to help them get ready.

The key to making screening less draconian was to precede it with in-tensive social services. The problem with this admirable experiment of "pulling people who were living in a dark closet all these years and trying to bring them to the light," as one CHA employee put it, was that there was too little money for the front-end interventions. Thomas Sullivan was hired to monitor and evaluate the implementation of the Chicago Housing Authority's Plan for Transformation, including the programs meant to get residents ready for the new mixed-income com-munities. He wrote in his report: "The information I received from many, many sources is that the Service Connector Program in Phase II was grossly underfunded, and therefore was grossly understaffed, with the result that it was only marginally effective in assisting a relatively few residents. I have been told that the number of successful long term outcomes was minimal."[23] While the CHA has responded to these criti-cisms with more funding, its hands are also tied by a shrinking federal commitment to adequately fund public housing.

On the specific issue of crime, the new developments that will include public housing will do ten-year criminal background checks on potential residents. Households are not eligible for the new public housing units if *any household member* has a felony record within the last ten years. The Chicago Urban League reports that 55 percent of the adult male African American population in Chicago has a felony record. (This includes both those currently incarcerated and ex-felons.)[24] While the purpose is to select residents who will not contribute to crime in the neighborhood, this criterion has a very wide impact. Some families will have to choose between their sons, grandsons, brothers, and boyfriends and housing. At the public hearing to receive comments on these selection criteria, one North Kenwood–Oakland resident gave an impassioned speech:

> My question is this. Ten years is too far to be checking on criminal background for activities for someone. What about a juvenile? Are you all going to punish a young adult who is trying to do the right thing for themselves even when they paid for the crime when they were a teenager? And my final question is: all applicants and members of the applicant's household age eighteen or older must pass a drug test to demonstrate that they are not currently using illegal drugs. Now, what kind of question is that. Why do families have to submit to a drug test? If these housing developments are built for the upper middle class and the rich folks, are they going to have to take a drug test too or is this just for our poor people that you all are just trying to chase out of the neighborhood? Because these are some things that I would like for you all to consider, because this is something like being in prison. Last, I thought we were in America. This is something like I would expect would be over in Russia or over there in Afghanistan or—I forgot, Bush is y'all president, so y'all support taking people's rights. That's all I got to say."[25]

North Kenwood–Oakland was raising the bar for entry into the neighborhood not just in terms of sheer economics—that is, who could afford to buy or rent—but also with regards to behaviors, past and present. It was assumed that the escalating sticker prices on homes would be sufficient to ensure only the best class of buyers, but more proactive steps were needed to pick the working-class and lower-income families in the large, subsidized apartment buildings and public housing communities.

Without a doubt, a lack of responsible management is unfair to the majority of tenants and neighbors who abide by both the official criminal laws and the subjective local norms. Michelle Campbell complained about the subsidized complex where she used to live. When she came back to Chicago after years away, she avoided her old building. But for reasons of familiarity she moved in just across the street. From that perch she could observe the flagrant mismanagement.

> So managers, if they know somebody that know somebody, then they will go ahead on and just move somebody in. So you got young people in there, you got people sellin' drugs. They don't care. I mean, I'll be honest with you—management knows that they sell drugs. They make statements like, "Well as long as you sell marijuana and not hard drugs like cocaine." And to me that's sad. It's all still the same thing. This is your building. You have people comin' in and out to buy these drugs. Why would you let anybody in the building sell drugs. And that was one of the reasons I didn't want to get back over in there. It's because I don't have to be subjected to that drug shit.

Campbell is of course right. She should not have to tolerate drug deals and whatever violence might go along with them. And having accountable management who stick to the rules, indeed, to the laws of the state, is one route by which to rid the neighborhood of the illegal acts that undermine safety. As community leaders turn to tenant selection and building management as the next frontier of anticrime activism, long-term, working-class residents like Campbell will be the definite beneficiaries. But as this chapter argues, the scope of efforts to make the neighborhood safe goes beyond prohibiting illegal behaviors to policing moral selves.

"Discipline" is a word that one resident used when imagining what would be necessary to bring low-income and working-class renters in line with the new prevailing codes of conduct. It is an interesting term because it encompasses both external and internal stimuli and motivations, both social strictures and individual agency. "If they go in and recruit the right people and discipline them, that's all it is," remarked Melvin Lewis about how he hoped the selection of new public housing residents would proceed. "And if you discipline 'em right—tell 'em what you can and cannot do—they'll do it." Using *discipline* as a verb, Lewis envisioned the use of both training and punishment in enforcing the rules for living in the mixed-income communities. To discipline someone is to set parameters for action as well as clear penalties for noncompliance. These are the forces that would *act upon* public housing residents in Lewis's schema. The example he gave to illustrate his point is in line with this connotation of discipline: "Now you know we [are] death on grass. Now you know that. You go into some neighborhoods, people be sitting on the porch, grass is just—no grass period. Especially [with] the number of kids, the children, that's out there playing. [But] you go by [Lake Parc Place, the renovated high-rises that mix poor and working-class tenants] and you look at that grass—it's perfect. That's because of discipline. If you do this, this is what's gonna happen." Lewis emphasized the fact that when disciplining tenants, there must be repercussions for breaking the rules.

But *discipline*, especially in its noun form, also suggests *self-regulation*, or internal playbooks that guide behavior. Such inner states are definitely fashioned by the social context within which the individual is rooted, but soon they persist without their external social moorings. Discipline was a characteristic that building managers searched for in potential tenants. One manager described her inspection protocol: "In that home visit we have to have everyone in the household there. And we get the opportunity or the chance to see how the family relates to each other. How well disciplined, you know. We don't discriminate against anyone, but the housekeeping and home visit is the most important part of the screening process." Using family interaction as a gauge for neighborly interaction, this manager looked for outward expressions of internalized normative guides. Such cues would help her sort out the troublemakers from the respectable tenants.

Imposing discipline to encourage discipline is the guiding principle of screening and management as anticrime tools. But not everyone will be on board. Some will see "discipline" as a form of tyranny, while others will be "undisciplined" for material reasons—not having air conditioning will push people to "loiter" outdoors; lack of a lawn mower, or a crumbling back porch, will prompt people to barbecue on the street; overcrowded living conditions lead to "private" behaviors in public places. As Melvin Lewis well knew, "You gonna have problems. Some people just can't change because of change." Controlling crime through these mechanisms entails exclusion. The designers of the conservation area legislation in the 1950s recognized the fact that "conservation" was based on the exclusion of the poor,[26] and proponents of mixed-income communities are equally aware that success relies on the exclusion of the *poorly behaved*. When I asked Charles Lear, a manager of a mixed-income development in another Chicago neighborhood, about whether the screening criteria rule out many public housing families, he answered:

> I've had this question asked of me all the time because people ask themselves, "Well, the people that you don't select, what happened to them?" I said, "I don't know." I really don't. Because when you do projects like this and you do any kind of housing and tenant selection, you want the best. Yes, it is somewhat of a creaming process because you're taking the best that you can get because you want to be successful. You don't want to just put [in] any and everybody that you got to put out the next week or [who are] just going to run everybody else away. Because you want to be successful. I had to do the best job I possibly could with selecting these folks because I would be the guy to take the blame if I ran away all those condo owners. For Sale signs would be going up everywhere and then they'd be looking at me and saying, "Boy, have you failed." Then, I would not have a contract with anybody. . . . This is the wave of the new public housing throughout the country, is mixed income, so you got to be successful. There are going to be some people who [are] going to get left out. Where they go, I really don't know. That's going to be for somebody else to figure out. I have to figure out how I'm going to make this process work.

Lear felt acutely the eyes of many onlookers judging him and the community he was trying to form in his handpicking of public housing residents. The Chicago Housing Authority, the home owners in the development, the City of Chicago, and indeed the nation were all watching. He had to succeed. But while all eyes are on the mixed-income experiment, who is monitoring the fate of those who don't make the cut? Lear is a subcontractor with the job of selecting tenants for one development; such a big-picture question is not his concern.

That responsibility is similarly, and perhaps even rightly, shunned by North Kenwood–Oakland residents. Leonard Watson envisioned a system of tenant inspections every six months, with the understanding that "you'd have to follow those rules or you leave." When I asked him where the evicted people would go, he answered:

> I don't know where they live. But they have to live. You are right they have to live. That's what they should think about when they're doing—

see I'm not on that committee. . . . It's hard to say, but I do care and I don't care. I do care in one way, and I don't care in another. If you going to bring down me, I don't need you around me.

In its all-out effort to be a neighborhood on the rise, North Kenwood–Oakland does not want residents who might bring the community down. Through the related approaches of tenant selection and management, the architects of the neighborhood's future work to lower the incidence of crime and otherwise unwanted activities.

The University to the Rescue

My final example of anticrime activism in North Kenwood–Oakland is the request made to the University of Chicago to extend its police patrols into the neighborhood. The hearty welcome of the University of Chicago police in 2003 was a strong indication of gentrifiers' desire to quell disorder by any means necessary. "There's a new generation now," said Jonathan Kleinbard, former vice president for community affairs at the University of Chicago. He was surprised to hear of the expanded patrol, which would have been unthinkable during his tenure at the university. "I just resisted [expanding the police boundaries], and I thought it would be like declaring war. And it's now happened." Kleinbard's astonishment at the requests for the university's police services by "ministers and home owners" in North Kenwood–Oakland is rooted in the tumultuous historical relationship between the university and its surrounding communities, mostly as a result of its aggressive urban renewal efforts in the 1950s. Given this background, the vision of Kirk Clemons, a middle-class home owner who moved to North Kenwood–Oakland in 1997, is nothing short of amazing:

My grand scheme, what I would have been pushing for from a political point of view, is: You've got three big rental courtyard buildings. I would have loved to have seen the University of Chicago buy one of those, make it a dormitory, forcing integration. Now, that would have immediately added $10,000 to $20,000 in appreciation of property values because [before] you didn't have a mixed income. You also would have had the extra services that would have came with that. The University of Chicago police would have had jurisdiction north of 47th Street. It would have had a higher level of security.

Clemons's vision—illustrative as much for its multilayered attention to racial and class integration, property values, and crime, as for its ahistorical cheerfulness—is now a reality. When the university came to the Conservation Community Council in June 2003 to present its proposal to begin patrols of NKO, the reception was as ebullient as Clemons had imagined it might be. Alderman Preckwinkle presented the proposal as coming at her request. She was not being selfish in taking the credit, but rather making herself liable for the blame if there were a backlash based on the historical suspicion of the university. She repeated her spiel that when people attempt to revitalize a neighborhood, two things are especially important—public safety and good schools. The university had already opened a charter elementary school, and now it was willing to assist with public safety. The latter commitment would cost the university approximately $300,000 a year, plus the cost of installing emergency phones throughout the neighborhood at roughly $10,000 each.

"Why expand into North Kenwood–Oakland?" asked the chief of the University of Chicago police as a set up to his own three-part answer: the neighborhood is getting better, the university feels a greater responsibility for its contiguous neighborhoods, and it's a win-win situation. NKO wins by receiving university police services on top of those of the Chicago Police Department. And the university wins by further "stabilizing" its surroundings, extending the range of neighborhoods in which faculty, staff, and students may choose to live.

After the alderman and the police chief concluded their presentations, the meeting was open for questions from CCC members and residents at large. I was the only person to ask a skeptical question: "Have there been any complaints since the university has started patrolling Woodlawn?" I asked. Woodlawn is the community to the south of the university, and is also predominantly black and low-income. "Three that I can remember," answered the chief. "Two were from people who were arrested for selling drugs, and those were unfounded. The third was when two young men were stopped on the way to church, and that one needed to be addressed." I then queried the audience, "Are people in the audience generally supportive or skeptical?" I asked, not wanting to misinterpret the considerable silence. My neighbors looked at me as if I had landed from outer space. For the residents at the meeting, a preponderance of home owners and newcomers, this was a no-brainer. The offer of patrols was unanimously approved. The generations had been replaced in North Kenwood–Oakland, and the young pioneers welcomed any assistance in their increasingly successful efforts to tame the neighborhood.

The Next Level: Quality of Life

In his presentation to the community, the chief of the University of Chicago police made explicit the new direction of crime-fighting efforts in North Kenwood–Oakland. He told community residents that the university police planned to be helpful not just in fighting major crime incidents, but also in attacking loitering, bottle breaking, and the like. The university specializes in "quality-of-life" policing, he told the audience, ceaselessly observing and investigating nuisances until perpetrators are so bothered that they stop. The steady progression in what behaviors are subject to policing, from violent and property crimes to softer crimes such as loitering and littering, brings us to a turning point beyond which some residents, mostly those who have low incomes and have been in the neighborhood longer, switch from *being part of* the policing effort—complaining about drug dealers, calling 911 when they hear gunshots, taking precautions when walking through the neighborhood for fear of robberies or other assaults—to *being the targets of* policing.

The list of behaviors that evoke the contempt of residents is long, and they are frequent topics of conversation and attention at block club meetings, in casual neighborhood conversation, and at the Chicago Alternative Policing Strategy beat meetings. The vignette opening this chapter already raised the issue of where the appropriate place is to barbecue in the summer. Other such concerns include littering and broken glass, loud music, public drinking, fixing cars on the street, "loitering" and other kinds of congregating (which could include standing in front of one's own apartment building), porch sitting, honking horns, double-parking, and unauthorized home repairs. Residents' responses to these activities increase in earnestness from inaction, to making polite pleas to offending neighbors or building management, to making organized efforts through block clubs or approaching offenders as a group, to lodging complaints with or calling the police, to insisting that the police take action. At some point, all of the behaviors in the list above have been raised at beat meetings, and thus all have reached the level of being subject to official policing and official sanction.

The rhetoric around managing neighborhood behaviors is unabash-

edly normative and charged with the class tensions expected under gentrification. "This again [is] a problem with the CHA," began Robert
Blackwell as he explained why he was skeptical about the reconstruc-
tion of public housing. "There is very little punishment for bad behavior. And that's what people, I think, are really worried about. I don't
think it's the idea of I don't want to live around anybody who doesn't
have as much money as we do. It's how are these people going to behave." Blackwell's comments are interesting because he initially denies
that his evaluation of appropriate behaviors is based on class considerations while simultaneously setting up his categories based on class,
specifically public housing residents versus non–public housing residents. Soon after this comment, he realizes his inconsistency, noting,
"So there's a little bit of classism—not a little bit, a lot of classism."

Moreover, his emphasis here is on bad behaviors, like property upkeep, that are not criminal but that, in his view, require sanctions nonetheless. These kinds of behaviors fall into the list of quality-of-life issues that residents often rehearse. Blackwell was quick to add that he
has been pleasantly surprised by just how inconspicuous the new public housing and its residents have been. Despite his initial protests, he
now sees the mixed-income experiment in North Kenwood as a success.
Part of the reason for this positive evaluation is of course the stringent
screening and behavior management to which residents are subjected.

Defining the objectionable behavior more clearly, resident Paul
Knight argued about loiterers:

> They don't know what they're doing. And it looks bad. And they're not
> educating themselves or distinguishing themselves in any way or con-
> tributing to the greater good. Hanging out in front of a liquor store
> makes the neighborhood look bad [even] if it wasn't. I go over on Narra-
> gansett [a street on Chicago's predominantly white northwest side], you
> know, they're inside the liquor store, or sitting in the tavern, or what-
> ever. Bridgeport even [a white and Latino working-class neighborhood],
> there's nobody hanging out in front of a liquor store.

Soeurette Hector was even more adamant in her dismay over the bad
behaviors of fellow residents.

> There are several nuisances, but two I would say would be the top priori-
> ties. The first one is the undesirables. You know, either they will have to

be taught how to live correctly or they will have to find where they feel comfortable to do whatever they're doing. It's nothing against them, but if they don't know the meaning of community, either they get someone to teach them or they need to go someplace where they can behave, you know, have the same behavior.

Hector illustrates the confidence with which many newer residents assert their vision of proper neighborhood comportment. She went on to give examples of such breaches of residential etiquette, including driving motorcycles at 2 AM, public urination, and drinking in the neighborhood park.

A liberal (or perhaps libertarian) response to Soeurette Hector's protestations can be offered for each of these behaviors: For one thing, not all people are on the same waking and sleeping schedule. Some people work variable shifts, young people have summer vacation, and the self-employed work when they want to. Hence leisure activities at 2 AM, including riding motorcycles, do not interrupt the sleep of *everyone*, just those with nine-to-five jobs. As one resident of public housing said, "Sometimes on a hot summer night, I don't blame them [for being in the park after the 10 PM closing time]. Me and my kids don't come in the house at nine o'clock. Yeah, they be woke at eleven. Yup. In the summer, what else you got to do with them? You don't want them woke at eight o'clock in the morning." Children playing outdoors at 11 PM is likely to annoy neighbors who must rise early for work. The point of this exercise is not for me to decide the ideological, moral, or legal high ground of different kinds of behaviors, but rather to expose the subjective and prescriptive contours of defining what is "undesirable." Moreover, Hector has relatively more power to actualize her values. Her story about the undesirable young men drinking in the park ends with an action that made her proud. Her ten-year-old son flagged down nearby police officers to report the bad behavior. "I was, like, so thrilled," she recalled. "I remember when I was a little girl, we used to have those things and the police used to be our friends."

Property managers (of private and publicly subsidized buildings) are also subject to the complaints of gentrifiers and are under pressure to keep their tenants in line with the desires of the new neighbors. Tenant screening and selection is just the first step in ensuring a certain kind of resident. Next, building managers see themselves as actively participating in behavior modification. Some of their strategies are structural, such as installing barbecue pits behind a building so that residents do not barbecue out front, as one manager told me. Another manager told me she installed individual air conditioning units to cut down on outdoor socializing in the summer. Many managers make sure that certain rules, such as those prohibiting loud music, are written into their leases and discussed with tenants so that there is no confusion over what infractions could result in eviction. These are relatively routine forms of building management and are appreciated as much by the tenants of the buildings themselves as by their new middle-class neighbors.

Yet sometimes these efforts become more austere and elicit greater resistance from low-income residents. Jenine Harris, manager of a project-based Section 8 building, was very cognizant of, perhaps even stressed out by, the gentrification of the neighborhood. Her awareness was heightened when the apartment building adjacent to the one she managed was converted to condominiums:

> It's been hell because I'm trying to get people to maintain this building in a certain way, but people aren't ready for the change. The tenants aren't ready for the change. They're not ready to live in a certain way that now the new residents of this area are accustomed to, or they expect. Like the condo association next door. You know, they don't hang out in front. But the culture of a lot of the residents in [this] building is they hang out [because] they come from areas or developments that that was the norm. So that was a big change for me to adjust to the hanging out and to not be so aggressive in asking them not to. You know that's been a change. I got a lot of resistance when I first got here because, you know, they gonna buck the system. My approach is a little different from the other management. I don't try to dictate to them, you know, what they should do and how they should live. I just try to incorporate them and show 'em different things and give 'em different things to do. But it's been very, very hard trying to get the residents to understand that there's, you know, no smoking in the hallways, smoke-free environment, drug-free environment, not to hang in front of the area and just some behavioral things.

Harris tried to be a sensitive landlord, but still felt there were certain rules that needed to be enforced, especially given the added scrutiny of the new condo owners next door.

What might have been the response of the tenants in Jenine Harris's building to her gently prodding them away from hanging out? Or the reaction of the young men who were asked by the police to leave the park at the behest of Soeurette Hector's son? "I'll tell you what. When you start paying our taxes, my taxes, then you tell me where to barbeque," was the response of one middle-aged man who had lived in NKO for decades when his new neighbor asked him not to barbecue on his front porch. There was a similar feud about barbecuing on the front porch on Emma McDaniel's block. A new neighbor did not like it, and the old neighbor did not care. McDaniel gave me her interpretation of the whole thing.

> If it had've been me, I'm telling you, honey, they'd have called the police on me. And I said, "You know, what kind of stuff is this?" You know, these are things that they have been doing all these years. And some of our back[yards] aren't like other people. And I can understand if you're out there and you got clowns out there with you and they're acting up and they're cursing and they're all disrespectful. Nobody wants that. Nobody wants that. But, I mean, it's the point that, honey, anything you do in your house or around your house, you don't annoy me. You're not bothering me. I'm not going to bother you, honey, because that is your place to enjoy. To do what you want to do. And I mean, I just said, "What's going on?" You know.

Her frustration with the new rules on her block is palpable. Not surprisingly, she too has a limit. She does not condone cursing, clowns, disrespect, or general "acting up." But the new rules, in her opinion, had gone too far. Her family had personally experienced not only the condescension of her neighbors but, more seriously, the pressure of the police when neighbors complained about her son repairing cars on the street. McDaniel feared for her son, who had spent time in jail and could not risk being on the police radar for even the most minor infraction. Despite her feistiness, she ultimately acquiesced. Emma McDaniel instructed her adult children not to antagonize the new neighbors and to follow the new block rules if confronted. She was already struggling financially and surely did not need any more headaches in the way of complaining neighbors and watchful police officers.

Andrea Wilson took the opposite approach when the management of the apartment building where she, her mother, and her grandmother had all grown up grew progressively more strict. "The management, now, I don't particularly care for," she began. "They don't want the kids

running around. They can't play in front. They don't want you standing in front of the building. You can't do this, you can't do that. It's like
you a prisoner in your own home. Basically, they don't want you to do
anything." Wilson was in her twenties and had a young son whom she
felt had nowhere to play, even though the U-shaped building enclosed
a large grassy courtyard. Her extended family combined the income
from her job at a record store and her mother's nursing salary to pay
the modest rent. Her grandmother had her own apartment, which she
paid for with a Section 8 voucher. But they saw changes coming. Wilson
commented on nearby buildings being converted to condos, the new
construction, and the remodeling. She appreciated that the vacant lots
were being filled, but as a result, she said, "it's getting more expensive to live around here." Furthermore, along with the new housing
came new rules, and the landlord began hassling her, her friends, and
her family about standing in front of the building. Wilson fought back,
and planted herself in front of her apartment building.

> Like where I live, my bedroom face the front of the building. So I used to
> go outside a lot to sit up under my window. [The landlord] didn't want
> anybody to sit there. My mom felt that if I'm paying rent why can my
> daughter not sit there. She [was] like, "Well, just go out there and sit
> anyway. And if he have something to say, tell him to come talk to me."
> And it was like he'll come, he'll do things like just sit there and watch us
> to see if his staring'll make us move. We just sit there and not pay any
> attention to him. And then finally he'd just drive off. I guess he just got
> tired of it.

Contrary to Emma McDaniel's experience, where she feared police re-
prisal, Andrea Wilson and her family felt emboldened by their long
tenure to defy rules that they perceived to be excessively rigid. Still, the
success of Wilson's stoop-sitting protest was short-lived. The landlord
got the ultimate revenge, not through the criminal justice system, but
through the prerogatives of ownership.

> He wanted to raise our security [deposit] from $75 to $900. He wanted
> to raise our rent to $1,100. We were already paying $875. So by the first
> of November we had to have $900 rent and a $900 security which is no
> way. Got to move. So within a month we were packed up and moved in
> here.

The Wilson family was able to find an apartment that was still near Andrea's grandmother's in a subsidized building a few blocks away. Andrea Wilson's run-in with her landlord, which she sees as connected to the changes in the neighborhood, exemplifies the turning point, where established residents, who initially benefited from change—seeing fewer vacant lots, having more retail options, and so on—start to be hurt by it, either through law enforcement or market forces.

Conclusion

Sociologists, especially of the social constructionist ilk, have long argued that something is a crime only if the people who guide public opinion and make laws say that it is.[27] There are some quite egregious acts, murder for instance, but even murder has not always been considered a crime that deserves harsh punishment. Lynchings, for example, drew cheering crowds of "law-abiding" white citizens. Even more socially constructed, historically contingent, and thus variably enforced are rules concerning things like jaywalking, drinking ages, drug use and sales, and panhandling. It is in this ambiguous and malleable realm that social power is most determinative of what will be deemed criminal, or abhorrent but legal, or somewhat distasteful, or perfectly acceptable.

The story in North Kenwood–Oakland begins at the extreme end of this spectrum, with old and new residents joining together, for the most part, to combat the more flagrant behaviors—gun violence, robbery, assaults, and home break-ins. The middle-class gentrifiers are concerned with their own safety but also greatly interested in protecting their investment and ensuring the future marketability of their homes. Established home owners—who may or may not be poor—have watched the neighborhood succumb to high crime rates but stayed put. They too want to feel safe, to be able to recoup their financial investment and, moreover, they have a certain nostalgia for the neighborhood as it was before gangs and drugs were so evident. Research on public housing residents illustrates that they are also deeply dissatisfied with its condition and management; foremost they desire safer surroundings.[28] All are of one accord in fighting serious crime.

Yet public housing residents are less successful in joining the coalition of new and old home owners against crime because they reside within what is purported to be the physical instantiation of the problem itself. Their absence and silence (or silencing) allows for the revanchist sentiments documented in this chapter—the verbal and ultimately literal condemnation of public housing and by extension its residents. Once headway has been made in lowering crime rates and erasing its signpost, the rhetoric easily shifts to the new terrain of lifestyles, values, tastes, and behaviors. The rules in this domain are as vehemently enforced as those employed to combat more serious crimes, through either legal, management, market, or planning mechanisms. The social and political clout, financial leverage, and activism of the gentrifiers ensure that their visions of appropriate neighborhood behavior reign, and the laws on the books—made by others like themselves—are there to back them up. This is the point at which the benefits of gentrification do not flow equally, and established poorer residents feel, and indeed are, increasingly supervised and disciplined so that the new residents can fully enjoy the neighborhood as they desire.

For decades, Chicago's South Side has been the iconic representation of black urban poverty in the United States. Today, the poorest but best-located parts of black Chicago, where land and homes could be had for a pittance two decades ago, are being celebrated by the city, eyed by developers, and featured by the media for their rise from the dust. They are also being reclaimed by more affluent African Americans. In this book, I have tried to highlight the class and lifestyle fractures within black identity, while affirming the persistence of blackness as a collective experience and endeavor. The gentrifying black middle and upper classes act as brokers, well-connected to the centers of elite power but grounded by their upbringings and socialization in more humble black surroundings. By framing this story within a discussion of urban politics and power, I hoped to show that the distinctions made by African Americans, which marginalize the behaviors and interests of their poor black neighbors as contrary to the respectable image of the race, have real consequences for the distribution of neighborhood resources.

Consider the contrasting remarks made by two residents of Berkeley Avenue in North Kenwood.

> *Emma McDaniel:* I know the block had to come up [i.e., "improve"].
> I understand this, and I don't envy the people. But, I mean, it's just that

they're just so different. Because I have a job where I've had a position too, but I didn't look down. You don't look down on anyone. Because all of us know where we've been, honey, but we don't know where we're going.

Shannon Howard: Then there's like this component on the block of the people who have, like, more than two or three generations in the house, and not keeping up their house. You know, fifty cars on the street, that kind of stuff, which I hate. Sitting on the porch all the time, staring at you from like the time you walk out of your door till you get to your car. I'm just like seeing them and it's like, oh, yuck. So that's how my neighbors are.

I lived on Berkeley between Ms. McDaniel and Mrs. Howard. It was clear in these separate interviews that they were talking about each other. A few houses to the north of me was the McDaniel household—headed by Emma McDaniel and including her two sons, her daughter, and her daughter's young son. The extended family members frequently sat on their porch, talking on the phone or talking to each other, entertaining visitors, barbecuing, or just passing the time. A few houses to my south was Shannon Howard, her husband, and their new baby. They had built an addition to the back of their house, including a beautiful deck off of the kitchen, so they rarely sat in front of their house. Some other neighbors thought Mrs. Howard was somewhat aloof, but no one denied the intensity with which she worked on issues of block improvement. Of course not everyone agreed on what "improvement" meant, and Ms. McDaniel felt like it sometimes meant "looking down on people." That disdain is apparent in Mrs. Howard's own words.

These are the diversities of lifestyles that I have highlighted throughout this book. French sociologist Pierre Bourdieu theorizes the role that distinctions between and among lifestyles play in reinforcing and reproducing class stratification. He writes:

As a consequence, the space of life-styles, i.e., the universe of the properties whereby the occupants of different positions differentiate themselves, with or without the intention of distinguishing themselves, is itself only the balance-sheet, at any given moment, of the symbolic struggles over the imposition of the legitimate life-style, which are most fully developed in the struggles for the monopoly of the emblems of "class"—luxury goods, legitimate cultural goods—or the legitimate manner of appropriating them.[1]

This book is concerned with the sphere of lifestyle distinctions not for the mere fact of describing how different people live and what they value, but rather because lifestyles both reflect and impact the lived realities of stratification. On Berkeley Avenue, Ms. McDaniel, a part-time bus driver, clearly felt the downward gaze of Mrs. Howard, a corporate executive, but resisted it by both asserting her own previous occupational authority ("I've had a position too") and calling into question the belief in status security at all ("but we don't know where we're going"). Mrs. Howard, on the other hand, was unwavering in her judgment of Ms. McDaniel and her vision of proper neighborhood conduct, to which Ms. McDaniel and her family did not conform. These contrasting viewpoints are produced by the material resources that each person has at her disposal. Ms. McDaniel's family sits on their front porch at least in part because they can't afford air conditioning. Mrs. Howard, by contrast, completely rehabbed her home to include central air, then built the deck for the days when she preferred a fresh breeze. Both of their behaviors are borne of their economic resources or lack thereof.

But lifestyles are not only structured by one's income or education, they also *act upon* or *structure* them. Ms. McDaniel's and Mrs. Howard's decisions about how to spend their leisure time and how to use outdoor space matter because they are differentially punished and rewarded. As Bourdieu writes, there are "legitimate" lifestyles, which necessarily means that others are illegitimate. As North Kenwood–Oakland makes its transition from a poor neighborhood to a mixed-income or perhaps an affluent one, Ms. McDaniel's habits and customs are often deemed illegitimate and seen as grounds for sanction. As other examples have shown, renters and public housing residents are particularly vulnerable to the discriminating tastes of newcomers. But while no one can kick Ms. McDaniel out of her house for sitting on her porch, she can be ostracized and made increasingly uncomfortable in the neighborhood in which her family has lived for over forty years.

This quasi-exchange in the testimonies of my two neighbors illustrates my first thesis: distinction-making characterizes the black community, and lived class schisms constantly challenge attempts at racial solidarity. Of course, class and status conflicts have always been apparent and well-documented in black communities. St. Clair Drake and Horace Cayton concoct a fictionalized account based on one of their experiences in studying black Chicago in the 1930s. In their narrative, a black doctor is called to the house of a poor black family after a domestic dispute turned violent. They narrate: "For a moment, Dr. Maguire felt sick at his stomach. 'Are these my people?' he thought. 'What in the hell do I have in common with them? This is "The Race" we're always spouting about being proud of?'"[2] Such ridicule by the black middle class directed at poor blacks is common in the scholarship, literature, and the arts of past and present black America. W. E. B. DuBois lamented the fact that the white gaze at blacks was suffused with "contempt and pity," but those sentiments have always also been present *within* black America, held by a contingent of African Americans who, based on their class, status, and lifestyles, see themselves as respectable representatives of The Race. The difference between the pre– and post–World War II periods, I argue, is that middle-class blacks now constitute a numerically larger and thus more politically significant interest bloc of brokers and middlemen, more able to deliver resources to black communities in need, but also more able to translate their disdain into disadvantages for the targets of their contempt.

As a result of moving into schools, institutions, and occupations from which they were once barred, blacks have forged legitimate alliances with powerful white elites and can consequently act to exclude and dominate other, more marginal groups. Political scientist Cathy Cohen refers to this process as "secondary marginalization," whereby members of a disenfranchised group establish bases upon which they are superior to members of some subclass of that group who command even less moral or political legitimacy or power. In this vein, the practices of differentiation in NKO are ultimately political acts, as they privilege certain modes of action, define "out-groups," specify which voices will be heard, and determine how resources will be distributed. The resources at stake are such things as affordable housing, commercial amenities, use of the parks, and access to good schools. As Bourdieu writes, "The power to impose and to inculcate a vision of divisions, that is, the power to make visible the explicit social divisions that are implicit, is political power par excellence."[3] The politics of neighborhood change in North Kenwood–Oakland is occurring not only at the level of city bureaucrats and developers, who wield electoral or financial power, but also among residents—new and old, formally educated and not, owners and renters, rich and poor—who vie for the ability to name what is acceptable and what is not, who should stay and who should go.

Distinctions are only half the story, however. Drake and Cayton's account of the frustrated doctor in 1930s black Chicago continues:

He had a little trick for getting back on an even keel when such doubts assailed him: he just let his mind run back over the "Uncle Tomming" he had to do when he was a Pullman porter; the turndown he got when he wanted to interne at the University of Chicago hospital; the letter from the American Medical Association rejecting his application for membership; the paper he wrote for a white doctor to read at a Mississippi medical conference which no Negroes could attend. Such thoughts always restored his sense of solidarity with "The Race." "Yeah, I'm just a nigger, too," he mumbled bitterly.[4]

This passage illuminates the second thread in *Black on the Block:* simultaneous to the work of difference, distinction, and sometimes even dislike, exists the primacy of race as a unifying social category, fostering allegiances across class and similarities in worldviews and political attitudes. The black middle class has not abandoned the black poor, either ideologically or geographically. To the contrary, it maintains a deep sense of racial responsibility that is sometimes translated into return migrations to poor black neighborhoods. This is the most important distinguishing feature of black gentrification relative to white gentrification. Moving back to the black ghetto is part of a racial uplift project. In her study of the gentrification of Harlem, Monique Taylor finds similarly that the "black gentry negotiate class differences and antagonisms through a racial discourse that downplays the class conflicts inherent in the struggles of gentrification." Newcomers are nothing short of messianic in their neighborhood improvement fervor. One of Taylor's informants commented: "It's an easy community to become visible in because there are so many things to be done. And it's an easy community to win over if you have the right words. It's easy because its been hurt so many times. It's like a baby waiting to be nurtured."[5] This nurturing spirit is one reserved for family, for racial kin.

One way that the claim to racial sameness is apparent in North Kenwood–Oakland is in the discussion of potential white neighbors. Despite Ms. McDaniel's and Mrs. Howard's mutual critique, they were of one accord when discussing the growing presence of whites in the neighborhood. "Honey, naturally they want to get back here," McDaniel said. "And that's why I'm so determined, if it's God's will, to hold on." Worried that many whites were moving into North Kenwood–Oakland to reclaim attractive real estate, she righteously anchored herself in her home as a way to maintain a black presence in the neighborhood. Howard agreed: "I do want my neighborhood to remain predominantly black, because I like it that way. So [whites] can move if they want to, but I don't want this to be where it's more white people and then it's like just a few black people." The prominence of race as a structuring category in American society, manifested most starkly in space through rigid and persistent racial segregation, compels African Americans toward some basic recognition of shared historical and contemporary oppression, as well as some core values, practices, and beliefs, however changing and internally contested. While affluent blacks form a faction of middlemen that is now able to structure power in its favor—sometimes to the detriment of poorer African Americans—they do so within the boundaries of shared racial identity.

Overall, "the black community," and blackness itself, are not fixed realities. They are projects. The words exchanged between black professionals and black public housing tenants in North Kenwood–Oakland were painfully harsh. To parents of teenagers whose test scores were below average, the conversion of King High School to a magnet school was misguided. Home owners with gas grills in their fenced back yards find serious fault with renters (with no back yards) who pull their old charcoal grills onto Drexel Boulevard for a barbecue. North Kenwood–Oakland is fraught with debates over what makes a community a community. And in this case, what makes a *black* community a black *community*. But instead of listing the top ten things that constitute racial identity and membership in this community, I conclude that the engagement itself is the definition.

However exclusionary the new schools in the neighborhood might be, the black leaders and professionals who brokered them intended for them to better educate black students. And when black newcomers made comments like the following—"What I wanna know is for the 25 percent that's gonna be low income are there going to be some guidelines for these people that when I go to work I don't need to worry about anything going on in my house. That people won't be up partying all night when some of us need to go to work?"—the sting for poor residents was particularly bad because they clung to a notion of racial solidarity that such statements seemed to violate. But in just these moments, when the black community threatened to be torn apart, other voices spoke up: "These people? Wait a minute, wait a minute, what is 'these people'?" The points and the counterpoints, the suggestions and the countersuggestions, the values and the other values all make up the ongoing project of blackness, the constant pulling apart and pushing together that characterizes the black community. There is no unitary black political agenda and there is no "black" way of doing things. There are only the manifestations of a blackness project in the discussions and debates like those taking place in North Kenwood–Oakland.

North Kenwood–Oakland yields a portrait of the complexities of boundary making among African Americans. Black newcomers are moving into NKO and aligning with some old-timer home owners to resist the building of public housing and to reinforce attempts to control the behaviors of low-income neighbors in and out of public housing. Poor old-timers and public housing renters assert their presence and refuse to disappear. Indeed it is their very public use of what others define as private space (barbecuing on porches, partying all night next door) that fuels controversy. "Each lifestyle can only really be constructed in relation to the other, which is its objective and subjective negation," writes Bourdieu.[6] These mutually contested lifestyles reflect distinctions of capital resources—employed versus unemployed, taxpayer versus free rider, home owner versus renter. These evident distinctions necessitate a reconsideration of monolithic and static depictions of black communities.

Yet just as boundaries exist *within* this black community, they also work on its *outside* to contain its members within a community of solidarity. Residents in NKO recognize the short shrift that African Americans have been given by the wider society. In light of this, they demand racially specific benefits, regardless of class status, and are unwilling to turn the neighborhood over to the whites who are moving in. An implication of these findings is that we have undertheorized complex processes of racial domination, which position some groups as simultaneously dominated and dominators. The issue has not gone entirely unnoticed. E. Franklin Frazier's *The Black Bourgeoisie* deals with the contempt toward poorer blacks manifested by middle-class blacks. The historical research of Evelyn Brooks Higginbotham shows how black middle-class women's assistance to poor blacks was conditional on the latter's conforming to middle-class norms and codes of behavior. Yet the contemporary growth of the black middle class, and the presence of middle-class blacks in positions to broker power, as architects, city planners and elected officials, real estate developers and speculators, and social service providers—as middlemen and middlewomen—raises a new prospect in the quest to understand racial and class inequalities and hierarchies. Efforts to "uplift the race," contained historically mainly within the black community of churchwomen and a small intelligentsia, may now be articulated within much larger systems of power, within urban regimes, within growth machines. Bishop Arthur Brazier, who heads an organization involved in housing and commercial development in North Kenwood–Oakland, told one reporter: "When we were picketing and marching in the 1960s, we were doing it to get a seat at the table, a piece of the pie. We think we have been able to achieve that." As a result of this incorporation, the preferences of middle-class blacks—not to have people fixing cars on their street, to live far from public housing, to screen potential neighbors on the basis of their employment and housekeeping standards—now gain legitimacy from financial investors, from legal frameworks and sanctions, and from the enforcement of the state.[7]

A Theory of the Middle

Any study of gentrification, or neighborhood change in general, is likely to feature battles over land use, home maintenance, the diversity of shops and restaurants, public schools, and what counts as a crime. *Black on the Block* is no different in this respect. The story of *black* gentrification in North Kenwood–Oakland, however, is even messier. The added complexity can be explained by focusing on the power, promise, and precariousness of "the middle." Chapter 3 introduced and the rest of the book elaborated the middleness of North Kenwood–Oakland's newcomers, with their extensive educations, lucrative jobs, strategic contacts, and racial legitimacy. But it is also a concept that appears widely in the analysis of social phenomena, and thus, I argue, merits additional consideration and prominence in studies of inequality. There are, after all, many middles.

There are historical middles in the evolution of ethnic identity. In his sprawling history of eastern European Jewish immigration to the United States, Irving Howe locates a moment in the 1950s and 1960s when the second and third generations of the original immigrant families were looking both backward and forward. "They were reaching toward ease and comfort, while wanting also to retain fragments of their Jewish past." Surely theirs was as much a class middle as it was a historical one, and a spatial transition as well, since the place of this middle moment was decidedly suburban, far from the densely settled New York

City neighborhoods in which their forebears had lived. Skillfully rolling together all of these middles, and more, Howe observes, "They moved far enough into the pleasures of assimilation almost to feel ready for the pleasures of nostalgia." Movement across time, space, and identities, but still not quite there yet. "Since they were, after all, Jews," Howe adds, "many of them seem to have had some awareness of the oddity or the humor of their condition."[8] There is always dissonance and incongruence in the middle, a sense of being drawn in two directions.

There are transnational middles. Peggy Levitt studied families in Miraflores, Dominican Republic, and families in Jamaica Plain, Boston, who had migrated from Miraflores. Neither group was fixed, with frequent moves between the two cities creating communities of part-Americans in Miraflores and part-Dominicans in Boston. This required the reconciliation of many values and worldviews, which differed in the two places. One such example was the place of women in families and communities. In Miraflores, there were clear and separate spaces for men and women, and roles were well defined and distinct. But in Boston, "men spent less time with other women and more time at home. It was too cold for them to be out on the street during most of the year. It was too expensive to drink beer in the Irish bar on the corner (where they were not welcome anyway). And because women worked, men normally helped out with some of the cleaning and childcare." When families who had lived in Boston *moved back* to Miraflores, they brought these experiences with them and shook up the settled order of the sexes. Not completely, however, but through "incremental changes." "Roberto's solution," writes Levitt about one informant who had lived in both places, "was to do chores inside the house where no one could see him. He washed the dishes, he said, but he would never be caught hanging the laundry."[9] The middle is a site of negotiation and experimentation.

There are colonial middles. Historian Ruth Rogaski studied the occupation of the Chinese port city of Tianjin by several quasi-colonial foreign powers at the beginning of the twentieth century, focusing on outsider attempts to modernize China through an emphasis on health and hygiene. In particular, the Western and Japanese administrators who imposed foreign formulations of sanitary practices and disease prevention on Chinese cities were aided by Chinese elites, who were relegated to a middle function vis-à-vis the dominant occupying powers. These middlemen, as Rogaski explicitly calls them, stood "between

the [foreign] authorities and the Chinese population." Given their educations and material resources, these local elites were not affected by
the most violent and coercive hygienic practices imposed by the semi-
colonial rulers. In fact, they often appreciated the ordered regime that
the foreigners demanded, such as "the remarkable phenomenon of a
single-file ticket queue at the Tianjin train station, maintained by policemen who whipped anyone who stepped out of line." These alliances
with the occupying forces did not, however, constitute a freedom for
the still-subjugated Chinese elite. Instead, they were *in the midst* of
the project of "distancing themselves from a perceived chaotic Other
and obtaining for themselves . . . a position in the new order of 'modern civilization.' For both Chinese and Japanese elites alike, this chaotic
Other was primarily defined as a 'superstitious,' 'backward,' deficient
China." The Chinese elite in Tianjin were like middlemen across the
colonial world who staffed the police forces, worked as translators, and
doled out to their fellow colonial subjects whatever scant provisions
were allotted by the imperial government, whose actors were often absent. The interventions of powerful outsiders, notes political scientist
James C. Scott, "will typically be mediated by local trackers who know
the society from the inside and who are likely to interpose their own
particular interests."[10]

Finally, there are middles within social networks. Whereas actors
in the middle of a colonial arrangement seem particularly hemmed
in—used by their superiors while they themselves exploit and mis-
treat those below them—sociologist Ronald Burt investigates people in
the middle as particularly *free*. The middle, Burt argues, is the sight of
creativity and "vision advantage." "People connected across groups are
more familiar with alternative ways of thinking and behaving, which
gives them more options to select from and synthesize. . . . Some frac-
tion of these new ideas are good." Middleness is thus generative and
productive. It opens up new worlds, occasions new exposures, and invites novelty. Using commercial firms as his empirical case, Burt finds
evidence that employees who fill the "structural holes" of an organizations' social networks tend to have better ideas for solving organizational problems, and they are often better compensated as a result.
Their ideas are fresh not necessarily because people in the middle are
smarter than others, but rather because they have translated the com-
monsense knowledge of one group and applied it in the domain of another. "It is creativity as an import-export business," Burt observes, but

creative nonetheless.[11] When the middle is the person where two otherwise noncommunicating groups intersect, that person is the source of synthetic and multivocal new ideas, and thus a node of significant influence.

Reviewing these various middles makes visible an array of characteristics about middle status that helps in understanding instances of mobility and systems of inequality. The middle is a place of *relative* power because it is subjected to the power, and thus the *constraints*, of some higher entity while still maintaining authority over the littleman. Power is often conceptualized in binary terms—an oppressor and an oppressed—ignoring the reality of multitiered inequalities that create middles, which are both. Theorist Erik Olin Wright makes this point in his accommodation of the slippery "middle class" to Marxism. He decides that the middle class is defined by contradiction, for "they are like capitalists in that they dominate workers [and] they are like workers in that they are controlled by capitalists and exploited within production."[12]

The middle has similar proscriptions and duties outside of the labor market, and most especially in the realm of politics, where native elites in colonies, migrants returning to home countries, and black gentrifiers in poor black neighborhoods hold this same contradictory place. The work of spanning two worlds is rewarded by the "pleasures of assimilation" or the "competitive advantage" that a person achieves by identifying and filling structural holes. Other rewards come from the satisfaction of delivering much needed resources to one's less advantaged constituency or from representing the challenges they face so effectively that those in power actually become sympathetic and make just reforms. But the job of the middleman is also stressful because he or she is on the front lines, carrying out the initiatives of a largely invisible collection of corporate and governmental actors. Sometimes she thinks the goods she's selling are the right things for the community and sometimes she doesn't. But he has signed on to make the pitch nonetheless. The point is that the allegiances and preferences of middlemen are variable and perhaps even unpredictable. What is consistent is their presence as mediators, conduits, brokers, and enforcers, at one moment upholding the status quo, at another helping the rich get richer, and at still another moment demanding that the littleman get his due. In essence, the middle is the place where the actual face-to-face work of inequality transpires.

Introduction

1. In his analysis of Harold Washington's election and administration, and the scramble for power that followed his death, Abdul Alkalimat (1988, 53) concludes, "Washington gave people hope, but that ended when he died. White power then installed a black mayor and shocked the community into realizing that middle class black power did not have [to] be based on the will of black people." For other interpretations of the Washington era and its aftermath, see Grimshaw 1992; Bennett 1993.

2. Cohen 1999; Gaines 1996; Reed 1999.

3. See Boyd 2000 on the "racial nostalgia" of black gentrification.

4. I stop short of placing Chicago in a global context, which I leave to scholars with expertise in the impact of globalization on cities. See Abu-Lughod 1999; Clark 2000; Sassen 2002.

5. Wyly and Hammel (1999, 741) might argue the opposite, namely that the immigration of high-income families *precedes* the development of public housing into mixed-income housing: "Where the class transformation of neighborhoods tightens the housing market in the vicinity of public housing, mixed-income redevelopment is both feasible and profitable if the parcel is configured in such a way that higher-income residents do not feel threatened by the proximity of poor families. By contrast, public housing developments that are distant from areas undergoing private-market revitalization will have difficulty attracting market-rate residents."

6. Conservation areas were first contemplated in the 1943 Master Plan for the city of Chicago (see Chicago Plan Commission 1943). Yet at the federal level, the first piece of legislation did not address conservation. Title I of the federal 1949

Housing Act established federal support for slum clearance, including land acquisition, demolition, and relocation (see von Hoffman 2000). Subsequently, the Housing Act of 1954 changed urban "redevelopment" to urban "renewal" and "conservation," shifting the focus to areas that were threatened by blight but were not yet slums, and enlarging the kinds of construction the federal government would support beyond residential. The states were often ahead of the federal government on urban initiatives; Illinois had already enacted the Urban Community Conservation Act of 1953, which granted public dollars to imperiled communities (see Hirsch 2000). Together these state and federal acts granted powers of eminent domain for the "removal of dilapidated buildings and other obstructions"; zoning powers for the "discontinuance of property uses that downgrade the neighborhood"; aggressive code enforcement with the ability to place liens on private property; and state and federal loans for rehabilitation and new construction (Community Conservation Board [1957?], 10–11, 16). Some elements of conservation area legislation were amended in the Urban Renewal and Consolidation Act of 1961. For the conservation plan in North Kenwood–Oakland, see Community Development Commission 1992.

7. Urban Services and Development, Inc. 1978, 1.

8. While the 1978 document was *not* a conservation plan, a plan authored by KOCO in 1968 asserted that "Kenwood-Oakland should be declared a Conservation Area to make Federal 312 loans available" (Kenwood Oakland Community Organization 1968, 27). In the 1978 plan, KOCO actually changed its position to lobby for a Slum and Blighted Areas designation from the City of Chicago. The introduction read, "The best statistics available present a picture of poverty and deterioration, and justify the classification of the area as an urban slum ghetto neighborhood" (Urban Services and Development, Inc. 1978, 2). A contingent of community representatives strongly opposed the slum designation as it could lead to the demolition of dozens of homes. Alderman Tim Evans was also opposed. (See testimony of Mary Bordelon to the Chicago Plan Commission, February 23, 1989; also see letter to Alderman Timothy C. Evans from KOCO executive director Robert L. Lucas, July 2, 1988, both in North Kenwood–Oakland Conservation Area files at the Chicago Department of Planning and Development, hereafter cited as "DPD files"). Still, in April 1988, the Department of Urban Renewal designated the area from 44th Street to 47th Street and Greenwood to the lake as a "blighted and vacant project area." However, the Neighborhood Planning Committee, which convened soon after the blighted area designation, took community planning in the conservation direction. Support for conservation area designation eventually trumped that for the blighted and vacant project area plan. KOCO switched its support to the conservation idea "because it was consistent with the community's wishes and the original plan of 1978, and it put community residents in the driver's seat, enabling them to protect their community and develop it in a reasonable way that would prevent displacement." See Lucas letter to Evans, July 2, 1988, DPD files.

9. McClory 1993, 14. The article called Bordelon "the scourge of North Kenwood" and clearly meant it as a compliment.

10. Letter to Mayor Richard M. Daley from Sandra Chapman, November 15, 1990, DPD files.

11. On the University of Chicago and urban renewal, see Hirsch 1983; Rossi and Dentler 1961. For contemporary discussions of universities and neighborhood change/revitalization, see Gilderbloom and Mullins 2005 and Maurrasse 2001.

12. Dávila 2004, 3. For a general discussion of neighborhood revitalization, with several examples, see von Hoffman 2003.

13. In this book "public housing" refers to apartments and buildings constructed with federal dollars by the local housing authority. I use "subsidized housing" or sometimes "affordable housing" to refer to a larger category that includes units built using city, state, or federal funding. Examples of these programs are Low Income Housing Tax Credits, Section 221, and Section 236.

14. For 1990 community area data, see Chicago Fact Book Consortium 1995. There have been a few attempts to identify the community areas in Chicago that are undergoing gentrification using comparable demographic indicators. Taylor and Puente (2004) list both Kenwood and Oakland among the "most gentrifying areas" from 1990 to 2000. Hudspeth and Smith (2004) include Kenwood but not Oakland on their list; in personal communications, however, one of the authors wrote, "Keep in mind this is all based on census data—2000 is the most current and a lot has changed since then. We are seeing gentrification in many near south areas now, including Grand Blvd. (Bronzeville), Douglas, Oakland and Bridgeport." Wyly and Hammel (1999) do not list either Oakland or North Kenwood as core or fringe gentrifying areas based on data from 1960 to 1990, although they do list South Kenwood.

15. Data for Low Income Housing Tax Credit buildings and federally funded subsidized housing are from http://www.huduser.org/datasets/lihtc.html and http://www.uic.edu/cuppa/voorheesctr/IHARP%20information.htm. Data on public housing units are from Chicago Housing Authority (2004).

16. These two buildings were initially rehabbed as affordable housing in 1987 by the nonprofit Kenwood Oakland Development Corporation, in collaboration with a real estate syndication firm, Chicago Equity Fund, Inc., using the Low Income Housing Tax Credit Program. With the federal contract set to expire in 2002, the developers proposed to sell the condominium units at market price, but said they would consider working with the city to receive subsidies to make the condominiums affordable to moderate income families. See minutes of the Conservation Community Council (hereafter cited as "CCC minutes") for meetings held July 5, 2001, and February 3, 2005. Chicago Rehab Network (2004) reports that one hundred project-based Section 8 units will expire in Kenwood and five hundred will expire in Oakland between 2004 and 2009.

17. While the suburbs still account for more than 85 percent of total mortgage investments in metropolitan areas, Wyly and Hammel (1999) show that gentrifying areas and other nearby neighborhoods saw considerably more *growth* in investments during the 1990s than did the suburbs.

18. Cashin 2004; Taylor (2002, 62) finds considerable evidence of integration exhaustion among Harlem's black gentrifiers: "In interviews with Harlem's black gentry," she writes, "it was not uncommon for me to hear stories about negative experiences on the job and with white neighbors that in part prompted the move

to Harlem. Some had endured slights as subtle as whispered comments. Others had weathered more severe attacks in the form of racial slurs and, for one family, the firebombing of their new home in a white neighborhood." See also Daniels 2004; Lacy 2002.

19. Street 2005, 29–30. Mortgage lending data for 2003 show that of the 127 loans made in the Oakland neighborhood, 32 percent went to families with annual incomes between $56,000 and $82,000, and 39 percent to families with incomes above $82,000. I report only the data from Oakland, because the Kenwood data is complicated by the mixing of North and South Kenwood. See Woodstock Institute 2003.

20. I use the term "liberal whites" because data from Boston, Los Angeles, Atlanta, and Detroit show that only 31 percent of whites would move into a neighborhood that was just over half black (Krysan and Farley 2002, 960). North Kenwood–Oakland is still over 90 percent black, which suggests that the percentage of whites who would be willing to move in is even smaller.

21. Street 2005, table 14. Mortgage lending data for Oakland for 2003 show that 65 percent of the applicants for loans in the neighborhood were black, 12 percent were white, and 20 percent did not report their race. See Woodstock Institute 2003.

22. Research on mixed-income public housing sites across the country is relevant here. Each HOPE VI plan, each site's surrounding neighborhood, and each city's racial history is so different that it makes it difficult to generalize across the HOPE VI developments, but Zielenbach's (2003) study of the changes in eight HOPE VI neighborhoods found that on average the proportion of white residents increased from 8.6 percent to 9.8 percent. Theodoric Manley Jr. and his colleagues present simulations of the future racial composition of Bronzeville, a majority black community adjacent to North Kenwood–Oakland (Manley 2004; Manley, Buffa, and Dube 2005). They predict that 14 percent of the population of Bronzeville will be white for the 2010 census, increasing rapidly to 25 percent by 2015. These authors argue that "the Black middle class role is temporary at best in the larger scheme of the gentrification process occurring in Bronzeville. As housing prices and property taxes increase in Bronzeville, we predict that a second wave of gentrification will usher in a more stable White elite upper class" (Manley, Buffa, and Dube 2005, 7). For a brief summary of changes in Bronzeville, see Bennett 2005.

23. See Blau and Duncan (1967) for the classic formulation of class. On "hard and soft facts" of class, see J. L. Jackson (2001, 126) and Weber (1946, 193, 181). For class as lifestyles and distinctions, see Bourdieu 1984; DiMaggio 1982; Lareau 1987, 2003; Lamont 1992. There has recently been considerable attention to the study of boundaries in the social sciences. Lamont and Molnár (2002) review this literature with an emphasis on the distinction between "symbolic boundaries" and "social boundaries," where the former are conceptual, affective, rhetorical, interpretive, and discursive and the latter are inscribed into patterns of social (political, economic, and institutional) relations, often through processes of stratification or hierarchy. Symbolic boundaries can be used to produce social boundaries. The labels in this "boundaries" approach differ from those that Weber uses. Lamont and Molnár's "symbolic boundaries" are similar to Weber's "status," while their

"social boundaries" are what Weber would more narrowly define as "class." While these differences in terminology can be confusing, the analytical imperative is the same. Both approaches highlight the importance of distinguishing between: (1) the symbols, signs, and markers that are used to classify people, places, and times—that is, symbolic boundaries or statuses or lifestyles—and (2) the "objectified forms of social differences manifested in unequal access to and unequal distribution of resources . . . and social opportunities" (Lamont and Molnár 2002, 169)—that is, social boundaries or classes.

24. Gans 1995; Katz 1989; Small and Newman 2001; Wacquant 1997; Young 2004.

25. In Harlem's black gentrification, J. L. Jackson (2005) talks about home owners as split between the "old guard that never left and a newer group that has recently arrived. For many of the Harlem activists, these two black middle classes represent diametrically opposed interests—not least because the older guard views the younger set as a threat to their local authority" (51). One dimension on which the old and new guard sometimes overlap and sometimes conflict is in their interest in realizing Harlem's full market potential versus their interest in realizing a sense of racial community and collective responsibility.

26. Logan and Molotch 1987, 141.

27. See Duneier 2001 for an even more labor-intensive model of consulting interviewees for their reactions to a draft manuscript.

28. For reviews of the gentrification literature, see Atkinson 2002; Kennedy and Leonard 2001; Zukin 1987. For studies of gentrification and middle-class movement to cities, see Abu-Lughod 1994; Dávila 2004; Florida 2005; Lloyd 2005; Mele 2000; Pérez 2002; Smith 1996; Spain 1993; Zukin 1982. On the gentrification/displacement debate, see Atkinson 2000; Freeman 2005; Freeman and Braconi 2004; Henig 1980; Marcuse 1985; Vigdor 2002.

29. The Urban Institute is studying the HOPE VI development in North Kenwood–Oakland. See Popkin, Cunningham, and Woodley 2003; Popkin, Eiseman, and Cove 2004. University of Chicago researcher Mark Joseph is studying Jazz on the Boulevard, another mixed-income development in North Kenwood–Oakland, but no research reports are yet published. On HOPE VI more generally, see General Accounting Office 2003; Keating 2000; Kingsley, Johnson, and Pettit 2003; National Housing Law Project 2002; Popkin, Katz, et al. 2004; Zielenbach 2003. On a non–HOPE VI mixed-income project, see Goetz 2003.

30. Boyd forthcoming; Dávila 2004; Hyra 2006; Jackson 2005; Pérez 2004; Prince 2004; Taylor 2002.

Chapter One

1. Commission on Chicago Landmarks 1992, 39 ("[sic]" in original; the developer of these lots, discussed later in the chapter, was actually G. F. Swift). The street was named "Berkeley" in gratitude for a $10,000 gift from the City of Boston after the Great Chicago Fire of 1871. Berkeley was a major thoroughfare in Boston named after Lord Berkeley of London (Commission on Chicago Landmarks 1992,

25; Chicago History Museum, "Chicago Streets," http://www.chsmedia.org/ househistory/nameChanges/start.pdf [accessed July 1, 2005]).

2. Classified ads, *Chicago Tribune,* April 5 and September 25, 1891.

3. Commission on Chicago Landmarks 1992, 2, 3.

4. Quoted in Commission on Chicago Landmarks 1990, 25.

5. "Realty and Dinner: City Improvement Is Discussed by Real Estate Men," *Chicago Tribune,* September 26, 1893, p. 5; classified ad, *Chicago Tribune,* May 11, 1891, p. 7. The Chicago Commission on Race Relations (1922, 207) described the speculation in the area and the following real estate bubble as follows: "The World's Columbian Exposition, held in Chicago in 1893, was near the Hyde Park neighborhood. To accommodate the millions of visitors at the Exposition hotels and apartment houses were built in that district far in excess of the normal need. The apartment houses, moreover, affected the exclusiveness of the residence streets. The buildings were speculations. Large sums were expended in the hope of immediate exceptional profits. . . . After the Exposition the removal of the first residents to the North Side and to suburbs steadily increased."

6. The Commission on Chicago Landmarks (1992) officially attributes the development of 4432 South Berkeley to Gustavus Swift and his son Louis F. Swift, and thus I follow their lead. However, property records show a number of investors were involved in developing the Berkeley block; I could not find Gustavus Swift's name among them. I found it only in the newspaper entry quoted in the Landmarks Commission's pamphlet on the neighborhood. It is possible that Swift purchased the land even before it was annexed to the City of Chicago and then sold it, taking his profit quickly. The other possibility is that he was never involved in the building of 4432 Berkeley.

The confusion may have arisen because of the similarities between the name of his son—Louis Swift—and M. Lewis Swift, who is certain to have played a role in building and selling the house and who, as far as I can tell, was no relation to Gustavus Swift. The first listed deed activity for the parcel was a quit-claim deed from George M. Bogue to M. Lewis Swift and William H. Cairnduff. Bogue was a prominent Chicago real estate broker and principal in the firm Bogue & Hoyt, later Bogue & Company. Cairnduff was also a very active real estate investor and broker, and a prominent member of the Chicago Real Estate Board, a group of men who thought of themselves as the "men who owned the earth." Both Cairnduff & Co. and Bogue & Co. advertised several properties in the Kenwood and Oakland neighborhoods around this time. More specifically, a July 1890 newspaper article announced that architect Robert Rae was building eight homes for Cairnduff in the 4400 block of Berkeley Avenue ("Real Estate Transaction," *Chicago Daily Tribune,* July 13, 1890). While Cairnduff's role in the Berkeley block was obviously key, he was better known for developing other parts of Chicago around the same time. In particular, he developed "Cairnduff's Addition to Edgewater" on the city's north side (Edgewater Historical Society, "2004 Fall Tour of Homes," http://www .edgewaterhistory.org/tour040919/index.html?11.html [accessed July 1, 2005]).

M. Lewis Swift was less prominent across the city than the other two men in this transaction, but he was the most closely tied to the neighborhood. He lived at 4458 South Ellis, in a house that predated 4432 Berkeley by no more than one or two years and was located just one block west. M. Lewis Swift was involved in various projects on the South Side, including another row of houses in the 4500 block of Ellis (see Commission on Chicago Landmarks 1992, 30). He also placed ads in the *Chicago Tribune* that identified him as the "Owner and Builder" for 4430, 4434, 4436, 4440, and 4444 Berkeley (classified ads, April 5 and September 25, 1891); 4432 was built with the rest of these, but perhaps it sold before Swift could advertise in the paper. Deed records confirm that there were various early investors/owners.

Unlike Bogue and Cairnduff, who show up in searches of various Chicago Who's Who guides, I was able to find only one reference to M. Lewis Swift in the numerous historical sources I consulted. He was listed in the *Book of Chicagoans*, 1911 edition (Marquis 1911), by which time he had retired from the real estate business. The entry documented Swift's humble upbringing as the son of a general store owner in Dresserville, New York, and his wandering employment as a postmaster and hardware store proprietor in various Michigan cities. Aside from the hint of distinction accorded by his membership in Chicago's elite Union League Club, the listing concludes unceremoniously: "came to Chicago and engaged in real estate and building until 1897, when retired. Republican. Mason (K.T.). Club: Union League. Residence: 4458 Ellis Av."

7. Sandburg 1916.

8. Commission on Chicago Landmarks 1992, 38, 13.

9. Commission on Chicago Landmarks, North Kenwood File, form #39-04-10-073, April 6, 1987.

10. Deed records indicate that M. L. Swift conveyed the property in early 1892 to Marc S. Holmes, who in turn conveyed it to Agnes A. and Oliver P. Stoddard in 1893. Stoddard was a partner in the Chicago Real Estate and Investment Company, which ran ads in the *Tribune* listing their many homes for sale on the South Side, suggesting that he might have been a speculative owner. One realtor in the greater Hyde Park area gave the following description of the glut of houses and apartments that likely contributed to the early difficulty in selling 4432 Berkeley: "Buildings that were put up three and four years after the Fair, along in 1894, 1895, and 1896, could be built at about 30 percent cheaper than those that were put up during the World's Fair. The consequences were that you could rent a flat cheaper in a brand-new modern building than you could in a building that was put up during the World's Fair, and as the older buildings could not be rented, the owners finally had to come down in their rent more and more; they got in less and less desirable tenants until finally the whole territory became undesirable" (quoted in Chicago Commission on Race Relations 1922, 207).

11. Stuart 1997, 270.

12. Advertisement, *Chicago Tribune*, August 31, 1902, p. B31.

13. Lindsey 1942; Steeples and Whitten 1998.

14. Commission on Chicago Landmarks 1992, 39; classified ad, *Chicago Tribune*, April 3, 1898.

15. "Mary Quinn On Trial," *Chicago Tribune,* August 3, 1895, p. 4. "Is Her Story True?" *Chicago Tribune,* June 13, 1895, p. 1.

16. Classified ad, *Chicago Tribune,* November 6, 1892.

17. U.S. Census Bureau, "Historical Census of Housing Tables: Homeownership," http://www.census.gov/hhes/www/housing/census/historic/owner.html (accessed July 1, 2005); classified ad, *Chicago Daily Tribune,* September 23, 1912; "News of Chicago's Society," *Chicago Sunday Tribune,* May 10, 1914.

18. "Official List of the Dead and the Injured in Chicago's Race Riot," *Chicago Daily Tribune,* July 30, 1919, p. 4. See also Chicago Commission on Race Relations 1922, 657; Cook County Coroner [1920?].

19. Chicago Commission on Race Relations 1922, 1, 8.

20. Lawrence 1993.

21. It is difficult to give a blanket characterization of race relations during the time of the formation of the Black Belt. Spear (1969, 203–6) argues that the schools were relatively harmonious despite the fact that school officials were contemplating a segregated system, whereas parks, playgrounds, beaches, and other cultural facilities were aggressively contested. The Chicago Commission on Race Relations (1922, 109) paints a more sanguine portrait of the core of the Black Belt, referring to it as an "Adjusted Neighborhood," a place where "the Negro population has increased gradually without disturbance for many years." The commission presents photographs of black and white children playing and working together and statements by whites affirming their comfort with new black neighbors as proof of this racial accommodation; nonetheless, the study's map of homes bombed in the period 1917–1921 includes homes in the area it describes as relatively well integrated, and racially mixed areas saw intense rioting activity during the 1919 riots. Still, the commission underscores the important point that this was a period when most of what is often referred to as the Black Belt was not yet predominantly black. It gives the example of the area from 12th to 39th Streets and Lake Michigan to Wentworth Avenues, where 42,797 whites and 54,906 blacks lived in 1920.

22. "German 'Kultur' Spreads 'Over East,'" *Chicago Defender,* October 19, 1918, p. 1; see also "Bomb Explosion Wrecks Windows of Negro's House," *Chicago Sunday Tribune,* October 13, 1918, p. A1. The *Defender* article described the Andersons and Wallers as "people of the highest character [who] will compare favorably with any of their neighbors." (The white family that replaced the Wallers at 4143 Berkeley seemed to confirm this assertion. James Kerrigan, a white suspended police officer and onetime chauffeur, was charged in 1932 with assaulting and attempting to kill his wife and son ["Policeman Will Be Arraigned in Shooting Case," *Chicago Daily Tribune,* July 6, 1932]). Other buildings in the neighborhood were also bombed during this period, including two multiunit buildings: 4117–4119 Lake Park, on March 19, 1921, and 4212–4216 Ellis, on April 7, 1919 ("Bomb Breaks Windows in Flats of Colored Families," *Chicago Daily Tribune,* March 19, 1921, p. 1; "Bomb Set Off in Negro Flats," *Chicago Daily Tribune,* April 7, 1919 p. 1).

23. Chicago Commission on Race Relations 1922, 118, 591. The northern part of Oakland was covered by an adjoining early property owners' association, the Lake

Front Community Property Owners' Association, which covered the area east of Cottage Grove from 33rd Street to 39th Street (ibid., 118).

24. Ibid., 592.

25. Plotkin 1997. On racial covenants in Chicago and in the Oakland neighborhood in particular, see Plotkin 1999; Schietinger 1948; Washington 1948. For a general history and analysis of covenants in Chicago and nationally, see Plotkin 2001; Weaver 1945; Brooks 2003.

26. Chicago Commission on Race Relations 1922, 210.

27. White 1919, 296.

28. "Wounded Heroes Back from France," *Chicago Daily Tribune*, January 7, 1919, p. 7, and census records; "Brothers Who Helped Win the War," *Chicago Daily Tribune*, January 19, 1919; "Start on New St. James' M.E. Church Shortly," *Chicago Daily Tribune*, August 31, 1924, p. A9; "Former Cooper-Monalah to be Made Sutherland Hotel," *Chicago Daily Tribune*, June 21, 1925, p. F24; "Women's Club Page; Women Voters Plan Three Day Institute," *Chicago Daily Tribune*, February 20, 1927, p. I3.

29. "Oakland Starts House Cleaning for World Fair," *Chicago Daily Tribune*, April 9, 1933, p. SC2; "Cermak to Tell Oakland's Duty to Fair Guest," *Chicago Daily Tribune*, January 22, 1933, p. SC2.

30. Linehan 2004, 854; "Police Report 84 Saloonmen as 'LID' Tilters," *Chicago Daily Tribune*, October 25, 1915, p. 15; "New Campaign Starts to Clean Up South Side," *Chicago Daily Tribune*, June 5, 1922, p. 21; "10,000 Oakland District Men to War on Vice," *Chicago Daily Tribune*, June 6, 1922, p. 19. The "New Campaign" article included both the early-1920s statistics and the report of Thrasher's speech. The "Oakland district" referred to in these documents was larger than the contemporary Oakland community area. It spanned from 35th Street to 43rd Street (the same as today) and from Lake Michigan to present-day Martin Luther King Jr. Drive (then Grand Boulevard), four blocks west of Cottage Grove Avenue, the current western boundary.

31. Genevieve Forbes, "Color Line Lost in Abandoned Revels at Ritz," *Chicago Daily Tribune*, July 19, 1922, p. 12; "Girls of 16 Reel through Dance in 'Tan' Resort," *Chicago Daily Tribune*, July 14, 1922, p. 17. On black and tans, see Bachin 2004.

32. "Kidnap Couple; Rob Husband's Store of $300," *Chicago Daily Tribune*, February 4, 1929, p. 1; "Doctor Held on Charge of Murder by Abortion," *Chicago Daily Tribune*, December 1, 1928, p. 9; "Girl Collapses, Dies at Dance with Her Fiance," *Chicago Daily Tribune*, May 20, 1929, p. 16; "Tavern Shot Up; One Wounded; Seize Suspect," *Chicago Daily Tribune*, July 14, 1939, p. 4.

33. From the beginning the *Defender* questioned the police investigation. Its first headline read: " 'Somebody Did It,' So 2 Youths Who 'Might Have Done It' Are Arrested" (David Orro, *Chicago Defender*, May 28, 1938). Even when Nixon was convicted, the front-page headline read, "Nixon Found Guilty: Brick-Murder *Suspect* Given Death Penalty" (David Orro, *Chicago Defender*, August 6, 1938, p. 1; emphasis added). All along, the *Defender*'s coverage was more thorough, if

not more skeptical, than that of the *Tribune*, including information not reported in the *Tribune*, such as the fact that early fingerprint evidence did not match Nixon's fingerprints (see *Chicago Defender*, May 28, 1938, p. 24).

34. "Brick Slayer's Confession up at Trial Today; Criminal Court," *Chicago Daily Tribune*, July 29, 1938, p. 8.

35. "Brick Moron Tells of Killing 2 Women," *Chicago Daily Tribune*, May 29, 1938; "Fasten Double Murder in West on Brick Killer," *Chicago Daily Tribune*, May 31, 1938, p. 3; "Brick Slayer Is Likened to Jungle Beast," *Chicago Daily Tribune*, June 5, 1938, p. 8; "Sanity Tests Arranged for Nixon, Hicks," *Chicago Defender*, July 2, 1938, p. 4. The description of Nixon stood in stark contrast to the depiction of his fellow burglar Earl Hicks, which emphasized Hicks's lighter complexion. Hicks was not believed to be the murderer and was ultimately sentenced to fourteen years in prison.

36. Wright 1993, 532; see also Rowley 2001, pp. 152–53. I thank Ms. Ruby Harris for first making me aware of this incident and its connection to Richard Wright's novel.

37. "2 Accuse Each Other in Brick Killing," *Chicago Daily Tribune*, May 30, 1938, p. 1.

38. "Sift Mass of Clews for Sex Killer," *Chicago Daily Tribune*, May 28, 1938, p. 1.

39. Park 1936; Duncan and Duncan 1957, fig. 23 and table E-1. The 1950 census reports 3,021 Japanese residents in Oakland and Kenwood out of a total population of over 60,000 (Hauser and Kitagawa 1953). Although the Japanese presence barely topped 5 percent, they had a strong institutional presence. In 1948, the Ellis Community Center opened at 4430 Ellis to serve the "approximately 10,000 Japanese-American residents on the south side" ("Jap-American Center Opened on Ellis Av.," *Chicago Sunday Tribune*, March 7, 1948, p. S2). The Ellis Community Center eventually merged with the Kenwood Church and formed the Kenwood-Ellis Community Center and the Kenwood-Ellis Community Church, where 80 percent of the membership was Japanese and the Reverend George Nishimoto was the pastor. See Kenwood-Ellis Community Center 1956a.

40. Schietinger 1948, 20, 22, 25.

41. Hirsch (1983, 145) documents the role of the University of Chicago in establishing the Oakland-Kenwood Property Owners' Association and other similar groups. Through its financial and technical support, Hirsch writes, "More than a passive supporter of these groups, the university was the spark and driving force behind them." A 1952 address to the Oakland-Kenwood Planning Association by its president, Bradford W. Alcorn, gives a similar account: "George Fairweather, who was at the time Business Manager of the University of Chicago, felt that the South Side needed a certain group of strong local organizations which would work out local problems and carry them to the City Authorities for action." See Oakland-Kenwood Planning Association, "A Report to the Oakland-Kenwood Community," 1952, in the collections of the Chicago History Museum (formerly the Chicago Historical Society).

42. Long and Johnson 1947, 46. Thirty percent of those organizations also

thought Asians were objectionable, and 12 percent thought Jews were objectionable; see also Mikva 1951. For a discussion of home owners' organizations on Chicago's West Side, see Seligman 2005.

43. "Citizen Group Shows How to Prevent Slums," *Chicago Daily Tribune*, February 12, 1939, p. 20.

44. "South Side Leaders Consider New Approach to Blighted Area Problem," *Chicago Daily Tribune*, Tribune, April 7, 1940, p. B11; Richard Durham, "Farr of YMCA Calls 'Negroes Undesirable,'" *Chicago Defender*, February 17, 1945, p. 1 (also quoted in Plotkin 1999, p. 93, n. 60). In 1940–1941, according to the "South Side Leaders" article, OKPOA explored the possibility of forming a corporation to raise private capital to purchase large amounts of property that was "tending toward becoming a liability in the neighborhood." They planned to demolish the existing buildings and build new housing. These and similar discussions, taking place all over Chicago and in other cities, were the precursors to "slum clearance" legislation that allowed for comprehensive urban renewal projects (Hirsch 1983). Black residents definitely saw this land assemblage as a way to remove them from the neighborhood, even though OKPOA gave assurances that existing residents would be able to move back in once the area was redeveloped (see Mikva 1951, 67–68).

45. Long and Johnson 1947, 48.

46. Weaver 1945, 250. Mikva (1951, 66) reported even greater expenditures on enforcing restrictive covenants. She writes: "During 1944 [OKPOA's] budget was $13,243, over one-fourth of this spent on legal fees."

47. Washington 1948, 22.

48. On the ineffectiveness of covenants, see Hirsch 1983. But Brooks (2003) argues that restrictive covenants were effective in slowing black in-movement and had an even greater impact on housing prices, even decades after they were found unconstitutional. He emphasizes the role of covenants as indicators of neighborhood preferences above and beyond their legal enforceability: "Covenants were signals to realtors (who directed blacks to non-covenanted neighborhoods), lenders (who would not grant mortgages to blacks in covenanted neighborhoods), federal housing agencies (that would not issue or guarantee mortgages granted to blacks in covenanted neighborhoods), and insurers (who would not insure blacks in covenanted neighborhoods). These intermediaries used unenforceable covenants to coordinate transactions to maintain the racial exclusivity of traditionally white neighborhoods" (Brooks 2003, 22).

49. Ernest Lilienstein, "Mayor Kelly Threatened By Kenwood Ass'n," *Chicago Defender*, February 9, 1946, p. 1. I am amazed by Baird's unabashed racism given the fact that he was being interviewed by a *Defender* reporter, who I assume was black. This either raises doubts about the veracity of the quote or makes an even stronger case that white NKO residents were unashamed in their efforts to keep blacks out and of their justifications for doing so.

50. While the Commission on Human Relations (CHR) was clearly the convener and the executive director of CHR, Thomas Wright, acted as the chairman of the meetings, there was some suggestion in the minutes that OKPOA itself had

requested that these meetings be organized because they had been unsuccessful in communicating and negotiating with the black community—both the new arrivals into Kenwood-Oakland and the black leadership of the NAACP and Urban League. See Commission on Human Relations, Memorandum on Community Conservation Agreement, January 20, 1948, p. 5, and minutes, June 24, 1947, p. 1, both in the Metropolitan Housing and Planning Council Papers, University of Illinois at Chicago (hereafter cited as "MHPC papers").

51. Commission on Human Relations minutes, July 13, 1947, p. 1, and Memorandum on Community Conservation Agreement, January 20, 1948, p. 8. Both in MHPC papers.

52. "Home Owners End Race Ban in Community," *Chicago Daily Tribune,* January 24, 1948, p. 7; "Plan Spells End of Covenants: New Agreements, Ignoring Race, Are Substituted," *Chicago Defender,* January 24, 1948, p. 1. Ken-Oak Improvement Association press release, Memorandum on Community Conservation Agreement, p. 10, MHPC papers.

53. Weaver 1945; Hughes 1995. The *Oakland-Kenwood Neighbors* newsletter tried to emphasize the negative ramifications of not adhering to certain occupancy standards, as illustrated in the article "Sneak Conversions, Zoning Violations, Threaten Slums for Oakland-Kenwood" (*Oakland Kenwood Neighbors,* vol. 2, no. 2, pp. 6–7, April 1950, in collections of the Chicago History Museum). Commission on Human Relations minutes, May 7, 1948, p. 1, in MHPC papers; Abrahamson 1959, 122. In 1949, OKPOA changed its name to the Oakland-Kenwood Planning Association. OKPA undertook a community housing survey in hopes of attracting FHA financing to rebuild the more dilapidated parts of the neighborhood, specifically the small area east of Ellis Avenue between Oakwood Boulevard and 40th Street, where members of OKPA owned vacant land. They hired Evert Kincaid, former director of the Chicago Plan Commission, to do a survey of the redevelopment area. There were discussions of both rehabilitation and significant demolition within this area, with a focus on the area at Oakwood and Lake Park, especially east of Lake Park ("Lay Foundation for Controlling Growth of Area," *Chicago Daily Tribune,* December 19, 1948). The plans stalled due to a lack of financing (see Oakland-Kenwood Planning Association, "A Report to the Oakland-Kenwood Community," 1952, in the collection of the Chicago History Museum). Ultimately, this became the site for the first public housing high-rise in the neighborhood, the Victor Olander Homes. In 1949, OKPA inaugurated a community newsletter called *Oakland-Kenwood Neighbors.* Its approach was conciliatory and promoted racial harmony. The first page reads, "This first issue is an attempt to tell in words and pictures the story of a community in transition, a community made up of people who do not only happen to live and work together, but who are trying as neighbors to work out techniques of living together happily in peace and safety, maintaining in their community the residential values which are the basis of fine family living" (*Oakland-Kenwood Neighbors,* vol. 1, no. 1, November 1949). For 1950 and 1951, the hot issues were crime, the threatened closure of the Kenwood el line—which did eventually happen in 1958 (see Commission on Chicago Landmarks 1992, 4)—and a zoning case regarding overcrowding in the southern half of Kenwood.

The activities of OKPA had begun to retreat to South Kenwood before it disbanded completely in 1953.

54. Duncan and Duncan 1957, 118.

55. Muddy Waters was not the only famous person to live in North Kenwood–Oakland, but his time there is particularly well documented because there was so much activity always going on at his house. Thomas Dorsey, the father of modern gospel music, owned a house in Oakland at 4154 South Ellis Avenue and used it as his studio and publishing house. Michael W. Harris, author of *The Rise of Gospel Blues: The Music of Thomas Andrew Dorsey in the Urban Church* (1992), remembered conducting most of his interviews of Dorsey at the Ellis house in the 1980s. Its current occupant, Pamela Schneider, found reams of Dorsey's sheet music in the shed during a rehab. One, "An Angel Spoke to Me Last Night," listed 4154 Ellis as the address of the recording studio, as do most of the songs included as sheet music in a Dorsey songbook (Dorsey, Smith, and White 1951). I thank Professor Harris and Pamela Schneider for sharing their information. Also, soul singer Sam Cooke grew up in the northernmost corner of Oakland in the 1930s and 1940s (Guralnick 2005).

56. Gordon 2002, 127.

57. Many others have chimed in with their memories of 4339 South Lake Park. Nineteen years old at the time, Sonny Boy Lee, an aspiring white blues musician from Minneapolis, remembers the warm reception he got from Muddy Waters in the early 1960s:

A couple of times after his gigs Muddy invited me and my friend and some other kids hanging around the club to his apartment on Lake Park Drive South [*sic*]. We sat around his living room, listened to the phonograph, passed bottles around and talked about music. There was always somebody picking on a guitar, or blowing a harmonica, or tapping out rhythms on a table or chair. One early morning after a gig a kid picked up a guitar, intent on impressing Muddy, and ripped off a bunch of rapid-fire, run-together, stock blues riffs. When he got done, he was quite pleased with himself and glanced at Muddy and around the room with a "I'm really slick and aren't you impressed" look on his face. Muddy just sat in his chair taking it all in. After a moment of silence, he said: "You white boys play too many notes." That was the best advice anybody ever gave me on how to play the blues. (Sonny Boy Lee, "Sonny Boy Lee on Muddy Waters," http://www.sonnyboylee.com/muddy.htm [accessed July 1, 2005])

Harmonica player Mojo Buford was similarly befriended by Waters:

1956. I was living on the same street as Muddy Waters, Lake Park (in Chicago) . . . and somebody told me: "Muddy Waters live right down the street there." I'd been wanting to see him, but I was kinda shy, you know. So I run up on Otis Spann, his piano player, in a liquor store. He was talking, then he said: "I'll take you down there and let you see Muddy Waters." I say, "Then take me on down." And so we went on down there. They fed us, me and him too. We drank a few drinks and talked. We was friends from then on. (Jacquie Maddix, "Interview: Mojo Buford," Blues on Stage, http://www.mnblues.com/review/2001/mojobuford9-25-01-jm.html [accessed July 1, 2005])

58. When the neighborhood got too dangerous and the gangs too unruly in the 1970s, Waters moved his family to the suburbs (Gordon 2002, 237). Westmont, an hour west of Chicago, was all-white at the time and is still only 3.5 percent black. His kids complained about how boring it was compared to North Kenwood.

59. "Hotel Invests $300,000 to Meet Change," *Chicago Sunday Tribune*, April 15, 1956, p. 140. See also http://microgroove.jp/mercury/column/ CannonballInChicago/; Jazz Institute of Chicago, "Paul Wertico—Stereo Nucleo-sis," http://www.jazzinchicago.org/Default.aspx?tabid=43&newsType= ArticleView&ArticleID=88&PageID=170 (accessed July 1, 2005), for interviews of jazz musicians about the Sutherland; Reich 1997.

60. There were three main shopping areas in the 1950s and 1960s: 47th Street, 43rd Street, and 39th and Cottage Grove. "The best facilities are on 43rd Street, from Ellis to Lake Park Avenues, where the largest chain, both grocery and variety, and clothing stores are located. This shopping section appears to be improving as a retail center for the area" (Kenwood-Ellis Community Center, 1956a, 21).

61. For a discussion of the construction of the Olander Homes, see Bowly 1978, 87. "1,000 New Apartments in CHA Projects to Be Completed in First Half of 1957," *Chicago Housing Authority Times*, December 1956; "Competition for CHA Award Spurs Neighbors in 'Spruce Up' Drive," *Chicago Housing Authority Times*, April 1959. On the "paradise" metaphor for early public housing, see Fuerst 2003.

62. "Falling Saw Horse Perils Mayor, 200 at Housing Dedication," *Chicago Daily Tribune*, October 30, 1952, with a picture of the building under construction.

63. See Hirsch (1983, 223–29) for a discussion of the debates in 1950 over proposed sites for public housing, which included the Olander Homes. See also Alex Wilson, "Leaders Rap 'Joker' in New Housing Deal," *Chicago Defender*, April 29, 1950, p. 1. On black resistance to sites in Oakland, see Thomas Buck, "Disclosure Plan of Compromise on Home Sites," *Chicago Daily Tribune*, April 26, 1950, p.15. "Public Housing Hearings Echo Past Debate," *Chicago Daily Tribune*, July 14, 1950 p. A13. Meyerson and Banfield (1955, 110–11) quoted an interview with the leader of the Southwest Neighborhood Council, a white home owners' group fighting against integration and public housing: "You know, a lot of people say it's the colored we don't want, but the kind of whites who live in public housing are just as bad. It's not the colored alone. It's the whole class of people who live like that. I talked to a colored woman who spoke against the site at Lake Park and 43rd [*sic*]. She called me to ask if we could give her any help. I asked her what her reasons were for being against public housing, and she said, 'We're high-class niggers, Mr. Stech, and we don't want any low-class niggers living next to us.'"

64. "Kenwood-Ellis Open House to Be Held Today," *Chicago Daily Tribune*, February 24, 1955, p. S8; "Call Meeting on Crowding in South Schools," *Chicago Daily Tribune*, November 12, 1953, p. SA1; "Groups Plead for More Schools," *Chicago Daily Tribune*, January 2, 1958, p. S9; "Classes Underway at Unfinished School; Judd School Not Finished but No Gripes," *Chicago Daily Tribune*, October 25, 1959, p. S2; "Doniat School Addition Plan Ok'd by Board," *Chicago Daily Tribune*, April 9, 1959, p. S2; "School Board Defers Action on Boundaries," *Chicago Tribune*, April 4, 1963, p. S2. Charles H. Judd, at 44th and Lake Park, was built in

---

1960; Florence B. Price, at 44th and Drexel Boulevard, in 1963; Jackie R. Robinson, at 42nd and Lake Park, in 1975; and Martin Luther King Jr. High School, at 45th and Drexel, in 1971.

65. The Kenwood-Ellis Center was a merger of the Ellis Community Center, which had served the Japanese community since 1948, and the Kenwood Community Church, and its mission and programming reflected this multicultural fusion. See pictures in *Chicago Daily Tribune*, February 24, 1955, p. S8. See also Tjerandsen 2003. On the Hyde Park–Kenwood Community Conference, Abrahamson writes about the early discussions of renewal in Hyde Park in 1948 and 1949 that "much of the northern section of Kenwood had already become an extension of the Negro ghetto" (Abrahamson 1959, 9). However, the 1950 census shows North Kenwood to be about a quarter nonwhite, with much of the nonwhite population being Asian. "Do You Know Your 'YW'? Pictures Tell Story of Chi Centers," *Chicago Defender*, February 4, 1956, p. 11; "These Units Will Be in Parade," *Chicago Defender*, August 3, 1963, p. 17.

66. Duncan and Duncan 1957, 29.

67. Roi Ottley, "Community Center Doubles in Brass in South Side Area," *Chicago Daily Tribune*, April 28, 1957, p. W13. See also Kenwood-Ellis Community Center 1956a, 18.

68. The choice of 1965 as the end of the neighborhood's golden era is somewhat arbitrary. There was wide consensus in the interviews I conducted that it was around then—some said the mid-1960s, others the late 1960s—that gang activity increased and violence prompted many people to leave. I use 1965 for two reasons. Local historians cite this date as when the Blackstone Rangers began to branch out of Woodlawn (just south of Hyde Park). Lance Williams writes: "The Rangers talk about the period '59 through '65 as being their period of 'creation.' From then on, they definitely have a strong identity and they begin to grow" (Williams 2001). By 1967, the Blackstone Rangers had already staked out turf in North Kenwood–Oakland. Robert Gordon's biography of Muddy Waters has the following description: "The Blackstone Rangers, a 'community service' group that carried weapons openly, set its territorial line at Forty-third and Lake Park—Muddy's block. South of Forty-third belonged to the Stones [the Blackstone Rangers]; the Devil's Disciples—the 'Ds'—had the North" (Gordon 2002, 201). Also in 1965, the Kenwood Oakland Community Organization was founded. This group, unlike the Ken-Oak Improvement Association or the Kenwood-Ellis Community Center, was conceived as an explicitly black organization to address issues of unemployment, poor housing, and the lack of urban investment. It was very much a War on Poverty organization, indicating that the neighborhood had segued from a predominantly working- and middle-class black community to a poor one. I use 1988 as the end date because this is the year that the Neighborhood Planning Process began. Although there were planning efforts before 1988, the Neighborhood Planning Process was the most comprehensive and inclusive.

69. "Riders on 'L' Terrorized; Nab 13 Youths," *Chicago Daily Tribune*, February 5, 1968, p. 5.

70. Pattillo-McCoy 2000.

71. "Gang Blamed in Shooting of 2 Boys, 10 and 12," *Chicago Tribune,* June 15, 1968, p. 7; "Strike Charge against Youth in a Shooting," *Chicago Tribune,* November 4, 1969, p. A6.

72. On the integration of gangs into neighborhood life, see Pattillo-McCoy 1999; Venkatesh 2000; Jankowski 1991. At least two residents I interviewed had a theory that the University of Chicago was behind the growing gang violence in North Kenwood–Oakland in the 1960s and 1970s. Anne Boger said: "Like in the 60s, then they said that the university wanted this property. . . . That's why they say that the University of Chicago hired them gangs to terrorize the black people in this neighborhood." Ruby Harris was somewhat less direct in the following exchange:

> *Ruby Harris:* And I'm sure that you've heard that the gangs were paid, that the guns were stored in places. And you know this was a very poor community, they needed the money.
>
> *Mary Pattillo:* I haven't heard this at all. So gangs were paid for what?
>
> *RH:* They were given money to buy weapons. And at one time—I don't think you'll ever find this research.
>
> *MP:* Where was the money coming from?
>
> *RH:* I'm not sure. You know, [my neighbors] didn't research this, you know, but they just knew that it was wrong. I was in Woodlawn and I saw the same thing happen. And there are questions in my mind of how things like this happen. Both sides of the university. But then, later discovering that there's a plan to actually redevelop up to 67th Street [and] down to 35th. You understand what I'm saying? And you need to check your, the plan that we talked about, as well as to read a book called *The Making of the Second Ghetto.*

I have read, indeed scoured, Arnold Hirsch's book many times but have not found reference to the University of Chicago employing black gangs to destabilize black neighborhoods, but at the same time the absence of proof does not mean it did not happen.

73. Wilson 1996, p. 30, table 2; Massey and Denton 1993.

74. Mohl 1993, 24. See also Dreier, Mollenkopf, and Swanstrom 2004.

75. Wacquant 2001. See also Miller 1996.

76. U.S. Senate Select Committee on Nutrition and Human Needs 1969, 5573–75.

77. On early public housing screening and changing standards over time see Fuerst 2003; Venkatesh 2000; Lemann 1992; Hunt 2000; Kotlowitz 1985.

78. To get a sense of how many stayed, roughly 11 percent of the households in Kenwood and Oakland in 1990 moved into their dwellings before 1969 (31 percent moved in before 1979). This is a lower-bound estimate since it does not account for people like Patricia Sanders who have lived in many places within the neighborhood over the years; children who grew up and moved from their parents' home to their own residence in the neighborhood; or people who grew up in the neighborhood, moved away, and later returned.

79. Gotham and Brumley 2002; Merry 1981; Rymond-Richmond 2004.

80. On KOCO's founding, see Anderson and Pickering 1986; Gordon and Mack 1971. On Model Cities, see Mary Ullrich, "Grand Boulevard Area," *Chicago Tribune*, June 16, 1968, p. SC1. Robert Lucas, who would later become KOCO's executive director, was head of the Congress on Racial Equality (CORE) during King's visit; he soon fell out with King, thinking that King was accepting negotiations with Daley too readily (see Cohen and Taylor 2000, 420–21). Also, many black leaders fought with Daley over control of the Model Cities program (Cohen and Taylor, 490–92). On the SCLC versus the Black Power movement, see Carson 1981. For KOCO's motto, see Kenwood Oakland Community Organization 1968.

81. Gordon and Mack 1971, 6.

82. "Low-Income Housing Plan Crippled," *Chicago Tribune*, September 2, 1987.

83. Gordon and Mack 1971, 15–16.

84. Addendum to Proposal for Construction Work on Lakefront Properties, p. 2, MHPC papers.

Chapter Two

1. Two physicians who had toured the neighborhood testified at U.S. Senate hearings in 1969: "There is no library or park in the entire Kenwood-Oakland area. . . . Recreation is in the alleys, the streets, the occasional fields of rubble where buildings once stood. The tour crossed one such 'urban park,' where perhaps 20 small children were playing in and around a rusting, abandoned car. This is their 'playground' " (U.S. Senate Select Committee on Nutrition and Human Needs 1969, 5574). The Kenwood Oakland Community Organization had also emphasized the lack of park space in its plans. See Kenwood Oakland Community Organization 1968; Urban Services and Development, Inc. 1978.

2. Frazier 1957, 194, 193, 27, 91–92, 95, 188, 27. For reflections on Frazier's *Black Bourgeoisie*, see Teele 2002. Frantz Fanon (1963, 150) was similarly harsh in his criticism of the black middle classes in former African and Caribbean colonies. He characterized them as "stupidly, contemptibly, cynically bourgeois."

3. Wilson 1987, 30.

4. A transcript of Cosby's statements was published in an issue of *The Black Scholar*, along with black academics' responses to his speech (Cosby 2004). See also Dyson 2005. On everyday discussions of class in the black community, see Harris-Lacewell 2004; May 2001.

5. Jackson 2005, 87.

6. A 1999 survey of North Kenwood–Oakland residents (Metro Chicago Information Center 1999) found that 93 percent of residents thought that the people moving into the neighborhood were people they felt "comfortable with as neighbors," and only two of the eighty-nine respondents reported having had a "bad encounter" with new neighbors.

7. Brown-Saracino 2004.

8. Pattillo-McCoy 1999.

9. Raley 1995; White and Riedmann 1992.

10. In January 2005, the Co-op closed due to "struggling sales and hefty oper-

ating costs." Alderman Toni Preckwinkle also believed the store had been poorly managed and had suffered from ongoing construction on Lake Shore Drive, which limited access by commuters. See Kat Glass, "Bleeding Money, 47th Street Co-op Shuts Doors," *Chicago Maroon*, February 12, 2005, http://maroon.uchicago.edu/news/articles/2005/02/12/bleeding_money_47th_.php.

11. National surveys show that African Americans do see the problems of blacks as stemming from systemic causes. Hughes and Tuch (2000) find that African Americans are more likely than whites, Asians, or Hispanics to cite structural causes such as discrimination and poor educational opportunities for the "economic and social problems" of blacks. African Americans were not, however, any less likely to also suggest individual explanations, such as lack of motivation. In the spontaneous discussions that I describe in North Kenwood–Oakland, I picked up more of the latter, individualist sentiments. In the Hughes and Tuch study, the surveyor offered a list of explanations for economic and social problems and asked respondents to state their level of agreement or disagreement. Had I initiated a discussion about racism or the labor market, perhaps I would have heard more such arguments. Also see Schuman et al. 1997.

12. Wilson 1987; Gates 1998; Dyson 2005. Gates is quoted in Burnham 1998.

13. Heflin and Pattillo in press; J. L. Jackson 2001, 86. To measure African Americans' sense of linked fate, Dawson asked respondents for their level of agreement with the following kind of question: "Do you think that what happens generally to the black people in this country will have something to do with what happens in your life?" (Dawson 1994, fig. 4.1). The percentage of African Americans agreeing "somewhat" or "a lot" has not changed much since the 1980s: 63 percent in 1984, 66 percent in 1988, 67 percent in 1993–1994 (Dawson 1994, fig. 4.1; Dawson 2001, table A1.1). On more educated blacks' feeling more linked to blacks, see Dawson 1994, 81–82. On middle-class support for economic redistribution, see Dawson 1994, table 8.3. On middle-class blacks' sense of obligation to the black poor, see Hochschild 1995, table 4.6. Also see Billingsley 1992; Tate 1993.

14. Simpson 1998.

15. Demo and Hughes 1990. Positive feelings toward other blacks were measured on the basis of agreement with statements such as "black people keep trying" and "black people love their families." On support for black autonomy not affected by education or income, see Dawson 2001, tables A2.1 and A3.1. On income and economic nationalism, see Dawson 2001, p. 130 and table A2.3.

16. Hochschild 1995; Gay 2004; Schuman et al. 1997, 276–77. Also see Cose 1993; Hughes and Thomas 1998; Simpson 1998.

17. Battle and Wright 2002, p. 655; Cohen and Dawson 1993; Dawson 2001.

18. Hochschild 1995, appendix B: table 4.4. Hochschild reports that 27 percent of poor blacks, compared to 17 percent of middle-class blacks, think that the black middle class is doing as much as it should to help poor blacks. Also see Schuman et al. 1997, 277. For a journalistic treatment of this responsibility, see Daniels 2004.

19. Looking at all 331 metropolitan areas in the country, Iceland, Sharpe, and Steinmetz (2005) report a segregation index of 61.5 for blacks earning $45,000 to $75,000 in 2000, compared to 69.7 for blacks earning less than $20,000. This figure

falls in what is commonly defined as the "high" range of racial segregation, and it means that just over 60 percent of middle-class blacks (or whites) would have to move to different neighborhoods for each neighborhood to match the racial composition of its specific metropolitan area. In Chicago, however, middle-class blacks are as segregated from middle-class whites as poor blacks are from similar whites (Street 2005, table 11). Blacks of all classes in the Chicago metropolitan area are highly segregated; over 80 percent of the population would have to move to make each neighborhood integrated. See also Pattillo-McCoy 1999, 2000; Pattillo 2003. For a review of this literature, see Pattillo 2005.

20. DuBois, quoted in Battle and Wright 2002, 656.

21. Hochschild 1995, table 4.6. Several ethnographies expound on these cross-class misunderstandings. See Johnson 2002; Ginwright 2002; Gregory 1998; Haynes 2001.

22. Kelley 1994. On respectability, see also Cohen 1999; Duneier 1992; McBride 2005; Smith 2004; White 2001; Wolcott 2001.

23. Gaines 1996, xiv, 75, 45–46, 3; Higginbotham 1993, 15; Cohen 1999. Frazier is less kind regarding the leadership of the black middle class in that he does not see it as stemming from good motives. He writes: "When the opportunity has been present, the black bourgeoisie has exploited the Negro masses as ruthlessly as have whites. As the intellectual leaders in the Negro community, they have never dared think beyond the narrow, opportunistic philosophy that provided a rationalization for their own advantages" (Frazier 1957, 194).

24. Wilson 1987. See also Anderson 1999; Brooks-Gunn, Duncan, and Aber 1997; Jargowsky 1997; Jencks and Peterson 1991; Sampson, Morenoff, and Gannon-Rowley 2002; Small and Newman 2001.

25. Wilson 1996, 54; Wilson 1987, 158.

26. Smith 2002, 99.

27. Stone 1989; Reed 1999; Reed 2000, 23. On urban regimes, see also Arena 2003; Fainstein and Fainstein 1996; Harding 1994; Imbroscio 1997; Orr and Stoker 1994; Shaw 2003. On growth machines, see Clark 2004; Gotham 2000, 2002; Hartman 2002; Logan and Crowder 2002; Logan and Molotch 1987; Wolch and Dreier 2004. Mollenkopf (1983) puts forth a similar concept of "dominant policy coalitions," although his study also fits well under the rubric of growth machines. For a review history of studies and theories of urban politics, see also Mollenkopf 1989.

28. The literature evaluating the national transformation of public housing is large and growing as more cities implement these programs. As would be expected (since income mixing should have an effect for poor people opposite to that of concentrated poverty), the results are generally positive in areas ranging from health to employment, albeit often modest and sometimes conflicting depending on the particular income mixing strategy. On mixed-income housing, see Joseph, Chaskin, and Weber 2005; Leonard 1997; National Commission on Severely Distressed Public Housing 1992; Rosenbaum, Stroh, and Flynn 1998; Smith 2002. On scattered-site housing, see Briggs, Darden, and Aidala 1999; Kleit 2001; U.S. Department of Housing and Urban Development 1996. On the Moving to Opportunity

program see U.S. Department of Housing and Urban Development 2003, and, for frequent updates, http://www.wws.princeton.edu/~kling/mto/. On Section 8 and mobility programs, see Fischer 2003; Rubinowitz and Rosenbaum 2000; Varady and Walker 2003. On HUD's HOPE VI program (and its relationship to gentrification) see Boston 2005; Keating 2000; Popkin, Katz, et al. 2004; Wyly and Hammel 1999. For a critique of relocation in Chicago, see Venkatesh et al. 2004.

29. There have been three recent surveys conducted in North Kenwood–Oakland: in 1991, the University of Illinois at Chicago surveyed 99 residents about their housing and commercial needs (Center for Urban Economic Development 1991); in 1993, researchers at the University of Chicago surveyed 244 residents to assess their needs and the neighborhood's organizational infrastructure (Wilson et al. 1994); and in 1999, the Metro Chicago Information Center surveyed 89 residents about perceptions of change, social networks, and community involvement (Metro Chicago Information Center 1999). These surveys provide interesting over-time data on the neighborhood. However, they often offer contradictory evidence, and it is hard to tease out whether the contradictions result from changes over time, differences in the wording of questions, different demographics of the samples, or actual changes of opinion. For example, in 1991, 36 percent of those sampled thought there should be more public housing in the neighborhood, but in 1999, 87 percent of the respondents said the Chicago Housing Authority buildings should be closed down. Since by 1999 four of the six high-rises had been demolished it is unclear what residents meant when they said they agreed with "proposals to close down some CHA high rise buildings in this area." The 1999 respondents also overwhelmingly supported "proposals to build housing to increase the economic diversity of the neighborhood, with more middle and high income families moving in." Perhaps the 36 percent of residents who had wanted more public housing simply did not want it contained in high-rises and also favored more middle-income housing, although in 1991 only 9 percent thought that new housing should be for home owners. Another example of contradiction: In 1991, 43 percent of respondents said that the race of their neighbors was not important to them, while 20 percent said that it was important to have black neighbors. The 1999 survey found, instead of this seeming indifference, substantial support for racial integration: 83 percent of respondents supported the notion of racial diversity in the neighborhood. Again, this could be real change, or it could be that the 1999 sample was significantly more affluent (32 percent of respondents earned over $30,000 a year, versus only 5 percent in the 1991 sample) or that the question was posed differently and thus elicited a different kind of answer. Respondents in the 1993 survey, 61 percent of whom were unemployed, listed the community's most pressing problems as drug and alcohol abuse, vacant housing, and unemployment. While they wanted the abandoned buildings improved, they worried that this would push rents beyond what they could pay. Hence, there was consensus in the focus groups that were conducted along with the 1993 survey that rehabbing buildings without providing job training and substance abuse counseling—the latter being what one resident referred to as "fixing the people"—would do little to help residents (Wilson et al. 1994, 32, 43). On the final point, concerning neighbors with a similar life-

style, 32 percent of the respondents in 1991 said this was not important, 31 percent disagreed with the prospect of having neighbors who shared their lifestyle, and 25 percent said this is what they preferred (Center for Urban Economic Development 1991, 51).

30. Lawrence Vale finds similar ambivalence among the 267 residents of Boston public housing he interviewed, two-thirds of whom expressed satisfaction with their communities, and many of whom had no desires to leave: "On the whole, the interviews with Boston public housing residents provide evidence that inner city public housing environments are far from unambiguously pathological places, deserving only the funds for demolition. Most respondents seem to regard themselves as living in *communities with problems* rather than as *problem communities*" (Vale 1997, 173). The lack of total dissatisfaction with their communities as they are sheds light on the ambivalence over impending change, especially when such change might be threatening.

31. Gans 1995; Katz 1989; O'Connor 2001; Piven and Cloward 1993.

32. Scott 1998, 342–43.

Chapter Three

1. It will be clear throughout this chapter that the man, the middleman, and the littleman can all be women, but I use the masculine form because it makes for simpler and catchier prose.

2. Cleaver 1968, 130 (emphasis added).

3. Hubert Blaylock (1967) and then Edna Bonacich (1973) first laid out a theory of "middleman minorities" as applied to immigrant ethnic entrepreneurs. Bonacich characterizes this group as "sojourners" and argues that "since they plan to return, sojourners have little reason to develop lasting relationships with members of the surrounding host society" (586). While this obviously differentiates immigrant middlemen from the indigenous black middlemen that I am exploring here, one continuity in the term is in the function of middlemen as "act[ing] as a buffer for elites bearing the brunt of mass hostility because they deal directly with the latter. In a word, middleman minorities plug the status gap between elites and masses, acting as middlemen between the two" (584). See also Light and Bonacich 1988; Lee 2002.

4. Lorde 1984, 110–14.

5. Park 1928, 893. Park's discussion of Jews—drawn from Georg Simmel's notion of the "stranger" and echoing the work of DuBois, but without acknowledgment—describes a scenario very much akin to the one I outline here for middle-class African Americans. He writes: "When, however, the walls of the medieval ghetto were torn down and the Jew was permitted to participate in the cultural life of the peoples among whom he lived, there appeared a new type of personality, namely, a cultural hybrid, a man living and sharing intimately in the cultural life and traditions of two distinct peoples; never quite willing to break, even if he were permitted to do so, with his past and his traditions, and not quite accepted, because of racial prejudice, in the new society in which he now sought to find a

place. He was a man on the margin of two cultures and two societies, which never completely interpenetrated and fused" (Park 1928, 891–92). Turner 1967; Alvarez 1995; Anzaldúa 1999; Burt 2004, 354. Also see Burt 1992. For a review of research on boundaries, see Lamont and Molnár 2002.

6. DuBois 1904, 5.

7. Lieberson and Waters 1989.

8. Lamont (2000) shows that money commands little respect as a measure of moral worth among those without it.

9. Morrison 1992.

10. Hanchard 1999; Sawyer, Peña, and Sidanius 2004.

11. Anderson 1978; Duneier 2001.

12. Alderman Daniel Solis, quoted in Sanchez 2006.

13. Fanon 1963, 150.

14. Lorde 1984, 112.

15. Burt 2004 finds that brokers who fill structural holes have higher salaries and are promoted more quickly than people whose social networks are more insular.

16. Dumke 2000. For a look at Chicago's Latino middlemen, see Sanchez 2006.

17. In his study on the microdynamics of community organizing and planning, Xavier de Souza Briggs writes, "When planners and other actors in a social setting share life stage, ethnicity, class level, and other social traits, the chance for code confusion and mistaken intentions are much reduced: *codes and scripts will largely coincide in homogenous settings*" (Briggs 1998b, 7).

18. Reed 1988, 164. See also Stone and Pierannunzi 1997; Swain 1993.

19. Given the available evidence that subscribing to the idea of linked fate does not vary by income and is stronger among more educated blacks, it is a reasonable assumption that middle-class blacks see their own fate as tied to any policy or program that affects blacks as a whole. See Simpson 1998, 23; Harris-Lacewell 2004, table 3.10.

20. Rankings are standardized to reflect total lending dollars per mortgageable unit. Rankings for North Kenwood are not reported because it is a part of the larger Kenwood community area. Lending data by census tract show that mortgage dollars in North Kenwood totaled $3.9 million in 1989 and rose to $30 million by 2000. Figures for the same years in South Kenwood were $13.7 million and $52.3 million. Investment in North Kenwood began earlier and has outpaced that in Oakland, although Oakland's lending trajectory is steadily upward and has considerably more room for growth. See Woodstock Institute 1991, appendixes 1 and 3; Woodstock Institute 2002, appendixes 1 and 2.

21. In the 1930s, the United States Federal Housing Administration (FHA) created "security maps" for every city in the country (Jackson 1985). The maps established some neighborhoods as high-risk areas for mortgage investments; such areas were given a "D" rating and were not eligible for federally insured mortgages. "A" neighborhoods, by contrast, were good bets for mortgages, ones that the federal government would insure. "B" and "C" neighborhoods fell between these two

poles. The FHA often marked off neighborhoods with red boundaries, or shaded whole areas red, to indicate parts of a city that banks should avoid when making loans. In 1938, the Chicago Housing Authority created a map of mortgage-lending risk in Chicago based on the FHA's evaluations. At this time, North Kenwood and Oakland were both still predominantly white but sat just at the eastern edge of the Black Belt. This proximity of "inharmonious racial groups," as the FHA warned its appraisers, made such areas less than appropriate for mortgage dollars. Consequently, North Kenwood and Oakland were both given C ratings by the FHA, meaning that the agency would insure only ten-year mortgages, as opposed to the thirty-year mortgages available in A neighborhoods. North Kenwood-Oakland was not alone in being deprived of mortgage capital; only a few sections of Chicago were given the coveted A rating. These included Hyde Park and South Kenwood, the neighborhoods that hugged the north-side lakefront, and the areas at the farthest edges of the city. The Chicago Housing Authority summarized the message of this map bluntly: "All Negro census tracts fall within the area where loans have not been made by the major loaning agencies, and loans will not be made" (Chicago Housing Authority 1938b; Chicago Housing Authority 1938a, 35). For a discussion of race and mortgage capital in Chicago and beyond, see Squires et al. 1987; Squires 1994; Stuart 2003.

22. Stuart 2003; Turner et al. 2002.

23. Cummings and DiPasquale 1999.

24. Nancy Ryan, "Gore Visits Revitalized Kenwood," *Chicago Tribune,* January 14, 1998.

25. Light and Gold 2000.

26. For a discussion of "social preservationists" who wish to maintain or "preserve" a gentrifying neighborhood's working-class, ethnic, or immigrant flavor, see Brown-Saracino 2004.

27. Immergluck and Smith 2004.

28. Freeman 2005.

29. For an extended story of a Harlem gentrifier working to clear her recently purchased building of its many tenants, see Taylor 2002, chap. 4.

30. *Gautreaux v. Chicago Housing Authority,* Nos. 66 C 1459, 66 C 1460 (N.D. Ill. June 3, 1996), 3.

31. Chicago Department of Planning and Development and the Habatat Company 2000, 9–10.

32. On its grant-making strategies in the area of public housing, the MacArthur Foundation's Web site reads: "Through its grantmaking and other work, the Foundation seeks to help Chicago take advantage of this historic opportunity to improve the quality of public housing; to diminish the isolation of public housing and its residents; to support the development of well-designed mixed-income communities where public housing is located; and to provide a model of neighborhood revitalization that will be useful to other cities." MacArthur Foundation, "Human and Community Development," http://www.macfound.org/programs/hcd/stable_housing.htm#housing_policy (accessed July 1, 2005).

Chapter Four

1. I ended chapter 3 with a discussion of my own position as a middleman. I have also been involved in a school reform effort in Chicago as a board member of the Urban Prep Charter Academy for Young Men, located in another poor African American neighborhood in Chicago. Thus my observations of the transformation of schools in NKO and the utilization of various reform tools is also informed by my own philosophical and political quandaries as I participated in the creation of a charter school in another Chicago neighborhood.

2. Klinenberg 2002, 139; Blomley 2004, 30; Brenner and Theodore 2002; Dávila 2004. For a popular endorsement of a neoliberal approach to transforming cities, see Grogan and Proscio 2000.

3. Lipman 2002, 409–10.

4. Ariel Mutual Funds, "Education Initiative," http://www.arielmutualfunds .com/aei/aei_0_index.htm (accessed July 1, 2005).

5. For a current definition of "small schools" in Chicago Public Schools parlance, see Chicago Public Schools, "Small Schools Get Results," http://www.smallschools .cps.k12.il.us/whataress.html (accessed July 1, 2005).

6. As full members of the urban regime, contemporary black politicos and businessmen and women are more in the tradition of William Dawson than Jesse Binga. The former was a United States congressman who represented and managed the Black Belt for Chicago's political machine in the 1920s and 1930s, whereas Jesse Binga's Binga Bank was primarily a Black Belt institution, and thus his power, though considerable, was similarly circumscribed.

7. Sue Duncan Children's Center, http://www.sueduncanchildrenscenter.org (accessed July 1, 2005).

8. "Charter Schools," 105 Illinois Compiled Statutes 5/Art. 27A (1996).

9. University of Chicago Center for Urban School Improvement, "About USI," http://usi.uchicago.edu/aboutnew.html (accessed July 1, 2005).

10. CCC minutes, October 2, 1997.

11. Caitlin Devitt, "Charter School Strives to Achieve Its Mission," *Hyde Park Herald*, December 9, 1998, p. 19. Maurice Lee, "NK-O Charter School Aims to Attract More Local Kids," *Lakefront Outlook*, February 5, 2003, p. 7.

12. For data on Chicago Public Schools, see http://www.cps.k12.il.us/. See also Deborah, Bayliss, "King Will Be Magnet School, Says Board," *Hyde Park Herald*, June 30, 1999, p. 3.

13. See http://www.cps.k12.il.us/ and http://research.cps.k12.il.us/.

14. Lenore T. Adkins, "King off to Strong Start as Area Magnet School," *Hyde Park Herald*, September 25, 2002, p. 3.; Lenore T. Adkins, "School Officials Pin Hopes on $25M King," *Lakefront Outlook*, December 11, 2002, p. 2. North Kenwood–Oakland residents were not the only critics of the magnet school approach. Parents across the city questioned the politics behind the plan for and placement of magnet schools. See Janita Poe and Abdon M. Pallasch, "Chicago Schools Reach for Best as School Officials Try to Retain the City's Top Students with New Magnet Schools," *Chicago Tribune*, August 25, 1998, p. 1. For a general history

and analysis of Chicago school reform, with a focus on equity and justice, see also Lipman 2002.

15. Personal communications with CCC chairman Shirley Newsome, December 8, 2004.

16. Adkins, *Lakefront Outlook*, December 11, 2002, p. 1.

17. Deborah Bayliss, "Charter Schools Asks Waiver for Neighborhood Kids," *Lakefront Outlook*, February 2, 2000, p. 5. The University of Chicago opened a second elementary school in Oakland in 2005. It is a charter school with *local* attendance boundaries, accepting all students who live within its catchment area. This was made possible by a change in the state law, which resulted from lobbying by the university, Alderman Preckwinkle, and state lawmakers from the area. The university's second elementary school serves an entirely new mixed-income HOPE VI community that is replacing the Ida B. Wells public housing project and other nearby projects. In an ironic twist, and despite the progressive intent of the change in the law, the new localism also has its problem. It guards the benefits of a well-supported, reformed elementary school for a community for which the designs stipulate that two-thirds of the new residents will be moderate-, middle-, and upper-income families, and one-third will be public housing families. The text of the amended law reads: "Enrollment in a charter school shall be open to any pupil who resides within the geographic boundaries of the area served by the local school board, provided that the board of education in a city having a population exceeding 500,000 may designate attendance boundaries for no more than one-third of the charter schools permitted in the city if the board of education determines that attendance boundaries are needed to relieve overcrowding or to better serve low-income and at-risk students" ("An Act in Relation to Education," Illinois Public Act 093-086, http://www.ilga.gov/legislation/publicacts/fulltext.asp?name=093-0861& GA=093; accessed July 1, 2005).

18. The Ariel proposal was also aided by the fact that the Conservation Community Council had many other controversies on its plate in 1996, when the Ariel team made its presentation to the community (see CCC minutes, June 20, 1996). Among other things, the community was embroiled in the debate about the placement of public housing to replace the high-rises, the demolition of which had just been approved. The CCC was also hearing presentations about the merging of the King High and Price Elementary School campuses, which many community residents protested. On the night that the Ariel school leaders presented their plans, they were last on the agenda and the building engineer was trying to close the building where the meeting was being held. Kennicott Park was supposed to close at 9 PM, but this particular meeting did not end until 9:45. The Ariel presenters were asked to come back to the following month's meeting because of the lack of time. They did not reappear but instead sent a letter updating the council on their progress and announcing that the school would be opening in September of that year (1996). See letter from Arne Duncan and Ruanda Garth to CCC members, August 16, 1996, DPD files.

19. Grogan and Proscio 2000, 215.

20. Wilson et al. 1994; Project on Human Development in Chicago Neighbor-

hoods, "Intricate Pathways," http://www.hms.harvard.edu/chase/projects/chicago/about/intricate.html (accessed July 1, 2005); Center for Urban Economic Development 1991; Rosenbaum, Stroh, and Flynn 1998; Mason 1998; Lester 1998; Metro Chicago Information Center 1999.

21. North Kenwood/Oakland Charter School, "Our History and Vision," http://charter.uchicago.edu/Information/Vision/Vision.html (accessed July 1, 2005); Randel 2004.

22. Some residents also protested the expenditure of $2 million on infrastructure and landscaping when both schools were failing academically. Despite attempted legal action and the involvement of the Rainbow-PUSH coalition, headed by Reverend Jesse Jackson Sr., the plan was carried out. Funds for the King-Price campus came from Mayor Daley's neighborhood beautification plan, which supported capital improvements only and thus could not be used for educational purposes. See Kevin Knapp, "Operation PUSH Intervenes in Plan to Expand Campus," *Hyde Park Herald,* January 15, 1997; Jacquelyn Heard, "To Foes, King High Plan No Walk in the Park," *Chicago Tribune,* January 30, 1997.

23. Barry Temkin, "King's Cox Leaves Behind a Royal Record: A career of Titles and Controversies," *Chicago Tribune,* June 27, 2001.

24. The year before, in 1999, the local newspapers reported that 237 of the 547 students attending King, or 43 percent, were "from the community," but offered no definition of *which* community. See Deborah Bayliss, "King Will Be Magnet School, Says Board," *Hyde Park Herald,* June 30, 1999, p. 3; Deborah Bayliss, "CPS Hands King $11M as the School Turns Magnet," *Hyde Park Herald,* December 13, 2000, p. 11.

25. In fact, a small group of disgruntled constituents did protest at King, but it was to try to force King to open as promised as a magnet school, not to call for general admissions. CPS had delayed the opening of King by a year in order to complete renovations and boost applications, and parents and students staged a rally to signal their anger that they would have to wait. See Gabriel Piemonte, "King Magnet Plan Delayed Another Year," *Hyde Park Herald,* May 23, 2001. It is not clear, however, how many of these protestors were from the immediate North Kenwood–Oakland community.

26. Lipman 2002, 401.

27. Quad Communities Development Corporation 2005, 18, 19; Bernita Johnson-Gabriel, "King Should Model Itself after Morgan Park," *Lakefront Outlook,* op-ed, March 15, 2006.

28. Low-income students are defined as those qualifying for free or reduced-price school meals. Eligibility for this program is determined at the federal level and is based on the national poverty income guidelines. Families who earn up to 130 percent of the federal poverty line are eligible for free lunches; those who earn up to 185 percent of the poverty line pay a reduced price. Families in both of these categories are classified as low-income. The upper limit for annual income for a family of three for the 2004–2005 school year was $28,990, and for a family of four was $34,873. U.S. Department of Agriculture Food and Nutrition Service, http://www.fns.usda.gov/cnd/governance/notices/iegs/IEGs04-05.pdf.

29. North Kenwood/Oakland Charter School, "The Application Process," http://nko.usi-schools.org/how_to_apply/index.shtml (accessed December 1, 2005).

30. Schaeffer 2000. For a description of the Chicago Public Schools reform plan, see Chicago Public Schools, "Renaissance 2010," http://www.ren2010.cps.k12.il.us.

31. Grogan and Proscio 2000, 215.

32. As a mentor to a Chicago Public Schools eighth grader, I experienced firsthand the immense work that must go into securing a suitable high school placement. Most local public schools are still failing in Chicago, and thus I spent many hours mining the CPS Web site for public school alternatives. Each charter school has its own admissions process, and applications for the selective enrollment schools are due in December of the student's eighth grade year. It was a harrowing process.

33. Klinenberg 2002, 142–43.

Chapter Five

1. *Gautreaux v. Chicago Housing Authority,* 265 F. Supp. 582, 583 (N.D. Ill. 1967).

2. Affidavit of Linda McGill, May 27, 1996, in *Gautreaux* files.

3. Sampson and Wilson 1995, 42. See also Adelman et al. 2001, 621; Alba, Logan, and Bellair 1994, 427; Alba, Logan, and Stults 2000; Logan and Stults 1999, 270.

4. Massey and Kanaiaupuni 1993, 118; Briggs 2005.

5. Flynn McRoberts, "Kenwood, Oakland Reject CHA Plan: Property Values among Concerns," *Chicago Tribune,* November 16, 1995. On white resistance to black neighbors, see Rubinowitz and Perry 2002.

6. Bobo, Kluegel, and Smith 1997, 17.

7. Oliver and Shapiro 1995; Rusk 2001. Metropolitan fragmentation is another ostensibly nonracial form of bias that stifles attempts to provide desegregated public housing options. Each city, suburb, town, and village makes its own decisions about what kind of housing to allow in its jurisdiction, and because public housing is allocated at the local, not the federal, level, some places can and do opt out altogether. See Powell and Graham 2002.

8. *Gautreaux v. Landrieu,* 523 F. Supp. 665, 668 (N.D. Ill. 1981). Suttles (1990, 62) erroneously predicted that the revitalizing area order would open up racially mixed far-north lakefront communities to public housing. "In this post-*Gautreaux* demography, the revitalizing areas were those along the north lakeshore, not primarily the better-off areas near the Central Business District but those weaker and poorer toward the north." These areas were predominantly white, but had a substantial black and growing Latino minority; hence Suttles forecast that they were "most likely to undergo transition." While some scattered-site public housing was built in the Rogers Park and Uptown neighborhoods as Suttles predicted, the most active use of the revitalizing area provisions has been to rebuild public housing in black neighborhoods.

9. I use the term "desegregation" to refer to specific efforts aimed at *undoing* the segregation created by racist laws or policies. "Integration," on the other

hand, connotes the ideological subscription to or practical application of the goal of increasing black/white contact, apart from redressing segregative practices. The rhetoric used in deciding and implementing *Gautreaux* was both desegregation-ist in its specific requirements that the Chicago Housing Authority "disestablish" its segregated public housing system, and integrationist in the more far-reaching language of the judge and plaintiffs' lawyers about black public housing residents being able to move out of the "ghetto."

10. *Gautreaux v. Landrieu*, 523 F. Supp. 665, 669 (N.D. Ill. 1981). While I am focusing on the "revitalizing area" portion of the 1981 order, the consent decree was perhaps more significant for its creation of a new program covering the entire metropolitan area, the Gautreaux program, whereby seventy-one hundred public housing residents would be given Section 8 vouchers to use in the private rental market (Rubinowitz and Rosenbaum 2000, 38–39). The relevance of this revital-izing area category for the construction of new public housing in Chicago did not become apparent until the 1990s, when the Chicago Housing Authority made rede-velopment plans for several of its projects, including the Lakefront Properties. The revitalizing area designation for the Henry Horner Homes, made in 1995, was the first such order (Seliga 2000, p. 1078, n. 151).

11. *Gautreaux v. Landrieu*, 523 F. Supp. 665, 668 (N.D. Ill. 1981). See also Rubinowitz and Rosenbaum 2000, 50. This capitulation is reminiscent of the position taken by various proponents of public housing in the 1950s when new high-rises were being proposed for black neighborhoods only because white politi-cians rejected planned public housing sites in their wards. Arnold Hirsch writes, "Ultimately, the most common judgment was rendered by the Metropolitan Hous-ing and Planning Council and the [Chicago] *Defender*. There were problems with the site package, the MHPC acknowledged, but they were not enough to 'outweigh the tragedy of continued inaction in starting housing in Chicago'" (Hirsch 1983, 225). The addition of majority black areas as places where new subsidized housing could be built was also in response to protests by *black* politicians and community leaders who felt as if they were being deprived of federal housing dollars because of *Gautreaux*'s desegregation mandates. See Polikoff 2006, 241–43; Rubinowitz and Rosenbaum 2000, 32.

12. May 1979 order described in *Gautreaux v. Landrieu*, 498 F. Supp. 1072, 1073–74 (N.D. Ill. 1980). See also Rubinowitz and Rosenbaum 2000, 13.

13. Venkatesh and Celimli 2004; Vale 2000, 387. For the history of the progres-sive roots of public housing, see Radford 1996. On the energetic political and social life of public housing residents, see Feldman and Stall 2004; Small 2004; Venkatesh 2000; Williams 2004.

14. Baron 1971; Bowly 1978; Dubrow and Garbarino 1989; Hirsch 1983; Massey and Kanaiaupuni 1993; Kotlowitz 1991; Lemann 1991; Popkin et al. 2000; Polikoff 1978; Rubinowitz and Rosenbaum 2000; Rybczynski 1993.

15. Goering, Kamely, and Richardson 1994. See also Bickford and Massey 1991; Goering, Kamely, and Richardson 1997; Gray and Tursky 1986.

16. On the status of the CHA, historian Devereux Bowly Jr. writes: "[The CHA] is not an agency of the City of Chicago, although its commissioners are appointed

by the mayor, and it has to submit an annual report to him. It is a municipal not-for-profit corporation, created pursuant to state statute, and operating within the boundaries of the City of Chicago" (Bowly 1978, 18). Historian Bradford Hunt (2000) points out that the Chicago City Council had been leery of CHA's autonomy as early as 1941, not only because of its ability to force racial integration but because placing public housing involved significant city resource outlays, which councilmen wanted to control. Hunt also points out other factors that led to the segregation of public housing, including the recognition by the CHA that the direst housing needs were in the black community and thus most projects should be erected there.

17. Bowly 1978, 27; Hirsch 1983, 230; Fuerst 2003; Cohen and Taylor 2000, 72–78.

18. Hirsch 1983, 214 (emphasis added).

19. *Gautreaux v. Chicago Housing Authority,* 296 F. Supp. 907, 910 (N.D. Ill. 1969).

20. Kirp, Dwyer, and Rosenthal 1995, 2. For a historical discussion of struggles for affordable housing and racial segregation, see Biondi 2003.

21. The use and definition of these terms—public housing, affordable housing, subsidized housing, etc.—is slippery because they are imprecise, lay words. For example, none of these terms is listed in HUD's Glossary of Terms because they do not correspond exactly to any one government program or policy. These concepts can represent developments built with a variety of state or federal subsidies, including units built and managed by federally funded Public Housing Authorities, the most common referent for "public housing." In extreme contexts, any multiunit rental building can be labeled "public" or "affordable" housing, even if it receives no public subsidies at all, just because home owners are wary of the supposedly transient or low-income population such buildings may house. At a practical level, then, terminological precision is lacking in these debates and all terms are open to manipulation. One resident's "Section 8" building is another's "public housing" is another's "apartments." No matter the appellation or connotation, the challenge faced by planners and investors is where to put them.

22. Rubinowitz 1992, 596; Polikoff 2006. For other accounts of the slowness with which the CHA complied with the judge's ruling, see Polikoff 1978, 147–59; Seliga 2000, 1057–58; Polikoff 1988, 459–60.

23. Cohen and Taylor 2000, 489.

24. Polikoff 1978, 88.

25. *Gautreaux v. Chicago Housing Authority,* 296 F. Supp. 907, 912 (N.D. Ill. 1969).

26. Quoted in Polikoff 1978, 157. See *Gautreaux v. Chicago Housing Authority,* 265 F. Supp. 582 (N.D. Ill. 1967).

27. J. P. Jackson 2001; Scott 1997.

28. *Gautreaux v. Chicago Housing Authority,* 296 F. Supp. 907, 915 (N.D. Ill. 1969). The language also echoes the opening line of the Kerner Commission Report, which was released the year before: "Our nation is moving toward two societies, one black, one white—separate and unequal."

29. Quoted in Hirsch 1983, 227. also see Hirsch 1983, 245–53; Venkatesh 2000, 7–9.

30. Neighborhood Planning Committee 1989, 12, 42 (emphasis added).

31. Testimony of Valerie Jarrett, Transcript of Proceedings—Status before the Hon. Marvin E. Aspin, May 22, 1996, p. 6, in *Gautreaux* files (hereafter cited as "Transcript, May 22, 1996").

32. Chicago Department of Housing 1990, table 5, p. 15; Community Assistance Panel 1989, 8.

33. Affidavit of Safiya Karimah, May 28, 1996, in *Gautreaux* files.

34. Affidavits of Safiya Karimah and Margarette E. Wafer, May 28, 1996; affidavit of Brenda L. Vance, May 27, 1996. All in *Gautreaux* files.

35. Testimony of Benjamin Starks, Transcript, May 22, 1996, pp. 38, 41, in *Gautreaux* files.

36. Massey and Denton 1993; Jargowsky 1997; Wacquant 1994, 1997; Wilson 1987, 1996; Polednak 1997; Yinger 1995; Squires 1994.

37. CCC minutes, November 2, 1995, p. 3; CCC minutes, October 5, 1995, p. 4. Both in DPD files.

38. Motion to Join as a Party Plaintiff, November 21, 1995, p. 2; Memorandum in Support of Motion, November 21, 1995, p. 2. Both in *Gautreaux* files.

39. CCC minutes, November 2, 1995, p. 3, in DPD files.

40. Testimony of Benjamin Starks, Transcript, May 22, 1996, pp. 37–38, in *Gautreaux* files (emphasis added).

41. Joint Motion of Plaintiffs, and Defendants Chicago Housing Authority and Department of Housing and Urban Development, for an Order Designating a North Kenwood–Oakland Revitalizing Area and Authorizing the Development of Scattered Site Public Housing Units Therein, May 15, 1996, p. 5, in *Gautreaux* files.

42. Ibid., p. 4.

43. Ibid.

44. *Gautreaux v. Chicago Housing Authority,* 304 F. Supp. 736, 737 (N.D. Ill. 1969).

45. Testimony of Alexander Polikoff, Transcript, May 22, 1996, p. 45, in *Gautreaux* files (emphasis added). The 1981 consent decree stated, "In any fiscal year in which HUD wishes to approve contract authority for . . . assisted housing that does not comply with the locational requirements of paragraph 5.8.1 [which laid out the allowable proportions of public housing in a neighborhood] HUD may petition the Court for a waiver of that provision" (*Gautreaux v. Landrieu,* 523 F. Supp. 665, 681 [N.D. Ill. 1981]). See also Seliga 2000, 1078–79.

46. *Gautreaux v. Landrieu,* 523 F. Supp. 665, 671 (N.D. Ill. 1981).

47. Testimony of Jarrett, Transcript, May 22, 1996, p. 16, in *Gautreaux* files.

48. Testimony of Polikoff, Transcript, May 22, 1996, p. 46, in *Gautreaux* files.

49. Polikoff 2006, 303.

50. Transcript of Proceedings—Status before the Hon. Marvin E. Aspen, March 8, 1995, pp. 4–5, in *Gautreaux* files.

51. Chayes 1976, 1298; Polikoff 2006, 303.

52. Massey and Denton 1993, table 2.3; American Communities Project, http://browns4.dyndns.org/cen2000_s4/WholePop/CitySegdata/1714000City.htm; Iceland, Weinberg, and Steinmetz 2002.

53. Comments of Judge Aspen, Transcript, May 22, 1996, pp. 50–52, in *Gautreaux* files.

Chapter Six

1. Scott 1998, 6.

2. Spear 1967, 147.

3. Hirsch 1983, 116; Drake and Cayton 1993; Grossman 1989. Allan Spear (1967, 52) makes brief mention of African Americans aspiring to send their children to kindergarten at the Armour Institute (the precursor to IIT) in the late 1890s, and local historian Dempsey Travis (1981, 88) remembers going to the Institute to inquire about taking aviation courses in the 1940s.

4. Hirsch 1983; Mollenkopf 1983.

5. Hirsch 1983, 207.

6. Wallace 1953, 268–70. A study by the Chicago Housing Authority (1955) about displacement from seven sites cleared to make way for new public housing developments found that 18 percent of the sample moved to Oakland, Kenwood, and Washington Park. These neighborhoods were even the destinations for 12 percent of the refugees from the CHA developments on the near northwest side—Cabrini, Abbott, and Horner. The study summarized, "The heaviest movement was directed to Oakland and Kenwood, where nonwhite occupancy has increased substantially since 1950" (CHA 1955, 3). A *Chicago Reader* article charts the journey to North Kenwood of one family "whose two gray stone houses on Cottage Grove had been seized by the city and demolished to make room for Lake Meadows" (McClory 1993, 16).

7. Jacobs 1961, 394. There was a particularly unusual structure on the land cleared for the Washington Park and Lake Michigan Homes, which were the second phase of the Lakefront Properties. The "Sphinx Kiosk" at 4044 Oakenwald Avenue was a peculiar mansion built to house the art collection of an eccentric millionaire named Washington Porter II. A CHA newsletter announcing plans for the demolition described the house as follows: "To be certain that the structure would be unique, Porter himself worked with architects incorporating designs and art motifs of several ancient cultures. He described the building himself as 'Egyptian with a touch of Italian Renaissance.' Adjoining the Kiosk is a 150-foot tower intended as an observation post for the Chicago World's Fair of 1933. Although less than thirty years old, the structure which cost about $350,000 to build is today a shambles" ("Famous Art Palace to Give Way for New Public Housing Project," *Chicago Public Housing Today*, June 1, 1957, p. 1).

8. Keating 2000. See also Fullilove 2005.

9. Lakefront Properties Task Force, Final Report, June 11, 1986, p. 2, in MHPC papers.

10. Stanley Ziemba, "CHA Work to Empty 6 Buildings," *Chicago Tribune,* Sep-

tember 19, 1985; "700 Families Face Move in Renovation Plan at CHA," *Chicago Sun-Times*, September 19, 1985.

11. Don Terry, "Tenants Cry Foul at CHA," *Chicago Tribune*, January 31, 1986. Stanley Ziemba, "CHA Won't Uproot Tenants, Board Retreats on Mass Move for Repairs," *Chicago Tribune*, September 27, 1985.

12. Lakefront Properties Task Force, Final Report, p. 5, in MHPC papers.

13. Ibid., p. 11.

14. Memorandum of Accord, 1986, p. 4, author's copy.

15. Quoted in Stanley Ziemba, "Key Supporters Bolster Plan to Raze CHA Sites," *Chicago Tribune*, November 25, 1987.

16. Jan Crawford, "Tenants Told CHA Rehab Will Begin a Year Late," *Chicago Tribune*, September 18, 1987.

17. Wille 1997, 62.

18. Hirsch writes: "Ferd Kramer, president of the Metropolitan Housing and Planning Council, manager of Lake Meadows, and developer of Prairie Shores, tried desperately to integrate his projects. He was determined that the 'fine modern apartment development which would be replacing a Negro slum should not in turn become a Negro ghetto'" (Hirsch 1983, 260). On the development of Dearborn Park, see Wille 1997.

19. The Kramer Plan was revised many times. One version (Illinois Housing Development Authority 1990) states that four high-rises will be demolished (p.2) and presents a Phase I development map that coincides with this point (p. 17), but in the narrative describing the CHA development it calls for "the removal of all three CHA towers and replacing them with low-rise buildings, thereby restoring the traditional neighborhood character" (p. 14). The reference to demolishing three rather than four buildings could have been just a typo. The *Gautreaux* plaintiffs made clear that they supported the demolition of four of the six high-rises, with replacement housing to be scattered about the neighborhood (see Memorandum in Support of Plaintiffs' Motion for Further Relief, January 21, 1990, pp. 7–11, in *Gautreaux* files). However, a memo presented to the board of the Metropolitan Planning Council for their approval in August 1988 suggests that all six buildings were at one time contemplated for demolition. It lists as one of the envisioned "essential elements": "Development of 900 units of public housing units, either by replacing all six of the high-rises with approximately 900 units of scattered site housing, or by rehabilitating the northerly two-high-rises and replacing the other four with 600 units of scattered site housing" (memo to board of governors from Mary Decker, August 26, 1988, pp. 1–2, in MHPC papers).

20. Stanley Ziemba, "CHA Urged to Raze 4 High-Rises," *Chicago Tribune*, November 24, 1987.

21. Stanley Ziemba, "There Are No Little Plans: Aging Kramer Pushes Kenwood Rebirth," *Chicago Tribune*, April 25, 1988.

22. Rossi and Dentler 1961, 151. Rossi and Dentler document that there was definitely a class-within-race feature to Hyde Park's urban renewal, writing that "upper- and middle-class Negroes, however, who had settled into some of the larger

and expensive apartments and homes in Kenwood and North West Hyde Park, and who were fearful of finding themselves once again in the 'ghetto,' did approve of the stabilization goal" (Rossi and Dentler 1961, 151). As in Hyde Park, it was primarily poor and some working-class blacks in North Kenwood–Oakland who felt a growing sense of powerlessness in the face of the Kramer Plan, while middle- and upper-income blacks were at the forefront of NKO's revitalization, with many supporting the Kramer Plan.

23. Stanley Ziemba and John McCarron, "Mayor Hits Developer's Plan," *Chicago Tribune*, November 25, 1987; Stanley Ziemba, "CHA Puts Condition on Razing High-Rises," *Chicago Tribune*, December 16, 1987; Patrick Reardon and Jorge Casuso, "CHA Draws Fire from Urban League," *Chicago Tribune*, July 21, 1988; John McCarron, "Pressure Mounting against Ald. Evans within His Own Ward," *Chicago Tribune*, July 9, 1988; Stanley Ziemba, "There Are No Little Plans: Aging Kramer Pushes Kenwood Rebirth," *Chicago Tribune*, April 25, 1988; Stanley Ziemba, "CHA Urged to Raze 4 High-Rises," *Chicago Tribune*, November 24, 1987.

24. Polikoff (2006, 284–85) writes: "In the latter part of the 1980s, following the lead of the Reagan and first Bush administrations, Congress cut appropriations for new public housing steadily and severely. Section 8 funding was also in short supply, and the diminishing amounts were committed for fewer than fifteen years. The result—virtually a Catch-22—was that it made little sense for public housing authorities to propose to demolish their high-rises when, with funding for replacement housing unavailable, HUD would not approve their applications."

25. Popkin et al. 2000, 200, nn. 6–8; Rainwater 1970; Wilson 1987.

26. The CHA basically wrote the regulations for the program and only Chicago won approval, although the legislation allowed for funding for three other cities as well. At Lake Parc Place, half of the families were low income (under 50 percent of area median income) and half were moderate income (50 to 80 percent of AMI). See Schill 1997; Rosenbaum, Stroh, and Flynn 1998; Ceraso 1995.

27. The court's authority over the construction and siting of units that replaced demolished public housing was confirmed in a 1998 ruling. See *Gautreaux v. Chicago Housing Authority*, 4 F. Supp. 2d 757 (N.D. Ill. 1998).

28. Memorandum Supporting Plaintiffs' Motion for Further Relief, August 5, 1991, p. 1; see also Memorandum in Support of Plaintiffs' Motion for Further Relief, November 21, 1990, both in *Gautreaux* files. Polikoff 2006, chap. 6; Blair-Loy 1994.

29. Memorandum in Support of Plaintiff's Motion . . ., November 21, 1990, pp. 9–10, in *Gautreaux* files.

30. Lakefront Community Organization, Petition to Intervene as a Plaintiff, February 12, 1991, in *Gautreaux* files. The Central Advisory Council did not attempt to intervene until the *Gautreaux* plaintiffs filed a second motion to try to stop the rehabilitation of the high-rises. See Plaintiffs' Motion for Further Relief, August 5, 1991, and Motion to Intervene, by the Central Advisory Council, February 14, 1992, both in *Gautreaux* files. A group of residents from North Kenwood–Oakland also filed a friend of the court brief in these proceedings. Members of the SouthEast Side Residents for Justice (SERJ) opposed the Kramer Plan because "the

only available area (North Kenwood) to implement the opportunity so passionately argued for by Plaintiffs is already saturated with federally assisted housing in
numbers far in excess of the 15% maximum of federally assisted units established
by *Gautreaux*. Additionally, the targeted area is already 97% black and should
Plaintiffs succeed in implementing their plan it is probable that the percent of black
residents will increase" (See SouthEast Side Residents for Justice, Amicus Curiae
Brief, February 19, 1991, p. 1, in *Gautreaux* files). The arguments made by SERJ
laid the groundwork for RRR's position five years later (see chapter 5). However,
while RRR stated its desire to see the buildings demolished with no (or very limited) replacement housing, it is unclear if SERJ wanted the buildings demolished or
rehabilitated.

31. Burt 2004, 354.

32. Abrahamson 1959; Rossi and Dentler 1961.

33. The university had somewhat more success with Woodlawn in the mid-
1980s. Bishop Arthur Brazier, pastor of the fifteen-thousand-member-plus Apos-
tolic Church of God and nemesis of the university during its 1960s urban renewal
attempts to expand into Woodlawn, approached the university in the mid-1980s
about partnering to economically diversify the neighborhood and provide social
services and better housing for low-income residents. These negotiations resulted
in the formation of the Woodlawn Preservation and Investment Corporation in
1987.

34. "Ferdinand Kramer, PhB '22, Was Awarded the University Alumni Service
Medal," University of Chicago online magazine, http://magazine.uchicago.edu/
9708/9708AwardsKramer.html (accessed July 1, 2005).

35. Metropolitan Planning Council, "Our Mission," http://www.metroplanning
.org/about/mission.asp (accessed July 1, 2005).

36. Jorge Casuso and Patrick Reardon, "CHA to Renovate 2 Vacant High-Rises,"
Chicago Tribune, August 11, 1988.

37. Lane 1994, 71.

38. Patrick Reardon and Jorge Casuso, "CHA Draws Fire from Urban League,"
Chicago Tribune, July 21, 1988.

39. Patrick Reardon, "Lane Brings Grand Plan to Oakland Area," *Chicago Tribune*, March 29, 1994.

40. This informal working group kept no minutes or other official records and
thus the specifics of these surely contentious debates reside only in the memories
of the participants. I interviewed four members of the group, in addition to consulting Polikoff's *Gautreaux* memoir (2006), which includes information about the
group.

41. Instead of being the face of change in NKO, group members saw themselves
as "enablers." An awareness that they—as white or black professionals, many associated with the University of Chicago—could not sell their plan to the mostly
black and working-class neighborhoods they sought to work with (or on) was apparent when the group established the Fund for Community Redevelopment and
Revitalization. The Fund's chairman of the board was Bishop Arthur Brazier, whose

legitimacy stemmed from both his race and his credentials as a community activist. Their enabling came in the form of a $1.4 million operating grant to the Fund from the MacArthur Foundation, where Ranney sat on the board and where Paula Wolff had been a distinguished visiting fellow.

42. Allie Shah, "CHA Starts to Topple Its High-Rise Image," *Chicago Tribune,* January 24, 1995, p. 1. I asked Lane directly, "When did your position evolve to demolition, because in reading the newspaper accounts in the early part of your administration you were against demolition?" Lane's answer was as follows:

> Yeah, right. I was. I believed in the early part of my administration, like I said, public housing was not my thing. It was developing affordable subsidized housing. And I'd seen tremendous feats achieved. Like Cochran Gardens [and its tenant leader] Bertha Gilkey in Saint Louis. And Kimi Gray in Washington, DC—I can't remember the name of her development. But I'd seen tenants really take charge and, when given the resources and the authority, do things that the public housing administration couldn't, wouldn't, could never do. And so I was from my task force days at MPC working with residents. I believed that that was the way to go. That we could take the buildings and with supporting the tenants figure out how to make them work. Well, once I got into it and I saw how organized gangs and drug dealers were, and how intractable the social situation was—even with the schools associated with public housing, 50 to 70 percent of kids dropping out before finishing high school—I changed my view. I said that this won't work.

Lane's account for why he changed his position, then, rests on the depth of the problems facing public housing. He came to the notion that the best strategy was to start from scratch.

Some illustration of the disarray of Chicago public housing at this time is relevant. In October 1992, seven-year-old Dantrell Davis was killed in gang crossfire as he walked to school in Cabrini-Green. In 1993, at least five children were killed or injured when they fell from windows at various Chicago Housing Authority buildings. (See Cameron McWhirter, "Boy, 7, Dies after Fall from Window at CHA," *Chicago Tribune,* August 9, 1993, p. 2; James Hill, "Boy, 5, Dies in Fall from Window," *Chicago Tribune,* July 19, 1993, p. 3; "Safety Goes out the Window at CHA," *Chicago Tribune,* May 24, 1993, p. 12; Jerry Thornton, "3rd Child Falls out of Window in Taylor Homes," *Chicago Tribune,* May 7, 1993, p. 9.) When workers went out to the projects to put safety bars on the windows, they were fired upon by gang members, prompting Lane to institute random gun sweeps across the CHA. Polikoff (2006, chap. 6) emphasizes the Davis murder along with changing federal legislation as the key factors affecting Lane's thinking. Polikoff mentions but downplays the importance of the informal working group.

My intention is not to deny Lane's own account. Instead, I focus on how proponents of the Kramer Plan influenced Lane even as he was making his own observations of public housing conditions. He was friends with many of the players in the working group, including George Ranney, who was central to getting Lane appointed as CHA CEO and remained one of his private sector advisors and partners once Lane assumed the post. Lane stated: "George Ranney came over [to work with me at CHA] because I knew I would need the support of the corporate community. And so we built those relationships where we had lots of corporate support." While Lane's early beliefs inclined him to save the high-rises, his experience pursuing ever more drastic measures to do so, coupled with the activation of personal, institutional, and bureaucratic networks that supported demolition, led him to the conclusion that some of the buildings needed to be demolished.

43. Stone 2006, 29.

44. Flynn McRoberts, "CHA Ex-Lakefront Residents Pare Differences," *Chicago Tribune*, September 16, 1994.

45. "Revised Agreement Regarding Former Residents of the Lakefront Properties and the Future Use of Those Properties," September 22, 1995, author's copy.

46. Joint Motion of Plaintiffs, and Defendants . . . for an Order Designating a North Kenwood–Oakland Revitalizing Area and Authorizing the Development of Scattered Site Public Housing Units Therein, May 15, 1996, pp. 3–4, in *Gautreaux* files (hereafter cited as "Joint Motion"). Regarding the support of Habitat and the city, the motion states, "Movants are authorized to represent to the Court that the Receiver supports this motion and that the City of Chicago has no objection thereto" (p. 5).

47. Lakefront Community Organization, Intervenor's Motion for Temporary Restraining Order, November 24, 1998, in *Gautreaux* files.

48. Judge Marvin E. Aspen, order denying LCO motion, December 10, 1998 (emphasis added), in *Gautreaux* files.

49. Judge Marvin E. Aspen, order in response to LCO's Motion for Clarification, May 6, 1999, in *Gautreaux* files.

50. Letter to Toni Preckwinkle, William Wilen, and Shirley Newsome, signed by Daniel Levin, *Gautreaux* receiver, and Alexander Polikoff, attorney for the *Gautreaux* plaintiff class, May 13, 1996, in *Gautreaux* files.

51. Judge Marvin E. Aspen, order in response to LCO's motion to reconsider, July 1, 1999, in *Gautreaux* files.

52. Letter to Stuart Kirchoff Jones, attorney for LCO, from G. A. Finch, CHA general counsel, June 14, 2001, in *Gautreaux* files.

53. The nine CHA executive directors were Zirl Smith, Brenda Gaines, Jerome Van Gorkom, Paul Brady, Vincent Lane, Kevin Marchman, Joseph Shuldiner, Phillip Jackson, and Terry Peterson. See Abt Associates 1998 for a chronology of the CHA.

54. Stanley Ziemba, "CHA Won't Uproot Tenants," *Chicago Tribune*, September 27, 1985.

55. HUD User, "FY 2005 Income Limits," http://www.huduser.org/Datasets/IL/IL05/il_fy2005.pdf (accessed December 1, 2005). The median family income of Oakland residents in 2000 was $16,908. Over 98 percent of Chicago public housing residents earned less than $20,000 when planning for Lake Park Crescent began (Oldweiler and Rogal 2000). Larry Keating writes that this kind of income tiering in public housing, made possible by the Housing Act of 1998, "has shifted public housing policy far from concentrating poor people to fostering gentrification" (Keating 2000, 396). It is quite an irony that under this framework new public housing residents might themselves be gentrifiers.

56. "Summary of Lake Park Crescent Property Specific Requirements," January 24, 2003, provided by the Chicago Housing Authority.

57. Briggs 1998a; Putnam 2000.

Chapter Seven

1. For the overall quality-of-life vision and the official mission statements that resulted from the work of the subcommittees, see Quad Communities Development Corporation 2005.

2. Commission on Chicago Landmarks 1992, 32.

3. I did not attend the meetings where the Drexel Boulevard plans were finalized, but the organization's Web site states the goal for the boulevard as being to "create a physical environment that promotes safety and well-being through increased levels of street lighting to deter drug activity, decorative trash receptacles to reduce litter, and seating specifically designed to discourage loitering." See New Communities Program, "Plan Calls for Drexel Blvd. Restoration," http://www .newcommunities.org/communities/douglas/articleDetail.asp?objectID=99& communityID=3 (accessed July 1, 2005).

4. Harcourt 2001; Sampson and Raudenbush 1999; Taylor 2001.

5. Smith 1996, 45, 211.

6. Covington and Taylor 1989; McDonald 1986; Taylor and Covington 1988. For theoretical explanations of how both increases and decreases in crime may be correct, see Merton 1938. O'Sullivan (2005) offers an economic model of crime and gentrification, but his case study of Portland can only show a descriptive, rather than a causal, relationship between gentrification and crime. For a discussion of the reciprocal nature of crime and neighborhood change, see Taub, Taylor, and Dunham 1984.

7. Smith 1996; Mele 2000; Hartman 2002; Robinson 1995; Anderson 1990; Pérez 2002; Williams 1989.

8. Anderson 1990. Venkatesh (2000) vividly portrays how residents cope with, avoid, and manage crime and violence on a day-to-day basis. See also Pattillo 1998 and Jankowski 1991 on the connections between gang members and other community residents.

9. Data on index crimes and homicides for the 21st police district and entire city of Chicago from 1990 through 2003, and for beats 2122 and 2123 for 1991 through 2004, are from a statistical and crime data request by the author to the Research and Development Division of the Chicago Police Department. Data for index crimes and homicides for the 21st district and Chicago for 2004 are from Chicago Police Department, "Annual Report: Year in Review, 2004," http://egov.cityofchicago.org/ webportal/COCWebPortal/COC_EDITORIAL/04AR.pdf (accessed March 31, 2006). Data for index crimes and homicides for the 21st district and Chicago for 2005 are from Chicago Police Department, "Index Crime Summary—Chicago, January–December 2005," http://egov.cityofchicago.org/webportal/COCWebPortal/ COC_EDITORIAL/Dec05Index.pdf (accessed March 31, 2006). Data for the conservation area were provided to the author by the South East Chicago Commission. The Chicago Police Department defines an Index Crime as "one of eight crime

categories collected as part of the Uniform Crime Reporting Program and considered representative of the most serious crimes. The eight index crime categories are split into two major subcategories, violent and property. Violent index crimes are those committed directly against a person—Homicide, Criminal Sexual Assault, Robbery, and Aggravated Assault/Battery. Property index crimes are those in which there is no direct threat or harm to a person—Burglary, Theft, Motor Vehicle Theft, and Arson" (Chicago Police Department, Index Crime Definitions, http://www.cityofchicago.org/police; accessed March 31, 2006).

10. Blumstein and Wallman 2000.

11. Merry 1981, 125.

12. John McCarron, "Voters Give CHA Slums a Reason for Life," *Chicago Tribune*, August, 30, 1988. For a history of the Fort, see Nashashibi 2002.

13. Pattillo-McCoy 1999.

14. Robert Blau and William Recktenwald, "El Rukn Razing Doesn't End Gangs," *Chicago Tribune*, June 7, 1990.

15. Robert Blau and William Recktenwald, "El Rukn Razing Doesn't End Gangs," *Chicago Tribune*, June 7, 1990.

16. William Recktenwald, "Seizure of Rukn Headquarters Stirs Change," *Chicago Tribune*, October 30, 1989, p. 3.

17. John McCarron, "Voters Give CHA Slums a Reason for Life," *Chicago Tribune*, August, 30, 1988.

18. For a history and evaluation of CAPS, see Skogan and Hartnett 1997; Skogan 2006.

19. Steve Johnson, "Lake Parc Place: New Look, New Tenants, New Face for CHA," *Chicago Tribune*, August 15, 1991; Ed Marciniak, "Why Perpetuate Chicago's High-Rise Hell?" (editorial),*Chicago Tribune*, November 26, 1993, p. 31; "No More CHA for Kenwood-Oakland," *Chicago Tribune*, June 2, 1996, p. 16. See Logan and Molotch 1987 on the participation of newspapers in the growth machine.

20. Gorman-Smith and Tolan 1998; Osofsky 1995, 1997.

21. Affidavit of Brenda Vance, May 27, 1996, in *Gautreaux* files.

22. "Summary of Lake Park Crescent Property Specific Requirements," January 24, 2003, provided by the Chicago Housing Authority.

23. Sullivan 2003. For an assessment of the difficulties some public housing residents face in meeting the site-specific criteria, see Cunningham, Popkin, and Burt 2005.

24. Street 2005, 101.

25. Transcript of Chicago Housing Authority public comment hearing, February 13, 2003, pp. 10–11, provided by the Chicago Housing Authority (punctuation edited for clarity).

26. The Metropolitan Housing and Planning Council studied the possibilities of conservation as a legal and practical development tool. It concluded: "Conservation based on any policy of racial exclusion is not only morally reprehensible, but practically impossible." Instead, conservation areas can be examples of "interracial communities maintained at a middle or upper middle class level. . . . This, of course,

means de facto exclusion of certain groups on economic grounds" (Metropolitan Housing and Planning Council 1953, 22).

27. Becker 1963; Loeske and Best 2003.

28. Katz, Kling, and Liebman 2000; Popkin et al. 2000.

Conclusion

1. Bourdieu 1984, 249. Prudence Carter's (2005) work is informative here on the cultural capital of young people and how it is affected by and affects their academic engagement and performance.

2. Drake and Cayton 1993, 566. For the classic description of class diversity within a black community, see DuBois 1899.

3. Cohen 1999; Bourdieu 1989, 23.

4. Drake and Cayton 1993, 566.

5. Taylor 2002, 87, 59. See also Hyra 2006; Boyd forthcoming. For a similar kind of concern on the part of a select group of white gentrifiers, see Brown-Saracino 2004.

6. Bourdieu 1984, 193.

7. Frazier 1957; Higginbotham 1993; Dumke 2000.

8. Howe 1976, 613. See also Sanchez 1993.

9. Levitt 2001, 102, 106.

10. Rogaski 2004, 183–85; Scott 1998, 78. See also Burawoy 1972; Fanon 1963.

11. Burt 2004, 349–50, 388.

12. Wright 2000, 16.

REFERENCES

Abrahamson, Julia. 1959. *A Neighborhood Finds Itself.* New York: Harper.

Abt Associates. 1998. Chicago Housing Authority Time Line: December 1996–August 1998. http://www.abtassoc.com/reports/D19980404.pdf (accessed July 1, 2005).

Abu-Lughod, Janet. 1994. *From Urban Village to East Village: The Battle for New York's Lower East Side.* Cambridge, MA: Blackwell.

———. 1999. *New York, Chicago, Los Angeles: America's Global Cities.* Minneapolis: University of Minnesota Press.

Adelman, Robert, Hui-shien Tsao, Stewart Tolnay, and Kyle Crowder. 2001. "Neighborhood Disadvantage among Racial and Ethnic Groups: Residential Location in 1970 and 1980." *Sociological Quarterly* 42:603–32.

Alba, Richard D., John Logan, and Paul Bellair. 1994. "Living with Crime: The Implications of Racial/Ethnic Differences in Suburban Location." *Social Forces* 73:395–434.

Alba, Richard D., John Logan, and Brian Stults. 2000. "How Segregated Are Middle-Class African Americans?" *Social Problems* 47:543–58.

Alkalimat, Abdul. 1988. "Chicago: Black Power Politics and the Crisis of the Black Middle Class." *Black Scholar* 19:45–54.

Alvarez, Robert R., Jr. 1995. "The Mexican-US border: The Making of an Anthropology of Border-lands." *Annual Review of Anthropology* 24:447–70.

American Communities Project. Chicago City: Data for the City in 1980, 1990, and 2000. http://browns4.dyndns.org/cen2000_s4/WholePop/CitySegdata/1714000City.htm (accessed July 1, 2005).

Anderson, Alan B., and George W. Pickering. 1986. *Confronting the Color Line: The*

Broken Promise of the Civil Rights Movement in Chicago. Athens: University of Georgia Press.

Anderson, Elijah. 1978. *A Place on the Corner.* Chicago: University of Chicago Press.

———. 1990. *Streetwise: Race, Class, and Change in an Urban Community.* Chicago: University of Chicago Press.

———. 1999. *Code of the Street: Decency, Violence, and the Moral Life of the Inner City.* New York: W. W. Norton.

Anzaldúa, Gloria. 1999. *Borderlands = La Frontera.* San Francisco: Aunt Lute Books.

Arena, John. 2003. "Race and Hegemony: The Neoliberal Transformation of the Black Urban Regime and Working-Class Resistance." *American Behavioral Scientist* 47:352–80.

Atkinson, Rowland. 2000. "Measuring Gentrification and Displacement in Greater London." *Urban Studies* 37:149–65.

———. 2002. "Does Gentrification Help or Harm Urban Neighbourhoods? An Assessment of the Evidence-Base in the Context of the New Urban Agenda." Center for Neighbourhood Research, paper 5. http://www.neighbourhoodcentre.org .uk./research/research.html (accessed July 1, 2005).

Bachin, Robin Faith. 2004. *Building the South Side: Urban Space and Civic Culture in Chicago, 1890–1919.* Chicago: University of Chicago Press.

Baron, Harold M. 1971. *Building Babylon: A Case of Racial Controls in Public Housing.* Evanston: Northwestern University, Center for Urban Affairs.

Battle, Juan, and Earl Wright II. 2002. "W. E. B. DuBois's Talented Tenth: A Quantitative Assessment." *Journal of Black Studies* 32:654–72.

Becker, Howard. 1963. *Outsiders: Studies in the Sociology of Deviance.* New York: Free Press.

Bennett, Larry. 1993. "Harold Washington and the Black Urban Regime." *Urban Affairs Quarterly* 28:423–40.

Bennett, Michael. 2005. "Bronzeville: Remaking a Community for the 21st Century." *Urban Focus.* http://ctcp.edn.depaul.edu/documents/ UF-Spring05-UrbanFocus.pdf (accessed July 1, 2005).

Bickford, Adam, and Douglas S. Massey. 1991 "Segregation in the Second Ghetto: Racial and Ethnic Segregation in American Public Housing, 1977." *Social Forces* 69:1011–36.

Billingsley, Andrew. 1992. *Climbing Jacob's Ladder: The Enduring Legacy of African-American Families.* New York: Simon & Schuster.

Biondi, Martha. 2003. *To Stand and Fight: The Struggle for Civil Rights in Postwar New York City.* Cambridge, MA: Harvard University Press.

Blair-Loy, David. 1994. "Comments: A Time to Pull Down, and a Time to Build Up: The Constitutionality of Rebuilding Illegally Segregated Public Housing." *Northwestern Law Review* 88:1537–81.

Blau, Peter, and Otis Dudley Duncan. 1967. *The American Occupational Structure.* New York: Wiley.

Blaylock, Hubert. 1967. *Toward a Theory of Minority Group Relations*. New York: John Wiley and Sons.

Blomley, Nicholas. 2004. *Unsettling the City: Urban Land and the Politics of Property*. New York: Routledge.

Blumstein, Alfred, and Joel Wallman, eds. 2000. *The Crime Drop in America*. Cambridge: Cambridge University Press.

Bobo, Lawrence, James Kluegel, and Ryan A. Smith. 1997. "Laissez-Faire Racism: The Crystallization of a Kinder, Gentler Antiblack Ideology." In *Racial Attitudes in the 1990s*, ed. Steven A. Tuch and Jack K. Martin. Westport: Praeger.

Bonacich, Edna. 1973. "A Theory of Middleman Minorities." *American Sociological Review* 8:583–94.

Boston, Thomas. 2005. "Environment Matters: The Effect of Mixed-Income Revitalization on the Socio-economic Status of Public Housing Residents: A Case Study of Atlanta." Working paper. http://www.econ.gatech.edu/seminarpapers/boston_environ.pdf (accessed July 1, 2005).

Bourdieu, Pierre. 1984. *Distinction: A Social Critique of the Judgement of Taste*. Cambridge, MA: Harvard University Press.

———. 1989. "Social Space and Symbolic Power." *Sociological Theory* 7:14–25.

Bowly, Devereux, Jr. 1978. *The Poorhouse: Subsidized Housing in Chicago, 1895–1976*. Carbondale: Southern Illinois University Press.

Boyd, Michelle. 2000. "Reconstructing Bronzeville: Racial Nostalgia and Neighborhood Redevelopment." *Journal of Urban Affairs* 22:107–22.

———. Forthcoming. *Jim Crow Nostalgia and Redevelopment Politics on Chicago's South Side*. Minneapolis: University of Minnesota Press.

Brenner, Neil, and Nik Theodore. 2002. *Spaces of Neoliberalism*. Malden, MA: Blackwell.

Briggs, Xavier de Souza. 1998a. "Brown Kids in White Suburbs: Housing Mobility and the Many Faces of Social Capital." *Housing Policy Debate* 9:177–221.

———. 1998b. "Doing Democracy Up Close: Culture, Power and Communication in Community Building." *Journal of Planning Education and Research* 18:1–13.

———, ed. 2005. *The Geography of Opportunity: Race And Housing Choice In Metropolitan America*. Washington, DC: Brookings Institution Press.

Briggs, Xavier de Souza, Joe T. Darden, and Angela Aidala. 1999. "In the Wake of Desegregation: Early Impacts of Scattered-Site Public Housing on Neighborhoods in Yonkers, New York." *Journal of the American Planning Association* 65:27–49.

Brooks, Richard R. W. 2003. "Covenants and Conventions." Paper presented at the John M. Olin Center for Law and Economics, University of Michigan, November 13, 2003. http://www.law.umich.edu/CentersAndPrograms/olin/papers/Fall 2003/Brooks.pdf (accessed July 1, 2005).

Brooks-Gunn, Jeanne, Greg Duncan, and Lawrence Aber, eds. 1997. *Neighborhood Poverty*. New York: Russell Sage Foundation.

Brown-Saracino, Japonica. 2004. "Social Preservationists and the Quest for Authentic Community." *City & Community* 3:135–56.

Burawoy, Michael. 1972. *The Colour of Class on the Copper Mines: From African Advancement to Zambianization.* Manchester, UK: Manchester University Press / Institute for African Studies, University of Zambia.

Burgess, Ernest, and Charles Newcomb, eds. 1931. *Census Data of the City of Chicago, 1920.* Chicago: University of Chicago Press.

———, eds. 1933. *Census Data of the City of Chicago, 1930.* Chicago: University of Chicago Press.

Burnham, Linda. 1998. "Home for Him Is Harvard Square." *Colorlines* 1. http://www.arc.org/C_Lines/CLArchive/story1_2_12.html (accessed December 1, 2005).

Burt, Ronald S. 1992. *Structural Holes: The Social Structure of Competition.* Cambridge, MA: Harvard University Press.

———. 2004. "Structural Holes and Good Ideas." *American Journal of Sociology* 110:349–99.

Carson, Clayborne. 1981. *In Struggle: SNCC and the Black Awakening of the 1960s.* Cambridge, MA: Harvard University Press.

Carter, Prudence L. 2005. *Keepin' It Real: School Success beyond Black and White.* New York: Oxford University Press.

Cashin, Sheryll. 2004. *The Failures of Integration: How Race and Class Are Undermining the American Dream.* New York: Public Affairs.

Center for Urban Economic Development. 1991. "Commercial and Housing Priorities and Needs in North Kenwood–Oakland." Unpublished report to the Kenwood-Oakland Development Corporation. http://www.uic.edu/cuppa/uicued/npublications/communityeconomicdevelopment/economicdev/commercialdev/EXECSMRY/nex314.html (accessed July 1, 2005).

Ceraso, Karen. 1995. "Is Mixed-Income Housing the Key?" *Shelterforce Online,* March/April. http://www.nhi.org/online/issues/80/mixhous.html (accessed July 1, 2005).

Chayes, Abram. 1976. "The Role of the Judge in Public Law Litigation." *Harvard Law Review* 89:1281–1316.

Chicago Commission on Race Relations. 1922. *The Negro in Chicago: A Study of Race Relations and a Race Riot.* Chicago: University of Chicago Press, 1968.

Chicago Department of Housing. 1990. *Report to the Department of Urban Renewal Board on the Designation of North Kenwood–Oakland Conservation Area.* Chicago: City of Chicago, Department of Housing.

Chicago Department of Planning and Development, and the Habitat Company. 2000. *Request for Proposals: Redevelopment of the 'Drexel Site.'* Chicago: City of Chicago.

Chicago Directory Company. 1915. *The Chicago Blue Book of Selected Names of Chicago and Suburban Towns.* Chicago: Chicago Directory Company.

Chicago Fact Book Consortium. 1984. *Local Community Fact Book: Chicago Metropolitan Area, 1980.* Chicago: Chicago Review Press.

———. 1995. *Local Community Fact Book, Chicago Metropolitan Area, 1990.* Chicago: University of Illinois / Academy Chicago Publishers.

Chicago Housing Authority. 1938a. *Information in Regard to the Proposed South Park Gardens Housing Project*. Chicago: Chicago Housing Authority.

———. 1938b. *Mortgage Risk Classified by District*. Chicago: Chicago Housing Authority.

———. 1955. *Relocation of Site Residents to Private Housing: The Character and Quality of Dwellings Obtained in the Movement from Chicago Housing Authority Slum Clearance Sites*. Chicago: Chicago Housing Authority.

———. 2004. "CHA Moving to Work Annual Plan for Transformation—Year 5 (FY2004)." http://www.thecha.org/transformplan/plans.html (accessed July 1, 2005).

Chicago Plan Commission. 1943. *Master Plan of Residential Land Use of Chicago*. Chicago: Chicago Plan Commission.

Chicago Rehab Network. 2004. "At Risk Housing Units in Chicago." http://www.chicagorehab.org/policy/pdf/Preservation%20Map_City.pdf (accessed July 1, 2005).

Clark, Terry Nichols. 2000. "Old and New Paradigms for Urban Research: Globalization and the Fiscal Austerity and Urban Innovation Project." *Urban Affairs Review* 36:3–45.

———, ed. 2004. *The City as an Entertainment Machine*. London: JAI.

Cleaver, Eldridge. 1968. *Soul on Ice*. New York: McGraw-Hill.

Cohen, Adam, and Elizabeth Taylor. 2000. *American Pharaoh: Mayor Richard J. Daley: His Battle for Chicago and the Nation*. Boston: Little, Brown.

Cohen, Cathy J. 1999. *The Boundaries of Blackness: AIDS and the Breakdown of Black Politics*. Chicago: University of Chicago Press.

Cohen, Cathy, and Michael Dawson. 1993. "Neighborhood Poverty and African American Politics." *American Political Science Review* 87:286–302.

Commission on Chicago Landmarks. 1990. *Oakland Multiple Resource District*. Chicago: Commission on Chicago Landmarks.

———. 1992. *Revised North Kenwood Multiple Resource District*. Chicago: Commission on Chicago Landmarks.

Community Assistance Panel. 1989. *North Kenwood–Oakland Neighborhood Planning Process: Community Assistance Panel (CAP) Report*. Chicago: Chicago Department of Planning and Development.

Community Conservation Board of Chicago. [1957?]. *Save Your Neighborhood: The Chicago Conservation Program*. Chicago: Community Conservation Board.

Community Development Commission. 1992. *The North Kenwood–Oakland Conservation Plan*. Chicago: Chicago Department of Planning and Development.

Cook County Coroner. [1920?]. *The Race Riots: Biennial Report 1918–1919 and Official Record of Inquests on the Victims of the Race Riots of July and August, 1919, Whereby Fifteen White Men and Twenty-three Colored Men Lost Their Lives and Several Hundred Were Injured*. Cook County (IL): Coroner of Cook County. http://www.chipublib.org/004chicago/disasters/text/coroner/45.html (accessed July 1, 2005).

Cosby, Bill. 2004. "Dr. Bill Cosby Speaks at the 50th Anniversary Commemoration of the Brown v. Topeka Board of Education Supreme Court Decision, May 22, 2004." *Black Scholar* 34:2–5.

Cose, Ellis. 1993. *The Rage of a Privileged Class.* New York: HarperCollins.

Covington, Jeannette, and Ralph Taylor. 1989. "Gentrification and Crime: Robbery and Larceny Changes in Appreciating Baltimore Neighborhoods during the 1970s." *Urban Affairs Quarterly* 25:142–72.

Cummings, Jean, and Denise DiPasquale. 1999. "The Low-Income Housing Tax Credit: An Analysis of the First Ten Years." *Housing Policy Debate* 10:251–306.

Cunningham, Mary K., Susan J. Popkin, and Martha R. Burt. 2005. "Public Housing Transformation and the 'Hard to House.'" Urban Institute. http://www.urban.org/UploadedPDF/311178_Roof_9.pdf (accessed March 31, 2006).

Daniels, Cora. 2004. *Black Power, Inc.: The New Voice of Success.* Hoboken, NJ: John Wiley & Sons.

Dávila, Arlene M. 2004. *Barrio Dreams: Puerto Ricans, Latinos, and the Neoliberal City.* Berkeley: University of California Press.

Dawson, Michael C. 1994. *Behind the Mule: Race and Class in African-American Politics.* Princeton, NJ: Princeton University Press.

———. 2001. *Black Visions: The Roots of Contemporary African-American Political Ideologies.* Chicago: University of Chicago Press.

Demo, David H., and Michael Hughes. 1990. "Socialization and Racial Identity among Black Americans." *Social Psychology Quarterly* 53:364–74.

DiMaggio, Paul. 1982. "Cultural Capital and School Success: The Impact of Status Culture Participation on the Grades of U.S. High School Students." *American Sociological Review* 47:189–201.

Dorsey, Thomas A., Julia Mae Smith, and Mary Belle White, eds. 1951. *Dorsey's Songs with a Message.* No. 1. Chicago: Thomas A. Dorsey.

Drake, St. Clair, and Horace Cayton. 1993. *Black Metropolis: A Study of Negro Life in a Northern City.* Chicago: University of Chicago Press.

Dreier, Peter, John Mollenkopf, and Todd Swanstrom. 2004. *Place Matters: Metropolitics for the Twenty-first Century.* Lawrence: University Press of Kansas.

DuBois, W. E. B. 1899. *The Philadelphia Negro: A Social Study.* Philadelphia: University of Pennsylvania Press, 1996.

———. 1904. *The Souls of Black Folk.* New York: New American Library, 1996.

Dubrow, Nancy F., and James Garbarino. 1989. "Living in the War Zone: Mothers and Young Children in a Public Housing Development." *Child Welfare* 68: 3–20.

Dumke, Mike. 2000. "Prophets or Puppets? Mayor Daley and the Black Church." *Chicago Reporter.* http://www.chicagoreporter.com/2000/9-2000/9-2000main.htm (accessed March 31, 2006).

Duncan, Otis Dudley, and Beverly Duncan. 1957. *The Negro Population of Chicago: A Study of Residential Succession.* Chicago: University of Chicago Press.

Duneier, Mitchell. 1992. *Slim's Table: Race, Respectability, and Masculinity.* Chicago: University of Chicago Press.

———. 2001. *Sidewalk.* New York: Farrar, Straus & Giroux.

Dyson, Michael Eric. 2005. *Is Bill Cosby Right? Or Has the Black Middle Class Lost Its Mind?* New York: Basic Civitas Books.

Fainstein, Norman, and Susan Fainstein. 1996. "Urban Regimes and Black Citizens: The Economic and Social Impacts of Black Political Incorporation in U.S. Cities." *International Journal of Urban and Regional Research* 20:22–37.

Fanon, Frantz. 1963. *The Wretched of the Earth.* New York: Grove Press.

Feldman, Roberta, and Susan Stall. 2004. *The Dignity of Resistance: Women Residents' Activism in Chicago Public Housing.* Cambridge: Cambridge University Press.

Fischer, Paul. 2003. *Where Are the Public Housing Families Going: An Update.* Chicago: National Center for Poverty Law.

Florida, Richard L. 2005. *Cities and the Creative Class.* New York: Routledge.

Frazier, E. Franklin. 1957. *Black Bourgeoisie.* New York: Free Press.

Freeman, Lance. 2005. "Displacement or Succession? Residential Mobility in Gentrifying Neighborhoods." *Urban Affairs Review* 40 (4): 463–91.

Freeman, Lance, and Frank Braconi. 2004. "Gentrification and Displacement: New York City in the 1990s." *Journal of the American Planning Association* 70:39–53.

Fuerst, J. S. 2003. *When Public Housing Was Paradise: Building Community in Chicago.* Westport: Praeger.

Fullilove, Mindy. 2005. *Root Shock: How Tearing Up City Neighborhoods Hurts America, and What We Can Do About It.* New York: One World/Ballantine.

Gaines, Kevin. 1996. *Uplifting the Race: Black Leadership, Politics, and Culture in the Twentieth Century.* Chapel Hill: University of North Carolina Press.

Gans, Herbert J. 1962. *The Urban Villagers: Group and Class in the Life of Italian-Americans.* New York: Free Press of Glencoe.

———. 1995. *The War against the Poor: The Underclass and Anti-poverty Policy.* New York: Basic Books.

Gates, Henry Louis, Jr. 1998. "The Two Nations of Black America." *Brookings Review* 16:4–7.

Gay, Claudine. 2004. "Putting Race in Context: Identifying the Environmental Determinants of Black Racial Attitudes." *American Political Science Review* 98:547–62.

General Accounting Office. 2003. "Public Housing: HOPE VI Resident Issues and Changes in Neighborhoods Surrounding Grant Sites." GAO-04-109. www.gao.gov/cgi-bin/getrpt?GAO-04-109 (accessed July 1, 2005).

Gilderbloom, John I., and R. L. Mullins Jr. 2005. *Promise and Betrayal: Universities and the Battle for Sustainable Urban Neighborhoods.* Albany: State University of New York Press.

Ginwright, Shawn. 2002. "Classed Out: The Challenges of Social Class in Black Community Change." *Social Problems* 49:544–63.

Goering, John, Ali Kamely, and Todd Richardson. 1994. *The Location and Racial Composition of Public Housing in the United States.* HUD-1519-PDR. Washington, DC: U.S. Department of Housing and Urban Development.

———. 1997. "Recent Research on Racial Segregation and Poverty Concentration in Public Housing in the United States." *Urban Affairs Review* 32:723–45.

Goetz, Edward G. 2003. *Clearing the Way: Deconcentrating the Poor in Urban America.* Washington, DC: Urban Institute Press.

Gordon, Andrew C., and Raymond W. Mack. 1971. *The Kenwood Oakland Community Organization and Toward Responsible Freedom: An Interim Report and Evaluation.* Evanston: Center for Urban Affairs, Northwestern University.

Gordon, Robert. 2002. *Can't be Satisfied: The Life and Times of Muddy Waters.* Boston: Little, Brown.

Gorman-Smith, Deborah, and Patrick Tolan. 1998. "The Role of Exposure to Violence and Developmental Problems Among Inner-City Youth." *Development and Psychopathology* 10:101–16.

Gotham, Kevin Fox. 2000. "Growth Machine Up-Links: Urban Renewal and the Rise and Fall of a Pro-Growth Coalition in a U.S. City." *Critical Sociology* 26:268–300.

———. 2002. *Race, Real Estate and Uneven Development: The Kansas City Experience, 1900–2000.* Albany: State University of New York Press.

Gotham, Kevin Fox, and Krista Brumley. 2002. "Using Space: Agency and Identity in a Public Housing Development." *City and Community* 1:267–89.

Gray, Robert, and Steven Tursky. 1986. "Location and Racial/Ethnic Occupancy Patterns for HUD-Subsidized Family Housing in Ten Metropolitan Areas." In *Housing Desegregation and Federal Policy,* ed. John M. Goering, 235–52. Chapel Hill: University of North Carolina Press.

Gregory, Steven. 1998. *Black Corona: Race and the Politics of Place in an Urban Community.* Princeton, NJ: Princeton University Press.

Grimshaw, William J. 1992. *Bitter Fruit: Black Politics and the Chicago Machine, 1931–1991.* Chicago: University of Chicago Press.

Grogan, Paul S., and Tony Proscio. 2000. *Comeback Cities: A Blueprint for Urban Neighborhood Revival.* Boulder, CO: Westview Press.

Grossman, James R. 1989. *Land of Hope: Chicago, Black Southerners, and the Great Migration.* Chicago: University of Chicago Press.

Guralnick, Peter. 2005. *Dream Boogie: The Triumph of Sam Cooke.* New York: Little, Brown.

Hanchard, Michael, ed. 1999. *Racial Politics in Contemporary Brazil.* Durham, NC: Duke University Press.

Harcourt, Bernard. 2001. *Illusion of Order: The False Promise of Broken Windows Policing.* Cambridge, MA: Harvard University Press.

Harding, Alan. 1994. "Urban Regimes and Growth Machines: Toward a Cross-National Research Agenda." *Urban Affairs Quarterly* 29:356–82.

Harris, Michael W. 1992. *The Rise of Gospel Blues: The Music of Thomas Andrew Dorsey in the Urban Church.* New York: Oxford University Press.

Harris-Lacewell, Melissa. 2004. *Barbershops, Bibles, and BET: Everyday Talk and Black Political Thought.* Princeton, NJ: Princeton University Press.

Hartman, Chester. 2002. *City for Sale: The Transformation of San Francisco.* Updated and rev. ed. Berkeley: University of California Press.

Hauser, Philip M., and Evelyn Kitagawa, eds. 1953. *Local Community Fact Book for Chicago, 1950.* Chicago: Chicago Community Inventory, University of Chicago.

Haynes, Bruce. 2001. *Red Lines, Black Spaces: The Politics of Race and Space in a Black Middle-Class Suburb.* New Haven: Yale University Press.

Heflin, Colleen, and Mary Pattillo. In press. "Poverty in the Family: Race, Siblings and Socioeconomic Heterogeneity." *Social Science Research.*

Henig, Jeffrey. 1980. "Gentrification and Displacement within Cities: A Comparative Analysis." *Social Science Quarterly* 61:638–52.

Henig, Jeffrey, and Dennis Gale. 1987. "The Political Incorporation of Newcomers to Racially Changing Neighborhoods." *Urban Affairs Quarterly* 22:399–419.

Herring, Cedric, Michael Bennett, Doug Gills, and Noah Temaner Jenkins, eds. 1998. *Empowerment in Chicago: Grassroots Participation in Economic Development and Poverty Alleviation.* Chicago: Great Cities Institute, University of Illinois at Chicago.

Higginbotham, Evelyn Brooks. 1993. *Righteous Discontent: The Women's Movement in the Black Baptist Church, 1880–1920.* Cambridge, MA: Harvard University Press.

Hirsch, Arnold. 1983. *Making the Second Ghetto: Race and Housing in Chicago, 1940–1960.* New York: Cambridge University Press.

———. 2000. "Searching for a 'Sound Negro Policy': A Racial Agenda for the Housing Acts of 1949 and 1954." *Housing Policy Debate* 11:393–441.

Hochschild, Jennifer L. 1995. *Facing Up to the American Dream: Race, Class, and the Soul of the Nation.* Princeton, NJ: Princeton University Press.

Howe, Irving. 1976. *World of Our Fathers.* New York: Harcourt Brace Jovanovich.

Hudspeth, Nancy, and Janet Smith. 2004. "The Effects of Gentrification in Chicago: Displacement and Disparity." Paper presented at the 2004 annual conference of the Urban Affairs Association, Washington, DC, March 31–April 3.

Hughes, Langston. 1995. "Restrictive Covenants." In *The Collected Poems of Langston Hughes.* Arnold Rampersad, ed. New York: Vintage.

Hughes, Michael, and Melvin E. Thomas. 1998. "The Continuing Significance of Race Revisited: A Study of Race, Class, and Quality of Life in America, 1972 to 1996." *American Sociological Review* 63:785–95.

Hughes, Michael, and Steven Tuch. 2000. "How Beliefs about Poverty Influence Racial Policy Attitudes." In *Racial Politics: The Debate about Racism in America,* ed. David Sears, Jim Sidanius, and Lawrence Bobo, 165–90. Chicago: University of Chicago Press.

Hunt, D. Bradford. 2000. "What Went Wrong with Public Housing in Chicago? A History of the Chicago Housing Authority, 1933–1982." PhD dissertation, University of California, Berkeley.

Hyra, Derek. 2006. "Racial Uplift? Intra-Racial Class Conflict and the Economic Revitalization of Harlem and Bronzeville." *City & Community* 5:71–92.

Iceland, John, Daniel Weinberg, and Erika Steinmetz. 2002. "Racial and Ethnic Residential Segregation in the United States: 1980–2000." U.S. Census Bureau, http://www.census.gov/hhes/www/housing/resseg/pdf/censr_3.pdf. (accessed July 1, 2005).

Iceland, John, Cicely Sharpe, and Erika Steinmetz. 2005. "Class Differences in African American Residential Patterns in US Metropolitan Areas: 1990–2000." *Social Science Research* 34:252–66.

Illinois Housing Development Authority. 1990. *Kenwood-Oakland Neighborhood Conservation Plan*. Springfield: Illinois Housing Development Authority.

Imbroscio, David L. 1997. *Reconstructing City Politics: Alternative Economic Development and Urban Regimes*. Thousand Oaks, CA: Sage Publications.

Immergluck, Dan, and Geoff Smith. 2004. "Risky Business: An Econometric Analysis of the Relationship Between Subprime Lending and Neighborhood Foreclosures." http://woodstockinst.org/document/riskybusiness.pdf (accessed July 1, 2005).

Jackson, John L. 2001. *Harlemworld: Doing Race and Class in Contemporary Black America*. Chicago: University of Chicago Press.

———. 2005. *Real Black: Adventures in Racial Sincerity*. Chicago: University of Chicago Press.

Jackson, John P. 2001. *Social Scientists for Social Justice: Making the Case against Segregation*. New York: New York University Press.

Jackson, Kenneth T. 1985. *Crabgrass Frontier: The Suburbanization of the United States*. New York: Oxford University Press.

Jacobs, Jane. 1961. *The Death and Life of Great American Cities*. New York: Random House.

Jankowski, Martín Sánchez. 1991. *Islands in the Street: Gangs and American Urban Society*. Berkeley: University of California Press.

Jargowsky, Paul A. 1997. *Poverty and Place: Ghettos, Barrios, and the American City*. New York: Russell Sage Foundation.

Jencks, Christopher, and Paul E. Peterson, eds. 1991. *The Urban Underclass*. Washington, DC: Brookings Institution.

Johnson, Valerie. 2002. *Black Power in the Suburbs: The Myth or Reality of African American Suburban Political Incorporation*. Albany: State University of New York Press.

Joseph, Mark L., Robert J. Chaskin, and Henry S. Webber. 2005. "The Theoretical Basis for Addressing Poverty through Mixed-Income Development." Paper presented at the Workshop on Social Structures and Processes in Urban Space, University of Chicago, April 21, 2005. http://cas.uchicago.edu/workshops/urban/Mixed-Income%20Development%20and%20Urban%20Poverty.pdf (accessed March 31, 2006).

Katz, Lawrence F., Jeffrey R. Kling, and Jeffrey R. Liebman. 2000. "Moving to Opportunity in Boston: Early Results of a Randomized Mobility Experiment." Princeton University Industrial Relations Working Paper 441.

Katz, Michael B. 1989. *The Undeserving Poor: From the War on Poverty to the War on Welfare*. New York: Pantheon.

Keating, Larry. 2000. "Redeveloping Public Housing: Relearning Urban Renewal's Immutable Lessons." *Journal of the American Planning Association* 66: 384–97.

Kelley, Robin D. G. 1994. *Race Rebels: Culture, Politics, and the Black Working Class*. New York: Free Press.

Kennedy, Maureen, and Paul Leonard. April 2001. "Dealing with Neighborhood Change: A Primer on Gentrification and Policy Choices." Discussion paper prepared for the Brookings Institution Center on Urban and Metropolitan Policy. http://www.brookings.edu/es/urban/gentrification/gentrification.pdf (accessed March 31, 2006).

Kenwood-Ellis Community Center. 1956. *Community Facts*. Report 1. Chicago: Kenwood-Ellis Community Center.

Kenwood Oakland Community Organization. 1968. *Alternatives for Planning Kenwood Oakland*. Chicago: KOCO.

Kingsley, G. Thomas, Jennifer Johnson, and Kathryn Pettit. 2003. "Patterns of Section 8 Relocation in the HOPE VI Program." *Journal of Urban Affairs* 25:427–47.

Kirp, David L., John P. Dwyer, and Larry A. Rosenthal. 1995. *Our Town: Race, Housing, and the Soul of Suburbia*. New Brunswick, NJ: Rutgers University Press.

Kitagawa, Evelyn, and Karl Taeuber, eds. 1963. *Local Community Fact Book: Chicago Metropolitan Area, 1960*. Chicago: University of Chicago.

Kleit, Rachel Garshick. 2001. "The Role of Neighborhood Social Networks in Scattered-Site Public Housing Residents' Search for Jobs." *Housing Policy Debate* 12:541–73.

Klinenberg, Eric. 2002. *Heatwave: A Social Autopsy of Disaster in Chicago*. Chicago: University of Chicago Press.

Kotlowitz, Alex. 1991. *There Are No Children Here: The Story of Two Boys Growing Up in the Other America*. New York: Doubleday.

Krysan, Maria, and Reynolds Farley. 2002. "The Residential Preferences of Blacks: Do They Explain Persistent Segregation?" *Social Forces* 80:937–80.

Lacy, Karyn. 2002. "A Part of the Neighborhood? Negotiating Race in American Suburbs." *International Journal of Sociology and Social Policy* 22:39–74.

Lamont, Michèle. 1992. *Money, Morals and Manners*. Chicago: University of Chicago Press.

———. 2000. *The Dignity of Working Men: Morality and the Boundaries of Race, Class, and Immigration*. New York: Russell Sage Foundation.

Lamont, Michèle and Virág Molnár. 2002. "The Study of Boundaries in the Social Sciences." *Annual Review of Sociology* 28:167–95.

Lane, Vincent. 1994. "Public Housing Sweep Stakes: My Battle with the ACLU." *Policy Review* 69:68–72.

Lareau, Annette. 1987. "Social Class Differences in Family-School Relationships: The Importance of Cultural Capital." *Sociology of Education* 60:73–85.

———. 2003. *Unequal Childhoods: Class, Race, and Family Life*. Berkeley: University of California Press.

Lawrence, Jacob. 1993. *Jacob Lawrence: The Migration Series*. Lonnie Bunch and Elizabeth Hutton Turner, eds. Washington, DC: Rappahannock Press.

Lee, Jennifer. 2002. *Civility in the City: Blacks, Jews, and Koreans in Urban America*. Cambridge, MA: Harvard University Press.

Lemann, Nicholas. 1992. *The Promised Land: Black Migration and How It Changed America*. New York: Vintage Books.

Leonard, Paul, ed. 1997. "Mixed-Income Housing: In Memory of Donald Terner." Special Issue of *Cityscape: A Journal of Policy Development and Research* 3.

Lester, Thomas. 1998. "Urban Revitalization or Gentrification? A Case Study of the Redevelopment of Chicago's North Kenwood–Oakland Community." Urban Studies Senior Seminar Research Paper. University of Pennsylvania.

Levitt, Peggy. 2001. *The Transnational Villagers*. Berkeley: University of California Press.

Lieberson, Stanley, and Mary Waters. 1989. "The Rise of a New Ethnic Group: The 'Unhyphenated American.'" *Social Science Research Council Items* 43:7–10.

Light, Ivan H., and Edna Bonacich. 1988. *Immigrant Entrepreneurs: Koreans in Los Angeles, 1965–1982*. Berkeley: University of California Press.

Light, Ivan H., and Steven J. Gold. 2000. *Ethnic Economies*. San Diego: Academic Press.

Lindsey, Almont. 1942. *The Pullman Strike: The Story of a Unique Experiment and of a Great Labor Upheaval*. Chicago: University of Chicago Press.

Linehan, Mary. 2004. "Vice Commissions." In *The Encyclopedia of Chicago*, ed. James R. Grossman, Ann Durkin Keating, and Janice L. Reiff, 854. Chicago: University of Chicago Press.

Lipman, Pauline. 2002. "Making the Global City, Making Inequality: The Political Economy and Cultural Politics of Chicago School Policy." *American Educational Research Journal* 39:379–419.

Lloyd, Richard. 2005. *Neo-Bohemia: Art and Commerce in the Postindustrial City*. New York: Routledge.

Loeske, Donileen, and Joel Best, eds. 2003. *Social Problems: Constructionist Readings*. New York: Walter de Gruyter.

Logan, John R., and Kyle D. Crowder. 2002. "Political Regimes and Suburban Growth, 1980–1990." *City & Community* 1 (1): 113–35.

Logan, John R., and Harvey L. Molotch. 1987. *Urban Fortunes: The Political Economy of Place*. Berkeley: University of California Press.

Logan, John R., and Brian Stults. 1999. "Racial Differences in Exposure to Crime: The City and Suburbs of Cleveland in 1990." *Criminology* 37:251–76.

Long, Herman, and Charles Johnson. 1947. *People vs. Property: Race Restrictive Covenants in Housing*. Nashville: Fisk University Press.

Lorde, Audre. 1984. "The Master's Tools Will Never Dismantle the Master's House." In *Sister Outsider: Essays and Speeches*, 110–14. Trumansburg, NY: Crossing Press.

Manley, Theodoric, Jr. 2004. "A Dream Deferred: Bronzeville at the Crossroads." http://condor.depaul.edu/~blackmet/ (accessed July 1, 2005).

Manley, Theodoric, Jr., Avery Buffa, and Caleb Dube. 2005. "The Revanchist City:

Downtown Chicago and the Rhetoric of Redevelopment in Bronzeville." Working paper. DePaul University, Chicago.

Marcuse, Peter. 1985. "Gentrification, Abandonment, and Displacement: Connections, Causes, and Policy Responses in New York City." *Washington University Journal of Urban and Contemporary Law* 28:195–239.

Marquis, Albert Nelson, ed. 1911. *The Book of Chicagoans: A Biographical Dictionary of Leading Living Men of the City of Chicago*. Chicago: A. N. Marquis & Company.

Mason, Maryann. 1998. "Mixed Income Public Housing: Outcomes for Tenants and Their Community: A Case Study of the Lake Parc Place Development in Chicago, Illinois." PhD dissertation, Loyola University of Chicago.

Massey, Douglas, and Nancy Denton. 1993. *American Apartheid: Segregation and the Making of the Underclass*. Cambridge, MA: Harvard University Press.

Massey, Douglas S., and Shawn M. Kanaiaupuni. 1993. "Public Housing and the Concentration of Poverty." *Social Science Quarterly* 74:109–22.

Maurrasse, David J. 2001. *Beyond the Campus: How Colleges and Universities Form Partnerships with Their Communities*. New York: Routledge.

May, Reuben A. Buford. 2001. *Talking at Trena's: Everyday Conversations at an African American Tavern*. New York: New York University Press.

McBride, Dwight A. 2005. *Why I Hate Abercrombie & Fitch: Essays on Race and Sexuality*. New York: New York University.

McClory, Robert. 1993. "The Plot to Destroy North Kenwood." *Chicago Reader* 23 (October 15): 1– 24.

McDonald, Scott. 1986. "Does Gentrification Affect Crime Rates?" In *Communities and Crime,* ed. Albert Reiss and Michael Tonry, 163–202. Chicago: University of Chicago Press.

Mele, Christopher. 2000. *Selling the Lower East Side: Culture, Real Estate and Resistance in New York City*. Minneapolis: University of Minnesota Press.

Merry, Sally Engle. 1981. *Urban Danger: Life in a Neighborhood of Strangers*. Philadelphia: Temple University Press.

Merton, Robert. 1938. "Social Structure and Anomie." *American Sociological Review* 3:672–82.

Metro Chicago Information Center. 1999. Community Capacity Survey Questionnaire. Provided to author by MCIC staff.

Metropolitan Housing and Planning Council. 1953. *Conservation: A Report to the Conservation Committee of the Metropolitan Housing and Planning Council*. Chicago: Metropolitan Housing and Planning Council.

Meyerson, Martin, and Edward C. Banfield. 1955. *Politics, Planning, and the Public Interest: The Case of Public Housing in Chicago*. Glencoe: Free Press.

Mikva, Zorita. 1951. "The Neighborhood Improvement Association: A Counterforce to the Expansion of Chicago's Negro Population." MA thesis, University of Chicago.

Miller, Jerome. 1996. *Search and Destroy: African-American Males in the Criminal Justice System*. New York: Cambridge University Press.

Mohl, Raymond A. 1993. "Shifting Patterns of American Urban Policy since 1900." In *Urban Policy in Twentieth-Century America,* ed. Arnold Hirsch and Raymond Mohl, 1–45. New Brunswick, NJ: Rutgers University Press.

Mollenkopf, John. 1983. *The Contested City.* Princeton, NJ: Princeton University Press.

————. 1989. "Who (or What) Runs Cities, and How?" *Sociological Forum* 4: 119–37.

Morrison, Toni. 1992. *Playing in the Dark: Whiteness and the Literary Imagination.* Cambridge: Harvard University Press.

Nashashibi, Rami. 2002. "Mighty in the Margins: The Blackstone Legacy and Resistance in a Global Ghetto." Paper presented at the Workshop on the Sociologies and Cultures of Globalization, University of Chicago.

National Commission on Severely Distressed Public Housing. 1992. *The Final Report of the National Commission on Severely Distressed Public Housing: A Report to the Congress and the Secretary of Housing and Urban Development.* Washington, DC: Government Printing Office.

National Housing Law Project. 2002. "False Hope: A Critical Assessment of the HOPE VI Public Housing Redevelopment Program." http://www.nhlp.org/ html/pubhsg/FalseHOPE.pdf (accessed July 1, 2005).

Neighborhood Planning Committee. 1989. *North Kenwood–Oakland Neighborhood Planning Process.* Chicago: Chicago Department of Planning.

Newman, Katherine S. 1999. *No Shame in My Game: The Working Poor in the Inner City.* New York: Knopf, Russell Sage Foundation.

O'Connor, Alice. 2001. *Poverty Knowledge: Social Science, Social Policy, and the Poor in Twentieth-Century U.S. History.* Princeton, NJ: Princeton University Press.

Oldweiler, Cory, and Brian J. Rogal. 2000. "Public Housing: Reading between the Lines." *Chicago Reporter,* http://www.chicagoreporter.com/2000/03_ 2000/032000plan.htm (accessed July 1, 2005).

Oliver, Melvin, and Thomas Shapiro. 1995. *Black Wealth/White Wealth: A New Perspective on Racial Inequality.* New York: Routledge.

Orr, Marion E., and Gerry Stoker. 1994. "Urban Regimes and Leadership in Detroit." *Urban Affairs Quarterly* 30:48–73.

Osofsky, Joy D. 1995. "The Effects of Exposure to Violence on Young Children." *American Psychologist* 50:782–88.

————, ed. 1997. *Children in a Violent Society.* New York: Guilford Press.

O'Sullivan, Arthur. 2005. "Gentrification and Crime." *Journal of Urban Economics* 57:73–85.

Park, Robert E. 1928. "Human Migration and the Marginal Man." *American Journal of Sociology* 33:881–93.

————. 1936. "Human Ecology." *American Journal of Sociology* 42:1–15.

Pattillo, Mary. 1998. "Sweet Mothers and Gangbangers: Managing Crime in a Black Middle Class Neighborhood." *Social Forces* 76:747–74.

————. 2003. "Extending the Boundaries and Definition of the Ghetto." *Ethnic and Racial Studies* 26:1046–57.

———. 2005. "Black Middle Class Neighborhoods." *Annual Review of Sociology* 31:305–29.

Pattillo-McCoy, Mary. 1999. *Black Picket Fences: Privilege and Peril among the Black Middle Class.* Chicago: University of Chicago Press.

———. 2000. "The Limits of Out-Migration for the Black Middle Class." *Journal of Urban Affairs* 22:225–42.

Pérez, Gina. 2002. "The Other 'Real World': Gentrification and the Social Construction of Place in Chicago." *Urban Anthropology* 31:37–68.

———. 2004. *The Near Northwest Side Story: Migration, Displacement, and Puerto Rican Families.* Berkeley: University of California Press.

Piven, Frances Fox, and Richard A. Cloward. 1993. *Regulating the Poor: The Functions of Public Welfare.* New York: Vintage Books.

Plotkin, Wendy. 1997. "Deeds of Mistrust: Shelley v. Kraemer (1948) and Restrictive Covenants in Chicago, 1927–1950." http//www.public.asu.edu/~wplotkin/DeedsWeb/newberry.html (accessed July 1, 2005).

———. 1999. "Deeds of Mistrust: Race, Housing, and Restrictive Covenants in Chicago, 1900–1953." http//www.public.asu.edu/~wplotkin/ (accessed July 1, 2005).

———. 2001. "Hemmed In: The Struggle against Racial Restrictive Covenants and Deed Restrictions in Post-WWII Chicago." *Journal of the Illinois State Historical Society* (spring), http://www.findarticles.com/p/articles/mi_qa3945/is_200104 ai_n8929165/pg_1 (accessed July 1, 2005).

Polednak, Anthony P. 1997. *Segregation, Poverty, and Mortality in Urban African Americans.* New York: Oxford University Press.

Polikoff, Alexander. 1978. *Housing the Poor: The Case for Heroism.* Cambridge, MA: Ballinger Publishing.

———. 1988. "The Federal Courts and the Community: *Gautreaux* and Institutional Litigation." *Chicago Kent Law Review* 64:451–78.

———. 2006. *Waiting for Gautreaux: A Story of Segregation, Housing, and the Black Ghetto.* Evanston, IL: Northwestern University Press.

Popkin, Susan, Victoria Gwiasda, Lynn Olson, Dennis Rosenbaum, and Larry Buron. 2000. *The Hidden War: Crime and the Tragedy of Public Housing in Chicago.* New Brunswick, NJ: Rutgers University Press.

Popkin, Susan J., Mary K. Cunningham, and William Woodley. 2003. *Residents at Risk: A Profile of Ida B. Wells and Madden Park.* Washington, DC: Urban Institute.

Popkin, Susan J., Michael Eiseman, and Elizabeth Cove. 2004. "How Are HOPE VI Families Faring? Children." http://www.urban.org/UploadedPDF/311074_Roof_6.pdf (accessed July 1, 2005).

Popkin, Susan J., Bruce Katz, Mary Cunningham, Karen Brown, Jeremy Gustafson, and Margery Austin Turner. 2004. *A Decade of HOPE VI: Research Findings and Policy Challenges.* Washington, DC: Urban Institute.

Powell, John, and Kathleen M. Graham. 2002. "Urban Fragmentation as a Barrier to Equal Opportunity." Chapter 7 in *Rights at Risk: Equality in an Age of Terrorism,* ed. Dianne M. Piché, William L. Taylor, and Robin A. Reed. Washington,

DC: Citizens' Commission on Civil Rights. http://www.cccr.org/publications/publication.cfm?id=1 (accessed December 1, 2005).

Prince, Sabiyha. 2004. *Constructing Belonging: Class, Race, and Harlem's Professional Workers*. New York: Routledge.

Putnam, Robert D. 2000. *Bowling Alone: The Collapse and Revival of American Community*. New York: Simon & Schuster.

Quad Communities Development Corporation. 2005. *Quad Communities: Connecting Past, Present and Future*. LISC/Chicago's New Communities Program. http://www.newcommunities.org/cmadocs/QuadCommQofL2005.pdf (accessed March 1, 2006).

Radford, Gail. 1996. *Modern Housing for America: Policy Struggles in the New Deal Era*. Chicago: University of Chicago Press.

Rainwater, Lee. 1970. *Behind Ghetto Walls: Black Families in a Federal Slum*. Chicago: Aldine Publishing.

Raley, R. Kelly. 1995. "Black-White Differences in Kin Contact and Exchange among Never Married Adults." *Journal of Family Issues* 16:77–103.

Randel, Don M. 2004. "Behind Every Charter School There's a Good Idea." *University of Chicago Magazine* 97:15.

Reed, Adolph, Jr. 1988. "The Black Urban Regime: Structural Origins and Constraints." *Comparative Urban and Community Research* 1:138–89.

———. 1999. *Stirrings in the Jug: Black Politics in the Post-Segregation Era*. Minneapolis: University of Minnesota Press.

———. 2000. *Class Notes: Posing as Politics and Other Thoughts on the American Scene*. New York: New Press.

Reich, Howard. 1997. "Venue Revivalist." *Down Beat* 64:10–12.

Robinson, Tony. 1995. "Gentrification and Grassroots Resistance in San Francisco's Tenderloin." *Urban Affairs Review* 30:483–513.

Rogaski, Ruth. 2004. *Hygienic Modernity: Meanings of Health and Disease in Treaty-Port China*. Berkeley: University of California Press.

Rosenbaum, James, Linda Stroh, and Cathy Flynn. 1998. "Lake Parc Place: A Study of Mixed-Income Housing." *Housing Policy Debate* 9:703–40.

Rossi, Peter H., and Robert A. Dentler. 1961. *The Politics of Urban Renewal: The Chicago Findings*. New York: Free Press of Glencoe.

Rowley, Hazel. 2001. *Richard Wright: The Life and Times*. New York: Henry Holt.

Rubinowitz, Leonard S. 1992. "Metropolitan Public Housing Desegregation Remedies: Chicago's Privatization Program." *Northern Illinois University Law Review* 12:589–669.

Rubinowitz, Leonard S., and Imani Perry. 2002. "Crimes without Punishment: White Neighbors' Resistance to Black Entry." *Journal of Criminal Law and Criminology* 92:335–428.

Rubinowitz, Leonard S., and James Rosenbaum. 2000. *Crossing the Class and Color Lines: From Public Housing to White Suburbia*. Chicago: University of Chicago Press.

Rusk, David. 2001. "The 'Segregation Tax': The Cost of Racial Segregation to Black

Homeowners." Brookings Institution, http://www.brookings.edu/dybdocroot/es/urban/publications/rusk.pdf (accessed July 1, 2005).

Rybczynski, Witold. 1993. "Bauhaus Blunders: Architecture and Public Housing." *Public Interest* 93:82–90.

Rymond-Richmond, Wenona. 2004. "Perception and Data on Violent Hot Spots." Paper presented at the annual conference of the American Society of Criminology, Nashville, TN.

Sampson, Robert J., Jeffrey D. Morenoff, and Thomas Gannon-Rowley. 2002. "Assessing Neighborhood Effects: Social Processes and New Directions in Research." *Annual Review of Sociology* 28:443–78.

Sampson, Robert J., and Stephen W. Raudenbush. 1999. "Systematic Social Observation of Public Spaces: A New Look at Disorder in Urban Neighborhoods." *American Journal of Sociology* 105:603–51.

Sampson, Robert J., and William Julius Wilson. 1995. "Toward a Theory of Race, Crime and Urban Inequality." In *Crime and Inequality,* ed. John Hagan and Ruth D. Peterson. Stanford: Stanford University Press.

Sanchez, Casey. 2006. "Building Power." *Chicago Reporter* 35:6–15.

Sanchez, George. 1993. *Becoming Mexican American: Ethnicity, Culture, and Identity in Chicano Los Angeles, 1900–1945.* New York: Oxford University Press.

Sandburg, Carl. 1916. *Chicago Poems.* New York: H. Holt.

Sassen, Saskia. 2002. "Scales and Spaces." *City & Community* 1:48–57.

Sawyer, Mark, Yesilernis Peña, and James Sidanius. 2004. "Cuban Exceptionalism: Group Based Hierarchy and the Dynamics of Patriotism in Puerto Rico, the Dominican Republic and Cuba." *Dubois Review* 1:93–114.

Schaeffer, Brett. 2000. "Some See Elite Schools as Drain on System." *Catalyst* 12 (4): 12–13. http://www.catalyst-chicago.org/news/index.php?item=256&cat=23 (accessed December 1, 2005).

Schietinger, Egbert Frederick. 1948. *Real Estate Transfers during Negro Invasion: A Case Study.* MA thesis, University of Chicago.

Schill, Michael. 1997. "Chicago's Mixed-Income New Communities Strategy: The Future Face of Public Housing?" In *Affordable Housing and Urban Redevelopment in the United States,* ed. Willem van Vliet, 135–57. Thousand Oaks, CA: Sage Publications.

Schuman, Howard, Charlotte Steeh, Lawrence D. Bobo, and Maria Krysan. 1997. *Racial Attitudes in America: Trends and Interpretations.* Cambridge, MA: Harvard University Press.

Scott, Daryl Michael. 1997. *Contempt and Pity: Social Policy and the Image of the Damaged Black Psyche, 1880–1996.* Chapel Hill: University of North Carolina Press.

Scott, James C. 1998. *Seeing Like a State: How Certain Schemes to Improve the Human Condition Have Failed.* New Haven: Yale University Press.

Seliga, Joseph. 2000. "*Gautreaux* a Generation Later: Remedying the Second Ghetto or Creating the Third?" *Northwestern University Law Review* 94:1049–1198.

Seligman, Amanda. 2005. *Block by Block: Neighborhoods and Public Policy on Chicago's West Side.* Chicago: University of Chicago Press.

Shaw, Todd C. 2003. "Race, Regime, and Redevelopment: Opportunities for Community Coalitions in Detroit, 1985–1993." *National Political Science Review* 9:186–205.

Simpson, Andrea Y. 1998. *The Tie That Binds: Identity and Political Attitudes in the Post–Civil Rights Generation.* New York: New York University Press.

Skogan, Wesley G., and Susan M. Hartnett. 1997. *Community Policing, Chicago Style.* New York: Oxford University Press.

———. 2006. *Police and Community in Chicago: A Tale of Three Cities.* New York: Oxford University Press.

Small, Mario Luis. 2004. *Villa Victoria: The Transformation of Social Capital in a Boston Barrio.* Chicago: University of Chicago Press.

Small, Mario Luis, and Katherine Newman. 2001. "Urban Poverty after *The Truly Disadvantaged:* The Rediscovery of the Family, the Neighborhood, and Culture." *Annual Review of Sociology* 27:23–45.

Smith, Alastair. 2002. "Mixed-Income Housing Developments: Promise and Reality." Joint Center for Housing Studies of Harvard University, Neighborhood Reinvestment Corporation. October.

Smith, Neil. 1996. *The New Urban Frontier: Gentrification and the Revanchist City.* New York: Routledge.

———. 2002. "New Globalism, New Urbanism: Gentrification as Global Urban Strategy." In *Spaces of Neoliberalism,* ed. Neil Brenner and Nik Theodore, 80–103. Malden, MA: Blackwell Publishing.

Smith, Shawn Michelle. 2004. *Photography on the Color Line: W. E. B. DuBois, Race, and Visual Culture.* Durham, NC.: Duke University Press.

Spain, Daphne. 1993. "Been-Heres Versus Come-Heres: Negotiating Conflicting Community Identities." *Journal of the American Planning Association* 59: 156–71.

Spear, Allan. 1967. *Black Chicago: The Making of a Negro Ghetto, 1890–1920.* Chicago: University of Chicago Press.

Squires, Gregory D. 1994. *Capital and Communities in Black and White: The Intersections of Race, Class, and Uneven Development.* Albany: State University of New York Press.

Squires, Gregory D., Larry Bennett, Kathleen McCourt, and Philip Nyden. 1987. *Chicago: Race, Class and the Response to Urban Decline.* Albany: State University of New York Press.

Steeples, Douglas, and David Whitten. 1998. *Democracy in Desperation: The Depression of 1893.* Westport, CT: Greenwood Press.

Stone, Clarence N. 1989. *Regime Politics: Governing Atlanta, 1946–1988.* Lawrence: University Press of Kansas.

———. 2006. "Power, Reform, and Urban Regimes." *City & Community* 5:23–38.

Stone, Clarence, and Carol Pierannunzi. 1997. "Atlanta and the Limited Reach of Electoral Control." In *Racial Politics in American Cities,* ed. Rufus Browning, Dale Rogers Marshall, and David Tabb, 163–78. New York: Longman.

Street, Paul. 2005. *Still Separate, Unequal: Race, Place, Policy, and the State of Black Chicago*. Chicago: Chicago Urban League.

Stuart, Guy. 2003. *Discriminating Risk: The U.S. Mortgage Lending Industry in the Twentieth Century*. Ithaca, NY: Cornell University Press.

Stuart, Jack. 1997. "A Note on William English Walling and His 'Cousin,' W. E. B. DuBois." *Journal of Negro History* 82:270–75.

Sullivan, Thomas. 2003. "Report #5 of the Independent Monitor." http://www.viewfromtheground.com/archive/2003/01/sullivan5.html.

Suttles, Gerald D. 1990. *The Man-Made City: The Land-Use Confidence Game in Chicago*. Chicago: University of Chicago Press.

Swain, Carol M. 1993. *Black Faces, Black Interests: The Representation of African Americans in Congress*. Cambridge, MA: Harvard University Press.

Tate, Katherine. 1993. *From Protest to Politics: The New Black Voters in American Elections*. New York: Russell Sage Foundation.

Taub, Richard D., D. Garth Taylor, and Jan D. Dunham. 1984. *Paths of Neighborhood Change: Race and Crime in Urban America*. Chicago: University of Chicago Press.

Taylor, D. Garth, and Sylvia Puente. 2004. "Immigration, Gentrification and Chicago Race/Ethnic Relations in the New Global Era." Paper presented at "The Changing Face of Metropolitan Chicago," Conference on Chicago Research and Public Policy, University of Chicago, May 12–13, 2004. http://www.about.chapinhall.org/UUC/presentations/TaylorPuentePaper.pdf (accessed March 31, 2006).

Taylor, Monique M. 2002. *Harlem between Heaven and Hell*. Minneapolis: University of Minnesota Press.

Taylor, Ralph. B. 2001. *Breaking Away from Broken Windows: Baltimore Neighborhoods and the Nationwide Fight against Crime, Grime, Fear, and Decline*. Boulder, Colorado: Westview Press.

Taylor, Ralph, and Jeannette Covington. 1988. "Neighborhood Changes in Ecology and Violence." *Criminology* 26:553–91.

Teele, James E., ed. 2002. *E. Franklin Frazier and Black Bourgeoisie*. Columbia, MO: University of Missouri Press.

Tjerandsen, Carl. 2003 [1980]. "Education for Citizenship: A Foundation's Experience." Santa Cruz: Emil Schwarzhaupt Foundation. http://comm-org.utoledo.edu/papers2003/tjerandsen/contentsd.htm#about (accessed July 1, 2005).

Travis, Dempsey J. 1981. *An Autobiography of Black Chicago*. Chicago: Urban Research Institute.

Turner, Margery Austin, Stephen L. Ross, George L. Galster, and John Yinger. 2002. "Discrimination in Metropolitan Housing Markets: National Results from Phase I of HDS2000." http://www.urban.org/url.cfm?ID=410821 (accessed July 1, 2005).

Turner, Victor. 1967. *The Forest of Symbols*. Ithaca, NY: Cornell University Press.

U.S. Department of Housing and Urban Development. 1996 (November). *Scattered-Site Housing: Characteristics and Consequences*. HUD User's Document Reproduction Service.

———. 2003 (September). "Moving to Opportunity for Fair Housing Demonstration: Interim Impacts Evaluation." http://www.huduser.org/Publications/pdf/MTOExec.pdf (accessed July 1, 2005).

U.S. Senate Select Committee on Nutrition and Human Needs. 1969. *Part 15: Human Needs in Health: Hearings before the Senate Select Committee on Nutrition and Human Needs.* 90th Congress, second session, and 91st Congress, first session. Washington, DC: Government Printing Office.

Urban Services and Development, Inc. 1978. *North Kenwood–Oakland Development Plan Proposal: Creating an Environment for Social and Economic Growth in a Planning Framework.* Chicago: Kenwood Oakland Community Organization.

Vale, Lawrence. 1997. "Empathological Places: Residents' Ambivalence toward Remaining in Public Housing." *Journal of Planning Education and Research* 16:159–75.

———. 2000. *From the Puritans to the Projects: Public Housing and Public Neighbors.* Cambridge, MA: Harvard University Press.

Varady, David P., and Carole C. Walker. 2003. "Housing Vouchers and Residential Mobility." *Journal of Planning Literature* 18:17–30.

Venkatesh, Sudhir. 2000. *American Project: The Rise and Fall of a Modern American Ghetto.* Cambridge, MA: Harvard University Press.

Venkatesh, Sudhir, and Isil Celimli. 2004. "Tearing Down the Community." *Shelterforce Online.* November/December. http://www.nhi.org/online/issues/138/chicago.html (accessed March 31, 2006).

Venkatesh, Sudhir, Isil Celimli, Douglas Miller, Alexandra Murphy, and Beauty Turner. 2004. "Chicago Public Housing Transformation: A Research Report." New York: Columbia University, Center for Urban Research and Policy.

Vigdor, Jacob. 2002. "Does Gentrification Harm the Poor?" Brookings-Wharton Papers on Urban Affairs. Ed. William Gale and Janet Rothenberg Pack. Washington, DC: Brookings Institution.

von Hoffman, Alexander. 2000. "A Study in Contradictions: The Origins and Legacy of the Housing Act of 1949." *Housing Policy Debate* 11:299–326.

———. 2003. *House by House, Block by Block: The Rebirth of America's Urban Neighborhoods.* New York: Oxford University Press.

Wacquant, Loïc. 1994. "The New Urban Color Line: The State and Fate of the Ghetto in Postfordist America." In *Social Theory and the Politics of Identity,* ed. Craig J. Calhoun, 231–76. Cambridge, MA: Basil Blackwell.

———. 1997. "Three Pernicious Premises in the Study of the American Ghetto." *International Journal of Urban and Regional Research* 21:341–53.

———. 2001. "Deadly Symbiosis: When Ghetto and Prison Meet and Mesh." *Punishment and Society* 3:95–134.

Wallace, David. 1953. "Residential Concentration of Negroes in Chicago." PhD dissertation, Harvard University.

Washington, Louis. 1948. "A Study of Restrictive Covenants in Chicago." MA thesis, University of Chicago.

Weaver, Robert Clifton. 1945. *Hemmed In: ABC's of Race Restrictive Housing Covenants.* Chicago: American Council on Race Relations.

Weber, Max. 1946. *From Max Weber: Essays in Sociology.* Ed. H. H. Gerth and C. Wright Mills. New York: Oxford University Press.

White, E. Frances. 2001. *Dark Continent of Our Bodies: Black Feminism and the Politics of Respectability.* Philadelphia: Temple University Press.

White, Lynn, and Agnes Riedmann. 1992. "Ties among Adult Siblings." *Social Forces* 71:85–102.

White, Walter F. 1919. "Chicago and Its Eight Reasons." *Crisis* 18:293–97.

Wille, Lois. 1997. *At Home in the Loop: How Clout and Community Built Chicago's Dearborn Park.* Carbondale: Southern Illinois University Press.

Williams, Brett. 1989. *Upscaling Downtown: Stalled Gentrification in Washington, D.C.* Ithaca, NY: Cornell University Press.

Williams, Lance. 2001. "The Almighty Black P. Stone Nation: Black Power, Politics, and Gangbanging." Lecture delivered at the University of Illinois at Chicago School of Public Health. http://gangresearch.net/ChicagoGangs/blackstonerangers/lance.htm (accessed July 1, 2005).

Williams, Rhonda Y. 2004. *The Politics of Public Housing: Black Women's Struggles against Urban Inequality.* New York: Oxford University Press.

Wilson, William Julius. 1987. *The Truly Disadvantaged.* Chicago: University of Chicago Press.

———. 1996. *When Work Disappears: The World of the New Urban Poor.* New York: Knopf.

Wilson, William Julius, David Campbell, Lena Lundgren-Gaveras, Mignon Moore, Bruce Rankin, James Quane, and Alicia Bassuk. 1994. "Communities in Transition: An Assessment of the Organizational Structure and Community Needs of the Woodlawn and North Kenwood/Oakland Redevelopment Areas." Unpublished report by the Center for the Study of Urban Inequality to the Fund for Community Redevelopment and Revitalization.

Wirth, Louis, and Eleanor Bernet, eds. 1949. *Local Community Fact Book of Chicago, 1940.* Chicago: University of Chicago Press.

Wolch, Manuel Pastor Jr., and Peter Dreier, eds. 2004. *Up against the Sprawl: Public Policy and the Making of Southern California.* Minneapolis: University of Minnesota Press.

Wolcott, Victoria W. 2001. *Remaking Respectability: African American Women in Interwar Detroit.* Chapel Hill: University of North Carolina Press.

Woodstock Institute. 1991. *1989 Community Lending Fact Book.* Chicago: Woodstock Institute.

———. 2002. *2000 Community Lending Fact Book.* Chicago: Woodstock Institute.

———. 2003. "Community Area 36—Oakland." In *Community Lending Fact Book—City of Chicago.* http://woodstockinst.org/document/2003-36.pdf (accessed July 1, 2005).

Wright, Erik Olin. 2000. *Class Counts.* Student ed. Cambridge: Cambridge University Press.

Wright, Richard. 1993. *Native Son*. New York: First HarperPerennial.

Wyly, Elvin, and Daniel Hammel. 1999. "Islands of Decay in Seas of Renewal: Housing Policy and the Resurgence of Gentrification." *Housing Policy Debate* 10:711–81.

Yinger, John. 1995. *Closed Doors, Opportunities Lost: The Continuing Costs of Housing Discrimination*. New York: Russell Sage Foundation.

Young, Alford A., Jr. 2004. *The Minds of Marginalized Black Men: Making Sense of Mobility, Opportunity and Future Life Chances*. Princeton, NJ: Princeton University Press.

Zielenbach, Sean. 2003. "Assessing Economic Change in HOPE VI Neighborhoods." *Housing Policy Debate* 14:621–55.

Zukin, Sharon. 1982. *Loft Living: Culture and Capital in Urban Change*. Baltimore: Johns Hopkins University Press.

———. 1987. "Gentrification: Culture and Capital in the Urban Core." *Annual Review of Sociology* 13:129–47.

Made in the USA
Middletown, DE
20 January 2016